D0853312

FEMINISM

WITHOUT

ILLUSIONS

FEMINISM

WITHOUT

ILLUSIONS

A CRITIQUE OF

INDIVIDUALISM

ELIZABETH

FOX-GENOVESE

WITHDRAWN

THE UNIVERSITY OF NORTH CAROLINA PRESS

CHAPEL HILL & LONDON

Tennessee Tech. Library
Cookeville, Tenn.

© 1991 The University of North Carolina Press

All rights reserved

Library of Congress Cataloging-in-Publication Data

Fox-Genovese, Elizabeth, 1941–
    Feminism without illusions : a critique of individualism /
Elizabeth Fox-Genovese.
        p.   cm.
    Includes bibliographical references and index.
    ISBN 0-8078-1940-9 (alk. paper)
    1. Feminist theory.   2. Individualism.   I. Title.
HQ1190.F69   1990
305.42'01—dc20   90-41044
                                                      CIP

Portions of Chapter 2 appeared in somewhat different form in "Ahistorical Admonitions," a review of Thomas Fleming's *The Politics of Human
Nature*, in *Chronicles: A Magazine of American Culture* 13, no. 1 (January
1989): 34–37.

An earlier version of portions of Chapter 3 appeared as "Women's Rights,
Affirmative Action, and the Myth of Individualism" in *George Washington
Law Review* 54 (1986): 338–74, reprinted with the permission of *George
Washington Law Review* © 1986.

Portions of Chapters 5 and 6 appeared in somewhat different form in
"Culture and Consciousness in the Intellectual History of European
Women" in *Signs* 12, no. 3 (Spring 1987): 529–47.

Portions of Chapter 7 appeared in somewhat different form in "The
Claims of a Common Culture" in *Salmagundi*, no. 72 (Fall 1986): 31–43,
and in "The Great Tradition and Its Orphans" in *The Rights of Memory*,
edited by Taylor Littleton. © 1986 The University of Alabama Press.

Portions of Chapter 8 appeared in somewhat different form in "Between
Individualism and Fragmentation: American Culture and the New Literary Studies of Race and Gender" in *American Quarterly* 42, no. 1 (March
1990): 7–34.

Portions of Chapter 9 appeared in somewhat different form in "For
Feminist Interpretation" in *Union Seminary Quarterly Review* 35, nos. 1
and 2 (Fall/Winter 1979–80): 5–14.

The paper in this book meets the guidelines for permanence and dura-
bility of the Committee on Production Guidelines for Book Longevity of
the Council on Library Resources.

Manufactured in the United States of America

95   94   93   92   91   5   4   3   2   1

FOR BECKY,

MY SISTER

CONTENTS

EIGHT

NINE

ACKNOWLEDGMENTS

Having developed through long years of reading, work, and conversation, this book embodies my innumerable debts to the support, interest, and encouragement of countless friends and colleagues. To the extent that it builds upon essays that have previously been published, it is especially indebted to those who have encouraged my thinking along the way: the editors of *Marxist Perspectives* (for chapter 1); the editors of the *George Washington Law Review* (for chapter 3); the editors of *Signs* (for chapters 5 and 6); Taylor Littleton and the editors of *Salmagundi* (for chapter 7); Gary Kulik of the *American Quarterly* (for chapter 8); and the editors of the *Union Seminary Quarterly Review* (for chapter 9). To the extent that the original essays were written in the interstices of and in interaction with my continuing work in Southern History and Women's Studies, they have very much benefited from the generous financial support I have received for other work. The American Council of Learned Societies, the Ford Foundation, the National Humanities Center, and the National Endowment for the Humanities may not have known all of the uses to which their support was being put, but I take great pleasure in thanking them for it now.

Without a year's leave from Emory University, the book, in this form, would probably never have been written. In thanking Emory, I especially thank David Minter, who as dean of Emory College and vice president for arts and sciences has provided not merely the leave but continuing support for my work, who as colleague and interlocutor has provided intellectual challenge and appreciation.

My colleagues and students at Emory, especially in Women's Studies, History, and English, have offered a rare sense of intellectual community that has helped me in innumerable ways to expand and deepen my thinking. Among my colleagues, Sheila Bennett and Eleanor Main, who share my combined interest in feminism, education, and politics, have talked issues, read drafts, encouraged, and helped me to think and rethink. And Martin Danahay, who shares my interest in individualism and autobiography, has read the manuscript with an invaluable blend of enthusiasm and criticism. It is hard for students to appreciate how much they teach their teachers. But I cannot begin adequately to thank mine. The undergraduates at Emory constantly remind me that teaching is one of our great privileges as well as our main responsibility. Their complex attitudes toward feminism have been an important influence on my own thinking about it. I owe a special debt to Saralyn Chesnut and Amanda Gable, who taught the first introductory Women's Studies courses at Emory with me, sharing the delights, wrestling with the issues, and helping me to think through and live the responsibilities of those demanding and rewarding courses. My graduate students have given generously of their interest and their questions—have always made me feel that they think what I am doing matters and have taught me to do it better. For these gifts of friendship and education during the past four years, I should especially like to thank Russell Andalcio, Nancy Barr, Lucie Fultz, Carmen Gillespie, Ginger Gould, Lisa Greenwald, Lisa Hill, Mary Margaret Johnson, Barbara McCaskill, Layne McDaniel, Fabienne McPhail, John Merriman, Magali Michael, Steve Paul, Jamie Stanesa, and Julia Williams.

This book depends heavily, in ways that the notes only begin to suggest, upon the work and ideas of innumerable colleagues in a variety of disciplines. Rather than excessively burden the text, I have chosen only to cite the works most directly relevant to my arguments. But I, like others, could not have begun to have thought the way I now think without the explosion of scholarly and theoretical writings, from very different points of view, inspired by contemporary feminism. Here, I can only acknowledge that I fully appreciate those debts. I must, however, more specifically acknowledge those who have directly contributed to my work. I have especially benefited from provocative discussions of the various issues with the wide variety of groups that have invited me to present aspects of my work: the fellows' seminar of the National Humanities Center, Auburn University, William Patterson College, Drew University, the Noun Symposium of Grinnell College, the Commonwealth Center for American Studies of the College of William and Mary, the Humanities Center of Vanderbilt University, the Madison Center, the Harvey Goldberg Center for Comparative History of the University of Wisconsin, Drake University, and the Center for Research on Women of Columbia University.

Research and writing are normally solitary occupations, but the thinking that informs them depends heavily upon the contributions of friends, and during the years that I have been working on this book, I have been blessed with many, who have challenged, stretched, and enriched my thinking more than I can ever acknowledge. Jean Bethke Elshtain gave the manuscript the kind of probing and appreciative reading that I had no right to expect. The members of the feminist legal studies group of the College of Law of Georgia State University, Anne Emmanuel, Pat Morgan, Mary Radford, Charity Scott, and Marjorie Knowles, read and discussed the chapters on politics and pornography, offering welcome encouragement as well as instruction in the legal issues. And Marjorie, along with a sustaining friendship, gave me the benefit of her fine editorial skills. Deborah Symonds read, queried, appreciated, and generally strengthened my courage. Christine Stansell's thoughtful challenges prompted me to rethink and revise. Joan Mandle's careful and sympathetic reading inspired many of the final revisions, even if I could not satisfy her request for a concrete political program. Jane DeHart persuaded me to try my hand at an initial version of chapter 8 for the annual meeting of the American Studies Association in 1988 and thoughtfully discussed the issues with me as I was preparing it. Through the years, Linda Kerber, who has been developing a similar line of thought, has generously shared work and ideas. Although she did not read this manuscript in draft, her work and correspondence have enriched my thinking. Dale and John Reed both read the entire manuscript, offering the inestimable support of friendship, appreciation, and hard questions.

It is a very special pleasure to thank Lou Ferleger and Bob Paquette for their painstaking readings of the manuscript, for innumerable references, and for long conversations about everything from the most sophisticated theoretical points to the smallest details. Even more, I thank them for long years of inestimable friendship—for always being there. Not least, I owe them for taking me into that quintessentially male world of the football pool—even if they have resolutely refused to give me a handicap to compensate for my sex. My friend Nancy Wilson, as always, read, discussed, enjoyed, and, more important, shared my quest for stories about what it means to be a woman.

My friends at the University of North Carolina Press have made the laborious task of preparing and editing the manuscript more of a pleasure than I should have thought possible. Matt Hodgson's confidence in my work has touched and strengthened me. Kate Torrey has proved a wonderful reader, a thoughtful interlocutor, and a patient and encouraging friend. Sandy Eisdorfer's interest in the manuscript has cheered me no end; Suzanne Bell's intelligent and painstaking copyediting has improved it in innumerable ways. The book would literally not have been completed without the devotion of my research assistants and the Emory Institute for Women's Studies staff. Linda Calloway and Fabienne McPhail protected my time, screened calls, kept the world at bay, handled duplication of the manuscript, and in general provided that tender loving care which all of us need and too few of us get.

Sharon McCoy proofread the entire manuscript with a skill that I shall envy until the day I die. And even as she read for detail, she read for content, picking up inconsistencies, asking for clarifications, and amazingly understanding what the book was about. To her, for better or worse, my readers owe the afterword, which, under the pressure of conflicting opinions, I was about to drop. Sharon convinced me that including a piece of myself mattered—that I owed the risk of a personal voice to the students who give me so much. John Merriman's devotion to the project continues to defy my understanding but has made everything possible. From my fractured, impressionistic notes, he reconstructed the bibliography. While I was writing and rewriting, he brought me new books and articles that he just thought I might want to see, the debonair manner in which he produced materials masking the determination, skill, and understanding that had gone into unearthing them. In the final push, he and Steve Paul checked the bibliography and notes. If I have ever underestimated how much I owe to his work and friendship, I was set straight when it dawned on me that he has spent so much time at the house that Josef and the little cats think he is a member of the family.

Like all of my work, this book has its roots in my own family. My parents, Elizabeth Simon Fox and Edward Whiting Fox, introduced me to literature and history and endowed me with an abiding belief that, in some way, they are part of who I am. My brother, Ted, shared that education with me, constantly providing me with a different perspective on the common story. My brother-in-law, William Scott Green, provided careful reading and intellectual friendship. Josef provided loving companionship during long hours at the computer, although by the end he had developed serious reservations about a project that required so many boring hours at work— and probably about feminism as well. Cleopatra and Georgia tolerated my absorption, provided I kept them well supplied with treats. Carolina finally learned to use the computer herself, although mercifully without making any lasting contributions. Gene, as always and in every way, has anchored it all, sustaining me with love and generosity that defy acknowledgment.

This book is dedicated to my sister, Rebecca Fox, who, from the time when I "carried her on my hip" and she called me by her toddler's version of

Acknowledgments

her own name, has embodied the true power of sisterhood—to which no words can do justice. But the words and stories that we have shared have brought me through dark hours, deepened my understanding of difficult issues, confirmed me in my personal and professional commitments, and, in every way, enriched my life. Because she is my sister, she knows.

FEMINISM

WITHOUT

ILLUSIONS

INTRODUCTION

Feminism enjoys a poor to middling press these days, among many women as well as men. One of my undergraduates at Emory University captured this unease in a paper she wrote for a Women's Studies course. When she had begun the course, feminism to her "meant the denial of femininity and womanhood. It suggested lesbianism. It led to 'bra burnings,' men-hating, and an almost irritating aggressiveness." She has not been alone in her associations. To many women, feminism even betokens the destruction of family values and the defiance of divine and natural order. In the time-honored tradition of blaming the victims of injustice and those who pro-tested against it for the consequences of injustice itself, some women and too many men find it easy to blame feminism for some of the most disturb-ing aspects of modern life: divorce, latch-key children, teenage alcoholism, domestic violence, the sexual abuse of children. From that indictment only a few short steps are required to arrive at an indictment of feminism for the collapse of academic standards and the decline of Western civilization. Many young women simply consider feminism outmoded—a relic of former times that no longer constructively affects their lives.

Feminists reply that only our vigilance protects and improves women's hard-won and still-precarious place in work and politics. Yet even those who call themselves feminists frequently disagree about the meaning and impli-cations of feminism. For some, feminism articulates women's rights as individuals and as women, women's needs as parents, and women's oppor-tunities as workers. Others insist upon the radical implications of women's experience for society as a whole, arguing that women speak "in a different voice" than men; have different "ways of knowing" than men; would, if given power, order the world more humanely than men. Some hold that justice can obliterate, or radically minimize, the differences between women and men. Others hold that those differences are fundamental and that our ideals of justice should be rewritten to take account of women's experience. Still others dismiss the very idea of difference as the product of invidious and hierarchical dichotomies that should be replaced by an appreciation of diversity.

The differences over the meaning of feminism reflect the larger confusion of our times. Less the cause of the unsettling changes in our world than their symptom, feminism embodies a variety of dissatisfactions with things-as-they-are and a variety of visions about how they could be improved. Above all, feminism represents different attempts to come to terms with women's changing position in American society, particularly the economy. Since the beginning of the twentieth century, women have steadily increased their participation in the labor force, most dramatically, married women with children, and most ominously, single mothers. American women are working outside the home in many cases by preference but in many cases because they have to—because they and frequently their families depend upon their doing so.

This century has also witnessed a steady increase in divorce, and analysts now project a divorce rate of 50 percent for all new marriages. And with the increase in the number of divorces has come the collapse of alimony and the erosion of child support. The most dramatic change in the lives of young women—although many have no wish to recognize it—is that marriage is not a viable career. Under favorable circumstances it remains a rewarding personal relation, but it no longer serves as a surrogate career. Today, no law, no father, no brother can force a man to support a woman, and the law is not successfully forcing him to support even their children properly.

Although the substance of feminism constitutes a response to harsh social and economic realities, much of its rhetoric and that of its opposition has focused on problems of sexuality and identity, rather than on problems of livelihood. Sexual freedom, sexual preference, abortion, figure prominently in public consciousness of the implications of feminism. Men and women understandably worry about radical transformations of our sense of what it means to be a man or woman. Accordingly, many men and some women intuitively respond to any talk of women's rights as if it portended the direst consequences. At the extreme, there are women who apparently oppose abortion out of a deep sense that sexual freedom for any woman exacerbates the pervasive threats to the security of married women; others more vaguely plead that if women would only be women, everything would return to normal. If women would only assume their ordained roles as the bearers and rearers of children and helpmeets to men, men would have to support them. There is no point in arguing with those who desperately cling to such illusions, for economic realities foreclose the return to that "normality" for most women.

The student who wrote of her initial distaste for feminism devoted the remainder of her paper to a discussion of what each of the books in her Women's Studies course had taught her about women's situations and possibilities. "Today," she concluded, "as I turn in my last paper, I consider myself a feminist. Maybe not an *active* feminist, but a definite proponent of feminism." The course, she avowed, had offered her a rare educational experience. "Although I am always academically challenged by my classes at Emory, rarely have I ever been personally challenged. Not only has my definition and attitude towards feminism matured and changed from what I have learned and studied about women in this course, but my own personal self has been affected; I have been challenged to think and reflect on my past, present, and future life as a woman. I have not just learned about women this semester, but I have also grown as a woman."

I shall not pretend that I was not pleased by her conversion, although I do not regard the teaching of Women's Studies as an excuse for proselytizing and do not require that my students espouse any particular ideology. Not all students who study the subject seriously become feminists, but few, if any, male or female, find it possible to dismiss feminism as intellectually unworthy of respect. And that, rather than an alleged and perhaps sometimes actual abuse of the classroom, may be the reason so many anti-feminists condemn Women's Studies courses out of hand and confuse, or pretend to confuse, Women's Studies with feminist ideological indoctrination.

The question remains: What do we want for our daughters, our students, the young women for whom we feel responsible? As the director of a Women's Studies program, I live with that question. As one who sees herself as temperamentally and culturally conservative, I harbor no consuming desire to turn the world upside down and by no means subscribe to all that is advanced in the name of feminism. But I am convinced that (1) the changes of which feminism is a symptom will not be reversed; (2) feminism is having a broad and profound impact on our society and our ways of thinking; (3) young women must be trained to support themselves, preferably by work that draws upon their talents and enhances their self-respect.

The impact of feminism on American cultural and intellectual life has been extraordinary, notwithstanding abiding resistance to it. But we have now reached a point at which what we make of feminism, and, above all, how we convince the majority of American women of its relevance to their lives, is everything. Many feminists have, since the late sixties, fought, with a measure of success, for a transformation of human consciousness and culture as well as social practice. A many-pronged attack on what is frequently called "the patriarchy" has resulted in sharp challenges to religious, educational, and cultural traditions and, yet more portentously, to our inherited ways of thinking, including our conception of justice.

The gains made by women in the academic world alone would have been unimaginable a scant fifteen years ago. Today, Women's Studies programs abound on college and university campuses. Conferences and sessions at professional meetings in such disciplines as English, Modern Languages, History, Religious Studies, Sociology, and even Political Science and Philosophy feature programs in which sessions on some aspect of women, gender, or feminist theory are steadily displacing traditional topics. Each of these disciplines now boasts at least one professional journal devoted exclusively to women, gender, and feminist theory, and interdisciplinary journals are addressing these issues as well. Most "mainstream" journals are devoting increasing amounts of space to Women's Studies and explicitly feminist scholarship.[1]

The heated debate over the canon, which is now being waged in books and on campuses and is being covered by the national press, directly testifies to the impact of feminist concerns. To be sure, these debates also reflect a concern with exposing students to the writings and experiences of working-class, nonwhite, and non-Western male authors, but feminist scholarship is now spearheading the challenge and is offering the most sustained theoretical program.[2] For if feminist scholarship argues that women have been excluded from the canon, it does not rest its case with rectifying that exclusion. It insists that women have been—and remain—fundamentally alienated from a culture that casts them as objects and with which they cannot identify.

Feminism has, in this respect, emerged as the cutting edge of postmodernist (a fancy word for contemporary) anxieties about the status of knowledge, certainty, subjectivity, the self. For feminism is increasingly challenging received notions about the fundamental structures of human knowledge. In particular, some influential feminists are rejecting all of our assumptions about knowledge on the grounds that they represent an oppressive and outmoded "binary thinking"—a way of thinking that rests on the delineation of difference as the foundation of all knowledge and therefore promotes hierarchy, notably the hierarchy that places men over women. Rather than thinking with reference to dichotomies—white/black, male/

female, self/object—we must, according to this version of feminist theory, learn to think with reference to pluralism and indeterminacy.

These complex debates cannot be ascribed solely to the influence of feminism, but feminism is emerging as a magnetic pole within them, for it potentially cuts across all boundaries of class, race, and nationality to confront the fundamental identity of the thinking subject. Although not all feminists focus on these debates or even accept their implications, the combined impact of various feminist projects has begun to erode our confidence in the culture we have inherited. Religious Studies provides an especially striking example. Christian feminist ethicists and theologians are formulating a searching critique of the Christian tradition. Insisting above all on women's right to become ministers, they are also wrestling with women's relation to a faith that represents God and the Savior as male. How, they ask, can women be expected to find a positive image of themselves in a faith that historically has excluded them from leadership and relegated them to secondary status?

If many applaud feminism for its contribution to the erosion of confidence in our inherited culture, others have been retreating into a rigid adherence to the time-honored status quo. Neither position will serve. Our inherited culture and values contain much that many feminists, including myself, cherish, as have innumerable women before us. Yet, we cannot hope to prepare young women to deal confidently with the world if we offer them a vision of themselves as dependent upon men for everything from material support to physical protection to a sense of their identities.

Another undergraduate student in Women's Studies wrote her final paper about the education that she had received at Emory. A joint major in English and Spanish, on the eve of graduation, she treated the paper as her private commencement address and assessed the place of women in the liberal education she had received. Never, she insisted, had she viewed that education as restrictive, but her Women's Studies class did open her eyes to "the limitations of my male dominated education." For until she read an article on the canon for that class she "would not have viewed the canon as a political statement."

From this perspective, she reviewed the syllabi for all of the courses in English and Spanish that she had taken during her undergraduate career to determine how many women authors had been included. (It is a measure of the value she attached to those courses that she had kept the syllabi.) Out of a total of 128 authors, her ten English courses had included sixteen women.

She believed it predictable that her courses in Chaucer and Shakespeare included only male authors—she did not comment on whether any feminist critics had been read—and also noted that the numbers of women authors had recently begun to increase in all courses. She was not complaining about, certainly not berating, her professors, whom she obviously very much admired, but she did hope that things might be different in the future. "If inspiration can take the form of a charge or revelation," she wrote in conclusion, "then my evaluations and this paper will have succeeded in creating a personal impact for me. While the insights that I have gained and the advances of any one woman do not make up for the countless and often unjustified exclusion of women and minorities from the canon today, it lessens the probability that such a reality will mark the canon of the future."

The feminisms of the eighties are raising a myriad of questions unlikely to yield easy answers, but one thing remains clear. We have a responsibility to train young women, as seriously as we try to train young men, to take their place in a complex world. I do not believe that we could—or should— entirely rewrite our history and our culture, even if we must significantly revise them, and even if we must acknowledge that they have been dominated by men. Now, perhaps more than ever, we need history, not myth. But, as many of our talented women students have the wit to agree, to accept the past does not bind us to a perpetuation of its wrongs. Our world is changing and so must our visions. Young women are entitled to an education that empowers them to make choices and accept responsibility— to realize their talents and to recognize their accountability.

This book has grown from my preoccupations as a woman, a teacher, and an intellectual who came of age just as the modern women's movement was coming into being. Betty Friedan's *The Feminine Mystique* appeared the year that I graduated from college.[3] Like many others, I did not immediately grasp its full implications for myself or for our society. My adult personal and professional lives have unfolded in tandem with contemporary feminism, to which I have been committed despite firm opposition to some of its tendencies that I regard as irrational, irresponsible, and dangerous. As a proud feminist, I confess to intense irritation over once more having to defend the term and explain its premises to a new generation. So much for irritation. Feminists cannot avoid the challenge, and I intend this book as a contribution to the defense and explication of feminism or, rather, of a feminism.

Introduction

The Supreme Court's recent *Webster* decision, which limited women's access to abortion and raised the possibility that *Roe* v. *Wade* might yet be reversed, is engaging the imagination of young women, who fear the implications for themselves, although that engagement does not guarantee their adherence to a broader feminist program, much less their concern with the problems of women of other classes and races. The fight for women's "right" to choice in the matter of abortion is being misguidedly waged in the name of women's absolute right to their own bodies and, ironically, on the grounds of reproduction as a private matter. It qualifies as ironical since so much feminist energy has been devoted to an insistence that familial relations are not private matters, that "the personal is political," and that women cannot, in justice, be excluded from the public business of society. But the fight over abortion is being waged more in the name of women's sexuality than in the name of their reproductive capacities. That confusion alone indicates the extent to which feminism has absorbed aspects of individualism, which, to be coherent, it must resolutely oppose.

This book offers a critique of feminism's complicity in and acceptance of individualism—or rather of its contemporary atomized version that replaces the early and glorious recognition of the claims of the individual against the state with the celebration of egotism and the denial or indefensible reduction of the just claims of the community. Throughout, I am using "individualism" to mean the systematic theory of politics, society, economics, and epistemology that emerged following the Renaissance, that was consolidated in the great English, American, French, and Haitian revolutions of the seventeenth and eighteenth centuries, and that has found its purest logical outcome in the laissez-faire doctrines of neoclassical economics and libertarian political theory. The political triumph of individualism has led to its hegemony as *the* theory of human nature and rights, according to which, rights, including political sovereignty, are grounded in the individual and can only be infringed upon by the state in extraordinary circumstances.

That hegemony has proved so powerful that most of us intuitively associate individualism with the defense of individual freedom, our highest value. Here I am arguing that individualism actually perverts the idea of the socially obligated and personally responsible freedom that constitutes the only freedom worthy of the name or indeed historically possible. Theoretically, individualism does not contain the possibility of establishing necessary limits on the will of the individual, on what Nietzsche called the "will to power." The problem lies at the heart of every modern discussion of democracy since Rousseau: What can be the relation between the will of the individual and the will of the majority? Theorists of individualism have not, in fact, arrived at a better definition of the social good than the individualistic notion that what more people want must be accepted as better. In practice, modern individualistic societies have significantly curtailed individual right in the name of the public good, but they have done so apologetically, defensively, not on the grounds of the prior rights of the collectivity. (To be sure, socialist societies have proclaimed the priority of society in a way that has stifled the just claims of the individual, but that deeply disquieting problem lies well beyond the scope of this book and is today being recast by events with unpredictable consequences.) Western societies, in any case, have, as some conservative and feminist critics are beginning to argue, failed to develop a notion of individual right as the product of collective life rather than its justification.[4]

The defense of individual freedom has properly prompted the most generous aspects of our national tradition, which includes the abolition of slavery and the growing recognition of women's rights. But we have had difficulty in separating the defense of individual freedom from the basic premise of individualism, namely that rights derive from the individual's innate being. The origins of the confusion lie in the theory of the social contract, dear to seventeenth- and eighteenth-century political theorists, according to which individual right derives from nature and, accordingly, precedes any form of social organization. The political institutions built on this theory did not, initially, expose the radicalism of the concept, if only because they did not acknowledge all people as individuals. Excluding propertyless men, slaves, and women from political participation, they perpetuated the illusion that individualism and collective life could coexist. But, as the dispossessed increasingly insisted that collective life depended upon the denial of their individuality, the last bastions began to fall and to expose individualism's growing inability to curtail any exercise of the individual will. No wonder, then, that free marketeers, who today call themselves conservatives as the result of a massive misunderstanding, probably choke when confronted with what they have wrought.

In our own time individualism, fueled by the capitalist market, threatens to swing the balance between the individual and society—the balance between personal freedom and social order—wholly to the side of the individual. In this process feminism has played an ambiguous and sometimes destructive role. The implementation of women's rights has whittled away at the remaining bastions of corporatism and community—notably the family—even as women, released to the dubious mercies of the public sphere, require new forms of protection from the state. The issues defy easy solutions but do suggest that we have reached a period in our history at which we can no longer deceive ourselves that individualism suffices to define our collective purposes as a people and a nation.

This book does not offer a political program. It explores some ways of imagining the claims of society—the collectivity—as prior to the rights of the individual, some ways of imagining and protecting the rights of the individual as social, not private, rights. I have attempted to identify aspects of our current political difficulties and to relate them to the history of the Western tradition in general and the American in particular. The first four chapters offer thoughts upon the relation between feminism and political life; the next five turn to feminism and intellectual life, notably the academic canon, which has emerged as the center of a heated debate.

These questions suggest the need for a reformed political practice but fall short of suggesting its content. In general, I believe that our political system does have the flexibility to meet the needs of women with justice but that for it to do so, we must rethink our basic assumptions about the relation between the individual and the collectivity and especially rethink our assumptions about the "freedom" of the market in a society as complex and interdependent as our own. Many of the most pressing feminist issues are, in truth, broadly social issues—for example, it seems extraordinary that we (or our legislators) are unwilling to recognize that in our time the "right to life" of our Declaration of Independence might not include comprehensive national medical insurance. The arguments against such insurance turn primarily upon expense—the rights of property—not upon the principles of democracy or upon our sense of collective decency and self-respect. At issue, in short, is how we interpret our political tradition and identify its most fundamental and admirable aspects.

The book as a whole has grown out of the thinking and research that have occupied me throughout my scholarly career, but especially during the last decade. Previous versions of my formulations of the main problems have appeared in essays and articles, but as they have succeeded one another, as our world has changed, and as the work of others has appeared, my thinking has changed. Having originally intended simply to republish a collection of essays, I decided that I had pulled too many punches and had been reluctant to press an argument that seemed out of step with some of the loudest voices in contemporary feminism. Although this book did not originate in, as it were, a clean slate, it does represent a distinct project.[5] Above all, it represents my conviction that the claims of feminism require the maximum clarity because feminism will shape our future as people—and whether it does so for good or ill entails a heavy responsibility.

At a number of points my arguments may seem to constitute opposition to what I in fact support—for example, the necessity for granting women the power to choose to have an abortion under socially determined conditions. I have proceeded on the conviction that honest readers will have no trouble in grasping the essentials of the argument—that one may accept that limited right to choice and yet emphatically deny that women have, or that a man has, an absolute right to the disposition of her or his body. For if we fight for a worthy goal on the basis of unworthy premises that could open the floodgates to undesirable and even vile consequences, we shall go down to a well-deserved defeat or, worse, have to assume responsibility for the destruction of the healthiest, as well as the unhealthiest, elements in civilized life. The greatest problems of our time arise from the need to get our premises as well as our priorities straight, and I intend this book as a contribution to that limited but essential task.

I

BEYOND

SISTERHOOD

Contemporary feminism has emerged from the crucible of the extraordinary economic and political developments of the twentieth century, especially since World War II. And high on the list of the many gains and casualties of these developments stands the erosion of our inherited doctrines of neutral, natural-rights politics. Gone are our illusions of rationality and objectivity; gone with them are our long-cherished dreams of the family as personal haven against struggle and competition. According to our newfound realism, the personal is political. The family, especially, is political. Grounded in hierarchy and domination, which it has historically reproduced, this most intimate locus of personal relations requires political response in the highly politicized age in which we live.

Feminism has led the way in demystifying personal relations, forcefully insisting that women's personal experience be recognized as political to its core. Many feminists have moved from naming their personal experience as political to naming established political norms and practices as personal—as the embodiment of men's perspectives and values—and, accordingly, as inappropriate models either for feminist politics or for a desirable social order. Since the late 1960s most feminists have been arguing that for the competitiveness and hierarchy of men's politics we must substitute the noncompetitive egalitarianism that they believe characterizes women's politics; for the rationality and positivism of men's thought, we must substitute an epistemology based on caring.[1] For feminism to thrive, the male model of individualism must be replaced by a female model of sisterhood.[2] For the world to survive—this argument continues—women's politics must replace men's as the model for all political relations. Where men, with their politics of "domination," have wreaked havoc and death, women, with their politics of "partnership," will bring a renewed commitment to life.[3]

Women, according to these feminists, speak in a different voice than men and have a different conception of politics, justice, morality.[4] They hold that women's experience has endowed them with an aversion to the competition and abstract standards that characterize our inherited models of justice and politics. Women's experience has led them to nurture life, to view moral questions in the context of personal relations and specific situations, to value mutuality and community.[5] Coming out of a common history of subordination and repression, women are supposed to have developed a tradition of sisterhood that offers a transformative model for society as a whole.

Since time immemorial, women have drawn upon the metaphor of sisterhood to express the quality of their relations with one another and to endure and resist oppression. In the United States during the early nineteenth century, the sisterhood of the women of the slave community constituted a dense network of everyday resistance to oppression.[6] These women, who joined together to do laundry by the brook or to hoe in the fields or to worship in church, spun sisterhood into a web of resistance that, if it did not produce violent revolts, did protect a minimum of living space and collective identity for themselves and their people. In the early twentieth century, Nigerian women drew upon their long-standing bonds of sisterhood to wage an outright revolt against British imperialists who sought to abolish their marketing privileges.[7] Such patterns of sisterhood existed in untold numbers of peasant societies, in which women conjoined in work, camaraderie, religion, and frequently in resistance to threats to their time-honored responsibilities as women. And with the growth of centralized states and capitalism, many women carried these bonds into urban life and new forms of resistance. Typically, women in early modern Europe engaged in bread riots in the name of the collective values that attributed responsibility for food to women and that held the state responsible for ensuring an adequate supply of grain at a reasonable cost.[8] During the Civil War, poor white women in Richmond, Virginia, drew upon comparable patterns in their protests against the exorbitant and escalating price of food.[9]

The tendency, practically and imaginatively, to divide the world by gender is apparently as old as human history and, in premodern societies, assumed even greater significance than in our own. Many feminist scholars, noting this tendency, have regularly emphasized the ways in which it devalued women; others have emphasized the ways in which it empowered them. But this focus misses the main point, namely the ways in which political imagery and institutions remained tied to a biologically based sexual division of labor. Modern states and institutions have tended, increasingly, to abstract from biology and to emphasize the (purportedly) impersonal or neutral roles of bureaucrats. That they invariably assigned those roles to men incontrovertibly testifies to male dominance but does not reduce the significance of the growing inclination to move away from a concrete, or personalized, image of power. The person of the president in our own time is far removed from the "body" of the king in the Middle Ages. And in Africa, the Ashanti long retained the position of queen mother as equal, in essential respects, to the king because she represented the women of the Ashanti people.[10]

Traditionally, the metaphor of sisterhood captured the distinctive bonds among women who lived in small communities in which family metaphors provided the most forceful justifications for social and political roles. Sisterhood thus asserted women's special loyalties to one another by claiming for women of different families the privileged status of "fictive kin."[11]

During the nineteenth century, as the public concepts of power became increasingly abstract, the metaphor acquired heightened resonance, especially for women who were active in the antislavery and nascent women's movements. Bonds of sisterhood entwined and empowered women, who sought understanding and support from other women like themselves.[12] The women's movement of the 1960s and early 1970s picked up the metaphor, extending the meaning and claims of sisterhood even further. "Sisterhood," announced Robin Morgan, "is powerful,"[13] thereby linking natural affiliation to power and underscoring the link between the personal and the political. Sisterhood is powerful because the personal is political, and it must bring the power of personal relations to bear against bankruptcy of politics.

At the core of the notion of sisterhood lies the affirmation of the solidarity and similarity of all women. As it unfolded in the consciousness-raising groups of the 1960s and early 1970s, this understanding became one of the most powerful weapons of the middle-class women's movement.[14] The groups themselves forged a practice of sisterhood by providing psychological space within which women could come to know themselves through knowing one another. Late capitalist society has contributed a particularly bitter twist to the centuries of female oppression. Consumerism, suburban residence patterns, declining family size, increased male occupational mobility, increased female education, declining parental control over children and their marital choices, rising divorce rates, and a host of other changes have been interwoven in a dense network of isolation and anxiety.

Not all of these changes have been *eo ipso* bad for women. But rising female individualism and opportunity have given with one hand, only to take away with the other. Stripping away the barriers that had simultaneously oppressed and sheltered middle-class women, and lightening the burdens of childbirth and physical household labor (although not necessarily reducing the time that it requires), they have failed to provide viable alternatives, notably rewarding and remunerative work and the daycare that would permit women to engage in it.[15] And they have encouraged greater competition among women to get and keep husbands, to consume with style, and to cultivate an appearance of youthful perfection by prevailing standards. The traditional world of middle-class women is being dismantled without adequate substitution and sufficient access for women to the world of men. That these same changes have provoked an increase in more or less veiled hostility and violence by men, wont to attribute everything unsettling to the increase in female independence, has hardly helped.

Sisterhood has helped middle-class women to break out of their walls of silence and has permitted women to forge a common language with which to express their hostility to men, to the constraints of their lives, even to their children. That language has provided a new vocabulary for female anger and, thus, opened paths through which women might turn natural aggression outward rather than upon themselves.[16] Sisterhood, miraculously, has allowed even the expression of women's jealousy of one another. The privately nurtured inadequacies, guilts, and fears have broken out in an orgy of recognition. Suddenly none was unique. One of the major traps of modern culture has been exploded. Women have recognized that strength lies not in being different—invariably presented as being best—but in being similar, even, or especially, if that means being no-better-than. Women came to see that they had been wasting their energies and talents on the wrong things. Dupes of the need to please men, they had become unable to like themselves, to like their sisters, to like anything.[17]

Sisterhood has thus afforded a network of mutual support—a fund of collective strength and affection from which women could draw upon for their still private battles in the home or on the job. At its most extreme, sisterhood has even flirted with proclamations of self-sufficiency. Learning to love and respect one another, women could do without men. Practically and emotionally, most women continue to regard this view as unrealistic and undesirable, but its mere existence has encouraged them to a new independence and to a new understanding of differences in sexual preference or style of life as variations on the shared identity of being women.[18]

Many middle-class women who came of age during the feminist wave of the 1960s and 1970s well remember the "click"—the moment of recognition—when these truths fell into place. For me it came at a party in the late 1960s when I recognized that I was more interested in talking to the women than to the men. Whenever or wherever that click occurred, it flicked on a light that chased the shadows from years of training to please socially dominant males. The sudden recognition that other women were not merely okay but important opened a new path to women's long-stifled sense of self-respect. The rising self-awareness brought many to confront how much of the early anger, presumably related to the male oppressors, in fact derived from childhood relations with mothers.[19] And, having learned to hate their mothers, women have come again to love them, as they have come to love the children against whom they had never been free to rage.[20] Recognizing and repossessing anger has gradually freed many women to function as whole human beings in the large world. In this respect, sisterhood has provided an inestimable ingredient in women's political coming-of-age.

Sisterhood has contributed to the creation of political female beings by freeing women from the continual replay of familial psychodramas, by freeing women from the necessity of continually reproducing their own childhoods and even their own narcissism.[21] So understood, sisterhood might be described as political. Common struggle against individual demons identifies those demons as social rather than personal. The struggle with an individual husband, mother, or child can indeed be understood as the struggle with the dominant pattern of reproduction in our society, but it must also be understood as a specific personal history. Most women, like most men, do not hate categories but people, frequently the very people they most love. The struggle remains personal, whatever its political implications.

Sisterhood has increasingly functioned as a sign for a vast network of ideas.[22] In perhaps its most important meaning, it has drawn upon a familial metaphor of politics to evoke an image of nonauthoritarian bonding among female peers. It thus sought to retain notions of attachment and loyalty associated with noncontractual family relations. In essential ways, therefore, its model for advanced capitalist society has rested upon a fundamental opposition to the principles of individualism. Sisterhood, accordingly, could be seen as a radical repudiation of that which it was proposing to reform, and indeed, it frequently has presented itself as such, albeit on the basis of a serious confusion. For sisterhood has proposed not the abolition of capitalism, the social foundation of individualism, but the abolition of patriarchy.

Our modern concept of sisterhood, like the feminism to which it is so closely related, rose from the ashes of patriarchy. Both concepts, in other words, emerged from the social and political transformations consolidated by the great bourgeois revolutions of the seventeenth and eighteenth centuries.[23] Both were "grannied," as Zora Neale Hurston would have said, by individualism.[24] Sisterhood perpetuates the struggle within the familial metaphor of politics that those revolutions repudiated in theory; feminism demands the realization of the democratic potential that they have failed to deliver in practice. Prior to the emergence of capitalism, Western societies relied heavily on the metaphor of family to justify political relations. The triumph of capitalism, at least in public discourse, replaced time-honored notions of patriarchy and dependency with the antithetical notion of individualism. To be sure, individualism, like any representation of social relations, did not so much abolish previous values as reformulate and transform them. And, in reformulating a general theory of society and politics, it appeared to leave many specific relations, notably those of the family, virtually untouched. In fact, the transformation included a significant reworking of the discourse of womanhood and of women's roles, but it did not noticeably alter women's subordination to men within families.[25] For women, the advent of capitalism and individualism proved paradoxical, simultaneously offering them a greater promise of full and independent social participation than had any previous social system and raising more systematic barriers to their social integration and self-respect.

There is no need to rehearse that contradictory and deceptive history. Suffice it to note that individualism, rationalism, and universalism were all interpreted in strictly male terms. Worse, in some measure, they all rested upon a more or less explicit repudiation of women as the opposite of the desired male norm and the celebration of them as the emotional anchor necessary to the functioning of that norm under conditions of intense competition. Having rejected dependency in favor of autonomy, the dominant male culture nonetheless itself depended, in the lives of individual men, upon a repressed domestic sphere that was represented as custodian of all the qualities the public sphere could not tolerate.

Throughout the nineteenth and twentieth centuries, sisterhood and feminism, although not always in the same ways, have helped women to identify the decisive features of their social, economic, and political vulnerability and to build foundations for their potential strength. Sisterhood has flourished even among women who remained uninterested in, when not actively opposed to, feminism, and it has also flourished among feminists, union women, and women who simply work to survive. It has flourished especially among black women, who have formulated their own understanding of its meaning under slavery and thereafter within their churches and communities. Frequently unnamed, sisterhood has provided both the model for and the substance of those bonds through which women have nurtured, supported, sustained, and valued one another. With time, the behavior and values of the so-called private sphere—the world of women—has come to offer an alternate model to that of a striving, competitive capitalism. The world of women has become a world of reproduction in the broadest sense, including not only reproduction of the species but reproduction of its values and level of civilization. Almost invariably, however, women's distinct activities, from charity and social work through the education of children and the sustenance of families to the support of culture and churches, have remained dissociated from, or in sufferance to, the world of men, understood as the world of real power.

Today, as in the nineteenth century, the model of sisterhood has drawn much of its force from the assumption that womanhood is a universal condition—an assumption that contradicts the reality of different women's lives. For if women, like men, share certain physical characteristics, they differ sharply in cultural, social, and economic realities. Those realities have decisively shaped contemporary American feminism, which, like all forms of resistance, arose and has developed within specific historical conditions. Even the language in which feminists formulate goals and ideals derives from the dominant language of our society.

No politics remains innocent of that which it contests. The politics of the contemporary women's movement remains hostage to the history as well as the contemporary reality of our advanced capitalist society. Specifically, the distinct notion of power and authority against which the feminist movement is reacting has derived from a widely accepted notion of the separation of public and private spheres.[26] Never as absolute as its formulators claimed, that separation functioned as an organic norm that helped to obscure the intense interdependence of public and private life and, especially, the significance of class and racial divisions. For individualism's model of the sexual division of labor, by tacitly assuming the same equality among women that the ideal of democratic individualism assumed among men, has tended to replace other forms of political and social hierarchy as the foundation of social order.

The ideological importance ascribed to the sexual division of labor has made it particularly tempting for women to consider their special oppression as deriving from their gender—to view themselves effectively as members of a distinct class—and thus to deny the importance of class and racial divisions within the public sphere. The temptation has led many to assume, first, that all women have been more united by gender than divided by class or race, and, second, that white middle-class women could legitimately speak in the name of all women. This assumption has had deadly consequences for the development of feminist politics, for, by assuming the right of middle-class women to speak in the name of Woman, it has blinded mainstream feminism to some of its most important responsibilities and simultaneously has alienated many lower-class and black women, who see their primary oppression as deriving from their class or race.[27]

Historically, feminism has embodied the premise that woman, like man, could be discussed in the abstract. To the extent that American laws and institutions have defined women by their sex, independent of their race or class, the fiction of woman has at least the same validity as the fiction of man. But many women, like many men, have never enjoyed the full opportunities assumed by the fiction. More important, slavery and then segregation ensured that most black women could not even claim the meager benefits of the fiction. Throughout most of the nineteenth century, married women were placed under the "protection" of their husbands and were thereby denied a myriad of independent public rights, including the right to vote. Yet black slave women, whose marriages were not recognized at law, enjoyed no such protection for their roles as wives and mothers. Even after they gained legal standing for their marriages, they had reason to fear oppression by hostile whites, male and female, as much or more than oppression by black men.

The experience of black women most sharply challenges the notion of a universal female experience, but so does that of poor women of all races and ethnicities, for whom no economically sheltered "mommy track" could sensibly be proposed.[28] Class oppression like racial and ethnic discrimination deprive many women of the "protection" under which many middle-class women have chafed. Forced by economic necessity to work outside the home, frequently deserted or abused by husbands or other male kin, poor women have never been restricted to a domestic haven. And whatever abuse they have suffered at the hands of the men of their own communities, most of them have understood that the greater oppression has come from outside that community—from a society that has denied their men as well as themselves the fundamental respect purportedly due to all Americans.

These women certainly have often experienced, sometimes with a vengeance, specific oppression as women within their communities. But they have also experienced a social oppression that has shaped their experience as women and excluded them from the advantages enjoyed by white, middle-class women. For women whose primary goals have included adequate food and shelter for their families or opportunities for schooling for their children, the wrongs against which middle-class women have railed might easily appear secondary or even as the fruits of privilege. Indeed, women who belong to socially oppressed groups might understandably see privileged women as their oppressors or at least as beneficiaries of their oppression.

The ideological claims of feminism are, at one level, universal. Therein lies their strength. The rights of woman, like the rights of man, speak for all women, independent of race or class. But to the extent that those claims abstract from the specific lives of many women, to the extent that they are enunciated on the basis of the needs of a specific group of women, they make a mockery of their own universality. When feminism fails to defend social and economic changes that can ensure decent lives for all people, the rights of women collapse into privilege for the few and exploitation for the many. In that configuration, personal politics, including the nature and role of sisterhood, lies on a narrow margin between commitment to social transformation and unintended succor to the social system that feminism explicitly criticizes.

Today, many feminists are repudiating the distinction between the public and private spheres, but it still throws a long shadow across present assessments of our situation, personal psyches, political possibilities, and, hence, on the allocation of energies. Historically, the politics of feminism has necessarily derived from the special place of women within the public and private spheres. In America women of all social groups have shared a systematic exclusion from the public world, and most, with the primary exception of black slave women, have shared a containment—in some instances violent—within the home. Feminism, in its various manifestations, has thus encompassed women's rights and women's liberation at home as well as in the public arena. By and large, victorious feminist struggles have advanced the entry of women into rights and activities previously reserved to men: property rights, the vote, education, improved access to employment and credit, divorce. Child custody rights constitute a special case since they can readily be assimilated to the image of nurturing womanhood, although in time and place women's right to child custody represented a significant victory, which is now again being challenged.

These fundamental gains have frequently had unintended consequences. For example, the right to divorce has, in many respects, more effectively freed men from the obligation of supporting women and children than it has increased women's independence.[29] In most instances, divorce leads to a substantial rise in the man's income and an even greater drop in the woman's. More ominously, some of the gains have tended to strengthen the class and racial divisions among women and have thus shattered the illusion of a collective movement. The decomposition of female solidarity in turn has tended at once to strengthen individual women's class and racial identification at the expense of their identification with other women and to strengthen many women's commitment to individualism. This individualist bias reinforces the dominant American belief that propertied individualism affords the necessary foundation for the middle-class conception of freedom and equality. And, not surprisingly, the women who have most profited from the new opportunities of uniform access normally come from the middle class or rapidly join it once they acquire a sufficient income to support themselves as individuals.

As an ideal, sisterhood has sought to transcend class and racial divisions by emphasizing the enduring relations among women bound together in a subordination that transcends class lines. Sisterhood has especially signified the commonalty of oppression and the nurturing, loving, mutually supporting network forged within oppression. As a metaphor, sisterhood has evoked the purportedly noncompetitive, noncontractual bonds of familial affection and devotion. But, whatever its strengths, the metaphor draws its model of women from women's experience within the family and therefore assumes that family relations, which feminists are committed to demystifying, inform women's vision of feminist politics.

Just as traces of the family have lingered in feminist thought, so has the myth of separate spheres, which has cast women as the softening antidote to the impersonal interaction of competing individuals. Feminists have found that myth especially tenacious because it embodies cherished and comforting middle-class views of the supposedly innate differences between women and men and because it embodies negative sanctions. The positive myth of women as innately nurturing and dependent derives much of its psychological power from its embedded message that women who do not conform to appropriate female behavior risk violence at the hands of men. In short, the social myth has been internalized by women, who have tended to view and transmit its values as central to female identity.

The formidable limitations on freedom at home and in the world that many women experience has endowed the negative or threatening aspects of the myth of separate spheres with genuine power. It may, accordingly, have informed the self-images of many women who did not benefit from its positive promises of protection and respect. Middle-class women may, in fact, frequently identify primarily with the positive aspect of the myth and only register its negative sanctions unconsciously. For many middle-class women have undoubtedly derived psychological comfort from the view of themselves as the softening antidote to the impersonal competition of the public world, while many others have agreed that if they obey the rules they will encounter no violence. Lower-class women are less likely to embrace such illusions, and their very skepticism confirms their more clear-sighted recognition of the negative aspects of the myth. For the mere existence of the illusions of the myth is widely taken to license special forms of male aggression and violence against those who transgress their bonds.

The legacy of these attitudes depressingly lingers among undergraduates today. For although the "sexual revolution" of the 1960s has "liberated" young women from many of the older constraints of propriety, it has also deprived them of the attendant protections. Young women no longer need worry (or worry as acutely as their predecessors did) if a young man will respect her if she has sexual relations with him or even other men before marriage. They do, however, have cause to worry that when they choose not to have sexual relations with a particular man, their "no" may not be respected. The ensuing confusion has given rise to an epidemic of "acquaintance rape" on campuses. And almost as distressing as the epidemic has been some of the response to it. For many young men and, worse, young women cling to the delusion that a woman who has been victim of sexual violence has, in some way, asked for it.

Like these deplorable lingering attitudes, sisterhood is the direct heir to the complicated and contradictory myth of separate spheres. As a myth in its own right, sisterhood has proclaimed the unity of women on the basis of radically different experiences and in the name of feelings that, like the family feelings from which they derive, mask the realities of power and opportunity. Sisterhood in itself has entailed no special political positions, although it has contributed to the rhetoric of every feminist upsurge. Because of its universal appeal, it has periodically supported a pervasive cultural feminism that, at its most mystifying, elaborates a universal ideology which in practice merely eases the passage of some privileged middle-class women into the public sphere. Thus, in an irony that few choose to recognize, the gains reaped in the name of sisterhood frequently result in the sharpening of class lines by pushing lower-class and minority women, singly or together with their men, further down the socioeconomic scale. There can, for example, be no doubt that what is increasingly being called the "feminization of poverty" has emerged during the years in which the women's movement has begun to make substantial gains for middle-class women.[30]

The rhetoric of sisterhood has deeply informed various feminist campaigns, notably the domestic feminism of the nineteenth century, various struggles for women's legal and political rights, and specific labor struggles.[31] Recently, it has contributed to the struggle for the ERA and the pro-choice movement and has especially strengthened the separatist tendencies within feminism. Throughout these campaigns sisterhood has been invoked in defense of various interpretations of feminism, including individual female privilege. Indeed, it could be argued that middle-class feminism has come to rely more and more heavily on the rhetoric of sisterhood precisely as the social and economic prospects for an inclusive feminism have been diminishing, for even the advancement of individual women profits from the illusion of a general female solidarity.[32]

The perceived cleavage between women's and men's modes of being and understanding, promoted by the ideology of separate spheres, has remained so broad and influential that no understanding of feminism or sisterhood is possible apart from it. On the basis of that perceived cleavage, many strong and self-reliant women have been able, in good conscience, to oppose feminism as either irrelevant to or corrosive of women's special mission. Feminists have not concurred. To them achievement of the vote and full access to political life has appeared of critical, if not unique, importance. But, beginning in the mid-nineteenth century and increasingly today, human equality even more than political equality has emerged as the decisive issue. Both female and male feminists of the late nineteenth century, accepting the distinct characteristics of female being, sought to combine it with aspects of male being to forge a model of human being that strongly resembled androgyny. They thus favored gender integration not merely in the social and political arenas, but in human consciousness as well. Their vision, which retains many attractive features and which persists among some middle-class feminists today, also exposed serious problems.[33] Specifically, it ignored the realities of class and race and obscured the fundamental differences and conflicts between the sexes.[34] Above all, their specific vision of female equality rested on a vision of society and human nature that repudiated the notion of power.

Power remained the fundamental issue, and simple denial could not wish it away. The nineteenth- and early twentieth-century women's movements confronted power on every front, beginning with the ubiquitous struggle with men that derives from the intractable differences between the sexes. They also faced struggles particular to their own society and culture, notably that with the anxious ghost of a patriarchy that had been repudiated in politics but that hung on in domestic relations. Confronting not the socially and politically embedded patriarchs of the distant past, nor even the relatively secure pseudo-patriarchs of the early modern period, but their increasingly market-dependent heirs, women had to contend with a male authority that increasingly depended for its very existence upon women—women whose internalization of their proclaimed inferiority and dependency alone could legitimate male authority. Hierarchy, banished from the public sphere, was transplanted to the domestic sphere and the individual psyche. To be sure, it did not survive intact. Social relations had changed, but, as often happens, their more superficial forms and a persistent rhetoric evoked a reassuring continuity. The growing disjunction between traditional values and changing social and economic conditions helps to explain the anxiety and "nervous diseases" that plagued both women and men, just as it helps to explain the violence that savaged domestic life and barred women's free access to the public world.

Understanding power as the issue, many feminists sought to secure its political weapons for women. They engaged the struggle for equal access to the public sphere, including the vote, legal equality, and employment. In addition, they struggled for respect for themselves and other women and for the recognition and implementation of what they viewed as women's values throughout society. In the most difficult instances they struggled with other women to ensure the triumph of their commitments. In almost all instances they struggled against male complacency, condescension, idealization, disdain, and abuse. In all instances they struggled against themselves—against the ingrained contradictions between the positive and negative views of women in which they had been reared.

The recognition of men's power led an impressive if undetermined number of middle-class women to struggle on behalf of their yet more oppressed sisters, for they understood the ways in which men's power oppressed women of other classes and races. Some fought valiantly against slavery. Others worked to protect working-class women against the abuse of working-class men and even against the undue exploitation of employers. But rarely, if ever, did they seriously consider the inequalities of power that separated them from other women whose causes they embraced. To the contrary, they normally took for granted that their view of women's rights and needs embodied universal principles—that their agenda should set the agenda for those less fortunate than they.

In these assumptions the confusion between the public and private roles of women remained paramount. In the eyes of men, women's private roles had a necessary public function and women's aspiration to a public role was taken to violate female nature itself. In the eyes of many women, however, the defense of women's private roles necessitated women's intervention in the public sphere. For, without women's public action on behalf of their private values, how could those values be defended? Yet how were women to act publicly without adapting to the public sphere? The growing participation of women in reform movements, organized charity, and social work inexorably led to a "feminization" of the public sphere, or to a "masculinization" of reforming women. In this complex process, the extension of female values into public life threatened to corrupt femininity as a public representation of strictly domestic values. How and where could the lines between home and market, between femininity and masculinity, be drawn?

These doubts, which plagued women as well as men, were deeply colored by an official—and predominantly male—view of the appropriate female role. The contradictions and tensions remain with us. Women today are more directly heirs of our predecessors than is often acknowledged. The history of their struggles, complete with victories, failures, and compromises, binds us, just as the history of the social relations and attitudes we oppose binds our opponents. That legacy colors the struggle for women's rights today.

Any feminist struggle draws much of its impetus from the inescapable conflict between men and women. As social facts, male strength and female reproductive power pit the sexes against each other in a conflict rendered only more poignant by the attraction that locks mortal adversaries in each other's embrace. Female self-definition, like female self-determination, remains informed by at least some trace of an elemental rage against the persistent threat of rape and physical violence. The motive force of feminism can never entirely be divorced from that psychological mainspring, even if most women are not conscious of it most of the time. But whatever the significance of those psychological traces, feminist language and goals are formulated in specific historical context and from the available political language of their society. Specific societies and polities establish the conditions, the limits, and, therefore, the forms, of feminism. Mary Wollstonecraft borrowed heavily from the eighteenth-century notions of individual right, just as some contemporary feminists are borrowing from postmodernist notions of indeterminacy.[35]

The relation between feminism and the dominant political language appears obvious. The quest for the realization of equal rights for all individuals regardless of gender or race draws directly upon the American political tradition and current social struggles.

Feminist theorists, especially socialist-feminists, have devoted considerable energy to arguing that capitalism and patriarchy in fact intertwine and even to arguing that patriarchy constitutes the older, more resilient, and more dangerous enemy. But their position rests on the dubious assumptions that the continuities in male power are more important than the discontinuities and that men's power over women is politically more significant than and effectively independent of all other forms of political, social, and economic power.[36] These assumptions cannot withstand scrutiny. The power that men exercise over women depends upon the polity, society, and economy in which it is embedded and which it articulates. Yet as Lynne Segal has argued, the "uneven, sometimes widening gap between what feminism had seemed to promise and women's still vulnerable, and for some increasingly impoverished, position in the world, fits most neatly with a biologistic and fatalistic interpretation of the inevitability of men's power."[37]

Sisterhood as the dominant metaphor for relations among women and, by implication, for relations among humans subordinates political to personal relations. In defining oppression as subjection to the law of the father, sisterhood defines politics as the domination of women by men. In rejecting the law of the father, sisterhood rejects the domination of the male. But since the great bourgeois revolutions, men have not generally accepted the law of the father as an adequate justification for political power. Indeed, those revolutions could instructively be viewed as the replacement of the father by the brotherhood. But where men had defended the principle of the equal division of the father's power among individuals—the brothers—women, in defending sisterhood, were advocating the egalitarian distribution of powerlessness. In so doing, they were, without acknowledging it, claiming the democratization not of the father's power but of the mother's (purported) lack of power.

Motherhood has deeply engaged the attention of many feminist theorists, notably Dorothy Dinnerstein, Nancy Chodorow, Adrienne Rich, Mary O'Brien, Sara Ruddick, and Jean Bethke Elshtain. Dinnerstein and Chodorow have especially called attention to the reproduction of mothering in capitalist society, and to the terrifying price it extracts from male as well as female children. Their work suggests that motherhood has afforded women considerable power, albeit largely unacknowledged.[38] Rich, independently exploring the question, similarly has concluded that motherhood affords women power and significant satisfaction. O'Brien, following yet another line, has insisted that the culture of childbearing binds women, including those who do not bear children, into a fellowship grounded in the practices of mothering. And Ruddick, pushing the argument to its extreme, has attempted to argue that women, whether or not they bear children, share a propensity to "maternal thinking," a commitment to nurturing life and an inherent opposition to its destruction in war.[39] Elshtain, too, believes that the values of care traditionally associated with women's mothering should be more broadly disseminated throughout social relations and places much more emphasis than the others on the complexities of psychological development.[40]

Feminist reflections on motherhood extend from a critique of the psychological consequences of pronounced gender roles and a split between public and private to a celebration of the values derived from women's distinct experience. In the first instance, the argument implicitly points toward an androgynous merger of the distinctions between women and men and more equal sharing of the responsibilities of child rearing. In the second, it points toward a recognition of the differences between women and men and, perhaps, a triumph of female over male values.[41] In both instances, the emphasis on love and nurture has in some measure masked the ambiguity of a power that is not normally recognized as power. According to prevailing feminist theory, the principal responsibilities of motherhood have traditionally consisted in teaching sons to free themselves from maternal bonds and values and in teaching daughters to internalize constraints and repress the angers against which the powerful mother herself has no recourse. The power of motherhood has, in other words, existed within the context and on sufferance of a system of political and economic power beyond its control. The power of motherhood is personal.

The limits of that personal power should be abundantly clear. Motherhood, as our culture has envisioned it, depends upon economic security and upon minimal protection of private life from public influence. Some conservatives persist in the illusion that traditional motherhood can be restored by fiat—primarily by eliminating supports for working women. Most of us know better, whatever our secret longings. The necessity for two incomes or, in the case of single mothers, for one, forces mothers into the workplace. Drugs, alcohol, child molestation, television, consumer culture, and peer pressure war against maternal influence on every front, penetrating the walls of even the most solid homes. Yet the illusion of maternal—and paternal—responsibility persists. In practice, most women cope as best they can. Children are left with baby-sitters or expensive housekeepers or placed in daycare centers, if available. But Americans have difficulty in portraying these solutions as a positive good. And then something happens: a fire is lit, a child drowns, a child is raped or terrorized or swallows pills. And many of us, in spite of ourselves, think that if only the mother had been there. . . .

Many feminists are quick to condemn the conservatives' nostalgia for a world that has gone beyond resurrection. They are less ready, if at all, to recognize it in their own thinking. Yet the celebration of women's maternal roles and instincts partakes of the same nostalgia, the same refusal to recognize the realities of political power. That refusal is all the more tragic and all the more deadly for coherent feminist politics because it ties feminism to a personal politics that cannot meet even middle-class women's needs and woefully ignores the realities that poor, especially minority, women confront every day.

Sisterhood, like motherhood, invokes nonpolitical relations, even as it claims to unite political and personal relations in a single struggle. In so doing, it misses the point. The call to understand the personal as political apparently demands the intrusion of competitive and conflictive relations into the purportedly nonconflicting personal realm. This call rests on the understanding that beneath myths of harmony and innate characteristics embedded in the myth of separate spheres there lies an intense political struggle. But for most feminists, that understanding reduces to the vision of the struggles between women and men as the essence of politics, rather than as the product of class and racial politics. The notion of sisterhood thus implicitly affirms a continuum between private and public relations, by affirming the primacy of the personal struggle between women and men over conventional political struggles, understood as the war games of boys.

But, many insist, the personal is political. Only fighting the personal battles will effect lasting change, for the struggle is for human minds. Of course. But while minds can only be won in the here-and-now of everyday life, daily life moves within the constraints of massive social, economic, and political forces. It should make feminists thoughtful that so many younger middle-class women have been refusing to align themselves with a feminist movement that they identify primarily with personal struggle, and that so many poor and minority women find it impossible to identify with a feminist movement that they perceive as largely impervious to their most pressing concerns, especially economic security and adequate daycare.[42]

The real lesson of the middle-class feminism of the 1960s and 1970s is that the personal is social—a proposition that conservative traditionalists and Marxists alike have always understood. The core of the myth of sisterhood lies in middle-class women's ability to recognize the similarity of their experiences. WASP and Jewish women from the towns and cities of the Northeast, the Midwest, and California readily found common patterns in their lives: childhoods in middle-class families; adolescent conflicts with mothers; self-discovery in college frequently foreclosed by a misguided first marriage; the unexpected constraints of motherhood; divorce; and, finally, a fresh start. Throughout the 1970s a spate of women's novels chronicled specific variations on that common experience.[43] Throughout the 1970s, middle-class women learned to recognize their own autobiographies in the lives of others—their sisters. And their recognition amounted to a release from the imprisoning silence that had led one woman after another to experience her problems as uniquely personal. Similar social backgrounds produced similar stories and responses.

Thus, the middle-class spokeswomen for the new women's movement, without fully recognizing what they were doing, established their own autobiographies as the benchmark for the experience of all women.[44] In so doing, they closely followed the lead of their brothers, who had long claimed that the experience of white middle-class men constituted the substance of and model for the experience of men in general. And like their brothers, they subordinated the experience of innumerable less fortunate Americans to their own and claimed for themselves the right to speak in the name of all. In this perspective, feminist politics of the personal unmistakably emerges as a politics of race and class that perpetuates the injustices of American society.

The experience of sisterhood has proved invaluable for the middle-class women lucky enough to have reaped its benefits. It has helped them to name their oppressors, including their unconscious ghosts, and to describe their social situation. In this sense, it has offered an invaluable experience of naming. And, since that naming has been collectively undertaken, it has helped women to forge ties of mutual respect and, yes, nurture. But it has not—and cannot—provide tools adequate to naming the real conditions of the oppression of all women. The language of sisterhood amounts to little more than a reversal of the language of oppression itself. Born of the capitalist split between the domestic and public spheres, it contributes, however inadvertently, to an internal transformation of capitalism that will afford yet more humiliating oppression for most, if not all, women.

The possibilities of even the most generous and inclusive sisterhood cannot extend much beyond prevailing social conditions. Some, mainly middle-class, women have made significant gains with respect to employment and financial independence, but their independence has tended to release them from the custodianship of individual men only to throw them into the arms of corporations and the federal government, which are increasingly replacing independent private institutions including family businesses and universities. The new mega-institutions can afford a much larger measure of heterogeneity than their predecessors could—can afford to hire women or minorities as well as, or even instead of, white men. But if the upper echelons of this new system can now indiscriminately employ men, women, and blacks, the lower echelons can, with equal arbitrariness, employ fewer full-time workers of any gender or race. In short, we are participating in an unprecedented widening gap between social classes, perhaps most dramatically captured in the proliferation of homelessness and the difference in life expectancy and infant mortality among classes, but also in the growing gap between the wages of high school and college graduates.[45]

These new conditions, which have a tremendous impact upon women's lives, should make us cautious in our hopes for a universal sisterhood. Among the new rich, financial security increasingly depends upon two salaries. If the woman does not work, the family confronts a declining standard of living. Among the new poor, women's work cannot cover the costs of decent childcare, much less education for the children and household help for the woman.[46] Hence many married women of the declining traditional working class understandably see their need to work as in conflict with their ability to mother their children and, accordingly, as a threat to the standard of living and culture in the next generation. Not surprisingly, as Kristen Luker and Sylvia Hewlett have argued, they see their only salvation in a strengthening of women's traditional domestic roles.[47]

The growing numbers of women consigned to the underclass of our cities face even bleaker prospects. Frequently unable to count on any support from men, inadequately trained for all but the most menial, part-time employment, many live on welfare in the maelstrom of a decaying public sphere from which they cannot hope to protect their children or even themselves. Crack, AIDS, and imprisonment are beginning to claim the lives of increasing numbers of women to whom American society offers no realistic hopes for the future.

How, under these conditions, can feminists seriously invoke sisterhood? Pious concern and benevolence go only so far, and certainly not back to the drug-infested projects and welfare hotels at night. What good does a middle-class woman's employment, raise, or promotion do her sisters? Many solid working-class women might argue that their middle-class sister's success merely threatens their own husband's or son's opportunities by taking jobs that were previously, and perhaps from their perspective correctly, reserved for men. Many underclass women would see no connection at all.

The myth of sisterhood has helped middle-class women, as it helped so many of their predecessors, to establish their presence in national life, but the unspoken premise of that dream of equality remains equality with men. "Which men?" poor women are entitled to ask. And what of equality among women? The sisterhood of "L.A. Law" includes Abby and Anne, and Gracie, when she is in a good mood, but not Roxanne, even after her marriage to a wealthy man. The worst nightmare that serious feminists must face is that in a decade or two the women's movement may be seen as having done the dirty work of capitalism—of having eroded the older communities and bourgeois institutions that blocked the way to a sinister new despotism. And if so, it should not be surprising to find many women, including many middle-class women, looking back to the older, oppressive bourgeois era as a golden age.

Academic feminists' celebration of diversity and indeterminacy in many respects captures the reality of poor women's lives. In a world that cannot sustain marriages, atomization governs everyone's lives. Welfare does not constitute an adequate substitute either for an employed husband or for economic independence, although welfare powerfully contributes to de-stroying gender hierarchy. That it may also increase random male violence is a matter that feminist theory has yet to explore. Women who face the conditions of the projects alone experience postmodernism in its most sinister guise.[48]

In the end, our politics must include the responsibility to forge a lan-guage and a practice that permits the objectification of personal relations and hard alliances among social groups. Politics bridges the gap between the particular and the general and constructs a nexus through which need may be translated into justice. By transforming the subjective impetus into an objective standard, politics permits the grouping of individual experiences into general goals. In our society, as feminist legal theorists insist, law (the universal category) has historically had a distinct male cast.[49] Part of the struggle, accordingly, must be to revise our standards to encompass wom-en's as well as men's experience. But to wage that struggle on the assump-tion that all women share the same goals, or on the assumption that women innately hold different values than men, or worse, on the assumption that no abstract standard is acceptable, is to jeopardize the outcome. Sisterhood, understood as natural affinity and solidarity among women, does not offer a strategy appropriate to the task.

Even the sisterhood that historically has proved effective within class and racial communities offers an uncertain basis for interclass and interracial alliances. The contemporary rhetoric of sisterhood has thus enjoyed its greatest success as a defensive posture among middle-class women, who can easily transform it into a rationale for political co-optation. For, in a crazy reversal, the politicization of the personal becomes the personalization of the political, in which individual women justify their own successes and arbitrary choices in the name of sisterhood: what benefits me necessarily benefits my sisters. The individual thus appropriates the being of others by claiming her individualism as the realization of collective purpose. But this identification only works if different women's opportunities are so comparable as to reduce the differences among women to simple personal variation. And they are not.

The claim that the personal is political has helped to expose the deep connections between individual experience and social context. It has assuredly exposed the ways in which the family and especially the ideal of motherhood does not belong to a sheltered private sphere, but depend heavily upon the vagaries of public life. But, as a legitimation of the political significance of the autobiographies of middle-class women, it leaves much to be desired.

To the extent that the personal is political, women need hard political wisdom and face hard political choices. If the myth of separate spheres is bankrupt, then how do we reconstruct adequate protections for families, and indeed other social institutions? The women's movement has primarily focused on enlarging opportunities for individual women. Some are now moving beyond that strategy, but they are primarily focusing on specific groups—African-American, Hispanic-American—rather than upon the complex relations among women of different groups. Meanwhile, popular feminism continues to draw upon the early personalist implications of sisterhood, especially upon the vision of distinct women's values. The real problem with this current, as Lynne Segal has argued, is that in representing "women as essentially virtuous and men as essentially vicious," it "serves the forces of reaction as surely as it serves the forces of progress."[50] The most daunting challenge remains to develop a new vision that underscores the claims of society as a whole. For without such a vision we risk a radical fragmentation that realizes the most Kafkaesque nightmares of solitary individuals at the mercy of sinister, faceless power.

2

WOMEN AND

COMMUNITY

Personal experience, Edith Klein argues, has led women to embrace the goals of the women's movement, whereas men have embraced them out of an abstract sense of justice.[1] Justice, however, has seemed an arid, inadequate goal to many women who came to the women's movement with a longing for a genuine transformation of their own lives in particular and American society in general. To such women, (male) justice looks more like the problem than the solution. Nor could politics as usual, even if put to the service of women's rights, serve. From this viewpoint, any adequate redressing of women's wrongs must reflect and build upon women's experience and values. Thus the implications of the metaphors of sisterhood and motherhood must be realized in a revitalized sense of community that transcends the instrumentalism of politics.

This sensibility has influenced many feminists, including many who do support the efficacy of conventional political struggles in support of women's goals, notably women who, finding the rewards of professional success less satisfying than they expected, are drawn to various forms of female community and spirituality. So no arbitrary distinction between politics and community can be drawn, especially since feminism has contributed so much to our ability to recognize the potential political implications and consequences of superficially apolitical activities. The attempt to draw a sharp line between politics and community becomes yet more problematical because of the imprecise meaning of community itself. For most of us use "community" heuristically to designate a group based on merging, on shared values, on shared attributes in contrast to atomized individuals, but we rarely if ever establish its precise boundaries. To the contrary, we tend to think of community, if anything, as resulting from the personal commitment of members rather than from the imposition of external legal and political limits. Yet historically, community has derived much more from imposed external boundaries than from internal commitments.

The Oxford dictionary indicates the complexity by including in its first meaning of community a state of being shared or held in common—joint ownership or liability—and fellowship. The definition thus moves from legal status to feeling. The second definition follows a similar progression, moving from an organized political, municipal, or social body to a body of people living in the same locality, having the same religion or profession in common, or otherwise sharing common interests.[2] Community, in other words, means a group of people who may be bound together by anything from a legal obligation to mutual sympathies. Thus although community may have a specific foundation in joint ownership or community property and may refer to political identity or structure, its implications diverge from those of formal political institutions and, especially, from the competition of political and market relations.

The nineteenth-century German sociologist Ferdinand Tönnies based his theory of social development and order on the distinction between community (*Gemeinschaft*) and society (*Gesellschaft*). Tönnies never doubted the superiority of community over society. In his judgment, community embodied organic, traditional relations, whereas society embodied the nefarious consequences of individualism, instrumentalism, and contractualism. With community, he associated the attributes of affectivity, particularism, ascription (quality), tradition, and family. With society he associated affective neutrality, universalism, achievement (performance), specificity, rationality, and contract.[3]

Tönnies's view of community and society has resonated widely among twentieth-century conservatives, notably southern conservatives from Allen Tate to Richard Weaver and M. E. Bradford.[4] Indeed the southern conservative tradition has largely defined itself in opposition to modern notions of society—specifically to capitalism and bourgeois individualism—and has forcefully insisted upon the claims of local groups bound by a common tradition and governed by indigenous principles. For these conservatives, individuality develops only in relation to the communities to which individuals belong, beginning with the family and progressing to village, town, and region.

Tönnies's notion of community has also been widely adopted by left-wing theorists, many of whom have shared southern conservatives' and other traditionalists' thoroughgoing opposition to capitalism and bourgeois individualism. No one, for example, more scathingly attacked the deleterious effects of unbridled individualism than Karl Marx, whose analysis of alienation underscored the ways in which capitalism divorced laborers from their own labor as well as from one another. Marx's theoretically specific, economically grounded discussion of alienation has led less rigorous left-wing theorists to embrace a general concept of personal alienation in an effort to capture the malaise of modern rootlessness.[5] Indeed the critique of the alienation of individuals—the loss of community—in capitalist society has led many on the left to romanticize premodern social relations as wholeheartedly as any conservative has ever done.[6]

Yet Marx, in ways he did not much reflect upon, was himself strongly influenced by the bourgeois individualism that attended the development of capitalism. And his less-talented and less-learned successors have felt that influence even more. The Marx that has most deeply influenced the recent left was the young Marx, who preached the utopian doctrine of the liberation of individuals from the constraints of society without fully considering the consequences of alternate claims.[7] Conservatives have had their own difficulties in coming to terms with the implicit individualistic assumptions in their thought, but, being fundamentally comfortable with social stratification and deference to authority, they have had an easier time forestalling individualism than those leftists who assume that personal liberation from all constraints constitutes the sine qua non of a desirable society.

These contradictions have cast a long shadow over the development of contemporary feminism, which rhetorically has tended to emphasize the values of community and to claim them for women. In truth, Tönnies's distinction between community and society very much resembles the nineteenth-century distinction between public male and private female spheres. The affective, noncontractual qualities that he associated with community sound disconcertingly like those traditionally associated with women, just as the striving, individualistic qualities that he associated with society sound like those associated with men.

Today, we recognize that ideology of separate spheres as, precisely, an ideology, rather than as a social analysis. The norms of separation, like those of the true womanhood closely allied to them, constituted a prescription for, rather than a description of, behavior.[8] Many white women, including many married women, worked outside the home, or inside it for other people's families. For most black women, at least until emancipation, the distinction had little meaning at all. And even after emancipation, married black women continued to work for wages much more frequently and to enjoy much less protection for their domestic status than their white counterparts of all classes. In this respect, as in many others, the ambiguity of the dictionary definitions of community reflect the ambiguity of the relations between purportedly separate spheres in modern times.[9]

Male theorists on the right and left who have, like Tönnies, preached the virtues of community have normally passed lightly over its foundations in legal and political relations to emphasize its qualities of fellowship and concord. The values, cohesiveness, and identity of community have been used to evoke care, neighborliness, solicitude, and even nurture and have thus widely been taken to provide the antidote to the brutality of the marketplace. For example, nineteenth-century Americans, moving westward, self-consciously sought to build communities, not way stations or labor camps. And women contributed not merely their share of the time and skills required to build them, but frequently the decisive commitment as well. Women, if anything, even more than their men, wanted churches, libraries, neat surroundings, a civilized existence grounded in responsible human networks.[10]

Historians of women have forcefully emphasized women's contributions to the building of communities. From the dawn of the republic, women pioneered in moral reform, especially in organizing community assistance to other women. It has become commonplace to recognize most of women's early activities outside their own households as exercises in community building. Suzanne Lebsock has documented the precocious incorporation of the Female Orphan Asylum in Petersburg, Virginia, in 1813, under women's leadership.[11] In the 1830s, women of New York City engaged in a systematic attempt to eradicate prostitution and to save its victims for upstanding womanhood.[12] Antislavery and abolitionist women, who especially emphasized the woeful effect of slavery on women in particular and community life in general, increasingly came to identify the condition of slavery with that of women.[13] During the antebellum period, the pace of women's reform quickened throughout the Northeast and increasingly the Midwest, although in the slaveholding South the women of Petersburg, as described by Lebsock, remained atypical if not anomalous. And, even in the Northeast, as Christine Stansell has demonstrated, working-class women, who were developing their own culture, values, and communities, did not unequivocally identify with the reformers' efforts.[14]

After the Civil War the pace intensified and the scope widened as black and white southern women inaugurated their own programs of reform. In different ways and for somewhat different constituencies, the Women's Christian Temperance Union, the Young Women's Christian Association, the General Federation of Women's Clubs, and the National Association of Negro Women's Clubs moved women's reform from the local to the national level, building ties among women of different communities and decisively altering the life of the nation.[15] The growth of cities in the late nineteenth and early twentieth centuries spurred women to extensive efforts to domesticate and contain the worst effects of capitalism. Beginning in 1908, Lugenia Hope, in Atlanta, built the Neighborhood Union to assure black children safe playgrounds.[16] The settlement house movement, under the special leadership of Lillian Wald and Jane Addams, worked to ease the plight of the urban poor, especially that of recent immigrants. Innumerable upper- and middle-class women worked to support charities, art galleries, theaters, operas, and other community institutions that would soften and civilize rampant capitalism. Others formed organizations that paralleled the growing number of men's fraternal organizations.[17]

The full record of women's contributions to community building still remains hidden, but even the part recently recovered reveals women to have been formidable participants in—indeed the bedrock of—every phase of the development of American communities. This partial record also reveals that many women were most successful and apparently most comfortable with public efforts that appeared to derive naturally from the domestic roles assigned them by society. Characteristically, women presented many of their most impressive accomplishments as "social housekeeping" and justified them in the name of prescribed domestic responsibilities.[18]

The ubiquitous association between community building and domesticity should make us thoughtful. Part of the mystique of community derives from its associations with organic relations and timelessness. "Community" has been used to signify the transformation or negation of contractual social relations. But, unless we accept a view of community as grounded in nature, instinct, or biology, it amounts to little more than an aura. Where women succeeded in creating community, they succeeded in creating a sense of belonging and bonding in contrast to the ruthless pursuit of individual self-interest. In this respect, community might better be understood as the opposite of individualism than of society. Indeed, that may well be what Tönnies meant to convey. For communities, like individuals, constitute the building blocks, or components, of societies and polities, albeit with radically opposed implications.

At an accelerating pace, since the mid-seventeenth century, capitalist societies in general, and American society in particular, have steadily repudiated community as the basic social and political unit, preferring, at least in theory but increasingly in law and in social life, to ground their public institutions in the individual. Law and social life especially lagged behind theory in a reluctance fully to open the opportunities of individualism—the category of the individual—to women and black people, notably married women and slaves. But, with the abolition of slavery, suffrage, and the increasing recognition of the individual rights even of married women, not to mention the increasing attention to the rights of children, Americans have moved inexorably toward the casting of all members of society and polity as individuals—toward the introduction of public norms into what had been viewed as the private sphere.[19] For how else are we to understand the implications of the current debate about the right of girls under eighteen to obtain abortions without the consent of their parents?[20] This "progress" has inescapably depended upon the complementary destruction of the rights of community—understood as binding claims upon individuals.

Americans, like others in bourgeois societies, have been loathe to recognize the inexorable erosion of community. If anything, that erosion has prompted a heightened nostalgia about the organic values of "the world we have lost" and a sentimental determination to restore community on a new basis. But the modern celebration of community must be recognized as primarily a defense against the actual social, economic, political, and legal conditions of modern life. As a defense, this celebration embodies serious contradictions that inform much of our political and social thought—especially feminism.

Both the idealization of community and the ideology of individualism as autonomy and privacy obscure the essential truth, which conservatives have generally recognized, that the history of men, like that of women, has been primarily the history of communities. Since the beginnings of human history, men and women have demonstrated a propensity to congregate in communities. The propensity runs so deep as to look very much like a fundamental aspect of human nature.[21] Whatever the intentions of nature, the development of human history has offered communities differing degrees of legal and political protection, until in our own time—with the noteworthy exception of corporations—they receive very little at all. Yet the human propensity to identify with community has outlived the persistence of community as an identifiable legal and political unit. Men and women as social beings still tend to perceive themselves as members of families, localities, races, churches, ethnic groups, neighborhoods, or other communities defined by a wide variety of criteria.

Feminist theory has drawn upon women's commitment to community building to argue for women's persistent tendency to define and represent themselves in relation to others rather than as individuals in the abstract.[22] A similar, although unlabeled, sense of women's primary identification with communities also seems to underlie the argument that women's sense of morality, in contrast to the abstract morality of men, derives from their perception of specific relations among people.[23] A significant group of feminist legal scholars are also developing a sustained critique of our prevailing (male) concept of justice on the basis of women's distinct experience. At its most theoretically sophisticated, as in the hands of Robin West, this work is moving feminist theory toward a probing critique of individualism. Thus for West, although the view of the individual as essentially autonomous and separate—as " 'epistemologically and morally prior to the collectivity' "—"may be true *for men*," it is "not true for women."[24]

These critiques, Jennifer Nedelsky has noted, embody a "rejection of liberal individualism" that intersects with a more widespread critique of "the individualistic premises of liberal theory." Rogers Smith and Christine Spaulding also suggest that liberalism is proving inadequate to sustaining community.[25] In general, however, feminist critiques have also remained tied, in ways that their authors do not always acknowledge, to the legacy of individualism. For, implicitly or explicitly, feminist theory has been unselfconsciously building upon the specific history of women's experience within individualistic societies and cultures. In these respects, feminist theory in large measure accurately reflects women's historical experience of exclusion from the polity and identification with the private realm, notably those families that conservatives consider the basic units of communities. In so doing, they risk falling into what Michael Sandel, criticizing John Rawls, has called the "sentimental" conception of community. In this conception, community is viewed as, in some sense, internal to the motivations and identities of the participants—a product of their commitment. This conception differs from a more instrumental or contractual view of community in attributing affiliation to benevolence or even identity rather than to instrumental self-interest, but it nonetheless continues to ground community in individualism.[26] And, in this respect, it very much resembles the dominant tendencies in feminist discussion of community.

The association of women with communities has a solid historical basis, but it has bequeathed much confusion to contemporary feminist theory. For if communities have afforded women a positive source of support and identification, communities, as reinforced and defined by states, have also figured as the immediate locus of women's domestic confinement. Feminism, in implicitly anchoring women's sense of community in their experience within families, which many feminists have identified as the primary source of women's oppression, perpetuates a fundamental contradiction and, especially, reinforces a sentimental view of community as emanating from the subjective intentions of individuals. For most feminists seek simultaneously to destroy the vestiges of families' control of women and to celebrate women's instinctive embodiment of the value of community that derived from their experience within families. The position of conservatives offers a valuable perspective on that of feminists. For conservatives, who also view families as the basic units of and models for community, tend to prefer a strong view of community as historically and legally, not just psychologically and morally, prior to the individual. And most feminists would not accept the easiest solution to the contradiction—namely that, by and large, women did not so much feel belittled as empowered by their ascribed position within families.[27]

From the start, an important tendency in feminist theory has resolutely championed women's rights as individuals—their absolute right to break free of the legal and political domination of communities. In this spirit, many feminists have insisted upon women's unilateral right to personal autonomy, sexual freedom, and divorce. But history has proved individualism at best a mixed blessing for women who, freed from community domination, face society with inadequate protection.[28] The growing consciousness of these deceptions has led many feminists to cling to an ideal of community while continuing to attack its specific manifestations. This nostalgia has tended to deflect feminist inquiry from a systematic discussion of community and has confused feminist positions on central theoretical problems.

When feminist theorists invoke the family as a primary source of women's oppression or more generally insist on the persistence of patriarchy, they treat women's oppression, even when they do not explicitly say so, as a consequence of their membership in communities. These denunciations of the role of community in oppressing and confining women cannot easily be reconciled with the conflicting view that women's distinct and supposedly more humane values derive from their association with communities. Indeed the attempt to conjoin the two positions, which few have attempted explicitly to reconcile, betrays the uneasy coexistence of communitarian and individualistic commitments in contemporary feminist theory and also betrays considerable confusion about the universal and the particular in the experience of specific women or groups of women.

In effect, much contemporary feminist theory asserts that women, independent of class or race, have historically shared the experience of oppression by and seclusion within communities. It asserts that the universal experience of dominance by men within small groups so outweighs the particular characteristics and experiences of the discrete groups as to constitute a universal principle of women's experience. This theory interprets the experience of oppression as a universal facet of women's experience and thus minimizes the specific characteristics of the oppression of black slave women, or Italian American working-class women, or northeastern middle-class white women, or even white southern slaveholding women; for in each instance the content of the oppression has been different. It emphasizes the universality of men's oppression of women and, in consequence, would have particular women identify themselves and their condition in relation to man in the abstract and, therefore, with the concept of woman in the abstract.[29]

The dominant tendency in modern feminist theory, at least since the late eighteenth century and the work of Mary Wollstonecraft, has closely followed the emergence of individualism in mainstream political thought in insisting on the universality of women's experience. Thus Wollstonecraft, in *A Vindication of the Rights of Woman*, used the singular to mean women in general, much as the familiar "Rights of Man" meant, in effect, "Rights of Individual Men."[30] But this determination to cast the experience of women as universal is not itself universal: it is a direct product of modern society and thought.

Universal models of womanhood are hardly new. All the great religions have included some representation of female nature. In the Christian tradition Eve and the Virgin Mary have figured simultaneously as distinct women and as general models. Broad cultural traditions similarly have developed archetypes of woman, such as the virgin and the whore, or the disorderly woman. And as these patterns emerged from and intersected with local cultures, they helped to establish norms. But we have scant reason to believe that most women took those norms to imply general equality or similarity among women. They more likely perceived their own womanhood as particular rather than universal, as one—perhaps the dominant—element of their membership in particular communities. For so long as differences in class and condition counted for more than biological similarity in the political definition of male status, they also counted for more than biology or cultural generalizations in female experience.[31] Thus even when precapitalist women defended their rights as women, they did so in the name of the rights of women within their community. Ibo women in Nigeria, in demonstrating in defense of their traditional marketing privileges, were defending the rights of Ibo women, not the rights of woman in general.[32]

Most communities have, in fact, shared some models of womanhood that are so common as to appear universal, notably those, such as mother, which derived from women's sexuality and family position. But, in creating their own versions of those models, they have cast them in the likeness and garbed them in the clothing of their own group. One need only think of the endlessly varied artistic representations of women to grasp this specificity. In Western culture, representations of the Madonna alone have changed significantly over time. As Anne Hollander has argued for painting in general, artists, like societies, see through clothes—that is, they see the embodiment of human nature through the specific conventions of their own culture.[33] Thus the most universal aspects of womanhood have always been represented as particular, as grounded in a woman's intertwining relations to the other members of a specific community. Daughter in one family, a woman becomes wife and mother in another, both linked by ties of production, locality, and religion. These ties simultaneously constitute her sense of community and her community's sense of her. To the extent that she identifies, as women frequently have, with communities of other women, she does so with women of the interlocking communities to which she belongs.

In premodern societies, women exercised only marginal choice about the communities with which they identified. In most peasant societies—the immediate reference point—women, like most men, belonged to communities by fiat rather than by choice and were unlikely to enjoy much choice about their religion, their husband, or even about how many children they would bear. In the premodern world, the harsh constraints of mere survival subjected men as well as women, but women in most societies normally suffered the additional constraints of being considered potentially dangerous and disorderly and were thus assigned to the strict control of the men of their families and communities. Never a voluntary matter for anyone, community membership was sexually asymmetrical and, increasingly with the advent of capitalism and imperialism, economically unequal.[34]

The modern world broke radically with this traditional practice in daring to propose that individual merit and individual choice should govern men's membership in communities. By the time such individualism had become a viable or even expedient basis for men's participation in society, the market had begun to erode the material foundations of traditional communities, although without immediately releasing women from their constraints. Modern bourgeois states and markets retained severe restrictions on women's mobility and independence, notably by denying married women the right to hold property and frequently even to control their own wages. Even protective labor legislation, which sought to shield women from the most demanding jobs and the longest hours, can, from one perspective, be viewed as limiting women's access to economic independence and as enforcing their dependence on men.[35] Individualism for women lagged far behind individualism for men, as individualism for the dispossessed of all races lagged far behind that for the propertied.

For Tönnies, one of the main distinctions between community and society was that between unity and conflict of wills. Community, he held, rested on the unity of wills. And he advanced the relations of man and wife in phrases reminiscent of Blackstone, who had insisted that at law the husband and wife are one and embodied in the husband.[36] Society embodies the conflict of wills. Stripped of its ideological claims, Tönnies's distinction faithfully describes important features of women's experience. Women did indeed remain subject to involuntary community membership long after men had, in principle if not always in fact, become entitled to self-determination. When women trespassed or were thrown upon the market, the consequences of the ideology of separate spheres followed them in the form of licensed violence against their persons, lower wages, and exclusion from opportunity.

Thus women's close association with the private sphere gave rise to the view that women who strayed from it became the legitimate prey of men—that, for example, women who are raped have "asked for it," not to mention the, if anything, more perverse notion that the rape of a woman is a crime against the man in whose keeping she belongs. The association also gave rise to the assumption that women who worked for wages were merely supplementing the primary income earned by the male head of their household or family. Thus the feminist struggles to identify rape as a crime against women and to defend women's rights to equal wages both embody the larger attempt to differentiate women as individuals from their roles within families—to ensure women the right freely to act as individuals within the public sphere.

From the start, the middle-class women's movement sought to improve women's access to voluntary membership in communities, beginning with the family. Women, including married women, required rights to their own property, to their own earnings, to their own persons. They, like men, must have a vote—or so many women came to believe—in order to shape the communities to which they belonged. Other women, fearing or mistrusting the implications of atomization, shrank from claiming full individualism for women, preferring to hold men and communities to high standards of caring for women.[37] The dilemma of individualism versus protection persists in social policy and politics, dividing women against one another as well as against men. Feminists today heatedly debate the desirability of claiming maternity leave as a specific right of women, rather than fighting for parental leave for men and women.[38] But such debates cannot fully mask the extent to which the market has completed its corrosive work. For communities retain little independent standing, and the premises of individualism have permeated most of our political thought, including the feminist.

Today, the opposition between community and individualism strongly resembles that between love and contract as the basis for marriage. Marriage, shorn of community, of religious and legal sanctions, is no more than a contract—and not a very binding one at that. Or it is no more than love. The two go hand in hand. Love offers the comforting illusion of choice, loyalty, and perhaps even continuity—who dares anymore to mention permanence?—to gloss over the fragility of the temporary alliance of interest of two individuals. Similarly, community has come to mean no more than the illusion of personal commitment and nonmarket ties in a world in which membership in practically all institutions results from the "voluntary" choices of individuals. A recognition that economic necessity influences the choices of some more than others in no way changes the principle. Nor has feminist theory systematically attempted to challenge it.

This historical perspective on women and community suggests a number of tentative generalizations: (1) community membership has indeed figured at the core of women's self-perceptions; (2) women's membership in communities has normally been involuntary rather than voluntary; (3) ever since women began to enjoy some measure of choice in their community membership, they have remained unequal or subordinate members of their communities of choice and more dependent upon them than their male counterparts; (4) women in modern times have been especially encouraged to identify with the ascriptive values of community rather than the achievement values of individualism; (5) within the confines of their community membership and attendant ascriptive values, women have accomplished marvelous works for their communities; (6) with the spread of contractual individualism as the mainspring of all social relations, community has become an increasingly nostalgic ideology rather than a legally guaranteed social reality; (7) women's growing participation in individualism has been undermined by their persistent inequality with their male counterparts, in part because of a legacy of the relations of men and women within specific communities; (8) the close association between community and the unity of wills that results from inequality has left an inadequate model for community based on gender equality; and (9) the contradictory legacies of community and individualism continue to inform contemporary feminist theory.

In modern times, men have enjoyed the opportunity to combine the struggle for individual achievement with some sense of security in their communities, especially the family. Women have carried heavier burdens of subordination and labor in order to enjoy comparable community support. In effect, men's commitment to individualism has, in the short run, made women, now dependent on men's market earnings, more unequally dependent upon communities than they were previously, even as it has, in the long run, decisively eroded those communities' independence. Throughout the nineteenth century, the expansion of capitalism promoted an increasing dependence upon wages and salaries. With the spread of the market, the economic independence of households and families of all kinds gradually eroded. More and more men went to work for others, following production's move from the household into the public sphere. Shoemakers, for example, who had been independent artisans, became laborers in shoe factories. And as this transition occurred for more and more kinds of work, as even farmers became dependent on the production of cash in contrast to subsistence crops, households in turn began to purchase more and more of the goods that women had once made at home as their economic contribution.[39]

With this transformation the economic value of women's unpaid labor within households inexorably declined, making women increasingly dependent upon men's earnings. Thus, although the rise in men's wages to the level of a "family wage" that could free women and children from the need to work for wages simply to ensure family survival represented significant progress, it can be seen from another perspective as having reinforced women's economic dependence.[40] Individualism, carried on the rising tide of capitalism, transformed community into a fiction that has largely benefited men by easing their transition into that rootless, atomized world that conservatives have so long prophesied and decried.

We have no call to bemoan the passing of traditional communities, which manifested their share of violence and inequality, but the persistence of community as an ideal does suggest that societies worthy of the name may not easily survive on the basis of radical individualism. In this respect, feminists rightly insist upon some community protection against the ravages of individualism, but they have sadly failed to attend to the consequences of their commitments. For in our world community cannot flourish in brave independence, much less on the uncritical acceptance of the individualistic premises that govern our economy and polity. It can only flourish when granted the minimal legal sanction that would recognize some measure of internal self-determination. Community can only flourish when, as Michael Sandel has argued, it is viewed as "strong" or "constitutive."[41]

Traditional communities constituted fundamental social, economic, and political units primarily by virtue of legal sanction. The same laws that subordinated serfs to lords, slaves to masters, and women to men ensured at least minimal community coherence. A society legally grounded in communities must be a corporatist—emphatically not an individualistic—society, and, by implication, must be based on particularist rather than universalist principles. To thrive, much less enjoy any genuine independence, communities must enjoy a large measure of legally sanctioned autonomy.[42]

Feminist theory has not advocated the legal restoration of traditional

communities. To the contrary, like the individualist theory from which, criticisms notwithstanding, it derives, it abhors the corporatism that the legal protection of communities implies. If part of this revulsion derives from feminism's commitment to individualism, another part surely derives from the conviction that legally protected communities have ranked as women's primary oppressors—that, despite rhetorical claims to the contrary, women have never been equal members of the communities to which they have been assigned. Jean Bethke Elshtain, confronting the issues directly, has in fact argued that the costs of unbridled individualism have proved so disastrous that feminists must seriously rethink the positive aspects of their historical association with the virtues of the domestic sphere.

Elshtain, who espouses a subtle and nuanced theory of human development, sees continuing value in women's ascribed and biologically grounded domestic roles and advocates an extension of their ethic of caring to society at large in order to ensure some measure of humanity to all of its members, especially to children.[43] Her perspective has failed to convince most feminists, who cannot accept her insistence on the abiding value of historical precedent, much less the social consequences of biology. And, theory aside, they cannot accept the price of her solution, which offers no concrete protections against the abuse that men have all too frequently wreaked upon women within families. But if Elshtain minimizes the mounting evidence of the ubiquity of men's abuse of women and children within families, she does so not out of mindless denial but out of the conviction that, for most women, independence in the public sphere has offered nothing better and could, conceivably, offer something much worse. More than most feminists, she takes women's special responsibilities to children in deadly earnest. More than most feminists, she assumes that the biological differences between women and men will have consequences not merely for the organization, but the quality, of our society. And even Elshtain has not yet explicitly urged the restoration of legally sanctioned communities.[44]

Although Elshtain, a feminist, hardly identifies herself as a conservative, her work intersects with that of traditional conservatives like Thomas Fleming, who bases his case for the restoration of community in biology, which he calls human nature. In *The Politics of Human Nature*, Fleming boldly undertakes to delineate a system of natural politics that would redress the consequences of the "collapse of Roman authority in the West," which, in his view, "created a crisis from which political thinking has never quite recovered."[45] Since that collapse, the vision of the lost unity of Rome's dominion has haunted political thinking, much as the vision of a lost Eden has haunted Christianity. In our own time, the destructive forces of modern technology have transformed that unrealizable, universalist dream into a nightmare that threatens our very survival. An Aristotelian, Fleming lays heavy blame on irresponsible bourgeois theorists who, since Hobbes, have developed a political theory based on abstractions that ride roughshod over our nature and social relations. Fleming especially protests the commitment of political theorists to the primacy of the individual, whom they have viewed as the basic unit of society and the fundamental embodiment of rights. He recognizes that the emphasis on individuality has not been entirely a bad thing, if only because it has fostered that insistence upon the moral responsibility of the individual upon which modern civilization depends. But, on the whole, he views the grounding of political and social philosophy on individual right as a grievous error that accounts for much of the woeful disarray of our own times.

Fleming's principal concerns about the price of "progress" in many ways resemble those of socially responsible feminists: high rates of family dissolution; ethical confusion and dissolution; sensationalist and homogenized mass culture; "and perhaps worst of all an apparent inability to agree on social priorities."[46] But, unlike most feminists, with the notable exception of Elshtain, he looks to strengthened families and communities as the necessary bedrock of politics and society. Insisting that modern peoples—those who live in bourgeois societies—have invariably perceived the relations between the individual and the state as antagonistic, he identifies the main problem of contemporary political philosophy as the balance between freedom and order: What rights must the individual relinquish for the good of the collectivity?

Fleming proposes to resolve that central dilemma of modern political theory by denying the legitimacy of its premises on the grounds that it derives not from nature but from the misguided history of our species. Like many romantic feminists and leftists he rejects the Freudian—and traditional Christian—view that the very essence of the human condition lies in the inescapable conflict between the individual and society.[47] But, unlike others, Fleming attributes our perception of that conflict to our deviation from the laws of nature, which he seeks in sociobiology. The modern view that human societies obey the laws of cultural rather than biological evolution, he argues, has blinded us to our inescapable biological roots. Rather than constantly struggling to escape nature, we should hearken to its fundamental law, as recorded in "the actual behavior and conditions of human life," namely in those customs and institutions that appear universal, notably male dominance and the incest taboo.[48]

Categorically rejecting the myth so dear to bourgeois political theorists, which feminist theorists have adapted to their own ends, that man was born free, Fleming argues that "our rights come not from nature but from our nature, human nature, and that natural law is the behavioral code of the human species." All evidence suggests that the human species has never been composed of solitary beings, but of families, which are frequently part of larger collectivities and which are invariably dominated by men. In effect, male-dominated households constitute the building blocks of any social system, and relations among men constitute the principles of social relations.[49]

This argument leads Fleming to his central assertion: "Society is natural"; "our social nature" is not a matter of choice, "it is a given," the essence of which lies in men's obligation to take care of women and children, which derives from the special relations of marriage and the family that lie at the root of all social order.[50] For Fleming, the family has persisted and should persist throughout history as the fundamental social unit. Families cohere in communities, communities in towns, towns in states, and so forth, but under no circumstances should the coherence be permitted to undermine the internal relations of the aggregate units. Following Tönnies, Fleming emphasizes the decisive difference between community and society and insists that our social and political health requires the protection of *communitas* in all its forms. On this basis, natural male aggression can safely and appropriately be channeled into the ritualized political and military contests characteristic of society.

Governance, in Fleming's view, is primarily a matter internal to families and communities and is violated by the practices of the modern state, which illegitimately intrudes itself into the affairs of families, intervening between parents and children and corroding the natural bonds of the family unit. Legitimate political relations require that we return to the kind of genuine federalism advocated by Althusius at the dawn of the sixteenth century, according to which society is organized into a pyramid of units, beginning with families and proceeding through corporations, towns, and provinces, up to the state itself. The constituent members of the state are not individuals but political units such as cities and provinces, and their constituent units are communities, which themselves are composed of families. Fathers, "the judges and foreign ministers of their families," represent their households to the next larger unit and beyond.[51]

Fleming's model thus follows the traditional, hierarchical pattern of the great chain of being. Conflicts within families should be resolved within families, conflicts within neighborhoods within neighborhoods, and on up the scale. Never should the state be allowed to intervene in matters best settled by the direct participants. In our accelerating departure from the laws of our own nature, Fleming continues, we are creating a monster that will level us all in the name of a chimerical and unnatural equality. By accepting the view of ourselves as atomized individuals we are inviting the destruction of our very humanity.

In the name of communitarian values, which many feminists might applaud, Fleming restores the subordination of women to men within families and communities. From a feminist perspective, his solution is unacceptable, not merely because men have so regularly abused their power over women, but because the social significance of men's physical strength and women's reproductive capacities has been so drastically modified by modern technology, including contraception. Even if men could be obligated to support women and children, even if men could be prevented from physically abusing the women and children who depend upon them, and even if we credit the biological differences between the sexes with significance, there is no longer any obvious biological justification for depriving women of the full development of their demonstrable capacities for socially, politically, and culturally useful labor of all kinds.

Withal, Fleming's argument demonstrates the extent to which the legal sanction of communities has been based on women's subordination to men. This quasi-universal association between legally sanctioned community and female subordination further reveals the ways in which feminism genuinely constitutes the logical consequence and cutting edge of individualism. In general, feminists, whatever their intentions, have inescapably committed their cause to the defense of the individual against the claims of society—to the defense of an unbridled freedom against the claims of any authority, whatever its claims to legitimacy. Yet, without some acceptance of the claims of authority, it is difficult to imagine an adequate defense of communities.

This standoff exposes a tragic, if unintended, consequence of feminist campaigns. The reluctance of men to grant women equality within communities has forced women to turn to the state to protect their rights. The measure in which men have identified legitimate authority with men's authority has led many feminists to dismiss the very notion of legitimate authority as a thin disguise for gender bias. In consequence, feminism has mightily contributed to the collapse of communities, even as the collapse of communities has left women exposed to their unequal position as individuals. One feminist issue after another runs up against the contradiction between individual and community values: reproductive choice, daycare, opposition to pornography, comparable worth.[52]

The feminists who support these causes frequently invoke community values but rarely develop the political theory and practice that their support requires. Socialist-feminists like Alison Jaggar have failed to elaborate a theory that would justify radical interventions in social policy.[53] And even those like bell hooks and Gayatri Spivak, who are most concerned with the plight of poor women and women of color in the United States and throughout the world, avoid specific political prescriptions.[54] To be sure, these feminists avoid the worst pitfalls of a complacent celebration of the existence of community among women, cogently insisting on the lines of race and class that divide women against one another. But time and again, even the most clear-sighted calls for the need to build community among women avoid the central political issues.

Many feminists have taken the defense of community, like the defense of humane values, as a distinct female mission. But they have been unable to reconcile that mission with their determination to free women from dependence on and oppression by men. For whereas the defense of community points toward a strengthening of authority within intermediate institutions, the liberation of women points toward a strengthening of individualism and, consequently, if paradoxically, of the state. Radical feminist dreams of revenge notwithstanding, it is impractical as well as politically dangerous to assume that we can stick to a course that would simultaneously promote women's freedom and increase the state's authority over men. In the end, the state's growing power over men guarantees its growing power over women, albeit as isolated individuals rather than as members of communities.

Some feminists do, intuitively, understand the problem. The most sophisticated feminist critiques of our concept of justice, most of which originate in feminist jurisprudence, are beginning to develop a full-scale attack on individualism. Robin West, especially, distinguishes between the male "separation" and the female "connection" theories of the human being, sharply exposing the inadequacy of the separation theory for women's lives. But West ends in explicitly advocating that feminists embrace a vision of a "utopian world" in which "a perfect legal system will protect against harms sustained by all forms of life, and will recognize life-affirming values generated by all forms of being."[55] Allowing that her model will not necessarily result in androgyny, West nonetheless comes very close to the position of feminists like Nancy Chodorow, who look to a more equal distribution of men's and women's productive and reproductive roles to ensure greater justice for women.[56] Similarly, Susan Okin argues that the revision of our notion of justice requires that it be extended to the family, "the linchpin of gender," to produce the equal sharing of all productive and reproductive roles. In her view, "a just future would be one without gender."[57] The prospect leaves me cold, although many other feminists might agree with her. But her world without gender could assuredly not be a world without individualism.

Individualism remains firmly ingrained in most feminist thought, notwithstanding feminists' distaste for individualism in the masculine mode. Most feminist theorists who criticize male individualism thus end by embracing the sentimental view of community. Their analysis assumes that since women more than men have historically been tied to community—to a notion of the individual as connected to others—the flowering of women's values would result in an individualism with a human face. Jennifer Nedelsky, who also begins with the assumption that women's experience of connection to others has endowed them with a distinct perspective on individualism as autonomy, differs from most others in beginning to explore the implications of the argument for the polity as a whole. Repudiating the notion that she is simply presenting the liberal model of the dichotomy between collective goods and individual rights in new guise, she insists that she is in fact proposing a new model of autonomy that will acknowledge the impossibility of separating it from the relations that make it possible and will thus build a social component into the meaning of autonomy itself. And yes, the implementation of such a conception would "involve a far greater role for collective power and responsibility than does our current system."[58]

Nedelsky is uncommon among feminist theorists in envisioning the possible political implications of a practical defense of the community values with which women have been associated and which many believe them to embody. But most feminists do not so much think about community in theory as they seek it in practice. Today, most feminists who celebrate community are referring to communities among women themselves. One of my dearest friends, an enormously successful professional woman, seeks out needlepoint stores in each of the many cities to which her professional responsibilities take her. There she finds an atmosphere of female community that provides welcome relief from professional meetings populated largely by men. And her pleasure in that community has much in common with the pleasure that women, throughout the centuries, have found in sewing, knitting, and quilting together. Communities of women, grounded in the fellowship of sharing work, childbearing, recreation, religion, are as old as human history. Women have also joined together in more formal communities such as religious sisterhoods, schools, or colleges. Such associations have generally strengthened women but hardly constitute a solution to the larger problems.

In an influential article, Carroll Smith-Rosenberg delineated what she called "the female world of love and ritual" among nineteenth-century American women,[59] arguing that the division of middle-class society by spheres increasingly bound women to one another for companionship and love. The legacy of separate spheres continued to foster such bonds well into the twentieth century, although in our own time at least some of them seem to be breaking down.[60] But even these female communities, like other persisting forms of community including those among men, have always been in some measure hostage to the legal and political relations of our society as a whole; they therefore depend increasingly upon acts of faith and personal commitment. To be sure, broad social developments continue to reinforce women's communities, if only those that result from extreme poverty and men's abandonment of families, but they are no less fragile and no less dependent upon the general trends than others. Female communities will doubtless persist and, under economic pressure, even increase. But whatever their strengths—notably the mutual support that their members offer one another—they do not offer a practical model for a society that still requires cooperation and fellowship across genders in order to survive and reproduce.

The path that feminism is treading leads inexorably to the final erosion of community, nor will any amount of nostalgic rhetoric be able to wish it back. And nothing could have poorer prospects than the attempts to reconstruct long-shattered communities of old types—whether those of puritan

New England or the Old South or the Italian or Jewish sections of Chicago or New York. The best of the old values and practices may yet be reinvigorated in new form, as prefigured by trade unions, universities, churches, and much else to which women have historically contributed and that could be accommodated to a modern economy and encompassed in a new and essentially corporatist social vision. Feminists have much to contribute to that work, but they will do so only to the extent that they reject the siren calls of nostalgic and utopian communitarianisms.

Neither the close historical association between women and communities nor the abiding need that most of us feel for some kind of community identification should lead us to romanticize the idea of community even as we let the reality slip from our grasp. The ideal of community in the abstract is hopelessly utopian and today amounts to little more than a metaphor for those bonds among individuals that the market is eroding. That erosion has granted women an unprecedented, if still incomplete, freedom from involuntary community membership. But it has also eroded the political and legal foundations for much that membership in specific communities could offer: roots, continuity, loyalty. Any comprehensive and compelling feminist theory must resolve feminist contradictions on these matters and contribute to a new vision of legally sanctioned communities that protect rather than exploit persisting sexual and gender asymmetry and that foster internal equality. Rogers Smith puts the matter clearly in writing, "I take the chief lesson of America's history of discriminatory citizenship laws to be that longings for a sense of the importance of particular communities and social roles pose many dangers—but that efforts to ignore such longings guarantee that those dangers will sooner or later come to pass."[61]

3

FROM FEMINIST

THEORY TO

FEMINIST POLITICS

Today, as in the past, feminists divide over whether women should be struggling for women's rights as individuals or women's rights as women—whether women need equality with men or protection for their differences from men. As Nancy Cott has argued for the feminists of the early twentieth century, the lines are difficult to draw, not least because feminists, like others, fall into inconsistencies.[1] Our predecessors, for example, campaigned for woman suffrage both on the grounds of women's entitlement to full standing as citizens (their equality with men) and on the grounds of the special contribution that they as women could make to the polity (their difference from men).

For Cynthia Fuchs Epstein, the evidence of recent history confirms the "overwhelming similarities between men and women." In her view, history therefore exposes the previous emphasis on gender differences as mere dichotomous stereotypes and encourages the hope that enlightened policies "may one day put an end to the self-fulfilling prophecy of differences between men and women."[2] Epstein suggests that women, above all, require equal access to abstract rights. For Catharine MacKinnon, in contrast, "Abstract rights authorize the male experience of the world." From her perspective, a feminist jurisprudence must repudiate those abstractions, including their claims to rationality, and maintain its particularistic and protectionist fidelity "to women's concrete conditions and to changing them."[3] Basing her theory on sexuality, which "is to feminism what work is to marxism: that which is most one's own, yet most taken away," Mac-

Kinnon argues for a fundamental difference between women and men. And, like many other feminist theorists, she assumes that the history of women's experience of biological difference has bequeathed them a distinct set of needs and perspectives fundamentally at odds with our prevailing standards of justice.[4]

This debate over equality versus difference lies at the core of contemporary feminist thought, not merely because of the way in which it divides feminist theorists but, perhaps more important, because of its ability to link theory and practice. The decision to fight for equality or to fight for the protection of difference impinges directly upon women's lives. Should women defend their right to maternity leave? Or should women insist on parental leave, which implies men's as well as women's responsibility to care for children?[5] Because so many "women's" issues—notably childcare—are also social issues, and because all women's issues affect men, feminist strategies theoretically and practically carry far-reaching consequences for our society as a whole. Nowhere are these consequences more apparent than in the legal struggles over affirmative action, comparable worth, and reproductive rights.

Many feminists understandably deplore the slow rate of progress in establishing either women's equality with men or the protection of their differences from men in the public arenas of the economy and politics. Even more deplore the persistent power of men over women's reproductive capacities. We have not come far enough. But we have, to borrow from an offensive ad, come a long way—come far enough to have changed decisively the contours of American society, and especially American law. We have not established complete equality between women and men; we have not established adequate protection for women's differences from men; but we have changed the way in which we and others think about both; and we are even changing the ways in which institutions function. For many feminists, this progress, such as it is, only underscores the intractability of what, for lack of a better term, we might call human nature. Women have gained a panoply of rights from which they were previously excluded, but their gains have not eradicated sexism or revolutionized the relations between women and men.

The perception of this gap between legal and institutional change on the one hand and persistent sexism on the other has, if anything, heightened many feminists' commitment to a radical transformation of our public values. If our existing jurisprudence cannot adequately encompass women's legitimate claims, then it must change. Men, who have dominated the development of our law, have shaped it in their image and to fit their needs. According to many, the transformation must begin with the (male) conception of the individual that undergirds the entire system.[6] But with rare exceptions, even the most searching critiques of individualism as a male stratagem perpetrated on women have difficulty in shaking individualism's fundamental premises.

Or to put it differently, most feminist critiques of individualism either propose to substitute female for male individualism or to transcend difference entirely. Few, in other words, follow conservatives like Michael Sandel in arguing that to reject the notion of the individual as prior to society means to strengthen the authority of society over the individual.[7] To the contrary, many feminists continue to found some of their most important claims—above all, the right to "reproductive freedom" and abortion—firmly in individual right, even as they ground others—above all, comparable worth—in a repudiation of individualism. And they ground arguments for affirmative action sometimes in one position and sometimes in the other. Either they do not perceive the contradiction or, worse, they cynically assume that others will not perceive it. In either case they serve their cause poorly and insult the intelligence of the American people.

These theoretical inconsistencies—not to say contradictions—at the heart of contemporary feminism derive directly from the history of women's experience of capitalism and individualism, from the tension between the conflicting principles of community and autonomy governing the private and the public spheres respectively. More important, they derive from the symbiotic relation between the two sets of values and the two spheres to which they were ascribed.

Historically, the myth of separate spheres promoted not merely a gender-specific division of labor, but a gender-specific division of values. The values of nurture, care, and mutuality that the myth ascribed to women could not be separated from the values of autonomy, competition, and abstract justice that it ascribed to men. The two sets of values, in other words, sustained and reinforced each other—made each other possible. For if the male values dominated public discourse, even that discourse always presupposed the existence of the complementary female values. Because women were represented as nurturing, caring, and compassionate, men could represent themselves as autonomous, competitive, and righteous. In theory, as in practice, nineteenth-century women and men, however much they were associated with other members of their gender in distinct spheres, were also linked to members of the opposite gender in a dense social and cultural network.[8] Together they embodied the essence of American individualism and democracy, just as contemporary feminists' concerns with equality and difference embody its legacy.

American democracy has grounded its hegemony in the theory and practice of individualism. All men, according to our founding text, are born free and equal. The term *men*, in time and place, produced some confusion, since some American men—black slaves—belonged to others. But men, in the constitutional sense, simply meant the individual on the understanding that individual referred to a social role, not an innate characteristic, or embodied the innate characteristic of moral equality, which need imply no equality in social relations.[9] Slaves, by virtue of their dependent class position, could not fill the role of individual, although free black men could do so, in principle if rarely in practice. From its origins, our reigning ideology has prompted confusion about the nature of the individual and individual rights. Confusion notwithstanding, our commitment to the ideal has fostered considerable mistrust of action by or in the name of groups perceived as defending special interests.[10] Especially since Tocqueville, commentators on American culture have noted the power of the myth of individual mobility and opportunity, although they have rarely noted its dependence on the complementary myth of gender relations. The defenders of slavery provided a sad exception, since they boldly announced that the biblical subordination of women to men preceded all other forms of social subordination. And they proved themselves perceptive and consistent by joining their theory of gender relations to a repudiation of the egalitarian dogmas that Mr. Jefferson had written into the Declaration of Independence.[11]

The nineteenth-century American commitment to individualism rested on an explicit repudiation of corporatism and hierarchy, which it viewed as fetters on individual opportunity. The political legacy of the American Revolution and the development of the capitalist market combined in an increasingly forceful defense of the freedom of individuals, including their property and their labor. In this respect, American history can be viewed as an ever-expanding defense of individualism against the vestiges of corporatism.

Corporatism, in various forms, characterized the political organization of European societies from the fall of Rome until the French Revolution.[12] Embodying pervasive particularistic beliefs, it identified individuals according to their membership in legally defined social and occupational groups and held the state accountable for acknowledging and representing—although not in a modern sense—their interests. Notwithstanding the tendency of corporatist societies to view the state as theoretically possessing absolute and divinely ordained authority (in the words of Louis XIV, "L'état c'est moi"), they did not develop strong states by modern standards. The vast majority of the functions that modern states have fulfilled were, in corporatist societies, assumed by the constituent groups, beginning with the family or household. Americans never knew the kind of fully developed corporatism that had prevailed in early modern Europe and that depicted all social relations as mediated by membership in larger groups, such as estates, guilds, or confraternities. The first settlers had brought elements of that tradition with them to the New World, especially the tendency to ascribe greater importance to the group—the family or household, the town or community—than to the individual, but the ratification of the Constitution effectively abolished its influence in the public sphere. In the one great exception to the general trend, southern slave society forged a kind of incipient corporatism, retaining some of the commitment to the hierarchy and particularism that informed European models.[13]

Southern proslavery theorists, whether secular or religious, regularly championed particularism and hierarchy as essential to social order. In the writings of a host of theologians, political and social theorists, moral philosophers, poets, and novelists, the proslavery argument emerged as an out-and-out attack on capitalism—and the individualism that inescapably accompanied it—in the name of corporate order.[14] These theorists spoke for a society composed of organic units larger than the individual and based on a hierarchy of rights and responsibilities. In striking contrast to northern individualism, antebellum southern corporatism celebrated its own version of personal liberty in the context of a commitment to the hierarchical inequalities that prevailed among men and women and among masters and slaves—inequalities it recognized as central to its concept of public order.[15]

The dominant northern culture also fostered inequality among household members, but a sleight of hand long permitted a coexistence of individualism and corporatism, primarily by distinguishing between public and private spheres. Northern views thus tolerated the exclusion of some persons from the opportunities of individualism on corporatist and hierarchical principles that were not taken to challenge the supremacy of individualism for free, propertied men. Tellingly, during the debates over the codification of New York law during the first half of the nineteenth century, some openly opposed any reform of married women's property law as an assault on the last bastion of harmonious, noncompetitive relations in society: the family. Others, in contrast, defended reform on the grounds that the principles of the law should be consistently applied to all, including married women. In effect, the debate pitted those who believed that the principles of family relations should remain distinct from those of market relations against those who believed that consistency required that the principles of individualism should apply uniformly to all.[16]

In the North, corporatism succumbed early to the mounting pressure of the capitalist economy; in the South it succumbed only after the fall of the Confederacy. But its demise did not lead to the triumph of equality and individualism in either North or South.[17] Indeed, the demise of corporatism may be said to have paved the way for the triumph of even less palatable, and purportedly universal, "scientific" explanations for excluding women and black people from individualism.[18] In this respect, sexism and racism, while prevalent and nasty, ran into severe limits in corporatist societies, which classified all people—the powerful as well as the weak, the rich as well as the poor, men as well as women—by their particularistic attributes.

Corporatism imposed inequality in the name of particularistic values very much like those that Tönnies had ascribed to community, on the assumption that individuals' positions and identities derived from their membership in the group, whose claims transcended that of any of its members. We, in contrast, are so accustomed to thinking of the individual as the irreducible unit of consciousness and sovereignty that the idea of the primacy of the group comes hard. It comes especially hard for those who see restraints on the individual as artificial and arbitrary interference with the free workings of natural law. In truth, our modern ideas of liberty might be said to depend entirely upon the concept of individual right. We have lost the habit of thinking of "liberties," in the plural, as the rights of communities or groups. In the Middle Ages, towns enjoyed liberties that, by virtue of membership in them, applied to their residents.[19] Thus, it was held, during the initial growth of towns, that town air "macht frei"—confers freedom. Today, in a remote echo of this sensibility, we speak of academic freedom, by which, in principle, we mean a freedom that derives from membership in a specific community or institution. Yet our fundamental concept of freedom remains the freedom of the individual.

In varying degrees the commitment to individualism permeates all modern political thought. Libertarians, or proponents of radical individualism, can be found within the right, left, and center. Conservative rhetoric still draws upon various aspects of corporatist theory, according to which there are natural reasons or innate attributes that fit different individuals for different degrees of freedom. But in sharp contrast to traditional corporatism, modern forms of conservative collectivism—notably fascism—have not revived a social organization based on membership in legally defined communities, even though they have espoused a corporatist rhetoric. Mussolini and his principal theorists waxed eloquent over "the corporate state," but they never could reconcile their invocation of corporatism, which historically and theoretically has required a limited state, with the demand for a leviathan state and indeed a "totalitarian" society. Socialists have rejected corporatist premises entirely and have insisted that restrictions, enforced by a powerful state, must, in principle, fall equally on all individuals independent of gender, race, or any other inherited attribute. In practice, both fascism and socialism have resulted in a decisive strengthening of the state at the expense of both individuals and local communities, although they have differed radically on the central question of property, with private property under fascism and state property under socialism.

Even the most traditional of modern conservatives have absorbed a large measure of individualism that leaves them pulled by conflicting tendencies. For, unlike earlier corporatists, most of them do not agree that social condition at birth should determine opportunity for men and that class should be a fixed legal category. Under the influence of individualism, the conservative commitment to particularism has largely been restricted to gender and race, and even southern conservatives increasingly agree that racism is unacceptable.

During the late nineteenth century, sexism and racism acquired vast new scientific pretensions that betrayed the influence of individualism and universalism by linking all black people and all women to their purportedly innate attributes and purportedly biological characteristics. Both racism and sexism embodied collective principles, albeit in negative form. The collective classification by race was especially pernicious, since, as Barbara Fields has cogently argued, race, unlike sex, is not, in fact, a biological category at all.[20] In practice, racism served to exclude all Americans of African descent from the opportunities of individualism, to subordinate them as individuals to an arbitrarily determined group.

The case of women as a group differed significantly from that of African-Americans in innumerable respects, although African-American women suffered liabilities on both counts. But women, too, found themselves excluded from individualism according to a rigid classification. Propertied white male defenders of individualism, who opposed labor unions because they interfered with the free play of the market, easily—to take examples at random—countenanced subordination of women within marriage, exclusion of women from lucrative professional opportunities such as medicine, and the perpetuation of Jim Crow. Logically, such men who subscribed to individualism and opposed collectivism on principle ought to have favored the admission of any qualified individual to any social role, even if they thought that few women or blacks would be able to compete successfully. Practically, they tolerated—when they did not openly propound—the exclusion of entire groups from individualism, without being much troubled by the contradiction. Indeed, this practice of negative collectivism probably strengthened their and others' conviction that American society embodied the maximum opportunity for individuals of all classes by maintaining that all white men shared equal opportunities to advance in the public realm, as well as equal opportunity to dominate their own women at home and equal opportunity to discriminate against blacks.

Although the negative collectivism of sexism and that of racism both expose the limitations—the bad faith—of individualism, they do so in different ways. Racism as an ideology originated at the time of the American Revolution in American individualists' uneasiness about their own acceptance of slavery, which manifestly contradicted their professed belief in individualism. Race, as Barbara Fields insists, permitted them to resolve that contradiction by effectively blaming those of African descent for their own enslavement, or at least by labeling them as innately so different from free, white men that their enslavement would not challenge the principle of individualism.[21] With the abolition of slavery, it then became convenient to substitute a legally enforced racism that would perpetuate their exclusion as a group from the benefits of individualism. To the extent that antebellum slave society took seriously its professed corporatist values, it acknowledged that a network of (unequal) rights and responsibilities bound masters and slaves. When the abolition of slavery snapped that thread of obligation, southerners, as northerners had before them, turned to a pseudo-scientific racism to bar African-Americans from the public sphere and to justify their exclusion from equal participation in the fruits of individualism.[22]

Like racism, sexism testified to and guarded against a particular group's access to full participation in individualism. But the condition of women within households, notwithstanding rhetorically strong analogies, had not been identical to that of slaves. For if more women than we like to think had suffered various forms of domestic violence and sexual abuse, more women than we like to admit had accepted their position within marriage as their natural condition. Marriage did subject women, including their property and their wages, to the authority of a man, upon whom they depended for support. Marriage did expose women to private forms of abuse against which they had little or no recourse. But, in many instances, marriage also offered women protection against the uncertainties of single life—offered them economic support and a social and personal identity that enhanced their self-respect. The residual corporatism of marriage excluded women from individualism, but at least for a time it also offered them important benefits in return. For many women, in short, marriage constituted a viable career, a more promising source of security than anything the individualism of the public sphere could offer.

Throughout the twentieth century, the irreversible intrusion of the market into the so-called private sphere has steadily eroded marriage as a career. There were nineteenth-century precedents but never of sufficient magnitude to challenge decisively the myth of separate spheres, which captured the realities of economic changes by associating women with the home and men with the market: men leave the household to work, while women remain within it. In reality, the growing hold of the market on all households and, especially, their growing dependence on salaries and wages generated a systematic devaluation of women's contributions to household prosperity since much of women's work was not performed for wages. Even the earnings of the large and growing numbers of women who did work for wages were generally perceived as secondary to men's, were invariably lower than men's, and were long subject to the control of the husband. Under these conditions, wage earning did not normally permit women to survive independent of male-dominated households and, accordingly, did not seriously challenge the prevailing myth of their dependence upon them. And those women who gradually gained the ability to support themselves did so more precariously than the men of their particular class and race.

The emergence of the "family wage" during the late nineteenth and early twentieth centuries belatedly offered some working-class women the welcome possibility enjoyed by middle-class women of treating marriage as a career—as a way of benefiting from an income for which they themselves had not directly worked. It thus reinforced the myth of separate spheres at the very moment at which its foundations were eroding.[23] The same period also witnessed the beginning of the end of marriage as a viable career, in large measure because of the liberalization of divorce, but also because of the beginning of what would prove an irreversible secular increase in women's participation in the labor force. Fueled in part by a growth in consumer spending that led even middle-class families to seek the benefits of two incomes, the increase in the numbers of women who work outside the home for wages has steadily grown; more portentously, an increasing number of married women and married women with small children are working outside the home. [24] By 1985, more than half of all women with children under six years of age were participating in the labor force.[25] Obviously, the wages of single mothers were necessary to support their households, but the wages of married women increasingly proved necessary for the maintenance of their family's standard of living. Thus in 1985, in nonelderly households, wives' earnings accounted for a 42.1 percent increase in family income since 1950.[26]

In practice, women's increasing participation in the labor force decisively undermined the distinction between public and private spheres, pushing women into the public world and drawing the public world into the home. The collapse of those distinctions in practice did not suffice to destroy them in ideology or at law and initially resulted in an increase in legal barriers, notably protective legislation. Women's acquisition of the vote formally acknowledged their rights to political participation, and, although it did not immediately result in a visible feminist upsurge, together with changes in women's participation in society and the economy, it did set the stage for the modern women's movement.[27]

An expanding access to individualism, uneasily combined with the legacy of separate spheres, and the attendant experience of the negative collectivism that greeted women's entry into the public world constituted the immediate backdrop for the campaigns of the modern women's movement, influencing its specific goals and its theory. Many feminists cling to the promise of individualism with all the tenacity of those long excluded from the candy store or, as Virginia Woolf would have had it, the senior common room.[28] Assuming that all they require is admission to the corridors of power in order to flourish as their brothers have flourished, such feminists have primarily sought the dismantling of negative collectivism. And the strategy has worked well for a privileged few.

To the dismay of many feminists, those for whom it has worked have had a disconcerting tendency to look very much like honorary men, much as Isabella, Elizabeth I, Catherine the Great, Maria Theresa, and other great queens—or "princes"—did. And like the great queens, those for whom it has worked have had a disconcerting tendency to identify more closely with their social class than with their gender. Thus, successful women stockbrokers see themselves as having more in common with their male peers than other white middle-class women, to say nothing of their own secretaries or with black single mothers in the inner city. And in many respects they do have more in common with those male peers. Yet even for privileged and successful women, unpleasant reminders of their gender in the form of unexpected encounters with discrimination have frequently provoked anguish and at least a temporary awareness of the disadvantages that all women as women share.[29]

The confusions that surround and are perpetuated by the American myth of individualism have influenced the kinds of gains women have made during the past two decades. Worse, they have distorted feminist theories of women's subordination and the strategies for overcoming it. As Catharine MacKinnon has angrily insisted, existing laws cannot take account of women's concrete experience, for, even in its strongest claims to objectivity, the law embodies men's experience: "When it is most ruthlessly neutral, it is most male; when it is most sex blind, it is most blind to the sex of the standard being applied."[30] It is not necessary to accept MacKinnon's blanket repudiation of the possibility for objective standards to recognize that our law has had difficulty in promoting an equality for women that would also take account of their difference from men. Women's equal access to divorce, for example, offers a case in point. Intended to decrease women's subordination to men within marriage, the feminist struggle for women's right to divorce has, however unintentionally, come to mean chiseling away at men's obligation to support and protect women within marriage. It remains a matter of debate among both men and women whether marriage historically has, on balance, more effectively fostered the subordination or protection of women.[31] But whatever that balance may have been in the past, by the 1960s the rising incidence of divorce brought about a decisive shift. Women could no longer afford to regard marriage itself as a viable career.

Full individualism for women has increasingly been understood to include equality both within marriage and in the workplace. Initially, the freeing of women from the crippling aspects of marriage only entailed the removal of legal disabilities.[32] But almost from the start, the promotion of women's equality in the workplace and such attendant arenas as educational institutions was taken to necessitate affirmative action. Removing barriers was not enough; the redistribution of scarce resources had to be promoted. Increasingly, the improvement of women's position within marriage is taken to require positive intervention.

The struggle to promote equality for women has starkly revealed the limitations of individualism at law, although perhaps not exclusively in the ways that feminist legal scholars are suggesting. Historically, individualism for men has depended upon the subordination of women. A commitment to the myth of separate spheres as the normative basis for American social and political relations has led many Americans to view any change in the relations between women and men as traumatic and socially disruptive. Indeed, it directly testifies to the power of the link between individualism and separate spheres that changes in gender relations have, to many, suggested threatening changes in social relations, mores, and individual behavior. For many the apparent increase in a variety of disquieting social symptoms (rape, family violence, incest, sexual and other abuse of children, runaway and kidnapped children, sexual harassment) should be directly attributed to the breakdown of separate spheres—to women's flight from their traditional domestic responsibilities—rather than to an extension of individualism.

Possibly women's growing participation in individualism has provoked some of these pathological responses, if only by increasing the anxieties of insecure men. But to lay the blame on women, or feminism, is to fail to understand that feminism itself is symptom rather than cause of the larger changes that are transforming our society. The pathological responses have resulted from those secular changes, notably the market's growing penetration into all kinds of private relations, which have also caused changes in women's position. We cannot even be sure that the pathological symptoms have increased, or increased as much as we think. Quite possibly, the principal change lies in our awareness of and propensity to report them, in part because we are less willing than our forebears to tolerate them, in part because, with the erosion of boundaries between public and private, they have become more visible. Whether or not the world has changed as dramatically as many of us think, our perceptions of it assuredly have.

Feminist Theory to Feminist Politics

The recent women's movement, in its various guises and from its various positions, has developed in response to these secular changes, waging war on many fronts against the multiple public and private obstacles to women's position in society and the economy. Frequently despairing of the slow rate of change in attitudes or perceiving a failure to change at all, feminists have turned to the government, the police, and the courts to support and enforce feminist goals. These struggles for women's equal treatment rapidly moved well beyond public institutions, leading to an unprecedented politicization of civil society—families, educational institutions, private clubs. These and other private institutions, which had customarily benefited from a residual corporatism, had long been treated as the equivalents of sanctuaries in which the internal relations of members obeyed discrete institutional principles.

According to the principles that govern families, for example, the father and husband spoke, voted, and earned a living for the family as a whole. Society expected disputes between husbands and wives, between fathers and children, to be settled internally. The myth of the home as haven from the struggles of capitalist society cloaked violence, injustice, and inequality: parents wielded authority over children and sometimes exploited or abused them; husbands wielded authority over wives, whose property, wages, and bodies the law entitled them to control. But until the twentieth century, these abuses were not normally taken to justify external intervention, and such intervention as did occur normally came from churches or informal community pressure rather than from the state.[33]

Growing state intervention in private institutions has resulted directly from the erosion of the barriers between public and private spheres, not merely from feminist pressure. But feminist insistence that the personal is political, that no private institution, including the family, has the right to oppress or abuse women has certainly contributed to justifying the state's and the courts' growing role in "private" relations. Women today owe much to the growing role of the police and the courts in disciplining rapists; in intervening in family violence, notably the battering of wives; and, in various ways, in helping women to claim some of the individual freedoms and rights a decomposing civil society has been unwilling or unable to grant them.

Civil rights and affirmative action legislation of the past three decades have vastly expanded the politicization of personal relations. Not many years ago, the very notion of marital rape would have been seen as a contradiction in terms. Now, women are demanding and getting a growing measure of protection in personal relations in which they frequently remain physically and economically unequal to men. Affirmative action legislation has embodied the dawning recognition that redressing a long history of inequality, not to mention such "natural" inequalities as pregnancy and childbearing, requires positive law and intervention in the workings of both nature and the market. And, during the past three decades, the law has begun to redress the balance of the physical inequality of nature and the economic inequality of the marketplace, although even the limited success of legal change has provoked resistance.

Many men, and women too, have failed to embrace the campaign for women's equality or even for greater opportunity, frequently out of the conviction that to admit a woman to a professional school, to give a woman a job, to promote a woman on the job, means, indeed, to deprive a man.[34] Others have simply believed that women's further intrusion into a "man's world" contravenes proper social order.[35] The first response reflects a keen awareness of the darker realities that underlie the optimistic view of individualism: an often well-grounded fear of the social effects of competition for limited resources. The second reflects devotion to one of the last bastions of corporatism and hierarchy in American life.

Affirmative action, according to its proponents, represents a strategy to redress previous injustices of racism and sexism in the name of the right of individuals who have suffered to claim their just share of the benefits of individualism, from which they had long been excluded.[36] Affirmative action programs, in other words, help to assure women access to positions for which they are qualified but from which they have been excluded because of systematic discrimination.[37] According to opponents, affirmative action programs constitute an illegitimate assault on individual opportunity.[38] They deprive men of positions for which they are qualified in the interests of increasing the numbers of women or African-Americans in particular groups, usually occupations. The difference between these two views reflects the confusion at the heart of affirmative action itself between individualist and collectivist principles.

In practice, affirmative action initially helped to strengthen the position at least of some, mainly middle-class, women, permitting them to claim an ever-increasing share of the places in professional schools and occupations of all kinds.[39] Increasingly, it is helping women of all classes to gain access to many nonprofessional employments once reserved for men. Even construction crews, police forces, and fire-fighting companies now include women. The armed services still exempt women from registration for the draft and still exclude them from combat duty, but are recruiting and training them in accelerating numbers for noncombat roles and are even sending them into combat officially designated as something else.[40] Women's access to promotion and positions of management or leadership in these and other employments, while less certain, is being realized. If the rate of progress looks slow and even pitiful to those who have waited so long, it looks impressive from a historical perspective.

In practice, affirmative action means that middle-class white young men now have to share the available places in colleges, universities, and professional schools with middle-class white young women, as well as with African-Americans, Hispanic-Americans, and others. More and more working-class white men are losing their monopoly of numerous employments, which they now share with women and men of all races. The sharing of those places means the sharing of incomes—of social resources. That was its purpose. Any individual case of redress may strike us as unfortunate: Had white Johnny Smith only been born a decade or two earlier, he might not have been refused admission to X Law School or Y Medical School. Why should he now be forced to pay for the sins of others? But turn it around. Why should he be allowed to profit from the effects of the unfair advantages his predecessors enjoyed?

Events since the passage of the Civil Rights Act of 1964 have solidified an identification between the interests of women as a group and the vicissitudes of affirmative action. The *Bakke* decision revealed the fragility of a sustained policy of affirmative action. Then, in one swoop, the *Grove City* decision effectively pulled the teeth of Title IX of the Education Amendments of 1972. *Grove City* has now itself been overturned by the Civil Rights Restoration Act, but the recent decision to bar quotas in the public employment of minorities has suggested to some that women's affirmative action gains may not be entirely secure.[41] In fact, they probably are secure in their essentials, for the Supreme Court, notwithstanding the reservations of some of its members, has built up a body of precedent that makes complete repudiation of affirmative action unlikely.[42] The grounds on which affirmative action is implemented may, however, be changing.

Some feminists have claimed a victory for women in the decision in *Johnson* v. *Transportation Agency*, in which the Supreme Court upheld the right of management to promote a woman rather than an equally qualified man to the position of dispatcher. That claim is hard to sustain, for the decision explicitly denied the validity of any claim of previous discrimination (and hence the right to back pay), holding simply that management had the right to promote affirmative action in conformity with its assessment of the composition of the local population. Rather than a victory for women, the decision constituted a major victory for business.[43] Perhaps more important has been the growing recognition of the limited ability of affirmative action programs adequately to redress the differences between women and men at all levels of income.

Mary Radford has argued, in a cogent analysis of the cases of *Craft* v. *Metromedia*, *Hishon* v. *King and Spaulding*, and *Price Waterhouse* v. *Hopkins*, that "three trained, competent professional women were denied admission to the highest levels of the professions due not to any failings in their abilities to perform capably, but rather to the fact that they were perceived to lack the personal qualifications which the decision-makers deemed necessary to success."[44] In each instance the missing personal qualifications concerned their (male) superiors' perceptions of them as women. Variously dismissed as "too feminine" and "too masculine," they were, in effect, found inadequate because they did not measure up either to their superiors' notions of proper womanhood or proper managerial presence—because they were women. Increasingly, open and covert opposition to Title VII of the Civil Rights Act and to the Equal Pay Act are leading many feminists to promote the concept of comparable worth as an alternative form of affirmative action.[45]

For most academic feminists, the case of the Equal Employment Opportunity Commission (EEOC) against Sears, Roebuck proved the most revealing and disillusioning. The EEOC failed to prove its claim that Sears sustained a nationwide pattern or practice of sex discrimination by failing to hire women for commission-sales positions on the same basis as men, by failing to promote women into commission-sales jobs on the same basis as men, or by paying women in certain job categories less than similarly situated male employees. The case provoked a furor among academic feminists, not least because two women's historians, Rosalind Rosenberg and Alice Kessler-Harris, testified as expert witnesses for Sears and the EEOC respectively. Although the substantive issue concerned the necessity for the EEOC to provide statistical proof of discrimination, the visible issue concerned Rosenberg's contention that women were less likely than men to seek jobs in commission sales, primarily because of a congeries of "female" values that included their preference for an assured lower, over an uncertain if potentially higher, income and their commitment to family responsibilities.

Rosenberg's testimony thus reinforced the popular feminist view that women's distinct values govern their choices in employment. In opposition, Kessler-Harris argued that women, like men, place a preference for higher income above other considerations. Notwithstanding the bitterness and incivility of the ensuing debates, which effectively earned Rosenberg ostracism by a large number of women's historians, the central issue that emerged from the case concerned the extent to which women's identities as women— their differences from men—influence their choices as workers and, consequently, how much employers' decisions about hiring and promotion should be allowed to reflect assumptions about them. However much one may disagree with aspects of Rosenberg's stand, as I do, the very viciousness of the attacks on her proved not merely disheartening, but wonderfully revealing. For, in effect, all she had done was to draw logical conclusions from many feminists' own favorite premises about gender difference. Those who do not share the premises need to challenge Rosenberg's argument at its root, but surely they owe her respect for furthering rational discussion by insisting that one cannot, if honest, draw individualist political conclusions from a scholarship that emphasizes women's collective identity and culture as women, or vice versa.[46]

If the laws that have encoded new commitments to women's civil and individual rights have failed to accomplish as much as their advocates hoped, they have accomplished more than enough to anger and frighten their opponents. For, as conservatives have claimed, the long- and short-term implications of this legislative and juridical innovation challenge fundamental attitudes and, perhaps, the fundamental structures of our society. Opposition to affirmative action has ranged from the pragmatic objections of right-wing liberals and neoconservatives, that it simply does not work, to the principled objections of southern and other traditional conservatives, that it undermines the Constitution and society. But whether the objections come from progressives like Michael Walzer, who insists that affirmative action interferes with individual opportunity, or from conservatives like Justice Antonin Scalia, who rejects "social engineering" on principle, they amount, in practice, to protests against tampering with the free operation of the market.[47]

Even the progressive legal scholar Ronald Dworkin holds that the "fairness—and constitutionality—of any admissions program must be tested in the same way. It is justified if it serves a proper policy that respects the right of all members of the community to be treated as equals, but not other-wise."[48] Yet, rather than mounting a cohesive and systematic attack on the principles of individualism, the proponents of affirmative action, if any-thing, have asserted that affirmative action represents a widening of the positive good of individualism.[49] Some feminists and black nationalists have been more willing to defend collectivist values, but even they have been shy about proposing a general critique of individualism.[50] Their collec-tivist visions have taken the narrow ground of separatism—collectivism for the members of their own groups but not for the society as a whole.[51]

The debates about affirmative action, notably the Sears case, have pushed feminists toward a sustained reconsideration of the respective places of "equality" and "difference" in promoting justice for women. Alice Kessler-Harris, socialist-feminist expert witness for the EEOC, has claimed to have learned much from her brush with Sears about the dangers of emphasizing the differences between women and men—"women's culture"—at the ex-pense of the differences among women or the similarities between some women and some men.[52] Similarly, Ruth Milkman has warned feminists about "the real danger that arguments about 'difference' or 'women's cul-ture' will be put to uses other than those for which they were originally developed." Milkman was not advocating that notions of difference be abandoned, merely that they be used with care.[53] But surely any such con-cept is a two-edged sword, with either edge at the service of those who wish to use it. Joan Scott, reproaching Milkman's implicit choice of equality over difference, has suggested that feminists would do better entirely to repudi-ate the dichotomy between equality and difference. Urging feminists to turn to post-structuralist literary theory for a new way of apprehending and analyzing language, discourse, and difference, she has suggested that to pair equality and difference dichotomously "is to accept an impossible choice."[54] For the dichotomous pairing "denies the way in which difference has long figured in notions of political equality and it suggests that sameness is the only grounds on which equality can be claimed."[55]

These discussions bear directly on large feminist concerns about the inadequacy of our prevailing model of justice to realize women's legitimate claims and to reflect their specific experience as women, but they generally fail to engage the more pervasive limitations of individualism as a model for justice.[56] Difference, as a concept, exacerbates the problem, for it can refer to infinite variability of personal characteristics and experiences (no two snowflakes are exactly alike), or it can refer to the differences that characterize groups, which are themselves composed of very different units (snowflakes are different from raindrops). The common denominator in these different uses of the concept lies in the element of comparison: difference is perceived as difference from some implicit norm. Individualism views women as different because they are different from men but does not normally view men as different from women.[57] Hence, the most common discussions of difference unintentionally perpetuate the illusion of the (white male) individual as the standard against which all others are measured by primarily seeking to expose its purportedly objective authority as subjective. This reasoning dangerously conjoins the exposure of purportedly neutral authority as partisan with an attack on authority per se.[58]

Randall Kennedy, writing of race rather than gender, has suggested that once difference comes into play, one is tempted to argue that difference itself should be represented in positions of power and prestige. In other words, it is easy to slip from the argument that women or African-Americans should have equal access to specific positions as defined by those (white men) who have controlled them, to the argument that the definitions of the positions are inherently inequitable. It is not enough for a woman, or an African-American, to gain the right to act or write according to prevailing (white male) "standards"; the woman or African-American must gain the power, prestige, and financial rewards that accrue to the position (equality) but retain the right to act or write out of personal experience (difference). In Kennedy's view the "eager yearning to perceive and celebrate moral and intellectual differences" is a general tendency, which, if left unchallenged, will "reinforce beliefs about 'natural' divisions that have, for too long, constricted our imaginations."[59]

Kennedy's argument also points to the ways in which affirmative action has been vulnerable to reinterpretation as entitlement. To the extent that proponents of affirmative action argue that the exclusion of women or others from desirable positions results not from their inability to meet "objective" criteria but from the corruption of the criteria themselves, they also tend to suggest that all established criteria are suspect and thus tend simply to promote the right of the previously excluded to a share of society's resources. They thus move from the original view of affirmative action as granting women (and others) admission to positions for which they are qualified and from which they have heretofore been (illegitimately) excluded, to a view of affirmative action as "enhanced opportunity" or even an alleged "reverse discrimination."[60] And the move is accompanied by a move from affirmative action as a means of implementing individual rights to a means of increasing social justice. For there can be no doubt that affirmative action has resulted in innumerable situations in which one qualified individual has been deprived of (his) individual rights in order to ensure the equal and conflicting individual rights of another.[61]

Affirmative action, in short, challenges individual right as an adequate standard for social justice. The most compelling arguments for affirmative action pertain to the collective social good. But to make those arguments, we need a conception of collective good that transcends the aggregate interests of competing, atomized individuals. For, as Elizabeth Wolgast shows, the language of individual rights repeatedly leads us to force issues into forms that are essentially alien to them.[62] Or, as Michael Sandel insists, without a coherent definition of the relevant community that will benefit from, and whose larger good will justify, interference with any existing individual right, we have no grounds for affirmative action programs at all.[63]

The balance sheet of recent decades is not easy to draw. Women have made progress, if the growing number of women who earn their own livings or who contribute to a family income is regarded as progress. Women have made progress, if the final dismantling of the time-honored limitations on married women is regarded as progress. Women have made progress, if to be treated as an independent, self-accountable individual is regarded as progress. But if married and single women can now cast votes, hold property, claim their own wages, keep their maiden names, and generally behave like independent individuals, they have also lost the host of protections that, in theory and to some extent in practice, sheltered their dependent status.

What legal change has accomplished for women is analogous to what the Fourteenth Amendment accomplished for former slaves. It has entitled them to most of the normal attributes of the status of individual. Yet for women, as for African-Americans, that vaunted and coveted status has, on the whole, failed to achieve equality. The stripping away of legal disabilities has neither revolutionized social relations nor eradicated social and economic disabilities. It has neither eradicated nor adequately protected difference, however defined. Formal acquisition of individualism has not produced the advantages that many naively hoped it would. Here lies the central dilemma of feminist theory and policy: Does our prevailing model of individualism provide an adequate theory and standard for the goals of the women's movement? Affirmative action, as its critics have been quick to point out, implicitly challenges the individualistic principles on which our society has operated by substituting collective values for unfettered individual competition. But the supporters of affirmative action, who have been quick to denounce its opponents as defenders of entrenched privilege, have been less willing to acknowledge the positive aspects of its collectivist implications. To the contrary, they increasingly defend it as the protection of different individuals' entitlement to their share of society's rewards. The real failure of affirmative action lies in the failure of its proponents to understand and defend what they themselves are about or would be about if they were thinking clearly.

Despite indications of some improvement, women still earn, on average, about 60 percent of what men earn. Recent figures suggest that younger women are improving their position relative to men, but even that improvement does not encourage optimism for the future. The most sanguine only predict that women may earn 80 percent of what men earn by the year 2000.[64] Although various federal measures, notably the Equal Pay Act of 1963 and Title VII of the Civil Rights Act of 1964, have helped to improve women's position as wage earners, they have not made a serious dent on the most pervasive problem: the tendency for women to be segregated into jobs that are tacitly regarded as "women's work" and that are paid at significantly lower rates than jobs held primarily by men.[65]

Comparable worth, picking up where affirmative action left off, has emerged as an alternative collectivist strategy for rectifying the disparities between women's and men's earnings by eliminating wage disparities between groups of women and groups of men that are caused by discrimination.[66] Affirmative action attempts to redress these disparities by considering all workers essentially as individuals and by insisting that, regardless of sex, they receive equal access to employment and equal pay for equal work.[67] But proponents of comparable worth, recognizing the limitations of affirmative action's strategy, propose that we consider women as a group. Certain forms of employment held overwhelmingly by women are consistently paid less than others held overwhelmingly by men. The issue, accordingly, transcends that of discrimination against individuals within the occupation or unequal pay for equal work. Librarians and janitors do different kinds of work. At issue is the scale of wages for an entire class of individuals—comparability rather than equality.[68] But how, on these grounds, can discrimination be determined?

Initially, feminists argued that discrimination occurs when an employer intentionally hires a man rather than a woman of equal qualifications because he prefers men. Or he might establish criteria, say height or weight, that favor men as a group over women. But neither of these strategies confronts the employer who exclusively or primarily hires women and treats them equally to one another. In the latter case, discrimination figures more as a social or community, than an individual, problem, as proponents of comparable worth tacitly recognize. For comparable worth implicitly accepts the legacy of separate spheres with respect to the stereotyping of jobs by gender and even with respect to women's special domestic responsibilities; it simply argues that now that women are working at female jobs in the public rather than the private sphere, they should receive wages equal to those for comparable male jobs.

Comparable worth exposes an especially difficult social problem. Tellingly, the most successful attempts to respond to the claims of comparable worth have been through state legislation that has raised the wages of female state employees to bring them closer to those of male employees. The federal government and the private sector have not proceeded at the same pace.[69] On this basis, comparable worth can be seen as a direct and unprecedented assault on the principle of a free labor market. To put it charitably, even without comparable worth the United States enjoys something less than a perfectly free labor market, but comparable worth represents a radical advance over all previous forms of collective bargaining and even over the most collectivist form of affirmative action as "enhanced opportunity."[70] Feminists could well respond that, in practice, the "freedom" of the market has always been as suspect as the "objectivity" of the individual, but whatever the justice of those claims, that response does not solve the problem of determining the grounds on which comparable worth can be defended. Sara Evans and Barbara Nelson bypass the problem of our larger conceptions of justice and rights by arguing that comparable worth should be understood as a technocratic or procedural reform—"not the same as creating new individual rights and leaving individuals to enforce them in the courts."[71]

David Kirp, Mark Yudof, and Marlene Franks, in contrast, implicitly accept comparable worth as a matter of rights when they criticize it on the grounds that "rights belong to persons, not groups."[72]

Comparable worth forces us to confront the difficult truth that our society has not been willing to pay for much of what it claims to value. We have not placed a high monetary value on the various activities, traditionally associated with women, that concern nurture, personal service, and many forms of education. The implementation of comparable worth could reinforce the association between women and service and nurturing occupations; or, as some argue, it could draw men into them. But in either case, the implementation of comparable worth in economic life would act primarily upon the supply rather than the demand side of the labor market. Eventually, comparable worth could result in a more equal distribution of men and women among various occupations, but we cannot be sure. Would men be more likely to become secretaries and nurses if the pay were better? To answer that question would require a strong stand in favor of the primacy of economics over gender hierarchy. But if economics, not gender hierarchy, is the basic issue, then why not assume that women, as individuals, should be encouraged to adapt themselves to the labor market's priorities? If the questions are not simple, the answers are even less so.

The campaign for comparable worth aims to reclassify the salaries or wages of entire groups of female workers who, it is argued, perform work of as much value to society as that of male workers who are paid at much higher rates. Intuitively, the notion that we should pay librarians, who are overwhelmingly women, as much as sanitation workers, who are overwhelmingly men, has genuine appeal. But the problems are considerable. First, the general implementation of comparable worth would be expensive and raises the question of who should pay the bill. Second, and more difficult, it would require an arbitrary determination of worth—or, rather, a collective determination about worth that a capitalist society, which relies on the market to determine worth, cannot easily make. Comparable worth would, in short, require the replacement of the market definition of value with a collective definition and would thus challenge the adequacy of the market as a basis for the social allocation of resources.

Neither men nor women enter the labor market as abstract units of labor or even as individuals in the abstract. They enter it as people who have been raised with expectations about their identities and roles as women and as men, with skills that they have acquired in large part because of their own families' and communities' expectations of women and of men. The labor market they enter itself embodies a long history of assumptions about the value that society attaches to certain kinds of work. How, in the absence of market demand, are we confidently to calculate the value of the kinds of work that comparable worth would reward more highly than the market has? In the cases in which comparable worth has been implemented, sophisticated calculations have, in fact, been developed; but no amount of sophistication can disguise the embodiment of nonmarket, and therefore arbitrary, determinations about the value of certain kinds of work. It has largely escaped comment that most of those—gender notwithstanding—directly engaged in the debates over comparable worth display an inherent bias in favor of secretaries and librarians over sanitation workers, if only because even those of us who devalue women tend to value education and mental labor over "mere" body labor. Whatever else comparable worth would accomplish, it seems likely to lower even further the prestige of manual labor and possibly even of productive labor in a society whose most serious economic problems include falling productivity.[73]

Conventionally, our system has rewarded labor power for what it is worth to the person who buys it, not for the inherent use or social value it embodies.[74] Whatever our position on the desirability of comparable worth as an appropriate strategy to rectify women's subordinate position in the labor market, we must agree with Justice Antonin Scalia that this strategy indeed constitutes social engineering. Mr. Justice Scalia's objections to social engineering—in which he includes all forms of affirmative action—presumably derive, in part, from his conviction that it violates our most fundamental constitutional principles, notably individual right. Feminists, insisting that comparable worth must be understood as rendering economic justice to women who cannot expect it from the market, have yet to meet his challenge squarely. Comparable worth cannot be defended on conventional individualistic grounds, for, as a concept, it rests not upon an ideal of allocative (individualistic) justice, but upon an ideal of distributive (particularistic) justice.[75] The distributive ideal assumes that justice, rather than applying equally or undifferentiatedly to all, should apply to each according to situation or classification, which means according to community. But to sustain an ideal of distributive justice, we must have legally sanctioned communities or groups that take socially recognized priority over individuals. More than that, we must have a collective conception of society that acknowledges the possibility that the good of the whole in some way transcends the good of individuals, as they themselves define it.

Although most Americans still behave and talk as if individualism and the free market shaped our society, they are living in a world in which neither individualism nor the market flourishes unfettered. Indeed, neither ever did. But we, like our predecessors, tend to regard limits on individualism and the market as lapses from the norm, as aberrations, and, consequently, the failure of feminist and other reformers to rethink basic premises has crippled their efforts to effect systematic reform.

Conservatives, like some romantic liberals, readily attack the instrumentalism that results from the collapse of the last enclaves of corporatism, notably the relations among members of such "private" institutions as the family. At the same time, they decry symptoms that logically result from the unfettered capitalism they cherish. If the market is to determine value, why should it not determine the value of a wife's services to her husband, parents' obligations to children, or any other personal relation? If individualism constitutes the foundation of our identity as a people, which of us should be entitled to determine where the individualism of one, say, the woman, should be sacrificed to the good of the other, the man? Historically, the law and the market have done that work by ensuring women's economic dependence upon men, but individualism itself does not supply the principles that would justify a view of the good of some hypothetical whole as superior to the good of any given individual. Utilitarianism tried to square that circle, but eventually ended in John Stuart Mill's early retreat to a facsimile of organic conservatism. And, as Gertrude Himmelfarb has cogently argued, once Mill's personal circumstances led him to take women's claims to individualism seriously, he rapidly moved on to a radical liberalism.[76]

An important tendency in feminism has followed his lead, linking the case for justice for women to an expanding notion of individual right. Comparable worth points in a different direction, arguing for restrictions on the individual right of some (sanitation workers) as currently defined by the market in the interest of others (librarians). Because of the nature of the kinds of work traditionally associated with women—librarianship, teaching, nursing, caring for the young, the elderly, and the infirm—the proponents of comparable worth are in effect arguing that we specifically reward those who contribute to our self-image as a moral and a humane society. Americans have long ascribed those values and activities to the private sphere, have attributed responsibility for nurture to women, while attributing responsibility for competition, notably in business and politics, to men. In so doing, we have been trapped in the notion that it behooves us to pay for the latter and not for the former. But if we continue to leave paying for the former to the market, we must recognize that we do not value highly that which, rhetorically, we claim to value most highly. For women, the question is no longer simply one of respect, but one of individual income. Since men cannot be held accountable for supporting women, as, for example, through alimony, women must be able to support themselves and often also their children.

For a time it looked as if women required only equal access to individualism to achieve equality, and many women still cherish that illusion.[77] But, as Elizabeth Wolgast has insisted, the arguments for equality rest on implied assumptions about androgyny and atomism, assumptions that women and men may and should be functionally interchangeable.[78] Such assumptions can appear to defy biology, history, and women's palpable needs. These arguments bring us back to the possible relations between legal equality and sexual asymmetry. In the past, to take account of differences of sex was to ensure women's subordination to and economic dependence on men. Today, many feminists are arguing that equality cannot eradicate the hierarchies that have been built on difference, but even in repudiating equality they have not decisively broken with the legacy of a theory of individualism that assumed that individuals' social rights derive from their innate natures.[79] From the start, the contradiction between innate rights and social rights has informed liberal and democratic theory, but as long as individuals were assumed to be free men it could be glossed over in practice.

The challenge of expanding individualism to include women has raised the contradiction to a higher level. The model of the individual as male would appear to have bequeathed women the unpalatable and unrealistic choice between becoming "male" or not becoming individuals. Theoretically, the individual need not be gendered male or female and should be understood as an impersonal entity—a unit of sovereignty. Historically, the individual, like the institutions developed to realize "his" potential, has been gendered. The weight of that history has made it extremely difficult for women simply to fit into social roles designed for men, but even more difficult for them to repudiate the ideal. Recent feminist strategies, notably affirmative action and comparable worth, have heavily if implicitly advanced the claims of collectivism against the market itself. In so doing, they have opened the possibility of a new political vision, which they regularly foreclose by clinging to individualism. Nothing more clearly reveals the confusions than the escalating debate about abortion.

The fight over women's right to abortion has emerged as the testing ground of the women's movement in the 1980s and threatens to dominate the 1990s. This fight, more than any other, exemplifies the chasm between feminist principles and politics. Abortion pits American women against one another in passionate combat. Those who favor reproductive choice for women have rested their case squarely on the ground of individual right. Women must be understood to have an absolute right to control their own sexuality and their own bodies. No woman should be forced to carry or bear a child against her will. The principle at stake, according to its proponents, is the same as that which led our founding fathers into the Revolution. Those who oppose abortion counter that it is nothing more nor less than the killing of babies. Most opponents of abortion are not, in truth, especially concerned with women's rights at all, but, to the extent that they are, they hold that the right of the woman must be balanced against the right of the fetus—that abortion concerns the respective rights of two lives, not the unilateral right of the woman. They are thus, as Faye Ginsburg argues, committed to a "pro-life view of the world."[80]

Any discussion of abortion proceeds in the midst of some ghastly social realities. The vast majority of women who seek abortions are still in their teens, unmarried, and poor. They have scant, if any, prospects of providing bare essentials for a child, and the attempt to do so almost invariably destroys their own prospects for education and, frequently, even for decent employment. The hard truth is that our society is not prepared to provide adequately for children, and those who oppose abortion are, in general, those least in favor of expanding social and family services. What social good can possibly be served by forcing a young, poor, unwed woman to bear a child she does not want and cannot provide for and for which society is unwilling to provide? The practical case for abortion is formidable.

The women's movement has raised the question of abortion to a high theoretical level and is coming close to tying the entire case for feminism to it. In one way, it is hard to fault feminist leaders for this tack. Especially in the wake of the *Webster* decision, the right to choice is drawing numerous fresh converts to feminist organizations, which had been having conspicuous difficulty in appealing to younger women.[81] Self-determination has proved a magnetic rallying point. But it is difficult to shake the impression that the right to choice is increasingly being presented as identical not merely to the right to freedom from all forms of sexual oppression, including incest and rape, but to women's right to liberation from the reproductive consequences of their own sexuality—their right to the male model of individualism. And we are now hearing claims—admittedly not yet all that widespread—that pregnancy "colonizes" a woman's body.[82]

The argument for abortion as a woman's individual right, by conflating pregnancy and child rearing, confuses sexual and economic issues, with potentially disastrous consequences. Pregnancy, the ability to carry a child in the womb, depends upon women's specific biological attributes. Child rearing, in contrast, depends heavily on economic resources and social support. Pregnancy itself does not long interfere with a woman's opportunities to live the life she chooses; child rearing frequently does. A woman can, in principle, afford to share her body—and even to give up drugs, alcohol, and tobacco—for nine months without serious consequences, although whether the state and society have the right to make her share it is in heated dispute. Rearing a child is another matter entirely. The responsibility for children drags women into poverty and keeps them there.

Opponents of abortion have done no better than its supporters in facing these issues. Most of those who oppose a woman's right to abortion do so on moral and religious grounds, and perhaps also out of a deep commitment to women's traditional roles as wives and mothers.[83] For these women, abortion "destroys the bases of gender difference" and thereby "threatens the union of opposites on which the continuity of the social whole is presumed to rest."[84] They hope against hope that marriage and motherhood can persist as the foundation for women's livelihood and identity, and they view other women who challenge those roles as a threat to their values and lives. They also tend to oppose any state intervention in the family and, hence, any notion of children as a collective social responsibility. They, like feminists, if for different reasons, invoke the power of the state in the name of collective principles to support individualism—albeit for men. In their vision, the family should retain extensive private rights over children. Their ideology has shown little concern with the lives of poor, frequently unwed mothers and their children.

With rare exceptions, both sides in the debate confuse issues of principle and policy, conflate pregnancy and child rearing, and argue within the broad context of individualism.[85] The debate as a whole reaches to the center of our social, political, and ethical life: the rights of the individual and the rights of the collectivity. For the collectivity does have a practical interest in the fate of children and a moral and political interest in the way in which we define and defend the right to life.

It is not easy to reconcile the feminist metaphors of motherhood and community with the feminist defense of abortion on the grounds of absolute individual right.[86] Surely, the special sense of human connection and nurture that so many feminists attribute to women derives primarily from women's special roles as the bearers and rearers of children. Jennifer Nedelsky has thus recently proposed that feminists reconceptualize the ideal of autonomy to ground it in child rearing.[87] Sara Ruddick has suggested that all women differ from men in their propensity to "maternal thinking."[88] Either abortion entails the killing of babies or it does not. If it does, then there are no legitimate grounds for allowing it, not even rape or incest. If it does not, then there are only the narrowest of pragmatic grounds for preventing it. The problem remains: Are we dealing with two lives or one? No precedent in individualist theory helps us to understand the issue, for the men upon whom individualism was predicated do not bear children.

It is not easy to reconcile the defense of women's right to abortion on the grounds of privacy with sustained attempts on the part of the women's movement to break down other aspects of what was traditionally viewed as the privacy of the family. Most of us applaud the state's growing willingness to help to protect women and children against sexual or physical abuse by husbands and fathers. But only very recently would all interference between a man and a wife have been viewed as an invasion of privacy. In effect, the defense of a woman's right to abortion as a matter of privacy represents a decisive reinforcement of the extreme individualistic view of society as composed of atomized individuals. More frighteningly, by implicitly identifying reproduction as a woman's individual right, it dismisses men's claims and dissolves their responsibilities to the next generation.

Abortion challenges feminists to come to terms with the contradictions in their own thought, notably the contradiction between the commitment to community and nurture and the commitment to individual right. Without doubt, the easiest way would be to reach some determination about our collective definition of life. Most Americans would probably accept a definition of life linked to the notion of viability and accept abortion on demand up to the twentieth week of pregnancy. Without some such agreement on the definition of life, the right to abortion opens the specter of any individual's right to kill those who depend upon her and drain her resources—elderly parents, terminally ill or handicapped children. Without some such agreement, the right to abortion—the woman's right to sexual self-determination—can logically lead to the right to murder with impunity. How are we to link women as the embodiments of "maternal thinking" with such a position?[89]

Many feminists, following Carol Gilligan, would argue that the abstract dichotomy between life and death is not the appropriate way to define the issue. In this view, women who espouse a relational morality grounded in immediate experience would emphasize the quality of life for the mother, the unborn child, and the other children in the family.[90] According to this reasoning, it would be no service to life to bring an unwanted child, or even a child for whose support there were inadequate resources, into the world. The decision not to have the child would, accordingly, be the moral decision. The main difficulty with this position lies in its repudiation of any attempt to define life in the abstract. For, if a rigid and abstract definition of life embodies dichotomous male thinking, it also embodies the highest standard of civilization—the greatest respect for human life in all its diversity—that human beings have been able to devise. Most of those who oppose capital punishment, including many pro-choice feminists, regard respect for life in the abstract as the most compelling argument against sentencing even the most hardened convicted criminals to death.

The second difficulty with this position lies in its assumption that one individual can determine another individual's desires. Many of us may think that we base such decisions on empathy—that we know that we would never want to live under a particular set of conditions, say with Alzheimer's disease, or as a paraplegic. But I, and presumably many others, have at one or another time known an elderly person who, earlier in life, had insisted on preferring death to living with loss of faculties, but, who continued doggedly to hang on to life long after most of the faculties had failed. It is as if the body takes on a life of its own, including a powerful determination to live. To say, in the face of such evidence, that we have a right to decide which living being would and would not want to live under which conditions is to assume precisely that arrogant disregard for another's subjectivity for which feminists condemn men's attitudes toward women.

Feminism's deep and uncritical commitment to individualism has left these matters unresolved. In our age of advanced medical technology, the lines between life and death are blurring. Today, many premature babies, for whom there would have been no hope as recently as a decade or two ago, survive and flourish. Today, many gravely ill children and adults, who would very recently have been given up for lost, recover and flourish. But in these and other instances, survival depends upon a massive expenditure of social resources. In a society in which people no longer agree on a single religious definition of life, such a definition must be a collective decision that risks a considerable measure of arbitrariness. For if we leave the definition of life to individual conscience or convenience, we open ourselves to the worst consequences of atomization.[91]

Abortion confronts us with a collective social, economic, political, and moral problem that we can only solve collectively and in frank acknowledgment that no solution will escape intellectual inconsistencies and some unresolved moral tensions. Abortion forces us to recognize provision for children as a collective responsibility. Increasingly, the responsibility for children penalizes women by curtailing their social and economic opportunities. By forcing women to bear and rear children they do not want and for whom they cannot adequately provide, society is pitting women's lives against children's and consigning women to social and economic marginality. But the difficulty and sacrifice do not constitute a moral, or even a political, justification for abortion. They constitute a justification for enhanced medical and educational programs for all children and hence for the acceptance of collective principles.

Feminists' recent emphasis on difference merely exacerbates the problem. There can be no doubt that the difference between women and men challenges the individualistic model of equality, but difference does not mean the same thing to all who invoke it. For some, difference reduces to narrow personal experience and thus signals an apparently unending process of atomization; for others, difference signifies the defining characteristics of particular communities or groups and thus, however unself-consciously, points toward some kind of modern corporatism. In either case, the invocation of difference implies direct concern with the community or collectivity within which it exists. This implication of difference has received very little attention in feminist thought, which has generally attacked the ideal of a single justice for all. But the specific limitations of our inherited ideal of justice, however blatant, do not justify repudiation of the ideal of an abstract justice. Indeed, if the proliferating claims of difference should teach us anything, they should teach us that if we need a justice sensitive to variations of gender, race, and class, we also need one that can transcend or at least discipline them. For without such an ideal, how do we expect to avoid Hobbes's nightmare of society as "the warre of all against all"?

The American version of the myth of individualism that promised success to those (men) who played by its rules assumed that unpaid female labor and devotion would buttress (male) individuals' efforts in the struggle to cope with the capitalist market. The myth never delivered as much as it promised, but its hegemony smoothed America's transition to full industrial capitalism and on to the age of great corporations and international conglomerates. The politics of the last decades, which have reinvigorated the myth of individualism, have also condemned innumerable individuals' dreams. The (collective) position of African-Americans has steadily worsened.[92] The proliferation of homelessness primarily testifies not, as some would believe, to individual failures—although doubtless they play some part—but to the collective failure of that greatest of all American dreams, the prospect of individual property ownership. This disappearance of the material foundations of individualism for growing numbers of Americans should be recognized as dramatic confirmation of the limits of individualism itself. Yet feminism continues to perpetuate the myth of individualism in defense of women's rights.

Minimal justice should offer women the same opportunities for individualism as men. The history of gender relations and the differences in male and female biology constitute powerful barriers to the simple inclusion of women in the individualistic market and polity. Women require discrete opportunities. Or, rather, they require a new conception of the economy and polity that can take account of sexual asymmetry without subjugating women to men. Women's needs cannot be defended in the name of atomistic individualistic principles. They must be fought for in the name of social justice for all—not individuals viewed as so many atoms, but individuals viewed as responsible and interdependent members of society, from which their rights derive. Like it or not, we are embarking on an age of distributive justice and social, in contrast to innate, rights. The measure of freedom and dignity that we manage to build into that inescapably collective society will depend heavily on the principles in the name of which we build it.

4

PORNOGRAPHY AND

INDIVIDUAL RIGHTS

Each society gets the pornography it deserves. Pornography, in the words of Alan Wolfe, "exists where sex and politics meet."[1] The proliferation of pornography in our society accurately mirrors the progression of our atomization. The pornographic imagination teases the boundaries of the taboos that we depend upon to define our humanity. Pornographic materials embody our actual defiance of taboos; their unlicensed circulation betrays our compulsion to test boundaries. The pornographer (and the consumer of pornographic materials) is, as Susan Griffin has argued, "obsessed with the idea of transgression."[2] Like small children, pushing to see how far they can go before being spanked, we are pressing against inherited authority. Like small children, desperate to find some limits that will help them to define themselves, we anxiously escalate our challenges, secretly hoping that someone will force us to stop. We have forgotten, or never learned, how to stop ourselves. So the fantasies multiply, blacking out the sun, leaving us flailing in a Sadeian world of nightmares.[3]

The proliferating and increasingly gruesome accounts of pornography seem to belong to some other world, but they do not. During the past twenty-five years, pornography has entered the mainstream of American society, mushrooming into a multibillion-dollar industry.[4] Reputedly, it accounts for 50 to 60 percent of all videocassette sales. Magazines that celebrate pornography abound on newspaper stands and even drugstore racks. Pornographic films show in theaters throughout the country; pornographic videos can be rented in any video shop and find their way into one in seven to one in ten middle-class homes.[5] Dial-a-porn services are advertised on cable television during prime time. The production of pornographic materials exploits untold numbers of women and children, and their contents are steadily becoming more violent. Even in the purportedly safe, privileged world of the upper middle class, tell-tale signs appear in such sanctuaries of taste as *Vogue*.

In its extreme forms, pornography represents an obscene degradation of women, increasingly of children, and of our conception of ourselves as a society. Even in its mild forms, it represents an objectification of women not merely as the objects of men's sexual gaze but as the objects of men's power. However difficult it remains to draw lines, I would ban the more extreme forms without a second thought, and with precious few worries about the public expressions of healthy sexuality that might be banned along with them. But we live in a society based on individualist principles that do not easily permit action in the name of the collectivity, and in a culture that is increasingly suspicious of any attempt to define standards. The curtailment of pornography, which does depend upon the implementation of standards, is, ultimately, a matter for the collectivity—and, accordingly, a matter that requires collective principles.

For those who, like myself, have been sheltered from the worst, the film *Not a Love Story* graphically introduced us to what we had been sheltered from. No wonder so many people reasonably give credit to the grimmest accounts of pornography's hidden empire and the, if anything, grimmer accounts of the by-products that many attribute to its influence—brutal rapes, "normal" fathers who rape their own daughters, day-school caretakers who molest children entrusted to their charge. No wonder advocates of women's rights to equality, dignity, and respect, and of children's rights to a protected childhood are demanding action.[6] Yes, at the risk of exposing my residual puritanism, I do count myself among pornography's instinctive opponents. Instinct, however, does not amount to a policy or even a clear understanding of the issues.

What do we mean by pornography? The simple answer is sexually explicit, violent materials that are apparently intended to provoke (frequently sado-masochistic) sexual response. Or, to paraphrase what has been said of art, I don't know much about it, but I know what I hate. Or, as Mr. Justice Stewart said about pornography itself, "I know it when I see it."[7]

Even those who have attempted to be more precise differ widely in their definitions. Edward Donnerstein, Daniel Linz, and Steven Penrod, for example, have attempted to categorize pornographic materials according to their content and apparent purpose. They distinguish among nonviolent sexually explicit stimuli that more or less intensely depict the degradation of women, sexually explicit stimuli that more or less explicitly depict women as desiring and benefiting from rape, and materials that although not sexually explicit juxtapose sex and violence or depict brutal rape.[8] Catharine Mac-Kinnon has no use for such discriminations. In her view, pornography "is an industry that mass produces sexual intrusion on, access to, possession and use of women by and for men for profit." Pornography "exploits women's sexual and economic inequality for gain." Pornography "sells women to men as and for sex." Pornography "is a technologically sophisticated traffic in women."[9] Pornography, in short, is "not a moral issue"; it is an issue of sexual hierarchy and oppression.[10]

The problems of definition reflect the complexity of different people's attitudes. Richard Randall has proposed a fundamental distinction between the *"pornographic within"* as "an imagistic resolution of erotic impulses or wishes to violate sexual taboos, mores, conventions" and *"pornography"* as a "material representation, portrayal, depiction, or other symbolization of the internally pornographic through a medium of expression, usually image, language, gesture, or sound."[11] His distinction thus usefully underscores the difference between what might be called the pornographic imagination and the pornographic commodity, but, unfortunately, the debates over the permissible place of pornography in our society have largely ignored it.

In the simplest terms, those who concern themselves with pornography can be messily divided between those who unilaterally oppose it and those who, whatever their personal distaste for its current manifestations, are squeamish about any attempt to curb it. Drawing the lines between opponents and tolerators yields some strange results and, specifically, yields no clear feminist position. By these criteria, some feminists end up on the same side as traditional conservatives in uncompromising opposition, whereas other feminists end up with civil libertarians, liberal and conservative, by viewing toleration as the lesser of the two evils of corruption and censorship or even viewing toleration as a positive good.

These strange alliances testify to our confusion about the relation between what we, in principle, believe we should do about pornography and what, in practice—given the constraints of the society in which we live—we can safely do about it. Pornography throws us directly into the morass of the untidy relations among morals, law, and politics, notably gender politics. Once we get beyond the intuitive horror that pornography evokes, what is at issue: our sexual mores? our sense of public decency? the domination and exploitation of women? our First Amendment rights of free speech? Or, to reverse the perspective, should pornography be viewed as obscenity? as sexual exploitation? as gender-specific sexual exploitation? as tyranny or domination? as self-expression? as an indication of sexual liberation? as speech? as, in legal parlance, a "nuisance"? or, again in legal parlance, as "defamation"? or perhaps even a "harm"?

Above all, the varied attempts to classify pornography testify to the disagreement about whether it represents an attack on morals or an attack on women, and, beyond that, how it can be defined in the most neutral or "objective" terms possible so that its regulation cannot be interpreted as an infringement of individual right.[12] (That a palpable attack on women is not automatically taken as an attack on community morals speaks volumes in itself.) The possibilities of definition, and this list does not exhaust them, further testify to the difficulty of disentangling pornography from the eye of the beholder, which is to say from the perspective of the individual—from the rights of the individual that lie at the core of our peculiar vision of social order.[13]

If attitudes toward pornography do not permit neat classification, we can nonetheless identify four general camps, two among its opponents and two among its tolerators. The first of those willing to curtail pornography legally and by force consists primarily of conservatives of various persuasions who view it as certain testimony to the degradation of our moral life; the second consists primarily of radical feminists who view pornography as one of the principal weapons in the systematic oppression, objectification, and degradation of women.[14] The first of those unwilling to ban pornography consists of radical individualists or libertarians, from the far left to the far right of the political spectrum, who celebrate the lifting of sexual repression and the rights of individuals of any age to participate in the sexual expression of their choice. The second consists of uneasy liberals who fear the consequences of censorship in any sphere.

Each of the four camps defines the salient issues differently. For the conservatives, the stakes consist of public decency, and, behind it, the institutions, notably family and church, that have sustained it in the past.[15] With varying degrees of enthusiasm, they are willing to risk the perils of censorship, which some view less as perils than as the reimposition of minimal social and political order. For the radical feminists, pornography can be understood exclusively as a support for men's brutalization and oppression of women, which some equate with male sexuality in particular and imposed heterosexuality in general. Like the conservatives, whose values they criticize but with whom they frequently find themselves uneasily allied, they do not fear censorship and willingly turn to the state to help enforce the curtailment of male brutality.[16]

In sharp contrast, the libertarians defend pornography as the embodiment of personal and sexual liberation. Viewing it as a question of individual freedom, they passionately oppose any form of censorship or restriction by whatever legal tactic. The liberals resemble the libertarians in their mistrust of censorship, but they remain queasy about whether it would be possible to place some limits on the spread and escalating violence of pornography. Accordingly, they anguish about the legal niceties: If pornography must be protected as speech, might it not still be curtailed as nuisance, defamation, or harm? Or is any such effort a subterfuge for an attack on the First Amendment that could be extended to other unpopular forms of speech?[17]

Even these differences do not account for all of the divisions among the groups. The conservatives, for example, view pornography primarily as a manifestation of social and moral disintegration, whereas radical feminists view it primarily as a direct attack on women and, as such, as nothing especially new. The distinction between these two positions may be difficult to draw but represents an important divergence in priorities, for the conservatives would like to restore women to men's protection, whereas the radical feminists would like to release them entirely from men's control. Their views, in other words, converge in identifying the split between public and private spheres as the central issue but diverge in their interpretation of it. Conservatives favor a restoration of a male-dominated private sphere; radical feminists favor denying the claims of privacy entirely. For, in MacKinnon's words, "The existing distribution of power and resources within the private sphere are precisely what the law of privacy exists to protect."[18]

Since at least the days of Montesquieu, it has been a commonplace of Western culture that a society's level of civilization can be measured by its treatment of women, who embody its standards of public and private morality.[19] But the association between women and public morality has not necessarily entailed a defense of women's equality, or even a defense of women's rights as individuals in the public sphere. Rather, it has been taken to rest precisely on women's exclusion from the public sphere and on their willing acceptance of male "protection," which is to say male domination.

Many conservatives still more or less explicitly and more or less punitively favor this view. They do favor respect for women—at least for the women of their own class and race—but they also impose stringent conditions. Of course no woman—read, no decent woman—should be raped or sexually abused. But women who willfully place themselves at sexual risk get what they ask for.

Conservatives oppose the sexual exploitation of those women who accept their proper place. They also oppose the public display of sexual exploitation, and sometimes even the public display of sexual expression. They favor, in short, a heavy dose of sexual repression in general. But they do not see the sexual abuse of women as a violation of women's rights as individuals, or as a reinforcement of women's subordination to men. To the contrary, they tend to believe that the renewed "protective" domination of women by men is the first step on the road to a decent society.

Radical feminists reject this premise a priori. For them, pornography consists above all—even exclusively—in men's domination of women. "Pornography is the theory, rape is the practice."[20] If their expression is occasionally shrill and their apparent goals more than a little chilling, up to a point their vision is compelling. Far from being a harmless fantasy—and expression of "natural" eroticism—pornography represents the sexual essence of male supremacy, which does indeed derive from male sexuality, or perhaps defines it.[21] Pornography embodies an erotic representation of male dominance and female submission, which it presents as the natural and inescapable relations of men and women. Gender is essentially sexual, and pornography defines that sexuality. "Men's power over women means that the way men see women defines who women can be."[22]

Pornography is not, by this logic, which has been most fully developed by Catharine MacKinnon, a crime against public decency; it is a crime against women. The problem is not one of sexually explicit material but of dominance. Obscenity laws, which define morals "from the male point of view, meaning the standpoint of male dominance," reproduce "the pornographic point of view on the level of constitutional jurisprudence."[23] Pornography, Susan Griffin elaborates, represents a logical extension of a culture that has silenced women and embodies not only the lie that the pornographer tells about women, but "the lie that a woman begins to believe about herself" or, even if she does not entirely believe, that she begins to mimic. "For since all the structures of power in her life, and all the voices of authority—the church, the state, society, most likely even her own mother and father—

reflect pornography's fantasy, if she feels in herself a being who contradicts this fantasy, she begins to believe she herself is wrong."[24]

Andrea Dworkin, whose conception of pornography has influenced MacKinnon, makes the case yet more rabidly. Believing, like MacKinnon, that sex is only power and only accrues to men, Dworkin views all men as beasts and all women as innocent (and strangely passive) victims. Men, from her tortured perspective, are incapable of compassion, decency, or honor and only refrain from the most brutal acts out of fear of revenge. This fear, which normally dissuades them from raping other men, does not operate in their relations with women, whom they brutalize without need to consider the consequences. Men see all women as whores and use them accordingly. What men do to women is worse than what the Nazis did to the Jews. For Dworkin, "Sex is the theory and extermination the practice."[25]

Radical feminists, in short, link pornography directly to, even blame it for, what they view as every crime against women, from mandatory heterosexuality, to job discrimination, to rape, and beyond. Pornography "is a form of forced sex, a practice of sexual politics, an institution of gender inequality." Together with rape and prostitution, to which it is linked, pornography "institutionalizes the sexuality of male supremacy, which fuses the erotization of dominance and submission with the social construction of male and female." Pornography is nothing more or less than the "meaning" of sexuality.[26] It must be eradicated because it plays a central role "in creating and maintaining the civil inequalities of the sexes," because it constitutes a violation of women's civil rights.[27]

One of the many difficulties with this view is that it extends the concept of civil rights beyond all meaning. The proposed remedy belongs to a frame of reference different from the purported cause. In 1983, Dworkin and MacKinnon drafted a model ordinance to ban the traffic in pornographic materials on the grounds that it constituted an infringement of women's civil rights. Actual ordinances of this kind were proposed in Minneapolis and Indianapolis but ultimately declared unconstitutional in both cities.[28] The attempts represented a significant departure from previous obscenity law, as well from First Amendment principles of free speech, and were, in both instances, rejected because of their discrimination on the basis of view point and, in the words of the appellate court that struck down the Indianapolis ordinance, because they represent "thought control."[29]

The fate of the ordinances faithfully reflected the spirit in which they were drafted. At the limit, radical feminists do see pornography as the embodiment of maleness, as the real expression of the relations between women and men—as malevolent in its effects but natural in its cause. On this understanding, the only successful curtailment of pornography must begin with limiting men's freedom of thought and action. And if we follow the argument to its logical conclusion, the only solution can be the elimination of men in anything that resembles the form in which we know them. Politics is reduced to sexual politics at the most fundamental level, and the invocation of civil rights reduced to a mockery.

Liberals and libertarians are less explicit about whether they view pornography as a social issue or as a women's issue, for both groups assume that a certain measure of sexual liberation has benefited women as well as men. The liberals, who include many feminists, will nonetheless also acknowledge that pornography represents a special threat to and a special degradation of women, even if most would be loathe to restrict its evils to its impact on women alone. Liberal feminists have, for example, attempted to distinguish between erotica and "violent, women-degrading pornography."[30] This attempted distinction reflects an abiding preoccupation with the relation between curtailment of pornography and the protection of individual rights and between healthy sexual self-expression and sexual degradation. Needless to say, the lines, which are blurred in theory, become even more so in practice. For, if in principle, most liberals would try to draw them so as to include some constraints on the exploitation of children, they cannot easily agree on where even those lines should be drawn.[31]

Libertarians, largely untroubled by these concerns, push the notion of individual right to its logical conclusion: no consideration of public morality justifies the violation of the individual right. From this perspective, pornography is not a women's issue but a social issue in the broadest sense, for it embodies a revolt against repressive authority. Sexually explicit material is thereby recognized as indeed the point and is judged inherently good. That is, each viewer may judge the content good or bad, but the presumed right of the purveyor to public self-expression is declared a transcendental good. There can be no question of pornography as a crime against women, for there can be no question of pornography as a crime. In the libertarian canon, women are simply individuals who should, like all other individuals, be free to follow whither their sexual predilections lead them, including into sadomasochism or anything else, and, more to the point, they should be free to parade their predilections and to proselytize. In its extreme form, this position defends the use of children in the production of child pornography on the grounds that children should have the "right," for psychological, sexual, or economic reasons, freely to consent to participate.

I suspect that intuitively most responsible adults find this position as offensive as I do, but its logic bears pondering. Note that I have just qualified "adult" by "responsible." Who am I, or anyone else, to judge the relative responsibility of other adults? By what criteria do we oppose proponents of "man-boy love"? Whatever our individual attitudes, do we have the right to impose them on others? The libertarians have logic on their side. Since individual right offers no compelling criteria by which to impose the views of one on another, we should give up the attempt to impose views. And since the libertarians' views are simply the conservatives' standards of decency by another name, we should give up the attempt to impose, or even to define, standards. If the libertarian position is, in effect, the polar opposite of that which I am calling the conservative (traditionalist) position, the libertarians nonetheless include many who identify themselves as political conservatives in today's crazy-quilt politics. Their flamboyant debates about the implementation of public morality cloak many points of agreement on other matters, notably economic policy.

To curtail pornography, we need some minimal agreement on the desirability of curtailing it and on the ways in which it could and should be curtailed within our own legal system. Conservatives, radical feminists, and most liberals would agree on the desirability but sharply disagree both on the justification of curtailment and the ways in which it could be effected.

The proponents of curtailment would have an easier time if it could be demonstrated that pornography actually causes, or even substantially contributes to, the perpetration of violent crimes in general and violent crimes against women in particular. Sadly, such proof is lacking, however strong the grounds for suspicion remain. It also cannot be demonstrated that pornography serves as a safety valve, in effect as a substitute for, the acting out of violent impulses.[32] All parties to the debate have attempted to bring the evidence of social and behavioral science to the service of their views, but at least on this matter, the radical feminists probably have made the best case simply by arguing that pornography celebrates the objectification, subordination, and dehumanization of women.[33] Indeed it does.

Pornography does depict women bound, beaten, writhing in subordination, accepting sex from one man, many men, and beasts—and enjoying it all. The spectacle is repulsive, offensive, and demeaning. But its purported vileness and loathsomeness cannot alone justify censorship or regulation without regard to the principles on which either would be imposed.

From the psychological perspective, the horrors of pornography testify, above all, to men's abiding struggles with the responsibility to respect and protect at least "decent" women that civilization has attempted to impose on them. I have a young friend who, when he was three years old, was informed that his mother was about to give him a wonderful present: another baby. My young friend pondered the news quietly, manifesting none of the signs of delight for which the script called, and then gravely informed his mother, "I eat baby." Shortly thereafter, he took his father aside and told him, with equal seriousness, "When I grow up I am going to marry Mommy and have babies with her." On the surface, his responses have little to do with pornography. Beneath the surface, they have everything to do with it, for he was expressing fantasies that defied the taboos of his world. In so doing, he delighted his parents and hurt no one—certainly not the new baby, a sister, whom he rapidly came to love and respect. His testing of the limits of the permissible remained in the realm of fantasy.

It may be objected that my young friend's fantasies were charming and innocent—the natural responses of a child to the threat of being displaced in his mother's affections. But they do have something in common with the pornographic imagination, notably the attempt to reimagine the world closer to the heart's desire. Western Christianity has always had a tendency, well exemplified in Saint Augustine, to believe that sins should be eradicated and judged at their root—in the imagination. But it has also had another, best exemplified in the Jesuits, that the sinner should be judged not by the intention (which is intrinsic to the inherently sinful human condition) but by the act.

If we are to regulate at all, we must agree upon what we are regulating. It is not enough to condemn pornography out of hand as, for example, the degradation of women—no matter how much it does degrade women. Our finest constitutional principles have included the protection of the individual and of the polity that individuals constitute. But, as feminists have been arguing, they make little or no allowance for women as a special class of individuals. And when they do make such an allowance, they show a distressing tendency to protect women by reinforcing rather than correcting their inequality with men.[34] How do we protect women, as women, without restricting their opportunities for individualism, notably the ability to support themselves? Must we change men's fantasies, or simply curtail their freedom to express them?

Even if we could constitutionally identify women as the special victims of pornography, we would still need to define pornography in order to act against it. Our obscenity law, as expressed in *Miller* v. *California*, embodied an attempt to define pornography as sexually explicit and violent material that has no purpose other than to cause sexual arousal or facilitate sexual satisfaction—in other words, as sexually explicit and violent material with no redeeming artistic or social value—and many, including many feminists, are attempting to adapt that definition to our current situation.[35]

As a first approximation, continued refinement of *Miller* works well enough. But the problem of updating cannot be dismissed lightly. How, in a world in which *Lady Chatterley's Lover* and *Ulysses* look tame, in which yesterday's hard-core porn is resurfacing as today's R-rated movie, in which glossy X-rated videos make their way into all manner of "respectable" homes, in which, to put it concisely, "yesterday's illegality is today's television commercial," do we determine artistic and socially redeeming value, and who does the determining?[36] Opponents of the regulation of pornography counter that it is dangerous to impose arbitrary definitions of artistic value and that sexual self-expression by whatever means is its own justification and hence should not be subject to others' criteria of social value.

Many of these arguments, which are legion and far more complex than this summary could suggest, rest on the assumption that pornography ought to be classified as a form of speech and, accordingly, ought to be only lightly regulated or allowed to flourish unimpeded, in conformity with the First Amendment principles that govern freedom of speech. From the perspective of the opponents of regulation, long, hard battles have been fought to extend the principles of freedom of speech, and they should not be jeopardized now. This view moves directly toward the arguments of civil libertarians who defend the right of Nazis to march in Skokie or the Klan to march in College Park or proponents of civil rights to march in Forsythe County. Many liberals and libertarians doubt the wisdom of attempting to regulate pornography even if it were divorced from speech and linked to sexual activity. Have we not also fought long, hard battles to free individual sexuality from the legacy of repressive puritanism? Do we really want to return to the days of the Comstock laws? Do we want to jeopardize women's right to abortion?

Some who have faced these difficulties have attempted to argue that pornography's great danger lies not in the printed word, the freedom of which should be protected at all costs, but in the immediate, graphic depiction of sexual violence on film. Visual representation differs radically from verbal representation and might well invite different kinds of regulation. But which ones? Would not the same principles of social consensus and public decency that justified the censorship of pornographic films also be used to justify the censorship of films on acid rain, or on Contra brutality in Nicaragua? The answers become all the more problematical when conservative ministers who oppose pornography also oppose any imposition of federal regulation on cable television channels because they fear that they would be obliged to give equal time on their own channels to political opponents. The question does not seem likely to admit of easy solution on democratic principles.

Some propose to cut through the difficulties that attend the regulation of pornography as verbal or visual representation by redefining it as act. This strategy has some promise, but it too rouses strong opposition. For, once again, who, in our democratic society, should be empowered to tell others what to do? The boundaries between thought and action remain frustratingly permeable. How do we draw the lines between acceptable and unacceptable sexual expression? Lesbians, like male homosexuals, would lead the opposition to any general attempt to regulate the expression of sexual preference, an attempt which many heterosexual feminists, like all libertarians, would fear as an invasion of individual right.

Another strategy consists in attempting to draw the lines between public and private in matters of representation, expression, and behavior. According to this logic, the behavior of consenting adults in the privacy of their own homes is their own business, while the defilement of public thoroughfares with garbage is the community's business. If pornographic materials can be shown to have an effect on the community analogous to the effect of a smelly garbage dump or a polluting factory or noisy runways, then they should be regulated.[37] These considerations would subject pornography to the equivalent of leash or defecation laws for dogs. But, as Elizabeth Wolgast insists, the harms of a smelly garbage dump affect the community as a whole, whereas the harms of pornography affect women in particular.[38]

The manifold difficulties with this position are not insurmountable. First, the nuisance must be proved: pornography must be shown seriously to inconvenience some individuals or groups of individuals. Second, the appropriate regulating authority must be determined: regulation would likely be a local matter, in the manner of zoning laws, rather than a national one.[39]

But even zoning, it can be argued, also impinges on rights of free speech, since, in the absence of an adequate supply of unrestricted land, how are adult movie theater operators, or others, to enjoy the free expression of their views, or, more to the point, the free marketing of their commodities?[40] And once the principles of local authority, which many conservatives enthusiastically support, were established, might they not, as many feminists and liberals worry, lead to abuses? Third, mindful of the lessons of Prohibition, many worry about the long-term benefits of driving offensive behavior underground. There are, after all, a number of people who favor solving the drug problem by legalization. But the most important problem concerns the escalating difficulty of drawing any boundaries between public and private at all, for, in the end, the community would be asserting its right to suppress behavior judged as an outrage against public decency. If so, could it not judge the advocacy of an ideology—fascism, communism, racism, racial integration—as just that?

The position of the radical feminists is instructive here, for their war against pornography admits of no distinction between public and private. If the crime of pornography were declared virulent misogyny, how much good could be served by regulating only its public expression and distribution? Their logic raises important theoretical questions, even if one does not entirely accept their premises. Are we prepared to sanction the private exploitation of women and children, provided that we can freely regulate its public celebration? That principle undergirded the free practice of the multiple abuses that festered beneath the public decency of Victorian society. Do we want to return to those "good old days"?

Feminists have fought a valiant battle to break down the barriers between the public and private spheres. Their efforts, abetted by important allies, have resulted in the recognition of marital and acquaintance rape as public crimes rather than private relations, resulted in a growing attempt to protect children from battering and incest, and resulted in growing awareness of the rights of battered wives. The public defense of at least minimal rights for women and children against the private privileges of men has figured at the core of the feminist agenda. But it has also irreparably undermined the barriers between public and private experience. The chickens of "the personal is political" have come home to roost. If the personal is political, then, by an implacable logic, the private must be public.

This general politicization of the private has also caught those feminists who support it in a frequently unacknowledged contradiction. The core of the argument for abortion lies in a defense of the rights of privacy. A woman's body is not merely her right, but her private right—a right over which the state has no jurisdiction at all. Logically, the defense of abortion on the grounds of absolute privacy carries potentially unpalatable corollaries, notably the difficulty of punishing men for abusing women or children, or even of holding men accountable for supporting women and children. Perhaps more important, it reinforces the individualistic view of rights as essentially a form of property.[41]

Many conservatives would reverse this tendency, and some feminists, notably Jean Bethke Elshtain, are prepared to join them in the endeavor. Elshtain, who also opposes pornography, has argued that women's preoccupation with the violence perpetrated against them by pornography is misplaced, that women are falling into a victim syndrome. For her, the solution lies in a strengthening of the private sphere. For, she insists, societies with strong private institutions manifest a much lower incidence of pornography than our own.[42] Elshtain has an important point, although there can be no doubt that restoration of that traditional bourgeois family on the old terms would come at tremendous cost to women and would not necessarily decrease men's violence against them. At the moment the prospects for the kind of renovated family and polity she favors, however desirable, appear slim.

Many feminists who do not share Elshtain's proposed solutions do join her in crediting feminism with the recent escalation in pornography. According to this analysis, the women's movement has put men on the defensive. By robbing men of their customary privileges and prerogatives and by exposing them to the direct competition of women as individuals, it has prompted them to try to reimpose their domination and to express their hostility by other means. The increase in pornography is said directly to reflect men's hostility to feminism.[43]

Radical feminists depart from this analysis primarily in their insistence that men's nature has always led them to oppress, vilify, and abuse women. From their perspective, pornography accurately embodies men's attitudes toward women in all times and places. The contemporary increase may be of passing interest but is of no special significance in the long-standing war between the sexes. In my judgment, their position fails to take account of the importance of historical change in the relations between women and men, but it does force us to ask whether pornography represents simply men's abiding fear of and hostility toward women or a historically specific version of that fear and hostility. It also forces us to develop a better understanding of the relation between the pornographic imagination and the pornographic commodity.

Those of us who accept the existence of fundamental differences between men and women suspect that at least some mutual hostility will always characterize relations between them. And those of us who also accept some notion, however secularized, of original sin, or who at least reject the utopian notion that the travails of the human condition can ever completely be transcended or reformed out of existence, recognize that the pains and conflicts of attempting to share love across those differences will always be with us.

The basic biological and especially sexual differences between men and women remain irreducible, but their forms and resultant relations change significantly over time. Pushed to its extreme, the argument that gender socially and linguistically constructs those differences has been taken by some to suggest that any notion of difference simply reflects the dichotomous thinking of a hierarchical society. And we know that in specific cases even such purportedly decisive aspects of biological difference as genitalia can be ambiguous. To take such marginal ambiguity as an adequate denial of fundamental biological differences between women and men is to distort the overwhelming pattern for ideological reasons. Let me confront the predictable objection directly: the existence of homosexual men, lesbian women, and transsexuals does not subvert the biological dichotomy between the sexes or justify talk of a "third" sex. The explanations for sexual preference are hotly contested and remain elusive. Heterosexual sexual preference itself reflects a mixture of psychology and biology. But notwithstanding the infinitely complex work of imagination and society in shaping individuals' sexual identity, the predominant biological pattern does rest on a fundamental (and complementary) difference between male and female upon which our reproduction as a species depends.

The issue, accordingly, is not the existence of differences, but the social consequences of those differences. As recently as the nineteenth century, men's physical strength and women's reproductive capacities were plausibly taken to dictate primary differences in male and female social roles. Today, under the influence of modern technology, including contraceptive technology, the plausible consequences of those differences are radically shrinking. But precisely as gender roles become increasingly interchangeable—what some seem to mean by "unisex" or "androgynous"—sexuality is apparently assuming increasing importance as the principal experience that differentiates men from women. In short, it seems likely that, however sensitive men and women may become to each other's condition and however many experiences they may share, both men and women still have great difficulty in grasping the other's experience of sex. Thus, since men and women must share the world, their attempts at accommodation and cooperation will inevitably be laced with tension. The recognition of such tension and even the high probability of its persistence need not trouble us much, but some of the forms that that inevitable hostility takes should trouble us deeply.

The forms are a product of historical change. The increase in the pornographic commodity and the escalating violence of the pornographic imagination must be attributed to our historical rather than to our human condition. Erosion of the barriers between public and private spheres has much to do with the unregulated proliferation of pornography. The women's movement probably has exacerbated men's frustration and hostility; it assuredly has helped to transform and overturn the laws, practices, and habits of mind that made men at least nominally responsible for women. Women's freedom to seek and obtain divorce looks, from one perspective, very much like men's freedom from the obligation to support women and their children. The liberation of female sexuality from the iron control of husbands and fathers therefore looks very much like men's freedom to do with all women as they choose. The list could be extended. But however long that list, it would still bring us back to the problem of distinguishing symptom from cause. Has the women's movement caused these changes, or is it itself the product of underlying changes, notably changes in technology and the market?

Changes in technology and the market have largely freed women's sexuality from women's reproductive capacities and have drawn women into the labor market in unprecedented numbers. They have also affected men. Specifically, they have radically reduced the importance of men's physical strength, absolutely and in relation to women's physical strength. One of the explanations for the explosion of pornography should be sought in the recognition that, increasingly, men's physical strength is irrelevant to the ordinary business of life, possibly even to warfare. Physical strength does not determine success as a corporate vice president, does not determine success on a highly mechanized production line, does not determine the ability to run a computer, probably does not much influence the ability to fly a nuclear bomber or pilot a nuclear submarine. Under these conditions, it is hardly surprising that men turn with growing urgency to one of the few remaining arenas in which their physical strength does yield an advantage— their sexual relations with women. Surprising, no. Deplorable and unacceptable, yes.

History has brought the latent hostilities between men and women to a crisis. Pornography is, as the radical feminists insist, preeminently an ideology of male violence, which, as they also insist, probably reflects a general tendency in the human condition. Certainly many feminists, notably but not exclusively those I am calling the radicals, accept violence as an innate male attribute. Some feminists, like Riane Eisler, attribute all historical manifestations of violence to men, but they nonetheless hold that in our time men could be redeemed by being converted to a "partnership" model of human relations.[44] Still others, who also accept the historical association between men and violence, believe that improved and shared child rearing by women and men will transform men through cultural practice.[45] And some, notably Jean Bethke Elshtain, come close to the position of conservatives like Thomas Fleming who believe that an innate association of men and violence could be turned to socially constructive purposes, although, unlike Fleming, Elshtain also believes that society desperately needs a much greater infusion of women's traditional values of care.[46] The various positions reflect various attitudes toward the respective roles of "nature" and "culture" in human personality.[47]

The debate between nature and culture is, in truth, revealing itself to be no debate at all, for almost no one holds either entirely accountable for human behavior. There are, nonetheless, sharp differences in the emphasis placed on one or the other, with most feminists aligning themselves on the side of a preponderant role for culture.[48] If only we could raise children more equitably and more lovingly, we would have a less violent world. At the same time, many feminists insist that women are naturally less violent than men. The record of women's behavior does not entirely support this position, for many women who have had access to power have displayed a disconcerting tendency to use it as ruthlessly as any man. But women like Margaret Thatcher, Golda Meir, and Indira Gandhi, not to mention Corazon Aquino or Imelda Marcos, do not figure prominently in feminist pages.[49] And most of us have, mercifully, repressed the very special psychological violence of the junior high school girls' clique.

The most thoughtful discussions of women's nurturing qualities normally focus more on women's cultural experience as nurturers of children, tenders of the sick, and comforters of the dying.[50] But, on the assumption that women have performed those roles because they have been excluded from others, it logically follows that their propensity to nurture derives at least in part from their history of subordination and victimization. And, as the disquieting evidence of abused women who themselves abuse others suggests, subordination and victimization do not constitute the best possible preparation for generosity, much less leadership.

We are not likely to legislate the human condition out of existence. Nor are we likely to restore previous relations between men and women. We are irreversibly engaged on a course that pits individuals, men and women, against each other as individuals in the workplace. It would be naive to assume that such a radical shift in the social relations between the genders will have no consequences for their personal relations.

This same history has been relentlessly stripping away all the institutions that constituted the private sphere. It has indeed politicized personal relations beyond anything previously imaginable. The consequences of that history for my argument lie in the inescapable conclusion that pornography, which has generally been viewed as a matter of morals, has also become a matter of politics and law. In this sense, pornography challenges our deepest sense of ourselves as members of a community that is willing to impose standards in the name of respect for its members and survival for itself.

At our most generous, we tend to view restrictions on individual right as the exception rather than the norm and tend to justify socially necessary restrictions with reference to the larger good of other individual rights. In other words, our view of the common good has more to do with the good of the majority of individuals than with the good of the whole, with the whole understood to have an existence in some way independent of, or logically anterior to, the individuals who compose it. This bias in favor of the individual has largely determined the development of our legal tradition, which we have attempted to separate from our various religious traditions by identifying religion as a matter of private (individual) conscience. But the confusions have been legion. Not least, we have had difficulty in disentangling religion as specific doctrine and observance from morality as public standard, for it is worth recalling that until the late nineteenth century, Americans typically favored the separation of church and state but no less typically assumed that such public institutions as the schools had a duty to promote the moral instruction of the young, where moral instruction was virtually equated with instruction in nonsectarian Christian values. And even in this secular age we might ask: Just what are our schools for, if not to foster in the young adherence to some minimal notion of common values and to impart some minimal moral instruction?

"The law," Justice Holmes once wrote, "is the witness and external deposit of our moral life." As an aspiration, Holmes's statement has much to commend it. Yet our laws have regularly tolerated, indeed supported, relations among individuals that many would consider flagrantly immoral. For while some would reduce morality to questions of decency and obscenity, others would insist that morality must take account of inequality and domination. It is, for example, possible to equate morality with men's protection of women in the context of manifest inequality between the genders and possible to equate morality with women's absolute equality to men as individuals. Morality, in short, has everything to do with the prevailing relations among individuals, including relations between women and men, in any society at any given time. A semblance of a moral consensus persisted as long as it did in the United States only because specific institutions, notably families and churches, embodied and enforced it. The free play of individual right alone could not ensure it. Indeed, it could be argued that the free play of individual right may well have acted as the single most powerful solvent of moral consensus.

"The best test of truth is the power of thought to get itself accepted by the market." That pearl of wisdom comes from the same Justice Holmes who insisted that law guarantees our moral life. Placed in sequence, his two assertions amount to the judgment that the market is the witness and external deposit of our moral life. And, sad to say, so it may be at this historical moment.

The deregulation of the pornographic commodity has as much to do with the freedom to buy and sell as with the freedom to speak or to act.[51] Yet most of the participants in the debate over pornography fall silent on the question of market regulation. This silence dangerously confuses the issues. As Lawrence Tribe has argued, the defense of free speech has never been uniform.

The speech of some has usually been taken to be more deserving of protection than the speech of others—the speech of capitalists, for example, more deserving than that of union members. Tribe argues that defense of First Amendment rights has been allocational rather than distributional. He means that the defense of First Amendment rights has been taken to apply to society at large without consideration for the inequalities that prevent some from benefiting from general social rights.[52] A distributional defense of First Amendment rights would also take account of the specific needs of specific, relatively disadvantaged groups.

The distinction applies to the case of pornography, which Tribe does not discuss in this context. In principle, it should be possible to curtail pornography without jeopardizing the right to express dissenting political opinions. But the possible in principle proves difficult in practice, not least because we should have to agree whether we want to curtail the expression of sexuality, perhaps viewed as obscenity, or whether we want to curtail the political freedom of men to express their hostility to women. And whatever our preferences in this respect, we would have to agree on whether we wanted to curtail the pornographic commodity or the pornographic imagination or both.

Because of the complicated relation between gender politics and more conventional politics, the odds are excellent that the regulation of pornography would be effected by a coalition of conservatives and radical feminists and that the price would be a general abridgment of First Amendment rights. The prevailing relation between allocational and distributional rights that Tribe describes reflects, above all, the ability of those in power to impose their views. It demonstrates that it is possible to take unfair advantage of our political and legal system, which favors some over others, without overthrowing the system as a whole. Tribe is pointing to the hard truth that in a system predicated upon the principles of individualism some are much more equal than others. He focuses on the fundamental tendency of the system to perpetuate economic inequality. It has, as radical feminists insist, with even greater success, perpetuated gender inequality.

In truth, our guiding individualistic premises have, in large measure, owed their long success to their coexistence with institutions based on radically different principles. The unparalleled triumph of individualism in our own time has seriously undercut the political effectiveness of individualism. Individualism has worked best—indeed has worked at all—when not all members of society could lay claim to the equal status of individual.

Pornography and Individual Rights

Individualism rampant has made it difficult for us to deal at all with pornography, as with much else.

Walter Berns, speaking from a white, male, conservative sensibility, has insisted that "concern for public morality requires censorship," even though concern for the arts may require abolition of censorship. Admitting the difficulty of drawing any precise lines between art and trash, he nonetheless concludes that the distinctions are necessary to survival of a decent society.[53] Berns supports the censorship of pornography, although he is not sure how to effect it; but then, his opposition to pornography does not rest on pornography's sanction of inequalities between women and men, much less its expression of male violence. Berns does not mention the market and rests his case on our intuitive and collective sense of decency. In effect he is trying to restore what Tribe would call an allocational attitude toward decency but disregards the distributional injustices his position conceals. His views have been widely attacked, largely because so many have come to reject decency as a relevant standard for our society or to doubt the possibility of defending any standard.

There are some grounds to sympathize with Berns's defense of decency and his commitment to the drawing of lines. For a society unwilling or unable to trust to its own instinct in laying down a standard of decency does not deserve to survive and probably will not survive. My quarrel with him concerns the assumptions about political, social, economic, and gender relations that underlie his views on pornography. He, like so many other conservatives, seeks to clean up our society and our culture, but he never questions how many of his own commitments on other matters have produced the outrage he deplores. We are not likely to restore decency by returning women, and violence against women, to the bedroom and the kitchen. Faced with the realities of our world, I must oppose Berns on important issues, however much I hate pornography and sympathize with the imposition of collective standards.

The hard truth remains: our prevailing individualistic principles and practices offer inadequate grounds for regulating, much less diminishing, the proliferation of the pornographic commodity. So long as we remain tied to our implicit conception of rights as themselves a form of property, we seriously risk confusing—indeed identifying—them with commodities. On the margin, we might impose some restrictions, as we have in other instances in which we have modified the free workings of the market. Our system of government embodies a remarkable flexibility in which the actions of the legislature are checked and monitored by the courts. Recently, for example, there has been a growing determination to treat as a crime the production of pornographic films and videos that depict children. After all, for such representations to be made, children have to do those things.

Yet even these modest measures increasingly raise complex questions of individual right.[54] Cannot even children, from the liberationist perspective, freely choose to do those things? Many would insist that children should not be permitted those choices and insist that children's psychological vulnerabilities should not be exploited. They might also insist that we should have to take account of the realities of our malevolent market and, perhaps more important, should have to rethink our notion of rights to include some vision of the rights of children other than simply extending to them the proprietary rights of atomized adults.[55] Today we confront the growing problem of how to protect children who live homeless on the streets with no guarantee of the next meal. Most would presumably agree that children should not be homeless, but with the decomposition of families, they are on the streets in substantial numbers. In permitting teenagers to be sentenced to death for murder, the Supreme Court has opened a wedge toward regarding them as self-accountable individuals.[56] On what grounds, other than the seriousness of the crime, can we distinguish between the teenage woman who chooses to play in a pornographic film and the teenage man who kills while executing a drug deal?

The example brings us back to the market. Pornographers are thriving off the degradation of our people. Pornography is obscene, not only because it exposes naked flesh in a manner that appeals to the worst in us but because it exposes our society naked. Yes, there is an element of human nature in anything—however "inhuman"—that humans do. But, from the dawn of time, part of what it has meant to be human has been the ability to define humanity as something more than the unmediated expression of human impulse. Even the most "primitive" societies developed principles according to which humanity should be measured. We, more than most societies, have tied our principles to unfettered greed, which we call the market and which we believe requires maximum freedom. In this respect pornography does nakedly reveal the extent to which our celebration of the individual intertwines with our enslavement to the market, and there is no necessary end to the escalation of atrocities. Society can, however, draw a line and prefer the risks entailed by the arbitrariness of some restrictions on individual freedom to a capitulation to flagrant degeneracy.

The principles of individualism do not readily permit the drawing of lines. Indeed, the case of pornography suggests that they make it almost impossible. Radical feminists are implicitly proposing that we draw the lines between men and women within our system. And the logic of our recent history may support their grim and bitter analysis but cannot support the underlying utopianism of their program. For the chasm between men and women results from the breakdown of an old society, rather than portending the birth of a new one. In short, the growing opposition between women and men itself results from the failure of individualism. To reverse it we need collective principles on the basis of which we can demand respect for women as distinct representatives of our humanity and as a necessary foundation for our society's respect for itself.

Traditional conservatives, who have always distrusted the market, appeal to religious absolutes or historically formed community sensibility. Traditional socialists appeal to the primacy of collective judgment and social need over the claims of the individual. Both, in principle, if not always in practice, recognize that society must also protect the rights of individuals against the penchant of the state to abuse its own prerogatives. They share a rejection of unbridled individualism and an insistence on the claims of the whole, both of which the rising tide of individualism has marginalized.[57] Political exigencies have led to the subservience of the traditional conservatives to a "Reaganism" that extols the very market mentality they mistrust; political exigencies have also led to the subservience of the traditional and socialist left to a radical individualism the basis of which is the very market they have always sought to rein in or depose. Thus on the left as on the right, the rising tide of unfettered individualism has swamped traditional visions of a society based on communities or alternate collectivities.

Feminism has the potential to challenge individualism, but the question of pornography reveals how deeply feminists remain divided among themselves. An important tendency in feminism has, in fact, begun to develop a far-reaching critique of individualism, but most of the contributors have primarily emphasized the bankruptcy of the male model of the individual as a standard for women.[58] Arguing from the responsibility of the law to take account of women's concrete situation and needs, such feminists have, in the main, contributed to a conception of law as relational rather than as absolute. The potential danger in this line of argument lies in minimizing the importance of the law as the embodiment of a general standard rather than being simply a reflection of existing conditions. The distinction between allocational and distributive justice is decisive in this regard. For a preference for distributive justice does not necessarily negate the ideal of law as universal, but it does take the interests of the community or collectivity, rather than the individual, as its linchpin.

At first glance, it is hard to view pornography as among the most pressing of feminist issues. Compared with the social issues of daycare, affirmative action, comparable worth, and even the right to abortion, pornography could plausibly be dismissed as primarily a cultural matter, a symptom rather than a cause. Today, many feminists reject that distinction, insisting that the intractability of cultural definitions of women lies at the root of our problems, although not all agree with MacKinnon that it is a primary cause of our disadvantages. MacKinnon and those who share her perspective find it irrelevant to distinguish between the pornographic imagination and the pornographic commodity. In contrast, I should argue that the pornographic imagination is a private matter and, like humor, from which it is sometimes difficult to separate it, is very much a matter of individual perception. But if we agree that it is not the business of the state to reform imaginations, we may nonetheless recognize that the forms in which imaginations are expressed is indeed a matter for public concern. Pornographic commodities embody a historically specific form of the pornographic imagination. As Susanne Kappeler has insisted, the feminist critique of pornography should properly focus on forms of exchange. "Part of a feminist strategy must be the elaboration of a concept of community that differs from male bonding over commodities and enemies."[59]

The Supreme Court's decision to give any individual the right to burn the American flag bears directly on the issue of pornography by extending the rights of free speech to what most Americans regard as an affront to our collective identity as a people and a nation. In this instance, Congress has responded rapidly, but the prohibition of flag burning does not obviously interfere with the freedom of the market. The regulation of pornography does. A comparison of the two cases conveys the message that respect for a public symbol requires immediate political action, whereas respect for women does not.

Yet the public degradation of women undermines all sense of community, including the sense of a national community that the flag represents. The Supreme Court's decision notwithstanding, neither flag burning nor pornography has anything to do with free speech, at least not with the free speech intended by the Founding Fathers and long upheld by the sober good sense of the American people. To those who, shaking with fear, argue that any limitation on freedom invites more and more limitations and threatens the imposition of a police state, we can only answer that no freedom could long survive unless the American people show an ability to distinguish sensibly among cases—which, despite many bad moments, they have overwhelmingly done.

I am not pretending that the suppression or regulation of pornography could come unaccompanied by political risks. But we need to accept those risks—not so much because pornography could be proved to cause specific crimes (although it may), but because it offers us an unacceptable mirror of ourselves as a people. In striking some balance between freedom and order, societies have always had to distinguish between liberty and license. By attaching the idea of liberty exclusively to the right of the individual, we have effectively destroyed the possibility for that distinction. At the extreme, the liberty of the individual inexorably becomes license. Only by grounding the idea of liberty in the collectivity—in the recognition that there has never been and cannot be any individual freedom unrooted in community discipline—can we hope to enact laws that recognize liberties as interdependent and as inseparable from social responsibility.

5

INDIVIDUALISM AND

WOMEN'S HISTORY

Who, George Eliot queried in the prelude to *Middlemarch*, "that cares much to know the history of man, and how the mysterious mixture behaves under the varying experiments of Time, has not dwelt, at least briefly, on the life of Saint Theresa?" Saint Theresa, whose "passionate, ideal nature demanded an epic life," Eliot insisted, was surely not the last of her kind. "Many Theresas have been born who found for themselves no epic life wherein there was a constant unfolding of far-resonant action." Many with such yearnings have found "perhaps only a life of mistakes, the offspring of a certain spiritual grandeur ill-matched with the meanness of opportunity," have known only a life of "tragic failure which found no sacred poet and sank unwept into oblivion." These latter-day Theresas "were helped by no coherent social faith and order which could perform the function of knowledge for the ardently willing soul." They alternated between "a vague ideal and the common yearning of womanhood; so that the one was disapproved as extravagance, and the other condemned as a lapse."[1]

Some, Eliot noted, have dismissed such blundering lives as confirmation of "the inconvenient indefiniteness with which the Supreme Power has fashioned the natures of woman." But things are not so simple. If all women shared a level of incompetence "as strict as the ability to count three and no more, the social lot of women might be treated with scientific certitude," but they do not. So imprecision persists, although the variations among women are in truth much greater than any could imagine "from the sameness of women's coiffure and the favorite love-stories in prose and verse." Here and there a cygnet appears among the ducklings. "Here and there is born a Saint Theresa, foundress of nothing, whose loving heart-beats and sobs after an unattained goodness tremble off and are dispersed among hindrances, instead of centering in some long-recognizable deed."[2]

Eliot's words poignantly capture the frustration of innumerable women for whose ambitions their society offered no outlet. Serving to introduce the tale of Dorothea Brooke's attempt to find a worthy and fulfilling life for herself, they especially signal the plight of many mid-Victorian women who confronted a model of male individualism that consigned them to domesticity as the only appropriate calling. Eliot does not suggest that the stifling conditions she is invoking have governed the lives of all women in all times and places. Saint Theresa, her example of realized female ambition, escaped that fate. But Saint Theresa did not live in the heyday of bourgeois individualism.

The sixteenth-century Spanish society to which Saint Theresa belonged might have discouraged her ambition and confronted her with monumental obstacles, but it nonetheless offered her, as a woman, some exceptional possibilities for excellence as her culture defined it. By Eliot's own time, female sainthood had been largely redefined as a domestic rather than a public calling, which, as Dorothea's story reveals, even the most determined would-be-saint could find only in the service of an individual man. Dorothea's problem lay less in the absolute suppression of female ambition than in the recognition that its realization would leave the woman "foundress of nothing." By invoking Saint Theresa as the template for Dorothea's story, Eliot was simultaneously underscoring the universality of women's temperaments and calling attention to the ways in which historical conditions shaped women's opportunities to express them.

In this tension between universality and historical specificity lies the crux of women's attempts to endow their lives with meaning and of the attempts to understand women's history, especially the direct historical legacy to which contemporary women are heir. Dorothea Brooke is recognizably our foremother. Her quest for a calling—for a realization of her ambition—has continued to reverberate in women's fictions and personal narratives down to our own time.[3]

The female self of which Eliot wrote and to which her own life testified was a direct product of an age that tantalized women with the model of individualism but denied them participation in it, that cast women not as individuals in their own right but as the appendages of individual men. Their situation, as Margaret George has argued for the case of Mary Wollstonecraft, resulted from the specific constraints of their historical moment, specifically the great eighteenth-century revolutions and the consolidation of capitalism, which together ensured the triumph of bourgeois individualism.[4] Long-standing customs and beliefs continued to influence the destinies of the women of the late eighteenth and early nineteenth centuries, but the politics of their age helped to recast inherited customs and beliefs, establishing new patterns for women as much as for men. For men, political individualism inaugurated a growing concern with self as agent and actor—self ultimately as public man and accountable citizen. For women, who were barred from those public roles and identities, it also inaugurated a new concern with self and identity, but within the confines of a comprehensive discourse of domesticity. For men's accession to bourgeois individualism allotted women a newly defined role as "other."

As George Eliot's linking of Saint Theresa and Dorothea suggests, the sharp opposition of male and female was not new to the nineteenth century but had constituted a dominant theme of Western culture. But, as she also suggests, it assumed a newly constraining character in the modern period in which the roles available to women had shrunk and changed. Culturally and practically, "traditional" societies differentiated between men and women, normally granting men authority over women, normally grounding many cultural and discursive patterns in that fundamental difference. But traditional societies did not grant any individuals absolute autonomy, viewing both men's and women's identities and rights as dependent upon the communities to which they belonged.

Natalie Davis has argued, for example, that sixteenth-century French men and women thought of themselves as members of collectivities, especially families. They thought of themselves in their connections to, rather than independence of, groups. More, they thought of the groups as prior to their individual members. Personal identity constituted an articulation or special case of a larger whole.[5] In effect, these people imaginatively participated in the general notion of a great chain of being that, however imperfectly, reflected a larger plan. They, like other early modern Europeans, appear to have anchored the sense of self in a different conceptual web than we do. Above all, they did not believe that authority emanated from the individual. Nor did they believe that individuals were interchangeable, much less equal. They viewed individuals as qualitatively different, with a myriad of attributes, including inherited social station.

Our early modern forebears thus adapted the apparently universal belief in the differences between men and women to their own social and cultural situation. Women in early modern European societies, as in the early North American colonies, imagined their own identities in the context of their people's vision of difference, which included a pervasive commitment to men's authority over and even superiority to women. But their commitment to gender differentiation and hierarchy intertwined with their commitment to particularism—the belief that each being had a discrete telos and should aspire to the specific forms of excellence appropriate to its own kind. Male and female represented two distinct forms of humanity. A woman, in this view, should aspire to be a good woman, not to be a good human being in the abstract, much less a good man.

In addition to emphasizing the specificity of each form of being, particularism presupposed a commitment to hierarchy in society as well as nature: some men naturally ruled over others and all men ruled over the women of their own family. That hierarchical vision, while consigning women to the rule of men, offered them discrete opportunities to excel as women and, because it envisioned the rights of collectivities as prior to the rights of individuals, even opportunities to serve as delegates or representatives of their communities. Thus a woman might, in the absence of her husband or father, (temporarily) occupy the role of "lord of the manor." In other words, as Laurel Ulrich has argued for early-eighteenth-century New England, women's roles included the possibility of serving as "deputy husband."[6]

Particularism also depicted social divisions as sharply hierarchical, assigning different social groups to different estates and giving social rank priority over gender. Thus noble women, although outranked by noble men, themselves outranked peasant men as well as bourgeois and peasant women.[7] The difference between women and men was taken as a constitutive aspect of all social groups and even of comprehensive ideologies or religious beliefs, but was not taken as an overriding or universal principle of social organization. Particularism, notwithstanding its endowing men with hierarchical superiority over the women of their own families and communities, did not relegate all women to a universal or undifferentiated position of inferiority.

Individualism flattened particularistic distinctions by positing a single, uniform, and universal model of excellence—the individual—and overthrew particularistic premises by assuming that the individual preceded all groups, which could only derive their meaning and legitimacy from their conformity to and respect for individual rights. The age of democratic revolution established individualism as a fundamental political as well as theoretical principle and inaugurated a historical transformation in gender relations by creating a model of "man" as free of community restriction. That individualist model, which has steadily gained currency and force since the eighteenth century, continues to shape the ways in which we envision the relations between individuals and the collectivity. Individualism in this sense must accordingly be recognized as a product of history rather than nature, and as distinct from what might be called our instinctive feelings of personalism.[8]

Systematic or bourgeois individualism has, from its origins, exercised a powerful sway on many women's imaginations, including those of feminist scholars who are attempting to recover the history of women's experience and identities. Few feminist scholars, however, have engaged individualism as the dominant ideology of a discrete historical period. Even the most thoughtful and accomplished have tended to take individualism for granted as a general feature of human consciousness, thus following the individualist proclivity to universalize human experience. This silence remains all the more puzzling since so much of the most insightful feminist scholarship has focused on the transformation of women's status in precisely the period that witnessed the triumph of individualism as a comprehensive ideology.

Women's historians have, for example, frequently debated whether the transition to capitalism or industrialization inaugurated an advance or a decline in women's position or status. But that debate misses the central point. First, the sea change in Western society and culture that we designate as the rise of industrialization or the rise of capitalism did not so much augur improvement or deterioration in women's position as it augured a transformation of their relation to society. Second, it transformed not only social relations but the social imagination, and hence the ways of imagining the female self.[9] Specifically, that sea change opened the way for at least some women to begin to think systematically about women as individuals and hence as possibly similar and equal to men. Yet many feminist scholars, writing out of the marrow of individualism, extend some modern women's concern with their identities and rights as individuals to the experience of all women. In this respect they implicitly conflate the qualities that individualism has attributed to the individual with the qualities of the self in general.

Normally, we tend to think of the self in the manner of Saint Paul's Epistle to the Galatians, "There is neither Jew nor Greek, there is neither bond nor free, there is neither male nor female: for ye are all one in Christ Jesus."

Many feminist scholars have cogently argued that that formulation, by abstracting from the self that inhabits the body and equating the self with the abstract essence of the person—something akin to the soul—denies women's discrete experience. Does not that abstract self, they have queried, also participate in everyday ("material") life? And, if so, does it really exist entirely ungendered? No. To insist upon the self's universality means to submerge woman in man. But only a few feminist scholars have extended their critique to ask if any self—male or female—exists entirely free of history.

How we conceive of the self touches upon all of our attempts to understand the specific and the general in women's experience, perceptions, and beliefs. An insistence upon the difference between the male and the female self restores attention to the (material) specificity of our lives in particular bodies. On this basis, feminist scholars are increasingly asking that we take account of the differences between women and men in all of our abstract legal and ethical standards.[10] Frequently building upon Carol Gilligan's argument that women have different standards and practices of morality than men, they insist that, at the least, any comprehensive morality must incorporate women's values as well as men's, and they sometimes even suggest that women offer a better model for a comprehensive morality than men.[11]

Rarely, however, do they explore the reasons for the differences between women's and men's moral reasoning. If in fact women (the plural stands as proxy for the encompassing singular, woman) have different moral attitudes than men, why do they? Because they are naturally different from men? Because they have had a different history? Or because men's tendency to cast women as the other has discouraged women from subjective identification with the dominant, male-fashioned culture? The various possible explanations for "women's" apparent alienation from "men's" standards of morality and justice carry portentous implications for all attempts to imagine a more just society, to say nothing of our attempts to understand the history and needs of women in the plural.

The question of women's morality intertwines with other aspects of their identities. Do women, as Margaret Homans has suggested, have a different discourse from men?[12] And, again, if they do, why? Such questions index a continuing tendency to view women's experience as particular—as categorically different from that of men—and perhaps even a lurking belief that women's consciousness remains shaped by their biology or their nature. But if answered in the affirmative, do these questions not also imply that men's consciousness is shaped by their biology or nature? Most feminists, however much they remain impressed by differences between women and men, would reject the full implications of that position, especially the implication that biology accounts for women's exclusion from the most demanding and prestigious endeavors. Even those who most emphasize the difference in male and female political and intellectual styles would likely insist that women have been excluded not by nature but by men.

This conviction should suggest that women's consciousness, like that of men, results in large measure from women's historical experience: the roles to which society has assigned them, their relations with men, and the prevailing discourses with which they have been invited to identify. But if so, then we should entertain the possibility that women's consciousness, like men's, has changed historically and that even contemporary feminist goals result from the history of contemporary women's situation. It is, in short, difficult to claim that women construct their fictions in total isolation from those of men, that they fashion their identities and live their everyday lives uniquely on the basis of their biology.

To the contrary, the history of women demonstrates that literate women in general and intellectual women in particular have always engaged the dominant discourses of their culture, even when they were primarily fashioned by and for men. In this history, the triumph of individualism ranks as a decisive bench mark, if only by its having offered women new justifications for the appropriation of aspects of the dominant discourse for themselves. For it justified men's excellence in a universal language that claims to apply equally to all.

Explicitly fashioned by and for men, the discourse of individualism has generally taken for granted that the individual is male and has treated woman, the other, as the problem. Most modern feminist scholars, even those who emphasize fundamental differences between women and men, have rejected that fiction, insisting that women have the same claims as men on the role of individual, or at least that men cannot claim their own status as individuals to speak in the name of humanity at large. Determination to expose the implicit link between the individual in the abstract and man in the concrete has led an important group of feminist scholars to insist forcefully that male and female can only be understood within the framework of gender, with gender understood as a social and symbolic category—not a fact of nature—as the social or symbolic construction of sexuality or biology.[13]

In practice, gender exists not as an abstraction but as a system of relations—the specific relations between women and men. Male and female genders always exist in relation to each other, never in splendid isolation. Societies ground prescriptions and practices in the specific roles that they assign to women and to men. But even when the roles most appear to conform to men's and women's biological attributes, they reflect the society's or the community's division of labor. Most societies believe that defenders and caretakers for infants are necessary to the infants' well-being, and in many societies there are biological reasons for assigning men and women to those roles respectively: men to the role of defender since fewer men than women are necessary to reproduction; women to the role of caretaker since they have a natural supply of milk. But even in the least complex societies, nature does not dictate those choices; humans make them. In more complex societies, like our own, technology has rendered the biological reasons obsolescent. Culture encourages women and men, neither of whose biology unconditionally dictates their acquiescence, to internalize those prescriptions and practices as gender identity.

A female child is born into a society that has its own view of the proper or normative relations between women and men. Those relations are grounded in the roles that the society offers to women and men respectively. All societies and cultures, through education in the broad sense, encourage women and men to identify with the roles available to them. When the process is successful, gender appears to both women and men as the seamless wrapping of the self. To be an "I" at all means to be gendered—to be male or female.[14] Particularistic societies like those of early modern Europe and the North American colonies generally emphasized the specificity of roles, which were normally reserved for one gender or the other. This proclivity persisted in naming practices that qualified the title of an occupation by the gender of those who normally occupied it, as in "policeman" or "seamstress." Particularistic societies also generally assumed that all people related to the society and polity through their particular roles, or their membership in defined communities. Individualism leveled those distinctions, substituting the purportedly universal role of individual for a myriad of specific roles.

Individualism did not emerge all at once as a full-blown ideology. It developed slowly and piecemeal. The Renaissance, the Reformation, the Scientific Revolution, and the rapid expansion of commerce have all been related to the growth of "individualism" in Western culture, although in significantly different ways. As cultural and ideological movements, the Renaissance and the Reformation both introduced a new emphasis on the individual into Western culture, although neither resulted in its political consolidation.[15] The Scientific Revolution fostered a growing confidence in the capacity of the human mind to understand and master the workings of nature.[16] The rapid expansion of commerce and colonialism, combined with the decline of feudalism and corporatism—that is, the growing separation between laborers and the land, between people and communities—fueled a social and economic transformation that encouraged the gradual application of aspects of secular and religious culture to political life and that eventually culminated in the series of political revolutions that inaugurated our modern world.

Both the ideological and the economic transformations were essential to that ultimate political result, but few scholars agree on the precise relations among them, much less on the causality.[17] The political discourse of individualism, notably the vision of the individual as the repository of all legitimate rights and as the basic element of sovereignty, also developed slowly, primarily as an aspect of early modern republican theory. In time and place its modern implications were not entirely clear, although Hobbes precociously pointed the way.[18] At best we can say that these developments were interrelated and that the gradual emergence of (male) individualism carried contradictory implications for women. Taken together, the economic and ideological transformations tended simultaneously to restrict women's access to political power by subjecting them to more rigidly defined male authority within smaller families and to introduce at least the literate to a concept of individualism that permitted them a glimpse of a new imaginative universe in which they might figure as authoritative subjects.[19]

In the end, political revolution, not gradual diffusion, effected the consolidation of individualism. The recognition that individual sovereignty constituted the necessary foundation of political and social order took its modern shape in the great eighteenth-century revolutions that enshrined it in political practice. The Americans' claim to the individual's allegedly self-evident right to life, liberty, and the pursuit of happiness paved the way for the French demand that government embody the rights of man and the citizen, which was followed by the yet more revolutionary claim of the black slaves of Saint Domingue that they, too, had innate rights, which slavery absolutely contradicted.

The eighteenth-century revolutions—most spectacularly the French—placed the nature and consequences of individualism at the center of Western culture. Henceforth, there would be no turning back, and conservatives as well as radicals would have to fashion their arguments in response to individualistic premises. Individualism did not easily sweep all before it, much less penetrate all social relations equally. The liberty of the individual in the abstract remained far from the equal liberty of individuals in practice. It rapidly became clear that the men who had resolutely claimed individualism for themselves had no intention of including large segments of humanity in the definition of individual. Women, children, slaves, and frequently men of insufficient property were not taken to be individuals at all—certainly not self-accountable members of the polity. Yet if full political individualism left women, children, slaves, and even some white men aside, it did not leave them untouched. In the end, that was the main story: the struggle to determine the proper relations between the individual and the collectivity in the absence of a divinely sanctioned authority.

From women's perspective the French Revolution codified the modern language of individual rights. In so doing, it drew heavily on French, British, and American precedent. But more cogently and economically—that is, less ambiguously—than any of its predecessors, it defined individual right as the indivisible unit of sovereignty and identified that right, at least in the abstract, as universal. The link between individual and universal lies at the heart of the matter. For in theory it depersonalizes the individual who, for political purposes, is stripped of particular attributes. The individual in the abstract—the man of political discourse—enjoys sovereignty by virtue of abstract and universal qualities, not by virtue of personal qualities.

Political individualism, understood as individual right, was an objective and impersonal category. It was a parcel of sovereignty under conditions in which all parcels of sovereignty were interchangeable. This aspect of individualism did not carry any necessary implications about personal attributes. If anything, it tended to depersonalize the individual, which it represented as simply a unit of society and the polity. But the emerging theory of individualism included another aspect that did concern personal attributes. From its origins in the Renaissance and Reformation, individualism had been concerned with the power of human rationality and, by the late eighteenth century, it was gradually insisting upon the power of the human mind to discover and order knowledge. The ultimate conclusion of this aspect of individualism was to substitute the mind of man for the mind of God as the locus of knowledge. Individualism thus came to associate a vision of society as composed of impersonal and interchangeable units of sovereignty with a model of human beings as rational, accountable, and autonomous. The complex development of this view proceeded unevenly and never triumphed unequivocally in practice. But qualifications notwithstanding, it did emerge as the dominant ideology of Western, including American, culture.

Many contemporary feminists have launched sharp critiques of this theory, especially of its emphasis upon the autonomy and rationality of the individual.[20] At the heart of the critique lies an insistence that any responsible concept of politics, justice, or cognition must take account of human beings as they are, especially of the differences between women and men. But however necessary and telling, these feminist critiques of individualism focus primarily upon the aspect of individualism that concerns personal attributes, rather than upon the aspect that concerns social and political organization. In truth, the two have been so confused as to defy disentangling. But in time and place the leveling of hierarchical and particularistic distinctions opened the way for the possibility of women's independent participation in society.

Revolutions and their aftermath rapidly established new constraints on many members of society to replace the legal hierarchies that were being destroyed. In the first dawn of revolutionary optimism many assumed that individual sovereignty implied both the liberty of the individual and equality among individuals, but they were abstracting from the actual conditions of individuals in the world. Once those conditions, notably property, were taken into account, liberty and equality were not easily reconcilable, for equality among individuals could directly threaten the liberty of propertied individuals to exercise their rights freely. In the extreme case, the liberty of slaveholders, defined as property holders, flatly contradicted the human equality of slaves, defined as property.

The tension between liberty and equality acquired special resonance for women and remains today at the center of the most heated debates in feminist theory. Initially, few even considered that the political discourse of individualism should apply to women at all. In the heat of the French Revolution, some women, most notably Mary Wollstonecraft in her pioneering *A Vindication of the Rights of Woman*, and even some men, made the case for the rights of woman.[21] Those precocious claims were soon repudiated, primarily by men who viewed either the liberty or the equality of women as an unacceptable threat to the stability of families—and to the psyches of men whose autonomy depended upon unquestioning female support.[22] By the end of the French Revolution, women in France, Britain, and the United States found themselves, if anything, more firmly and universally excluded from the political realm than they had been before it.

The swift quashing of those fragile political ambitions did not foreclose women's claims to individualism, although it did frequently push them into indirection. Most important, the redefinition of men as "man" was accompanied by a redefinition of women as "woman." Even those who most forcefully reproved Mary Wollstonecraft's presumption on behalf of her sex acceded to the view of women as (at least theoretically) equal and interchangeable in their womanhood. No longer distinguished by membership in legal estates, women, however much separated by class position, found themselves figuratively consigned to a common domestic identity—to submission, piety, and "passionlessness."[23]

No more than individualism did the ideology of domesticity, true womanhood, and separate spheres emerge fully formed at one moment in time. Beginning in the late seventeenth century and at an accelerating pace throughout the eighteenth, European and American culture, following the British lead, had been discovering the virtues of submissive womanhood and engaging in a substantive reworking of the prevailing notion of woman. During the Enlightenment, as Ruth Salvaggio has suggested, women were not so much excluded from culture as "the very idea of woman became a metaphor and figure of the essence of exclusion—of not being, of absence."[24] But also during this transformation, and in a surprisingly brief span of time, women, who had long been viewed as especially evil, began to be depicted as especially good. The new vision above all emphasized women's identities as dependent upon their specific relations with men within families: their roles as mothers, wives, daughters. Of the three roles, many male theorists unquestionably preferred that of mother, with its opportunities for minimizing female sexuality and for viewing women as primarily devoted to the nurture of men. In effect, the eighteenth century invented the modern concept of motherhood. There were precedents, but only in the eighteenth century did the ideal of motherhood crystallize as woman's highest mission—as her distinct career.[25]

Motherhood was, to borrow from Karl Polanyi, disembedded from the dense network of relations and activities in which it had previously been entwined.[26] The new concept of motherhood confirmed the new centrality of the individual, although not by endowing mothers with individualism. The purpose of motherhood was, rather, to nurture the individual. Literally, good mothers nursed their own children. Figuratively, they nurtured them. Early childhood education, which mothers alone could adequately provide, constituted the necessary foundation for individual character. Through love and measured discipline, mothers prepared their children to assume their places in the world. To this end, mothers were to educate their children in the ways of self-mastery. To mothers, in effect, was confided the formation of the self.

The ideology of motherhood that would rapidly develop into a full-blown ideology of bourgeois domesticity appeared to offer an ideal solution to the problem of women's place in the brave new world of individualism. Motherhood offered a new interpretation of female sexuality, which Western men had long castigated as dangerous and subversive. For motherhood was rapidly taken to neutralize women's sexuality. Rather than seeking personal gratification, women as mothers should seek the selfless gratification of nurture. No longer to be viewed primarily as breeders who produced male heirs for families, women as mothers came to be viewed as the guardians of individual character. The rhetoric remained ambiguous, but the message could hardly be mistaken. Motherhood subsumed all other female roles and attributes, emerging as the telos of women's "natural" and social destiny. As daughters and wives, women also contributed to reflecting and securing the male self, but motherhood increasingly subsumed the other roles in offering the dominant model for the mature female self.

The emphasis on women as mothers carried far-reaching implications, especially in its wedding of women's biological capacities to their social roles and self-perceptions. The ideal of motherhood attempted to conflate all possible aspects of the female self by proclaiming that women's relations with men, their social roles, and their personal identities converged in motherhood. The ideal perpetuated the myth of biology (sexuality) as destiny even as it held women accountable for embracing that destiny. While the ideal of motherhood derived much of its force from its close association with nature, the ideal of nature was represented through specific social forms. Motherhood endowed female sexuality with a purpose that minimized, when it did not entirely obscure, the potential force of women's own sexual desires. In this respect, motherhood became the reigning sign of the submission of the female self to the male individual.

Eighteenth-century culture did not ignore women as daughters and wives. If anything, fiction dwelt upon daughters and wives, especially daughters. From Richardson's Pamela to Rousseau's Julie and beyond, the daughter's story mesmerized the eighteenth-century imagination.[27] Titillating in her barely disguised sexuality, the daughter embodied all the promise of the nascent female self. One of the great dramas of the period concerned the daughter's appropriation of the right to choose her own mate. Yet the very selfhood mobilized in that choice was negated as soon as it had been made. For the daughter's choice led to the status of the wife, to submersion in a husband. To be sure, the status of wife and mother invited women's positive identification—invited them to find self-realization in devotion to husband and children—but tensions were unavoidable. For the deepest message of individualism was self-determination, yet the only self-determination open to women lay in the choice of the authority to which they would submit.

In some measure, the rhetoric of the self as a private being cloaked the starkness of this destiny. Women, to whom the laws denied individualism, were, in fact, enjoined actively to embrace their destinies and even in some sense to construct themselves. But the bifurcation of individualism colored their experience and influenced their sense of self. For the rhetoric of individualism ascribed women to the realm of nature rather than the realm of history and politics, to the realm of recurrence rather than to arenas of struggle and progress. Those who most forcefully enunciated the virtues of motherhood—notably men, but also some women—denied the novelty of their view of motherhood by presenting it as immune to historical and social change. In particular, they insisted that motherhood must constitute the universal condition of women, independent of time, place, or social class. Social standing and prerogatives could not be allowed to differentiate among women as mothers. From the castle to the cottage, women shared a common destiny, a common identity. Aristocratic women—the particular targets of anxious intellectuals like Rousseau—could not be permitted to escape the responsibilities of their gender. In women as in men, artificial distinctions of rank and station must be subordinated to a universal standard.

The universal pretensions of the ideal of motherhood firmly linked it to the new discourse of individualism but did not directly help to open individualism to women. If anything, the ideal of motherhood served to curb aristocratic women's pretensions to independence, to honor, to their own form of heroism.[28] It implicitly—and sometimes explicitly—criticized women's preoccupation with fashionable self-display, with frivolity, with worldliness. According to prevailing wisdom, aristocratic women betrayed a disconcerting tendency to lead independent lives. No sooner had they married and born the minimal number of children than they turned to a world of pleasure. If they deserved censure for taking lovers, how much more did they deserve it for behaving as if their own appearance and pleasure were the proper goals of their lives? No. They must retire to the country, remain faithful to their husbands, and, above all, nurse their children themselves. Motherhood demanded the virtues of retirement, restraint, and self-control. Above all, it directed women to define themselves in relation to others.

In the eighteenth century, specific public roles, like those of statesman, warrior, and lawyer, were by common consent reserved for men, while women were assigned to the roles of wife and mother. The bourgeois revolutions sanctified these distinctions but also developed the more general role of citizen. "Citizen" was, at bottom, nothing more than an abstraction, but an especially powerful abstraction for claiming the essence of legitimate authority. The analogous role for women, as Linda Kerber has cogently argued, was mother of citizen.[29] During the early nineteenth century, specific male roles continued to proliferate while the acknowledged roles for women did not. Early nineteenth-century bourgeois culture devoted its best efforts to encouraging men's and women's identification with their appointed roles. Inevitably, experience proved much more complicated than the ideology of separate spheres could allow, but the ideology retained a powerful hold on the collective imagination. Above all, it sought to promote a sense of continuity among gender relations, roles, and identities. Women were enjoined to find their identities in the domestic roles to which their society's gender relations assigned them.

This harmonious vision was vulnerable to challenge on two fronts, for both capitalism and individualism were revolutionary and self-revolutionizing forces. Absolute property proved something less than an absolute bulwark against the fluctuations of the market. Capitalism steadily eroded the independence of households, steadily penetrated the relations of the private sphere. Individualism, even in its most conservative forms, dictated at least moral self-accountability for women and frequently dictated their education as well. Capitalism even wrapped its tentacles around the discourses of individualism, which depended upon and were ever more broadly disseminated by the market. These complex processes inexorably drew women into a social and symbolic web in which their own individualism became a pressing issue.

Women writers and intellectuals of the late eighteenth and early nineteenth centuries, notably Mary Wollstonecraft, inaugurated the attempt to understand the female self within the context of individualism.[30] Their successors, down to our own time, have continued to wrestle with the problems they defined: Should the case for women's excellence rest upon their similarity to men or their differences from them? If the former, what became of the biological or sexual dimension of the female self? If the latter, on what grounds could women claim equality with men?

The case for woman's individualism, like the case for man's, required an implicit divorce between the category of self (understood as personal) and the category of individual (understood as impersonal). It also required the recognition that rights derive from the prevailing principles and organization of society—from the reigning system—and not from personal qualities or merits. In this respect, individualism implicitly repudiated the concept of particularism. As a self, the individual might be male or female, tall or short, rich or poor, nurturing or aggressive, for such attributes did not affect the individual's status as an individual. That status derived not from innate qualities but from social organization. Yet, in the case of women, particular qualities of femaleness seemed to amount to an essential and necessary modification of the basic quality of humanity. Thus during the eighteenth century the case for women's individualism foundered. Only during the first half of the nineteenth century would it gradually emerge as a clear if still hotly contested case of political individualism, just as antislavery would do. The ultimate case for the rights of woman nonetheless depended upon the prior case for the rights of man, for it depended upon the formulation of a view of rights as both innate and universal.

The linking of innate and universal decisively influenced perceptions of female individualism, as it has shaped subsequent feminist theory. For the concept of innate rights inescapably raised the question of gender. An important tendency in eighteenth-century thought, following the psychology of John Locke, held that the individual is born unencumbered by preconceptions of any kind but is, from the very moment of birth, formed by education. This theory, which promised potential equality for men, opened two new possibilities for women.

The first, as Catherine Macaulay and others insisted, was expressed in the view that there was "no characteristic difference in sex," or, in the words of Sophia, a Person of Quality, "In mind there is no sex at all."[31] The second, a much more widely embraced possibility, was expressed in the view that men and women are innately different but that women, as mothers, have a unique responsibility to shape the minds of their impressionable offspring. Although these two views pulled against each other in essential respects, they also combined to suggest a much more favorable view of women than Western culture had heretofore entertained. For the first, whatever its subversive possibilities, suggested that women, like men, were capable of learning, even if, as most men insisted, in lesser degree. The second suggested that women, as mothers, had important and beneficial social roles to play. Although few male writers discussed the matter directly, both views implied that a woman, like a man, had a self.

"Innate" thus seriously qualified eighteenth-century pretensions to universalism, for, with precious few exceptions, eighteenth-century thinkers did not imagine women as subjects of the new discourse of individualism. We might, with some justification, follow Simone de Beauvoir in dismissing the matter by saying that these men, like all men, simply cast women as the other.[32] But that age-old tendency was acquiring a new content with its new forms. Those who were trying to imagine a universal male subject abstracted from differences of temperament and station found it easy to fall back on biological difference as the sign of absolute otherness. Those who were trying to make their way in the newly competitive world of capitalism and individualism found it tempting to cast women as the natural custodians of harmony and nurture. For men to be fully self-realizing individuals, women must be self-denying.

Throughout the nineteenth century, the path from the moral and intellectual responsibilities of educating children to the right to write and speak publicly on moral issues, to the property rights of married women, to the right to suffrage and through it full citizenship, led some women increasingly to protest against those limitations on their identities and roles that they perceived as illegitimate. Or, more accurately, it led them to protest their exclusion from the role and identity of citizen. At least initially, most women who defended the concept of woman's rights did not insist that women should become like men. Some sought opportunities to become doctors or lawyers; others chose or were forced to work for wages; most, who accepted their allotted roles and still thought of themselves as fundamentally different from men, merely began to insist that the abstractions of citizen and individual should cover women as well as men. For some, that claim merely meant that women too were capable of moral accountability and had an independent self; for a small but growing number it meant that the new female self required a public presence.

From the early nineteenth century, the escalating campaign against slavery reinforced some women's awareness of the ways in which the implications of individualism were being restricted. The analogy between the position of women and the position of slaves forcefully engaged some women's imaginations. If women were denied full individualism, must they not also be considered slaves? Freedom knew no compromises. In the world of individualism, dependency in any form could only be viewed as a form of enslavement, however much disguised by a rhetoric of domesticity and true womanhood. Most women who espoused the cause of woman's rights did not intend to promote a social revolution but only to extend the rights of individualism to women. But whatever their intentions, by challenging women's dependency in marriage they were directly threatening marriage itself as an institution.[33] The full implications of their views would result in reducing marriage from the last bastion of institutionalized hierarchy to a contractual relation or even a spiritual union between two individuals.

The case of marriage cogently illustrates the problem. The logic of individualism offered no grounds for excluding women from its benefits, but in practice the subordination of women anchored individualism. This contradiction continues to plague—indeed threatens to explode—individualism in our time. Perception of the consequences of the contradiction accounts for the renewed interest in community on the part of some male conservatives.[34] But these conservatives have been slow to recognize that women cannot be restored to submission by fiat and even slower to recognize that the evolving situation of women lies at the center of the problem. For the failure to grant women full status as individuals was accompanied—if not partially caused—by an unacknowledged recognition that pure individualism could not anchor social cohesion, much less foster nonmarket values.

However legitimate our suspicions of misogyny on the part of the men who propounded the virtues of domesticity and women's exclusion from the public realm, we must acknowledge that they were attempting to preserve values they instinctively knew could not be sustained by individualism itself. We must also acknowledge that many women, at whatever cost to their own independence, willingly participated in men's project. But to the extent that both women and men were seeking to preserve some of the benefits of particularism, they effectively deluded themselves. With particularism destroyed in the public sphere, particularism in the private sphere increasingly appeared either nostalgic and sentimental or brittle and arbitrary, as did the attempts to exclude women systematically from the public world of individualism. Nor did these attempts to restrict women's access to the social, economic, and political benefits of individualism ever completely exclude them from the professed values of individualism, which many tried to adapt to their own situation. Drawing variously, and sometimes simultaneously, upon individualism's abstract language of rights and its specific celebration of domestic values for women, they fashioned a complex discourse. As Catherine Belsey has argued, women in modern society have participated in "contradictory discourses," in "both the liberal-humanist discourse of freedom, self-determination, and rationality and at the same time in the specifically feminine discourse offered by society of submission, relative inadequacy and irrational intuition."[35] For some, the realization of individualism came to mean women's equality with men. For others it came to mean the introduction of what were now viewed as distinct female values into the public sphere. For many it meant, however illogically, some combination of both. But even when women's discourses most sharply criticized individualism in practice, they remained tied to many of its fundamental premises, which shaped both the defense of women's public rights and the celebration of women's domestic identities.

Individualism's discourse of rights as dramatized in the French Revolution opened the way for Mary Wollstonecraft's *Vindication of the Rights of Woman* and thus for modern feminism. Wollstonecraft, who had incurred heavy debts to both male and female precursors, was not the first to write combatively of women's excellence or of the injustices that women suffered at the hands of men, but she was the most visible of the first generation to write of women's excellence and desserts in the language of individualism.[36] She was, that is, the first to combine a defense of women's political rights as individuals with a discussion of women's discrete domestic identities. Framing her discussion of women's entitlements in the new political language of individual rights, she poignantly explored women's social and psychological vulnerabilities. And, like her male contemporaries, who grouped all men under the rubric of "man," she generalized from her own situation in the name of "woman."

Not all feminist scholars agree that Wollstonecraft inaugurated modern feminism. The debate over her position in this respect reflects different definitions of feminism itself. Joan Kelly, for example, argues that a rich, coherent, and continuous feminist discourse had been developing for 400 years before the French Revolution.[37] Kelly locates the beginning of this discourse in Christine de Pizan's early fifteenth-century *Book of the City of Ladies*, which presented a passionate and learned defense of women's excellence, based on women's attributes as a sex, historical accomplishments, and intellectual and spiritual qualities.[38] Kelly then traces its development through the polemical writings of a group of seventeenth-century English women, who similarly defended the excellence of women's character, and the myriad of eighteenth-century writers who increasingly sought to demonstrate women's capacity for rationality.

As Kelly and other scholars have recovered these and innumerable other "forgotten" writings by women, it has become abundantly clear that for centuries—probably since women first began to write at all—at least some literate women had been writing in defense of their sex. The real issue for contemporary feminism is not that they did so with passion and conviction but how we should best understand their writings. In my judgment, the early modern "feminist" discourse of which Kelly writes did engage the nature, character, place, and representation of women, but did so within the language and presuppositions of the culture from which it emerged. It sought to defend women's character and nature against the deeply misogynist tendency to equate women with evil and to blame them for the sins of humanity, notably those of the flesh. And it sought to claim the emerging possibilities of rationality for women, especially insisting on women's need for education and possibilities for learning. These early "feminists" struggled to demonstrate that elite women should have the same opportunities as elite men to participate in "the Republic of Letters." Most were not noticeably concerned with social or political issues, nor even with a putative equality among women, although Mary Astell combined a strong defense of women's capabilities with an equally strong defense of conservative Tory politics.[39] They were directly concerned with women's possible position in what we would come to call the canon or the great tradition.

In an early and influential article, Joan Kelly herself criticized women's exclusion from the political and intellectual developments of the Renaissance. Noting a growing confinement of upper-class women in the Italian city-states, she angrily queried whether the so-called Renaissance qualified as such for women.[40] Kelly's subsequent article on early feminist theory thus reversed a previous position and tellingly identified the emergence of a coherent body of feminist thought in the period that she had originally identified as the seedbed of women's domestic confinement and loss of status. The contradiction between Kelly's two positions instructively exposes the problematic relations between the effects of ideological and social change on women's position and consciousness, and women's even more problematic relation to hegemonic (male) culture. However we evaluate the "feminism" of early modern women's writing, it is clear that at least some women managed to appropriate aspects of Renaissance thought to a consideration of their own situation, not least because they, like men, benefited from the renewed attention to education and the increase in vernacular literature.

Even before the Renaissance, women's intellectual and educational opportunities had been increasing in tandem with those of the men of their class albeit at a much lower level.[41] The rationale for educating women and the nature of the education they received are another matter. Historically, the incentives for educating women have depressingly tended to emphasize the need to prepare women to assume their ordained social roles and to be acceptable companions to the men of their communities. The attention to women's education expanded in conjunction with social and cultural changes in which their complicit participation was seen as desirable: the spread of Protestantism, the dissemination of the idea of the "mother-educator," and, eventually, the need for a minimally educated female labor force.[42] Women's education constitutes an important part of the history of women's intellectual life but remains episodic until the modern period. The systematic attempt to educate women emerged with the rise of capitalism and the modern, especially the democratic, state, although earlier, occasional women, notably Mary Astell in the late seventeenth century, formulated models for the education of elite women.[43]

Precapitalist European societies placed a low priority on educating women and actively discouraged women who sought an education or respect as intellectuals. During the Renaissance and Reformation, some Italian and English female intellectuals pieced together an education with the assistance of devoted fathers, brothers' tutors, or helpful local clerics.[44] But few if any women, even the most privileged, who alone had access to such opportunity, managed to acquire an education equal to that of the most learned men or managed to produce as much high-level work as those men. A disproportionate number of women would-be intellectuals ended their lives in silence, in illness, or in convents.

We should all like to know more about the personal and subjective histories of these women, but most did not leave autobiographical accounts. Women's possible impulses to chronicle their struggles presumably withered under the severe opprobrium attached to any authoritative female voice. There were exceptions, such as the *Book* of Margery Kempe, but Kempe did not write her autobiography herself. She dictated it and invoked the first person only because of a special, divine mission, not because of her own subjective worth.[45] Religious vocations apparently provided the most compelling justification for women's first-person narratives, presumably because women found it easier to speak authoritatively when they were speaking in the service of divine authority. Nor can we assume that women like Kempe were merely using divine authority as a subterfuge since the evidence we have suggests that they believed in and derived strength from the self-abnegating justifications that they invoked.

Not all female intellectuals followed the path of aspiring saints. To the contrary, many apparently sought recognition as what Simon Shepherd designates warrior women and cheerfully defied the conventions that normally circumscribed the acceptable actions of their sex.[46] Still others developed a satirical critique of marriage as a trap and a snare.[47] All of these elite female traditions apparently had popular counterparts, although lower-class women, who had very restricted opportunities for literacy, were much less likely to write. And women of all classes confronted male hostility to women's self-assertion. Church and secular leaders were quick to excoriate women who transgressed the spirit of their sex, most notably those whom some denigrated as Amazons.[48] But most female intellectuals, like most female saints, probably were less intent upon denying their sex than they were upon challenging the limits imposed upon women's striving for exemplary excellence as women.

Between the Renaissance and the eighteenth century, the models of female strength changed in conjunction with cultural change in general, especially the early manifestations of individualism. Similarly, persistent misogynist attitudes assumed different guises in different periods.[49] But during these centuries, European culture, despite deep hostility toward and mistrust of women, especially women's sexuality, recognized female strength and even allowed for the possibility of positive female, as distinct from male, strength. Further, as Hanna Pitkin has argued, even the most sophisticated political theory took account of gender.[50] The model of female virtue that dominated male views of female excellence throughout the Middle Ages and early modern period influenced women's own ideas and circumscribed their possibilities for effective action.[51]

Kelly's feminist tradition embodied women's early attempts to assimilate the new notions of individual excellence and subjective authority to their own sense of female excellence. From the fifteenth century a growing succession of voices defended the claims of women as a sex. Whether they defended those claims in the language of individual political rights is another matter. For early modern European and American women to have defined their claims for their sex in the language of individual right would have been revolutionary not because the claim threatened established relations between the genders but because it proposed a revolutionary model of society, politics, and individual identity. To the extent that these early feminist writings apparently hint at new social relations, they have much in common with aspects of feminist theory in our own time, notably a disinclination to move from quarrels with specific forms of oppression to a comprehensive theory of social change.

Women writers have always worked within a dominant discourse, however much they have been able to contribute to it.[52] Working within discourses largely fashioned by and for men, they have had to struggle against a hostile ideology of womanhood and for a language of women's being. Susan Schibanoff has argued that Christine de Pizan overcame the sense of self-alienation and self-hatred with which male theory swamped her by deciding that "her own feelings and thoughts about women . . . are more authoritative than the opinions of all the poets and philosophers she has studied" and by elevating "personal experience into a form of wisdom higher than anything literacy and authority can offer."[53] Schibanoff's reading of Christine de Pizan especially testifies to contemporary feminists' concerns with intellectual women's psychological experience of alienation from and objectification by dominant male discourses. Those concerns have led feminist scholars to explore exhaustively the ways in which women struggled to represent themselves. Schibanoff's reading thus underscores a tension within women's history that Christine de Pizan did articulate. For Christine de Pizan not only inaugurated a theoretical discourse of women's writing on behalf of the excellence of women but also a tradition of women's writing women's stories. The two traditions persist and also shape the ways in which we write our various versions of women's history.

The cultural transformations of the eighteenth century that converged in the consolidation of individualism and that included the new dominant image of woman also generated a new tradition of women's writing women's stories.[54] In what may have been the principal glacial shift since antiquity, prevailing images of shrew, harlot, and Amazon gave way to the image of the romantic heroine and loving mother, quintessentially celebrated by Rousseau and Goethe. This model accompanied the intellectual revolution of Enlightened thought and men's new sense of themselves and their needs as individuals in a harshly competitive world. It proposed a new generalized view of women as members of a species and a new view of female sexuality, the danger of which it whimsically denied or repressed. It extolled women as custodians of morality and religion, now reduced to the virtues of the home. And it explicitly generalized not merely women's essence as sexual beings but women's social roles as members of a gender. Although the new vision of women as domestic beings had precedents, it differed in granting women dominion in the home.[55]

Feminist scholars have demonstrated that many, perhaps most, women did not meekly accept the model of their own passivity, although most refrained from challenging it outright. Mary Poovey and Judith Newton have insisted that if eighteenth- and nineteenth-century women writers apparently represented women in conformity with prevailing conventions, they also manifested a growing ability to subvert conventions of female gentility and passivity—the image of the proper lady. Their narratives and representations of women embodied an implicit judgment on dominant male views of women.[56] With the steady increase in women's literacy and the circulation of women's writings, women gained new possibilities to share their stories, to write self-consciously for other women. And, according to Nancy Armstrong, by the mid-nineteenth century, women's concerns effectively dominated middle-class culture.[57] This burgeoning women's culture did not usually propound overt feminism in the sense of public rights but rather insisted on the distinct values of women's experience. Some have argued that the mere act of women's writing about women for women must be understood as feminist in the broad sense, although others prefer to restrict feminism to the attempt to claim the benefits of rationalism for women.[58]

The recent resurgence of women's intellectual history, by touching upon the history of ideas of womanhood and gender relations as well as upon the history of women's development of a distinctive discourse about themselves and their worlds, offers a new prism through which to consider the origins of modern feminism in particular and of women's thinking in general. It also highlights the theoretical controversies by foregrounding women's consciousness and opportunities for self-expression. Above all, it offers myriad opportunities to explore the interplay of gender and class struggles, the relation between experience and consciousness, and the complex and shifting roles of families, communities, and states in confining women's bodies and stunting their minds.

Confusion persists not least because those societies in which separate spheres had the least justification—those in which capitalism was most thoroughly undermining the significance of biological differences between women and men—insisted most firmly on their basis in biology and natural law. Societies in which the possibility of female competition for male places was becoming a real option, if not yet a general practice, pioneered in raising the doctrine of separate spheres to new ideological prominence and in using it to justify women's exclusion (frequently called protection) from the most lucrative employments, professions, and educational opportunities. The more advanced the economy, the more likely the society was to advance an ideology of separate spheres to justify separate and unequal education for women, the exclusion of women from the emerging professions, and women's exclusion from political life. This ideology of female confinement strongly influenced women's intellectual and organizational efforts on their own behalf.[59] Prophets of female emancipation or female excellence—the two claims occasionally intertwined—drew upon old dreams of ordered communities, new visions of communities of free individuals, and evangelical traditions. Some helped to lay foundations of subsequent feminist movements. Variously, they embodied the romanticism and transitional radical politics of their time.[60]

The experience of working-class as well as middle-class women confirms the tightening grasp of the doctrine of separate spheres as the model for gender relations and European society's growing preoccupation with sexual difference. The churches, the medical profession, and many conservative politicians and social theorists viewed women as suited for little more than marriage and motherhood. The discourse on sexuality intertwined with men's crass opposition to competition from women. The two are frequently difficult to disentangle, but they obviously concurred in viewing women's gender roles as inevitably dictated by their sexuality.[61] Women themselves remained deeply divided. Did they want equal relations between the sexes through promotion of greater sexual freedom for themselves, or did they want less for men?

The history of the twentieth century confirms that sexism, instead of receding with the triumph of modernity, has probably become more general and more difficult to locate in any single institution. If the so-called sexual revolution has loosened the grip of the nuclear family on female sexuality, it has not indisputably weakened sexism or acceptance of conventional gender roles.[62] Women have made vast gains in the possibility for an independent existence, but hostility to that independence has persisted. The waves of feminism that have punctuated the century also testify to women's own growing commitment to an ideal of "personal liberation." Feminists continue to debate whether women most need formal rights equal to those of men or a cultural and psychological revolution. They differ over whether women's liberation will mean freedom to be like men or freedom to be more like women—whatever those categories are projected to mean. Above all, they differ over what constitutes the authentic female voice, what we mean by women's culture and women's consciousness.

The political and theoretical concerns of contemporary feminism derive directly from this history. Feminism as an ideology developed in interaction with the development of individualism and cannot be understood apart from it. Feminist scholars have exposed the deceptions of individualism for women and have charted the ways in which women writers have wrestled with its demons. Today, the principal debates within feminism directly reflect the ways in which women, beginning in the eighteenth century, have attempted to claim the full status of individual without losing their identities as women. Feminists have nonetheless been slow to grasp the extent to which our specific ideas of woman's nature derive from the discourse of individualism. The ideas, for example, of women as the special custodians of the values of community or as natural nurturers paradoxically have their origin in the discourse of individualism and the attendant model of gender relations, roles, and identities that it promotes.

As a hegemonic ideology, individualism has been eminently successful in marrying its precepts to the identities of individuals. Just as men, immersed in individualism, tend to believe that the cultural (nonbiological) aspects of their maleness derive from their biology, so have women had difficulty in shaking the idea that the modern model of female identity is natural. To the extent that women have been "colonized" by the ideology of individualism, it has shaped their ways of thinking about themselves and the world. Modern feminism is no exception.[63] Born with the emergence of individualism, feminist theory has remained torn between two illusions: the illusion that the abstract possibilities of "autonomous" individualism could be fully realized for women (if indeed they ever have been or could be for men); and the illusion that the individualist view of woman-as-other can, by some miraculous transubstantiation, be converted into a general and "feminist" law of female experience.

6

THE STRUGGLE FOR

A FEMINIST HISTORY

"Between me and the other world there is ever an unasked question. . . . How does it feel to be a problem?"[1] Thus writes not Simone de Beauvoir, but W. E. B. Du Bois, speaking not of women but of black people—speaking as a black male intellectual in a white-dominated world. Du Bois answers his own question:

> The Negro is . . . born with a veil, and gifted with second-sight in this American world,—a world which yields him no true self-consciousness, but only lets him see himself through the revelation of the other world. It is a peculiar sensation, this double-consciousness, this sense of always looking at one's self through the eyes of others, of measuring one's soul by the tape of a world that looks on in amused contempt and pity. One ever feels his twoness—an American, a Negro; two souls, two thoughts, two unreconciled strivings; two warring ideals in one dark body, whose dogged strength alone keeps it from being torn asunder.[2]

Du Bois poignantly refuses to forego either side of his twoness. He claims for himself, and his people, the freedom to be black and American. But fidelity to that twoness requires holding fiercely to both its elements. It is the tension itself, the dialectic of his sundered identity, that he wishes to live: distinct, but equal; of, but not wholly assimilated to. And the free living of that tension necessitates full recognition of the black past, of a distinct African-American history.

It is no part of my intention to trivialize the particular meaning of Du Bois's words by equating female and African-American experience. But, however different the problems and histories of women and African-Americans, the living of twoness applies to both.[3] Joan Kelly has captured this dimension in referring to the "doubled vision" of feminist theory, by which she means the double perspective of social and sexual oppression that, in her judgment, must inform all feminist theory.[4] But Du Bois, who never slighted social or sexual oppression, meant something more. "Twoness," for him, especially referred to the doubled consciousness of all individuals who live between two cultures, who simultaneously identify with the dominant culture of their society and with the distinct culture of the community or group from which they come, or to which the dominant culture assigns them.

A sense of twoness has haunted women's relations to individualism. Cut off from direct participation in its political authority, as well as its most obvious social and economic benefits, women have also suffered a doubled vision of themselves through the prism of its culture. From the beginning, the Western tradition has tended to cast women as the other, but particularism mitigated the full force of that otherness, just as it mitigated the full implications of slavery, which was diluted in the general continuum that linked free to unfree labor. In the premodern world in which "unfreedom" was a matter of degree rather than an absolute, slaves were simply less free than other dependent laborers.[5] The dichotomy between male and female was more rigid, especially within cultural discourses, but even the most comprehensive of those discourses tended to differentiate among women according to estate or condition and rarely constructed an absolute dichotomy that transcended all other criteria to lump women in a single, transcendent category of womanhood. Or, perhaps ultimately more important, they rarely lumped men in a single transcendent category of manhood. Women were represented as women in relation to the men of their estate or community, and, in the absence of a universal concept of man, women escaped being relegated to an absolute concept of woman. There were exceptions to this tendency, notably in the churches, which enunciated universal claims about human identity, but even they, as George Eliot's evocation of Saint Theresa suggests, offered women special opportunities.[6]

Individualism, in this respect as in many others, flattened particularistic distinctions and constructed a newly stark opposition between woman and man, with far-reaching consequences for women's identities and self-representations. Significantly, it is to individualism that we owe the model of autonomy, which so many feminist theorists are beginning to criticize as an inadequate image—much less goal—of human identity.[7] But however much we are now beginning to recognize the limits of the model of individual autonomy, it has carried great prestige in the eyes of many women who have found themselves excluded from it, especially since the culture of individualism successfully associated it with a panoply of other virtues. Women's sense of twoness in relation to the dominant culture of individualism thus derived in large measure from their sense of exclusion from its promises and prestige. Under these conditions, many women, as Carolyn Heilbrun and Nancy Miller have convincingly argued, found it difficult even to represent themselves as an authoritative subject within the language of individualism.[8] For women autobiographers in particular, Miller suggests, "writing—for publication—represents entrance into the world of others, and by means of that passage a rebirth: the access through writing to the status of an autonomous subjectivity beyond the limits of feminine propriety."[9]

The attempt to understand women's distinct experience of twoness has motivated some of the most important feminist theory and scholarship, both of which have developed on the individualist premise of our culture that women and men have had fundamentally different roles in society and history, and perhaps have different natures as well. In this respect, feminist theory and scholarship have built upon the myth of separate spheres that has dominated Western thought since the Enlightenment and the great eighteenth-century bourgeois revolutions. That building has increasingly included searching criticism of the myth as an artificial limitation on women's capabilities and opportunities—as an instrument of men's power over women—but has nonetheless accepted its central tenet that public affairs, notably politics and "high" culture, have been defined and dominated by men. The myth of separate spheres has thus continued to influence much of the work of women's historians, who have been restoring women's indispensable, if largely unrecognized, contributions to the life of communities and the development of all aspects of society and culture.[10]

The coming of age of women's history has brought with it a welcome expansion in attention to various aspects of women's experience and an accelerating pace in the recovery of women's presence, roles, and perceptions. It has expanded knowledge of women's presence and behavior in previous societies and has forced renewed attention to problems of theory, notably those that concern women's motivations and perceptions.[11] The initial resurgence of women's history was closely allied to the proliferation of social history, with which it shares both the strength of recovering the texture of everyday lives and the weakness of insufficient attention to the politics that often intrudes decisively into those lives.[12] Recently, especially under the influence of the new historicism in literary studies, there has also been a growing interest in the intellectual and cultural history of women.[13]

Both tendencies in women's history, which have developed in conjunction with feminist theory, reflect growing analytic sophistication and attention to new concerns. The social history of women has moved from an initial preoccupation with adding women to the received record to a preoccupation with the role of gender in all societies. The intellectual and cultural history of women has moved from its initial concern with recovering women's voices to a concern with the fundamental relation between gender and discourse. The impressive quality and the quantity of this new work testifies to its growing hold on the scholarly and even public imagination. And, as the heated debates over the appropriate place of women in our tradition and teaching—the canon—testify, it has genuine political ramifications. The very success of feminist historical scholarship of all varieties brings to the fore difficult questions of theory and interpretation.

In general, women's historians have devoted more attention to writing history than to developing theory, although they have borrowed from feminist theory developed in other subjects, especially literature and anthropology. Feminism, in its many and ambiguous meanings, influences the work of women's historians but given wide divergence in philosophical and ideological assumptions results in disparate readings of the lessons to be drawn from it. Recently, especially under the political impact of the Sears case and the intellectual impact of post-structuralism and postmodernism, explicit theoretical discussions have begun to play a larger role in women's history, prompting women's historians to begin to discuss the more general problems posed by the very idea of a feminist theory.[14] Prior to these new developments, the more explicitly theoretical work tended to fall into two general groups: that which primarily emphasized patriarchy and that which primarily emphasized gender.[15] And even now, notwithstanding the emergence of new theoretical positions, both "patriarchy" and "gender" continue to influence feminist language and attitudes.

Feminist scholars who emphasize patriarchy regard male dominance as the most important constant in human history in general and women's experience in particular. They use patriarchy to refer to the system of men's persistent and universal domination over women on the grounds that, as an analytic category, it properly grasps the dynamics of persistently unequal gender relations across time and space. On this basis, many feminist theorists have argued that patriarchy constitutes a deeply rooted social system, analogous to but different from relations of race and class.[16] It has proven difficult to write a history of patriarchy in this general sense that takes account of the changing forms of male dominance. Gerda Lerner, for example, groups all institutionalized forms of male dominance under the rubric of patriarchy on the grounds that to restrict the term to genuinely patriarchal societies is "troublesome because it distorts historical reality."[17] To each her own distortion.

The only justification for such a view could be that the relations between men and women transcend all other social relations in importance and do not change over time. But, then, Lerner believes that the true emancipation of women will "enable women and men to free their minds from patriarchal thought and practice and at last to build a world free of dominance and hierarchy, a world that is truly human."[18] (But if so, on what grounds could her version of "a truly human world" be established?) Apparently believing that women are, by nature, free from aspirations to domination and hierarchy, she attributes gender inequality to innate human nature and thus effectively dismisses history. Yet suspicions of misogyny continue to haunt her work, if only because she, like others who focus on patriarchy, is more concerned with the abiding inequality and antagonism between the sexes than with the dynamics of specific social systems.

Misogyny can be found in all periods, all communities, all societies, and in many male texts.[19] Historically, misogyny has doubtless fueled much of the opposition to women's self-assertion and continues to do so today. But misogyny hardly constitutes an adequate theoretical explanation for women's oppression. To emphasize men's hatred and fear of women is to personalize gender relations and detract from the various forms of sexism that characterize them. To assume, as Riane Eisler and Gerda Lerner seem to, that inequalities of all forms have somehow arisen from men's nature is to slight the ways in which societies construct men's and women's roles and identities. To group all forms of male dominance under the single rubric of patriarchy is to fall into the similar trap of homogenizing all forms of male domination and thereby obscuring their specific characteristics. Patriarchy, like misogyny, exists within, not without, history and must be used with precise reference to historical relations of genders, races, and classes.[20]

Dale Spender, in an especially conspiratorial interpretation, has taken this ahistorical argument from patriarchy to its extreme, arguing that men have generally silenced women or, when they could not silence them, have suppressed evidence of women's voices. In so doing, men have ensured that male values are perceived "as the *only* valid frame of reference for society" and have prevented "women from sharing, establishing, and asserting their equally real, valid and *different* frame of reference, which is the outcome of different experience."[21] Her judgment rests on the correlative assumptions that the conflict between the sexes has dominated history and that women's intellectual work has reflected a distinctive female culture. Thus she, like others, implicitly treats men's opposition to women as historically invariable and, accordingly, deprives women themselves of a meaningful history. This general strategy promotes an essentialist view of women's history, according to which women's physical attributes, ostensibly more important than their social attributes, dominate the experience and consciousness of all women independent of class, race, or historical period.

The assumptions of Spender's argument notwithstanding, the ubiquity and significance of men's dominance of women are not the issue. In the measure that male dominance, like class and racial dominance, has obtained throughout human history, there is no women's history, nor forms of female power, apart from it.[22] Indeed, there is precious little men's history that can be divorced either from women's contributions or, perhaps more important, from men's pervasive consciousness of and attempts to enforce women's subordination.

Socialist-feminists, who are drawn to the concept of patriarchy primarily because they find conventional theories of social relations inadequate to explain women's position, have attempted to escape this trap by elaborating a theory of patriarchy that simultaneously emphasizes the oppression that all women share as women and takes account of its class dimension and even of class and racial divisions among women. They have, in other words, tried to resolve the tensions between second-wave feminism and Marxism by developing a "dual systems" theory that attributes independent, but interacting, influence to patriarchy and capitalism in determining women's position.[23] Increasingly, however, gender intertwines with patriarchy in socialist-feminist discussions, especially with the growing recognition of variations in the experience of women of different classes and races. Some socialist-feminist historians, notably Christine Stansell, Jeanne Boydston, Linda Gordon, and Ruth Milkman, who are placing more and more weight on the distinctions among women's experience of male dominance, seem to be repudiating the essentialist implications of a theory of patriarchy that ascribes primary responsibility for women's disadvantage to men's universal distrust and fear of women.[24]

As such work suggests, the more serious danger of grouping all forms of male dominance under patriarchy lies elsewhere, notably in homogenizing the experience of women themselves. As a familial metaphor, patriarchy holds that men exercise power—rule—as a consequence of their position within the family; it thus implicitly holds that men justify their rule over women on grounds of innate physical superiority. Accordingly, it reduces women to their physical attributes and thus reinforces precisely that view of women as innately "other," against which many feminists protest. Worse, as Elizabeth Spelman has cogently argued, it reduces the significance of differences among women and thus minimizes the social dimension of women's experience and identities.[25]

Those who emphasize gender normally avoid conspiratorial interpretations of men's subordination of women and emphasize the systematic but changing character of relations between women and men. The most promising work elaborates the ways in which women's experience and contributions interact with those of men to create and sustain social systems and the discourses that characterize them. The principal danger in this work, from a feminist perspective, lies in its concessions to functionalist models in the social sciences. It is easy for those who emphasize gender to lose the edge of righteous indignation that fuels the most passionate feminist scholarship—to assume that women's position has had to be the way it has been because of the social system as a whole—and to accept the basic framework and categories of academic disciplines—for example, economics—that many feminists view as inherently oblivious or even antagonistic to women's concerns.[26]

The prestige of post-structuralist literary theory has recently led some women's historians to reconsider gender in the light of literary theory. Joan Scott, a social historian, has proposed a definition of gender based on two propositions: "Gender is a constitutive element of social relationships based on perceived differences between the sexes, and gender is a primary way of signifying relations of power."[27] Under the influence of feminist literary theory and the new historicism, Scott seeks to develop a notion of gender that will simultaneously encompass historians' traditional concerns with describing past societies and literary critics' concerns with the problematic relation between language and "reality"—especially the difficulty of identifying any reality other than the language in which it is articulated.

Skepticism about our ability to identify any reality independent of language is hardly new, but it does constitute the cutting edge of much contemporary philosophy and dominates post-structuralist literary theory, especially deconstructionist theory as developed by Jacques Derrida. An important tendency in feminist theory has been deeply influenced by the post-structuralist attack on "logocentricism"—literally the exclusive focus on logic and, by extension, the commitment to the independent authority of a stable, pretextual subject. Such feminists have borrowed from post-structuralism the conviction that reality is inherently unstable and elusive and the complementary claim that language offers the only partial truth of it that we may hope to know. And they have expanded the attack on logocentrism into an attack on "phallocentrism."[28] Thus the illusion that the human mind can identify and understand any independent reality becomes a specifically male pretension to intellectual domination, which must inevitably end in the obliteration of woman, and all Western thought becomes inherently "phallocentric." In this spirit, they question the validity of a wide variety of our inherited intellectual assumptions, notably the concept of rationality, the notion of a stable self, and, above all, the practice of "dichotomous" thinking that informs the propensity to view the world in terms of such fixed oppositions as that between male and female.[29]

Such thinking intentionally calls into question precisely the kind of dichotomies that Frederick Tönnies relied upon in his juxtaposition of community and society. Were post-structuralist feminists to engage Tönnies's text, they would, in effect, argue that the opposition between, say, rational and affective constitutes nothing but an artifact of language, a convenience that permits people to divide attributes according to their political predilections—especially the determination to silence women.[30] From this perspective, the language in which the distinctions are expressed itself constitutes a political attempt to control human experience by insisting that it reflects a deeper reality. Gender, in this perspective, becomes nothing more than an aspect of language, albeit an especially powerful one. Thus for Scott, following Michel Foucault, gender should properly be studied as one among many epistemological phenomena ("economics, industrialization, relations of production, factories, families, classes, genders, collective action, and political ideas, as well as one's own interpretive categories") and be understood to mean "knowledge about sexual difference."[31]

Other postmodernist feminists make the case if anything more explicitly. Jane Flax has argued that any attempt to understand the underlying cause of gender relations in general or male dominance in particular may "reflect a mode of thinking that is itself grounded in particular forms of gender (and/or) other relations in which domination is present."[32] Flax enthusiastically endorses the purportedly radical implications of postmodernism, urging feminists to embrace "ambivalence, ambiguity, and multiplicity as well as to expose the roots of our needs for imposing order and structure no matter how arbitrary and oppressive these needs may be."[33] In a similar spirit, Scott argues that women's history can help to expose "such seeming dichotomies as state and family, public and private, work and sexuality" and to criticize history "not simply as an incomplete record of the past but as a participant in the production of knowledge that legitimized the exclusion or subordination of women."[34] At the heart of these concerns lies the conviction that the notion of difference has constituted one of the most powerful weapons in the subordination of women. Women have indeed, as Beauvoir insisted, been reduced to the status of other—the necessary opposite of the man. By this logic, deconstructing or, better yet, abolishing the notion of difference will launch us toward the abolition of hierarchy and domination—of authority in all its forms.

In this guise, feminist history now claims to be the cutting edge of what both supporters and opponents are calling a revolution in the writing of history, much as a decade ago cliometricians and psychohistorians claimed to be doing so. So much for the permanence of revolutions.[35] The primary source of the supposed crisis, which originated in literature and now extends to the humanities in general, lies in a preoccupation with the nature and legitimacy of power.[36] The lines between the post-structuralist and postmodernist critiques of power, notwithstanding divergent origins and agendas, are, in the work of historians like Scott, tending to blur.[37] At the risk of gross oversimplification of a complex debate, post-structuralism is primarily identified with a critique of the stability and referentiality of language, and postmodernism with a critique of the established structures and operations of power. In the words of Claire Dalton, postmodernism "focuses on the power that legitimates particular understandings and explanations of the world, on the link between power and knowledge, even while it also sees power as diffuse, and legitimation of power as local, plural and immanent."[38] But as postmodernists increasingly focus on the status of language as an intractable source of power in its own right, their analyses are tending to merge with those of post-structuralists.

Post-structuralist feminism originated in France, in the very special Parisian world of competitive intellectual fashion. It took longer to catch hold in the United States, where the feminist community was more focused on specific political issues and more closely tied to ensuring women's place in conventional, referential discourse.[39] Recently, a group of American post-structuralist feminists has begun to build on the work of French feminist theorists like Hélène Cixous and Luce Irigaray.[40] American post-structuralist feminists have especially focused on the related problems of difference and dichotomous thinking and have increasingly insisted that any dichotomous notion of difference is inherently oppressive. They have, in this respect, taken the conventional cultural distinction between woman and man as their primary target—as the very essence of that dichotomous or binary thinking that classifies human beings into rigid categories and arbitrarily curtails the possibilities of human development. Precisely because of its emphasis on the oppressive and arbitrary quality of the very categories of man and woman and of the difference between them, this aspect of post-structuralist feminism has proved eminently compatible with postmodernism.

Feminist theorists' initial distrust of post-structuralism and postmodernism resulted from their conviction that both were inherently inhospitable to their primary concerns, and, in fact, the leading figures in both camps displayed little interest in feminist issues.[41] For many, post-structuralist pronouncements about the "death of the subject" should be recognized as a direct reaction to a thinly disguised repudiation of the emergence of women and peoples of the non-Western world as authoritative subjects. In this conviction, Barbara Christian has forcefully denounced the intimidation of feminists by "the race for theory." In her view, the literary world has been taken over by "Western philosophers from the old literary elite, the neutral humanists" who deploy a language "that mystifies rather than clarifies our condition" and makes it possible for the few to control the critical scene. Significantly, that language surfaced "just when the literature of peoples of color, black women, Latin Americans, and Africans began to move to the center."[42] What, Christian and others are asking, have feminists to gain from a constellation of theories that prefer to kill off the male subject rather than leave him to face competition?

As some feminists, especially those working within the French literary tradition, have gradually begun to enter the post-structuralist lists, they have attempted to shift the focus in academic feminism from a concern with women's oppression to the oppressive character of the designation "woman" itself.[43] This tactic has led to a convergence of post-structuralism and postmodernism, encouraging some feminists to appropriate aspects of both. Certainly Joan Scott, who explicitly identifies herself with post-structuralism, increasingly articulates what appears to be a postmodernist agenda—or at least adopts a radically democratic, postmodernist rhetoric, which seems fundamentally at variance with post-structuralism's initial agenda. For post-structuralism's insistence on depersonalizing the subject— of divorcing texts from "experience"—implies no necessary assault on hierarchy or inequality within the academy or without. That inherent political agnosticism has been precisely what radicals of various stripes, especially feminists, reproached it for.

Scott, talking about the putative "crisis" in history at the annual meeting of the American Historical Association, explicitly identified her own position as an attack on those conservatives, notably Gertrude Himmelfarb, who protest any attack on a single central historical narrative "because it undermines the legitimation of their quest for dominance." Identifying the conservatives' defense of the traditional history of elites with their defense of "their own hegemony in the present," Scott dismissed the entire project as "a repudiation of the possibility of contest and conflicting interpretation, a refusal of change, and a rejection of the possibility for what I would call democratic history."[44] The conservatives' defense of their vision of history must in her view be understood as highly political and as having "profoundly exclusionary and elitist effects on the discipline."[45] For conservative elitism, Scott proposed substituting her own vision of democratic history— "a plurality of stories," the telling of which raises "contests about power and knowledge" and forces the recognition that "the historian's mastery is necessarily partial."[46]

Few conservatives or anyone else would quarrel with Scott's claim that good history should embody the conflict of social groups or include diverse stories, but that commonsensical claim masks a much more radical agenda with which many from all parts of the political spectrum do quarrel. Scott's embrace of postmodernism permits her simultaneously to obscure some issues and to personalize others. For Scott's insistence upon the centrality of politics in history has more to do with contemporary than with past politics. Gertrude Himmelfarb has a point in charging, albeit with slight exaggeration, that this emphasis on politics "reduces all historical controversy to *ad hominem* arguments, since all historians are presumed to be expressing or defending their own positions of power."[47] And Scott does regularly slip from politics in general into the specific politics of the historical profession. In Scott's telling, contemporary professional politics emerges as proxy for past politics, and contemporary historians emerge as the custodians of their predecessors' stories. This equation effectively elides the past and the present and comes perilously close, as Himmelfarb argues, to a "total indictment of all of history, in both senses of that word—the past itself and all of previous writing about the past—and an invitation to the total rewriting of history, again in both senses of that word."[48] It also cloaks an amusing irony, for many of those who most vociferously seek to expose the corrupt politics of the historical profession are today regarded, with good reason, as the dominant personalities and factions in the leading historical associations and college departments, to say nothing of the prize committees and grant-dispensing agencies.[49] As one who, like Scott, has herself benefited from the recent opening of the profession to women, I have no interest in perpetuating the *ad feminam* arguments, but surely, a privileged position in academia ought to make us all shrink from pretending that we are somehow the voice of the downtrodden.

Conservatives like Himmelfarb no longer dominate the academy; probably they never did. Indeed, a good case could be made that, as a group, they are more vulnerable to exclusion from or marginalization within the academy than even the most radical of their left-wing opponents. Today, the dominant politics of academia ranges from liberal to radical, with an anxious liberalism leading the way as it always has, but it is now firing to the right as it fired to the left in the McCarthy era. The shift, then, has less to do with a triumph of the left over the right than with a transformation of the liberal center under the pressures of our own confusing times. Pareto must be smiling. In a story as old as history itself, one establishment is giving way to another, not on the basis of a dramatic change in ideology, but on the basis of the establishment's internal transformation. Within the academy, Scott's charges notwithstanding, the transition is proceeding apace. In the narrow sense of professional politics, Himmelfarb has grounds for concern, however much she personally may enjoy an eminently secure—and well-earned—position.

The struggles within the academy, although intrinsically trivial, bear directly upon the struggles within our society at large, for they too derive directly from the legacy of individualism. The central contest between Himmelfarb and Scott can best be understood as a contest over the nature and political implications of knowledge. Himmelfarb adheres to the central Enlightenment conviction that the human mind is capable of rational knowledge and progress, both of which embody objective standards of excellence to which our society must subscribe if it is to prosper. In this respect, she fully accepts the classical liberal premise that the mind of "man" is capable of promoting the "rational ordering and organization of society" and thus "the public weal and the good life."[50] Scott rejects this premise on the grounds that it claims a monopoly on "the right way of telling the human story" and thus obscures the multiplicity of stories that make up our history.[51] Yet Scott herself remains as firmly tied to individualism as Himmelfarb; she is simply asking that we deconstruct it into its constituent parts—its multiple subjectivities.

Himmelfarb has declared unconditional war on feminism, as she has on Marxism and everything else she recklessly lumps as the "new" history. Her tactic exposes her to the risk either of being seriously misunderstood or of being correctly seen to promote an exclusionary vision of history. For Himmelfarb, like many of her liberal predecessors, has confounded the general notion of a coherent, politically informed history with its specific representatives—elite, white men and the few others acceptable to them. If, she seems to be saying, we are to preserve our notion of a common history, we must preserve it in precisely the form in which we have received it. As a result, with the passage of time and irreversible social change, her position becomes increasingly rigid and artificial; her politics has less to do with the flexible conservatism she is capable of espousing than with unthinking reaction. She thus grants unintended and undeserved plausibility to Scott's attacks and obscures the most important questions, which Scott does not help to clarify.

Scott's emphasis on a "democratic" history and a multiplicity of stories openly betrays her own commitment to individualism, in the narrow sense of personalism, but she combines it with a radical egalitarianism, apparently oblivious to the centuries-long association of those two quintessentially bourgeois concepts. She effectively argues that in our time we must recognize all stories as of equal value, although, somehow, she gives the voices of the elite short shrift. We have, she insists, no grounds for privileging one person's experience over that of another, for privileging one form of politics over another. She bases these claims not on the grounds of the practical politics of who has most power to determine the conditions of the lives of others but on the grounds of language. Since we can know nothing of "reality" except language, we must accept all language as equally valid.

Thus, with one fell swoop, she effectively dismisses the substance of oppression and injustice, which, presumably, can be righted by giving every voice a hearing. I am by no means sure that she intends such a conclusion; I am sure that it follows inexorably from her reasoning.

Although Scott champions a multiplicity of stories, she does not explicitly identify with any one of them. Her voice remains essentially academic—the voice of epistemology, if not that of an "objective" knowledge that, when probed, turns out to be radically subjective. The full implications of her argument emerge most clearly from the writings of those who spell out their concrete claims. Patricia Hill Collins, writing about the social implications of black feminist thought, takes Scott's arguments to their logical conclusion. "Living life as an African-American woman," she insists, "is a necessary prerequisite for producing Black feminist thought because within Black women's communities thought is validated and produced with reference to a particular set of historical, material, and epistemological conditions."[52]

Personal experience, in other words, constitutes the only valid basis for intellectual work. In this view, any attempt to perpetuate or even reconstitute a notion of universal knowledge misses the point. There is no value in the attempt to integrate black women's culture "into the substantiated body of academic knowledge, for that substantiated knowledge is, in many ways, antithetical to the best interests of Black women," which require a "recentering" of academic discourse to accommodate black women's claims.[53] Alternate or additional bodies of knowledge—in this instance the experience of African-American women—offer no serious challenge to conventional knowledge, but alternate epistemologies can challenge the basic processes of thought and legitimation. "If the epistemology used to validate knowledge comes into question, then all prior knowledge claims validated under the dominant model become suspect."[54]

These claims expose the individualist premises of Scott's position with a vengeance. If the individualism of our history and ideology has served the dominance of elite white men, then it must be dismantled by the competing individualisms that it has silenced. Heretofore, some privileged individuals have imposed their claim to speak in the name of all; now, each must speak in his or her own voice. And, in order for this proliferation of voices to triumph, we must abolish all criteria for distinguishing among them. As Allan Bloom has cogently observed, from a position about which I admittedly have deep reservations, "Indiscriminateness is a moral imperative because its opposite is discrimination."[55] Bloom, like Himmelfarb, scores

heavily in insisting that an unwillingness to discriminate betokens an unwillingness to praise the good or condemn the bad—to name excellence and
evil for what they are—although he seems to miss that his opponents, who
reject the legitimacy of imposing judgments on the past, are quick to pour
vitriol on those who do not share their views about it. But in Bloom's mind,
excellence and evil seem to depend upon an ideal of an absolute human
nature.

The defense of the absolute brings us back to the feminist attack. For the
mainstream of Western thought has generally regarded male and female not
as a linguistic convenience but as the signs of absolute nature. On this basis,
its ideals of excellence have been uncompromisingly male, its ideals of evil
too frequently associated with the female. Perhaps more important from the
postmodernist feminist perspective, the pretension even to name an absolute presupposes some form of authority, which has invariably been exercised by men over women, by the privileged over the dispossessed. In this
skewed, if not perverse, perspective, it follows that the success of feminism
requires nothing less than the repudiation of the Western tradition and,
beyond it, the repudiation of any notion of an accountable self or an ordered
collectivity. Thus feminism, which began with the attempt to claim for
women the rights that men were proclaiming for themselves, is moving
irrationally and at high political risk toward the repudiation of any notion of
right beyond that of personal experience.

  This move, ironically, strips feminism of its principal rationale, namely
the attempt to explain and to rectify systematic discrimination against
women. Mary Poovey, who attempts to combine deconstruction with an
abiding interest in the material conditions of women's lives, has explicitly
attempted to join the issue. Defending the techniques of deconstruction as
important tools of feminist criticism, she allows that unless we learn to turn
them back upon deconstruction itself, "deconstruction will trap us in a
practice that once more glorifies the 'feminine' instead of giving us the
means to explode binary logic and make the social construction of (sexed)
identities a project of pressing political concern." But Poovey's feminist
agenda would nonetheless "dismantle the system that assigns to all women a
single identity and a marginal place."[56] Thus even as she criticizes the
excessive depersonalization of deconstruction, she retains its essence. For if
the primary goal remains to expose the binary opposition of male and

female as fraudulent—as nothing more than an epistemological swindle—then there is scant need to concern ourselves with women as a group. From this perspective, women's experience of "twoness" can be treated as nothing more than the product of an oppressive linguistic politics. By extension, the "twoness" of African-Americans would be transformed from the subtle formulation of Du Bois, as a product of autonomous African-American cultural development within the constraints of a white racist society, into its opposite—a pathological response to oppression.

Most feminists, today as in the past, have grounded their case concretely in women's sexual, social, political, and economic oppression. Despite considerable disagreement among themselves, they have agreed that the history of such oppression or exclusion has endowed women with at least the rudiments of a common identity as women. Taken to its extreme, the position results in an "essentialist" interpretation that denies the significance of distinctions of race, class, and ethnicity. Neglect of the social dimension of women's oppression as well as of some women's privilege leads to a premature emphasis on the importance of what women as a sex share in contrast to what divides them by class, and puts undue emphasis on women's biology at the expense of their social positions and relations. But even in its extreme form, this position offers more than postmodernist indeterminacy.[57]

Historically, the notion of "twoness" has decisively colored women's experience and for this, if no other, reason, it continues to set the agenda for feminist theory. The twoness of which Du Bois writes constitutes primarily an attribute of consciousness grounded in specifically oppressive social relations. As such, it refers directly to an individual's sense of self in relation to the dominant culture of the society as a whole. For women, the sense of twoness bridges fundamental biological differences between the sexes and the cultural representation of those differences. A notion of twoness can, in other words, help to bind women, in beneficial ways, to the men of their communities—can capture an important aspect of our material existence as a species. The specific notion of twoness that many contemporary feminists are attacking is only a special case of the general notion, albeit an especially comprehensive one. That notion emerged in tandem with the individualism from which it cannot be divorced. It is a direct outgrowth of the concept of separate spheres according to which the theorists of individualism sought to codify male and female as the fundamental social categories.[58] The feminist critique of this legacy remains deeply implicated in its specific historical origins, and even the most radical rejections of it have not shaken the shackles of the individualism that engendered it in the first place.

Many feminist scholars recognize that women's specific social circumstances powerfully affect their perceptions of their cultural identities and even of their biology, that their sexual and social attributes converge in gender, loosely defined as the social construction of sex.[59] According to this argument, women experience their bodies and their identity in relation to the men and other women of their own communities, with whom they are more likely to identify than with women of other communities—especially of other classes and races. Slaveholding women in the Old South did not generally identify as women with slave women, whom they regarded as their social and racial inferiors. In most respects, they identified much more closely with the men of their class and race than with slave or even poor white women.[60] Yet the general representations of women as primarily members of a biological group did influence their identities as women among their own people.

This age-old idea of twoness in the sense of difference has acquired a special importance in the modern era. Individualism has in theory if not in practice eliminated all justification for hierarchy and inequality by emphasizing the importance of the self as an autonomous, accountable unit of consciousness. According to its premises, there is no reason that women, like men, should not be counted as individuals. Yet biological differences persist, as do their representations. The logic of postmodernist feminism points toward the denial of physical difference on the grounds that it, like other differences, exists solely in language. I remain unconvinced. A woman may only be able to represent her body through language, but its immediacy, however represented, exists. The problem is not the reality of physical difference between women and men but the estimate of its consequences. Those consequences constitute essential features of our laws, politics, and social relations, all of which are subject to change.

Viewing human nature as a constant, conservatives like Allan Bloom seek to bypass the social and political arena of struggle and change. They read all previous history through the prism of individualism on the assumption that it embodies transhistorical values. Imprisoned by their own ideology, they vitiate their own best insights by confusing interpretations of human nature with its essence. Their strategy apparently consists in divorcing our tradition from the social relations that produced it; they thus endow it with a status that denies the very history that they are purportedly defending. However unintentionally, by seeking to stop history in its tracks, they have opened the way to the postmodernist revolt. When Himmelfarb, who is much more concerned with social and political history than Bloom, accuses

Scott of being ahistorical, she fails to recognize how much she herself risks succumbing to the same temptation.

Both Bloom and Himmelfarb are writing out of the marrow of individualism but without acknowledging that the values they so admire are products of a specific historical conjuncture. Their strategy, at its most convincing, calls attention to the recurring or constant aspects of the human condition and invites us to read *Antigone* or *Hamlet* for their representation of human passions—human weaknesses and strengths. At its least convincing, that strategy enjoins us to read, say, Aristotle as a guide to contemporary political challenges. Both aspects of the strategy share a refusal to acknowledge the social—and hence the historical—constraints on representation. By refusing to credit the social and historical influence on behavior and representation, these conservatives seek to exempt their own values from the play of contingency. With enough reason to make the rest of us uncomfortable, they see the barbarians at the gates, but, intent on defending individualism against all comers, they fail to understand that, in the words of the Sicilian conservative Giuseppe di Lampedusa, "If things are to stay the same, things will have to change."[61]

Bloom, Himmelfarb, and their allies are conflating the defense of history as the custodian of our collective identity as a people with the defense of a specific version of history. They thereby invoke the idea of a common history, in contradistinction to a proliferation of personal stories, to legitimate the domination of some by others. Our history, in both senses of how things were in the past and how the past has been recorded, has indeed been one of domination by class, race, and gender. Revulsion at the iniquities does not make it any less our history. But the inherited record need not be enshrined as a blueprint for the present and future. Conservatives like Bloom and Himmelfarb are the last people who should need lectures on the freedom of the will.

Tragically the version of our history that they are trying to defend is decisively shaping the reaction against it. For conservatives, like radicals, are writing out of individualism's decomposition in our own time. Thus, in this respect, the conservatives' celebration of the autonomy of the individual does not substantively differ from the postmodernists' celebration of the proliferation of voices. Conservatives and postmodernists differ sharply over who should be able to claim the status of individual and even over the proper way to conceptualize the individual. But, in essential respects, they are as one in accepting the individual, however defined, as the constituent unit of society and in accepting the claims of the individual as prior to the claims of society. Neither group, in other words, has decisively broken with the individualist model of the unitary self. And, from the perspective of feminist concerns, neither has been able to imagine a world that could sustain the tension between equality and difference.

The problem of equality and difference, Scott has urged, should lead feminists to turn to post-structuralist literary theory for an illuminating guide to "analyzing constructions of meaning and relationships of power that called unitary, universal categories into question and historicized concepts otherwise treated as natural (such as man/woman) or absolute (such as justice or equality).[62] Deconstruction, in particular, she has suggested, offers feminists a new way of apprehending and analyzing language, discourse, and difference. For Scott, the sharp juxtaposition between equality and difference does not properly capture the most pressing issues that feminists confront. They would, in her judgment, do better to repudiate the dichotomy entirely. "When equality and difference are paired dichotomously, they structure an impossible choice."[63] Specifically, the dichotomous pairing "denies the way in which difference has long figured in notions of political equality and it suggests that sameness is the only grounds on which equality can be claimed."[64]

Scott is, in effect, proposing to substitute an analysis of language for an analysis of social and gender relations—of politics and class. In addition, notwithstanding her insistence that she is not simply advocating a happy pluralism, she is making a decisive move in the direction of postmodernism with its emphasis on the unmediated expression of diversity. Above all, her immersion in theory has blinded her to the historical specificity of the concepts of difference and equality she is attacking. Myra Jehlen has cautioned against the dangers of post-structuralist readings of gender, which she calls the dangers of the "vulgar linguicism" or "vulgar representationism" that result from "the collapse of the disciplines of literature and history into the common denominator of language." Rather than language, Jehlen proposes class as the appropriate common denominator for an interdisciplinary analysis, arguing that class "projects a world structured by relationships between human beings and property . . . and among human beings such that culture and social organization explain one another, and are contingent one upon the other."[65] There is, she reflects, "something profoundly conservative, both intellectually and politically (and the two can't be separated anyway) in the collapse of all levels of reality into the one level of representation."[66]

Since the idea of equality presupposes sameness, many feminists have argued that difference presents a challenge that no notion of equality has ever been able to meet. The challenge initially led some to endorse androgyny as the only possible model for meaningful equality.[67] As an ideal, androgyny abstracts from or obliterates difference and offers the illusion that women and men are not merely equal but interchangeable; it thus captures the essence of individualism in theory. In so doing, it also perpetuates the illusions of individualism, especially the illusion of autonomy. In our time, the ideal of androgyny captures the fantasy that we are free of all restrictions on the self, including material and biological restrictions. We can be, as so many self-development and New Age gurus are proclaiming, what we choose to be. Androgyny simultaneously perpetuates the extreme objective and subjective implications of individualism: that people are no more than irreducible units of sovereignty; that people are no more than their personal stories. It thus combines the worst aspects of formalism and personalism and bypasses the concrete politics of gender in our time. Androgyny embodies precisely what feminists have reproached the concept of the individual for—the denial of female being and experience. In this way, the appeal to androgyny risks the divorce of feminist theory from history.

The assumption that equality presupposes sameness itself derives from history, or, better, from individualism. For the equation of equality and sameness rests upon the notion of presocial individual rights in a world in which a supposedly free market allocates resources. If one were, hypothetically, to remove the market from the equation, there would be no necessary reason that very different kinds of people could not have equal claims on social resources. It is at least possible to imagine a conception of equality, or more accurately of equity, that would allow for difference. Christine Littleton, moving in this direction, has suggested that we replace the judicial model of "equality as assimilation" with a model of "equality as acceptance." In her view, the "theory of equality as acceptance requires social institutions to adjust themselves to the fact that people come in two sexes, not one, or one and a half." Even and perhaps especially, she insists, if we admit that "male and female are wholly social constructions, a society embracing equality as an ideal cannot fulfill that ideal by elevating one social category (male) to the level of public norm, and subordinating the other (female) to it."[68] Post-structuralist and postmodernist theory have, however, moved so far from any consideration of the social foundations of the linguistic practices they are criticizing that they have lost sight of the specific politics of our own and previous ages. Notwithstanding, or perhaps because of, the high level of abstraction at which they operate, they remain deeply implicated in the essence of that individualism the manifestations of which they deplore.

More than three decades ago, Richard Weaver, the great southern conservative social theorist, called for renewed attention to rhetoric in human understanding. Appalled by the one-sided concern with "dialectic," which he defined as abstract reasoning, Weaver insisted that rhetoric offered an indispensable attention to that persuasion which "tries to bring opinion into closer line with the truth which dialectic pursues."[69] Rhetoric, he insisted, "depends upon history."[70] Weaver viewed the dialectic as inherently revolutionary, rhetoric as inherently conservative. He never advocated abandonment of dialectical reasoning but did insist that it must always be coupled with rhetoric, for rhetoric alone has the power to make ideas concrete, to link them to the world we know. Hence the importance of history, for "the appeal to history is an appeal to events made meaningful, and the meaning of events cannot be conveyed through the simple empirical references that semantic analysis puts forward as an ideal."[71]

The argument for rhetoric assuredly does not require the repudiation of the unavoidable and frequently acceptable risks of dialectic or abstraction. Without abstraction, we should lose the ability to generalize and, hence, to identify significant patterns in human affairs. Feminist theory's conversion to the values of abstraction signals its intellectual coming of age, but it also places at high risk feminism's original moral and rhetorical power. In adopting postmodernism, even in the name of feminist values, feminism is opting for disproportionate emphasis on dialectic over rhetoric. It is jeopardizing the substance of its critique of individualism, forsaking its engagement with the politics of our time, and repudiating the history of feminism itself. The shift is neither accidental nor innocent in intent, for a politically effective rhetorical expression of postmodernist dialectics would immediately expose its intellectual bankruptcy and the vast gulf that separates a utopian and doctrinaire radicalism from the realizable aspirations of the overwhelming majority of women and perhaps even a significant number of feminists.

Feminism has, from its inception, wrestled with the problem of female identity and subjectivity within a dominant culture or discourse largely defined by men. Do women have a distinctive discourse, or is the very core of their self-consciousness fashioned by a discourse that is not of their own making? If women do indeed figure only as the eternal other—as mere objects—in an extended male monologue, how are they to represent themselves unless through that objectifying and murderous perspective? Within a discourse that defines the subject as male, they may represent themselves as women, but how do they (as women) represent themselves as subjects?

Feminist critics, differences notwithstanding, tend to agree that discourse cannot avoid being gendered—and that the discourses of Western culture have spoken in the first person masculine. The dualism of subject and object, presence and absence, thus "structures everything our culture considers thinkable."[72] Women, denied access as subjects to the symbolic, have, according to Margaret Homans's recent argument, remained tied to the literal, and thus, as writers, condemned to twoness.[73]

Feminism has thus built on cultural traditions that have taken the representation of biological difference as central to their concepts of humanity and subjectivity. Feminists who emphasize patriarchy as a constant feature of women's experience are insisting that this basic tendency to subordinate women to men in culture as well as in society and politics provides an essential unity to feminist theory as well as to women's experience. Feminists who emphasize gender, while not denying the ubiquity of male dominance, are placing more weight on the variety of forms that dominance assumes among different social and interpretive communities—among states, cultures, classes, nations, and races. Both feminists who emphasize patriarchy and those who emphasize gender, however, see twoness as structuring women's relations to culture and differ primarily in the importance they ascribe to the specific social context in which it is expressed.

Both tendencies exist within the general current of modern feminism that is a product of individualism. Feminists' attempts to come to terms with individualism expose the limits of individualism, which feminism, in turn, threatens to explode. For individualism has proved incapable of coming to terms with the most fundamental aspect of our humanity—the sexual difference that permits us to reproduce ourselves as a species. Twoness is indeed the biological grounding of all of our consciousnesses—those of men as well as women. Men, in abstracting from their own ties to biology, have tended to associate biology with women. In this perspective, the postmodernist feminists who are advocating the transcendence of twoness are claiming for women the same freedom from biology that men have claimed for themselves. They thus short-circuit the central problem, which remains not the abolition of twoness but its interpretation and the mastery of its consequences.

The twoness of which Du Bois wrote has resulted from a history of injustice rather than from the interpretation of innate difference. Race as a concept has a feeble basis in biology and might, accordingly, be eradicated.[74] Significantly, scholars today prefer the term *African-American* to *black*, thus emphasizing the national rather than the racial dimension of a people's experience. But even maximum intellectual honesty and maximum social justice would not eradicate the twoness that simultaneously divides and binds women and men. Conversely, although it is possible to make a plausible case for the national identity of African-Americans and, hence, a case for some measure of separatism, a comparable case for female separatism is utopian, not to say bizarre.[75]

Postmodernist feminists like Scott would argue that gender must be understood not as a sign of natural identity but as a linguistic convention—an epistemological phenomenon. In a limited way, this view of gender as a language provides a good heuristic model by calling attention to gender's systemic and semantic aspects. Above all, it exposes what feminist critics frequently call woman's objectification or absence as an ideological construct that exists only in relation to man's subjectivity or presence, and thus underscores the reverse. Woman and man, as the cultural or discursive codifications of women and men, remain interdependent. But this recognition constitutes only a first step, which must be succeeded by the recognition that the changing representations of woman and man correspond to the changing relations of women and men within and among social and interpretive communities—states and cultures, classes and races.

Even the apparently most timeless or unbounded representation of woman does not persist unchanging. It is reinterpreted by different communities—always as one pole in a system of gender relations. The appearance of persistence invites skepticism rather than acquiescence. As the discourse of the masculine changes, so does that of the feminine. Or rather, despite pretenses, there is no discourse of the masculine independent of a (possibly repressed) discourse of the feminine. And the reverse. This understanding does not justify a dismissal of the idea of twoness. To the contrary, its very persistence throughout so many centuries and so many cultures suggests a foundation in some intractable aspect of our being as a species.

The double recognition of the specific representations of man and woman—and hence of twoness—as the product of social and cultural relations and as signs of our underlying biological being defies reduction to simple formulas. Just because we recognize gender as a language, as the evidence of changing interpretations of the human condition—or, as

Thomas Fleming would have it, human nature—we cannot thereby dismiss its significance, much less decree its abolition. Just because we recognize the existence of basic sexual differences between women and men, we need not agree that previous pronouncements about eternal consequences must bind our future.

Gender has always constituted a "master" discourse, a primary interpretive map for participants in a culture as much as for its critics. But the core of that discourse lies less in the specific attributes it ascribes to woman and to man than in its insistence upon the difference between woman and man. Specific discourses articulate those differences differently, frequently emphasizing the specific manifestations more than the general concept of difference. Yet the general concept of difference necessarily informs and gives meaning to the specific manifestations. The question—which closely resembles the relation of form to content—remains the relative weight of the concrete and the general for members of specific communities. If all discourse is gendered, how do the specific and general forms of gendering respectively shape the relations between discrete discourses and the possibilities for women's self-representations?

Women, like men, construct self-representations through available discourses and in interaction with intended readers. For women, as for men, the self is represented within the context of one or more interpretive communities. Women, in other words, represent themselves specifically, not in the abstract, as particular kinds of women. Physical description explicitly identifies a woman as tall or short, fair or dark. Other descriptions, sometimes less explicitly, identify her as doing or not doing housework, as writing with a pen or with a computer, as making her clothing or buying it in a shop. Through these, and yet more subtle signs of time and place, women represent themselves in relation to other members of specific families, communities, societies. They also represent themselves as endowed with specific personalities and values, which are also shaped by their material and social circumstances. The abiding danger for women, especially in representing their character, remains that of being trapped into seeing themselves literally through men's eyes. The danger becomes, as Nancy Miller has suggested, especially acute when women attempt public self-representations such as autobiographies or self-portraits, for women can never free themselves entirely from the dominant discourses of their communities or cultures.[76] The engendering of discourses itself dictates their imprisonment: The "I," by its very evocation of humanity, is male or female. And the public "I" of Western culture has been predominantly male.

Those who attempt to transcend the constraints that discourses normally impose on the first person feminine risk a plunge into implicit or explicit identification with the first person masculine. By virtue of their being embedded in discourse—in language—the "I" female and the "I" male carry with them the attributes that the discourse ascribes to male and female. Escape from the constraints leads inexorably to abstraction, to the denial or ostensible transcendence, of humanity in place and time. Western discourses have, in fact, permitted such abstraction, as in Saint Paul's celebrated invocation of the soul. The concept of the self in principle knows neither male nor female. But the very act of self-representation implicitly modifies that abstraction with the contingencies of place and time—and gender—that make the self both recognizable and distinct. In this sense women construct self-representations within the conventions of specific discourses.

We must resist the temptation, so vigorously promoted by a male-centered culture, to read those conventions exclusively as evidence of the oppressive power of a unified—a totalitarian and totalizing—discourse of gender. For the discourses of gender themselves, whatever their pretensions to the contrary, are discourses of shifting relations and have even been turned to advantage by women.[77] They are also, however obliquely, discourses of sexual identity. The physical, social, political, and cultural dominance of men may have denied women the freedom to represent themselves as autonomous beings, may have encouraged women to represent themselves as men wished to see them, but the reverse has also been, if in much lesser measure, the case.

The root of the problem lies in our inability to shake the legacy of individualism. Today, any viable notion of the individual must expand to encompass the asymmetry of male and female—the central challenge to any idea of a unitary self that could serve as a proxy for all humanity. In this respect, gender does lie at the heart of our modern condition. I emphatically do not mean that gender is more important than other social categories, notably race and class, for in many instances it is not. But sex identifies a fundamental difference among human beings, and its consequences cannot be exorcised by a revolution in gender relations. Indeed, it may be the only difference that could not be effectively erased by a just and enlightened politics.

Inattention to this matter weakens even the most sensible and illuminating of recent work. Louise Tilly, who especially champions the social determination of women's experience, insists that women resist oppression or exploitation according to the same principles as men. They do not necessarily engage in the same kinds of resistance as men, although they may, but they, like men, will act in response to the possibilities that society shapes for them.[78] Her position follows logically from her commitment to social science and to the historian's presumed responsibility to aim for a rational and objective assessment of social structure and relations. She resoundingly castigates the flight from materialism into "feelings, attitudes, and unique symbolic acts" and warns against generalizing about the mentality of a group from the subjective experience of an individual. But Tilly's plea for a structural analysis that can explain how groups think and feel ends in a misguided condemnation of the attempt to study psychological states. She counterposes social relations and psychological relations as if they were in fact separable and indeed incompatible.[79]

The great strength of contemporary feminism has lain in its rejection of the divorce between social and psychological relations, of the divorce between politics and personal experience. The basis of that rejection lies in the insistence that women must be understood as members of interlocking groups—as sharing experiences and values with some other women and with some men. In this respect, the agenda for feminist history would seem to lie in a yet more complex understanding of the differences that unite and divide women. But above all, the struggle for a feminist history implies a critique of individualism that moves beyond its association with male dominance to criticize its theoretical assumptions about the relations between all individuals and society.

The various moves toward a feminist history alert us to the complex links between women's discourses and dominant (male) discourses. Physical attributes in general and sexuality in particular, as well as participation in society, lie at the core of every woman's experience of membership in a gender. But to be a woman in those ways is only the beginning, and even those ways are defined in a language fashioned by the others to whom women must relate. History confirms that consciousness is, finally, a matter of language, as are political and social goals. History also confirms that all three are matters of political and social relations—of power and its abuses. To equate feminist history with a critique of language and to assume that the transformation of language will ensure justice for women is to miss the point. Worse, it is to fall into the snares of the dominant (male) culture and its abstractions from life in specific bodies and communities. In this perspective, the claims of rhetoric appear compelling. A politically responsible feminist history must retain its engagement with women in the world. To accept a view of women as atomized individuals and simply to proclaim their right to tell their discrete stories obscures the structures—the specific social relations—that govern their lives.

7

THE CLAIMS OF A

COMMON CULTURE, OR,

WHOSE AUTOBIOGRAPHY?

Feminists, if we are to credit conservatives like William Bennett, Allan Bloom, and Gertrude Himmelfarb, must, among their other sins, answer for the collapse of American education—and beyond it Western civilization—primarily because of their broadside attack on the canon or the "great tradition."[1] Conservatives who defend the canon, if we are to credit feminists, must answer for the stifling of women's minds and the denial of their aspirations.[2] Nowhere perhaps have the passions inspired by feminism raged more heatedly than in this proliferating debate, which has torn apart faculties on campuses like Stanford and provoked national attention. If there is any comfort to be taken in this *"dialogue des sourds,"* it is surely the persisting importance that both parties attribute to the power of education.

Those who defend the canon view it as, in some way, the embodiment of the collective identity of civilized men and the collective values of civilized people—the foundation of political and cultural consciousness. The sanctity invoked by the very designation "canon" derives from these assumptions, which apparently also account for the passion with which feminists and others seek to dismantle it. And indeed, the purpose of the canon was to initiate aspiring members of the polity and the republic of letters, which has overwhelmingly consisted of elite, white men, into their future responsibilities. These assumptions endowed the canon with a prestige that far exceeded arbitrary pedagogical exercises. In studying it, the elite would learn not so much of cabbages as of kings, of the qualities of leadership and the perils of fortune, of statesmanship and character, of power and its corruptions, of civic duty and moral responsibility. The canon was fashioned by and for those who were to inherit the earth—not the meek, but the mighty. At its best, it introduced its heirs to an attractive set of values and to the perils of falling away from them. It offered a model of excellence and insisted that excellence comes at a price—that, in the words of the record about Prince Valiant I listened to as a child, "freedom also has its responsibilities."

The canon, as its critics insist, has never been the true and immutable body of sacred texts that both its defenders and detractors like to claim. Subject to "vision and revision," it has been modified by successive generations. The canon we have inherited and against which so many are warring did not always appear as reactionary and repressive as it appears to many today. It took shape as a body of privileged texts that encoded the rise and progress of the individual mind as the custodian of knowledge and standards of political and cultural excellence. Closely tied, in particular, to the notions of individual responsibility in politics, it encoded the triumph of rationality over superstition, opportunity over acquired status, universalism over particularism. It provided a common currency for "the Republic of Letters." Its fashioners and contributors generally assumed that membership in this Republic would be restricted, notwithstanding an occasional exception, by gender, race, and class.

Today the canon's prestige is wearing thin. The received notion of the responsible, autonomous, elite male individual seems alien even to many white middle-class young men. What have Socrates, Cicero, Saint Thomas Aquinas, Machiavelli, Descartes, John Locke, Voltaire, Goethe, Cardinal Newman, and all the rest to do with life in the late twentieth century? And if alien to young men, how much more so to women? The attack on the canon owes much to the quest for relevance that has its roots in the liberation movements of the 1960s but especially in the cynical instrumentalism that accompanied the political pseudoconservatism of the 1950s, which gave us J. D. Salinger's Holden Caulfield as the alter ego of the man in the gray flannel suit long before we got Mike Nichols's and Dustin Hoffman's graduate.[3]

Beyond its mission of initiation of the elite, the canon was also taken to represent civilization to the less privileged, who, if not viewed as its custodians, were expected to internalize its premises. And, in some measure, it did. Those who, like myself, were reared on the margins of privilege often took their own pleasure in knowing the general outlines of the story of the rise and triumph of Western civilization: the development of political philosophy, the flowering of chivalry, the growth and triumph of humanism, the emergence of Protestantism, the rise of the bourgeoisie and the liberal tradition, the dissemination of democratic values. Frequently, they took another and related pleasure in knowing, preferably by heart, the uncontested great texts of our tradition.

Those pleasures had long been shared by others in conditions that might today seem improbable. During the first half of the nineteenth century, southern slaveholding women, many of whom spelled and punctuated imperfectly, sprinkled their private writings with unacknowledged quotations from the Bible, Shakespeare, and other acknowledged "greats." "Slings and arrows" to evoke the uncertainty of fortune, for example, abounds. During the same period, Harriet Jacobs, an extraordinary slave woman who would make her way to freedom and write of her experience in the first person, signaled her period of hiding as a "loop hole of retreat," a quotation from the eighteenth-century poet Cowper.[4] Margaret Fuller and Marianne Evans, who would publish under the name of George Eliot, devoured German philosophy. Zora Neale Hurston immersed herself in Shakespeare.[5]

Women's pleasure in the canon did not normally derive from personal identification with the main players of a restricted group: Othello and Shylock paid the tragic price of their race and their religion, respectively; Portia, who pleaded infidelity to her modest woman's mission, triumphed because of her outsider's ability to push the letter of the law to its logical extreme, but in her triumph reaped her reward by resuming her subservient woman's role. But those who did not find personal models in the canon were invited to identify with its values in accordance with the roles assigned them—an identification that primarily demanded submission to the proper order, to the dominance of others in matters political and moral. Many of the upper- and, increasingly, middle-class women who were introduced to the great tradition effected that identification by abstracting from their situation as women and assimilating the values to the heritage of their class or community.[6]

This canon, like the great tradition it articulated, was constructed by particular groups to serve their particular needs. It embodied one of the many possible narratives of our collective past, not all of them and not the only possible one. From roughly the end of the eighteenth century until the Second World War it figured as the premier story of our civilization. And even when presented in the form of "Western Civilization," it had a special resonance for citizens of the United States, for whom it read something like an official story throughout most of the life of our republic. Americans could proudly see themselves as collectively realizing its most generous aspirations—as a collective representation of the first great triumph of "progress," "individualism," and "democracy" over feudalism, barbarism, bigotry, and all the other forces of darkness against which the great tradition was forged.[7] Perhaps the enthusiasm with which we embraced the canon as our own pedigree helps to account for our present disillusionment. But that disillusionment also, and more immediately, stems from the unprecedented ascent of women, and of those men whom the canon had ignored, to some of the benefits of that individualism which the canon itself celebrated.

For myself and others like me, the pleasures of the canon bequeathed a double legacy. The first derived from the heady delights of our introduction to that republic of letters from which so many of our foremothers had generally been barred. The second derived from our immersion in the cultural traditions of those foremothers whom the canon seemed to ignore or openly repudiate. Two sets of stories presided over our induction into literacy. Initially, many of us did not insist that they meet but more or less easily tolerated their coexistence in imagination and intellectual life. Of such coexistence is "twoness"—and, at the limits, schizophrenia—made. The recent disenchantment with the canon doubtless derives in no small measure from a growing recognition of and impatience with that schizophrenia. Feminism—to say nothing for the moment of African-American and "ethnic" scholarship—has sharply, probably irreversibly, challenged the canon's claims to be "everybody's autobiography." Clearly it is not.

I grew up on the canon. My father, who was uncommonly interested in the mind and education of his oldest child, and who, long before "shared parenting" was named as such, took charge of me for the long hours between 4:00 and 8:00 in the morning, gently inducted me into its pleasures. We began, when I was about two, with simple stories. As the years progressed, we went on to more complicated ones, moving from Edgar Allan Poe and Rudyard Kipling to Rousseau and on to Dostoyevsky and Albert Camus. Before I had finished college, we had started to work on Peter Abelard, Thomas Aquinas, and Georg Friedrich Hegel. Heady stuff for a mere girl, but I loved it. It did not, in those days, occur to me that my identification with the people and events that were unfolding before my imagination was of primary concern, although I did harbor a special fondness for Queen Elizabeth I. (Identification was reserved for fiction, to which my mother introduced me and which down the years I have pursued as a kind of shadow education with my erstwhile college roommate.)

I uncritically accepted the terms of the discourse presented to me. Struggling to grasp the dictates of morality, I trembled vicariously at the wrath of the Hebrew prophets. Struggling to grasp the complexities of citizenship, I pondered Rousseau's conception of the general will. Struggling to grasp the exigencies of heroism, I devoured Camus's thoughts on the rebel. Entranced with the unfolding of democracy, I cheered the victors of the American and French revolutions, never suspecting that in those days, when the modern world was aborning, some women and some of the dispossessed had also tried to claim their rights. I never heard of Mary Wollstonecraft and did not even suspect the existence of a Toussaint L'Ouverture. The appearance of Jane Austen and George Eliot never led me to question their apparent lack of precursors, or even to read them as offering a critique of prevailing views of women's possibilities.

In retrospect, I can see that I was torn by contradictions I had no words to express. I did not give much thought to women's having been excluded from the debates that engaged me, even less to the implications of their exclusion for myself. I suspended my disbelief and identified with the causes, the values, the characteristics of my heroes. I claimed the canon as my own. Today, I principally regret that my failure of personal identification with the actors led me to miss all the concrete lessons about dealing with power that might have proved valuable to me as an adult. But then, I took great delight in the knowledge itself, in understanding how we as a people had come to be what we are and to think as we do. The structure of the events, the quality of the texts, and my ability to grasp them pleased me. I appropriated the tradition as my own, even if I could not recognize that my own kind, in the direct sense, had been largely excluded from it.

The canon, in its various guises, assumes individualism, as defined by men for their own purposes, to represent the purpose and embodiment of civilization, and it assumes that the pool of potential heroes is restricted to white, elite males. In the measure that it considers the reasons for the failure of some and the success of others, it does so within the framework of individual ability and character. In the measure that it includes occasional improbable success stories—the odd peasant lad who rises to the position of adviser to kings or popes or who produces a work of genius—it invariably emphasizes the recognition and reward of extraordinary individual merit, rather than the larger patterns of exclusion by gender, class, or race that systematically foreclosed most members of entire social groups from exemplary roles. In this important sense, the canon has, in general, equated the progress of elite white men with the rise and triumph of civilization and sanctified their position as its elect representatives and interpreters. Small wonder, then, that feminists and proponents of other excluded groups have complained that our official story is not their own.

Feminist scholarship has developed in large measure as a revolt against the claims of the canon to reflect the values and legacy of society as a whole.[8] During the past decades, feminist scholars have recovered a vast store of information on women, none of which bears much resemblance to what the canon would have led us to expect. Much of women's history has concerned private, or at least mundane, matters: the bearing and raising of children, the cooking of food, the carrying of water, the tilling of the soil—a great deal of hard work and the ubiquitous risk of death in childbearing. Much of women's experience has not been of much concern to those who have written history. And if women did normally demonstrate deep commitment to the cultural values of their communities, especially religion, those values in return offered women negative, or at least passive and subservient, views of themselves and precious few opportunities for leadership.

More surprising, women's history has revealed that throughout time women have engaged in the most dangerous public employments, including military action. Women have participated in, and even led, a variety of riots and protests, have exercised political power, and have participated in the most advanced culture of their societies. No woman has ever been pope, but short of that, women have done almost everything that men have done, albeit not as regularly or in comparable numbers. But if individual women have proved their abilities to accomplish almost anything, women as a group have not been viewed as capable of such accomplishments. Worse, women as a group have been largely excluded from the opportunity to prove their abilities according to their society's most prestigious definitions of excellence.

As in life, so in letters. At least a few women have always participated in the "high" culture of Western societies, even if their contributions have been largely ignored or acknowledged with condescending surprise. There have always been women who prided themselves on their learning, no matter how hard they had to struggle to acquire it and how frequently they had to express it in private.[9] The emergence of "polite" urban society and, especially, the rise of the novel as a genre drew ever greater numbers of women into cultural life. Many feminist scholars argue that women novelists in particular tended to write for other women, thereby inaugurating a distinct female discourse. Be that as it may, women did turn to novel writing in steadily growing numbers, did sell large numbers of their works, and did not normally receive the accolades of the male writers we now view as canonical.[10]

Today the defenders of the canon are reaping the whirlwind their predecessors sowed. For if the canon has been less than hospitable to women, much recent feminist scholarship has been resolutely hostile in return. In extreme form, the argument runs that the canon has always been militantly male and that it has silenced, thwarted, even brutalized women.[11] This extreme view does not merely dissect the "misogyny" of the tradition, it explicitly challenges the standards of quality on which it has been based. According to the logic, men began by controlling women's bodies and proceeded to control their minds, silence their voices, and trample upon their values. Some feminists insist that the very ideals of quality that the tradition embodies are a swindle—a male conspiracy to devalue women.

This line of reasoning, which has grave defects to accompany its insights, contributes to the case for an entirely distinct women's tradition. Women, it is argued, speak "in a different voice." The generalizations concerning women's "difference" cloak a host of specific claims. Women, in the most common example, devote their lives to nurturing life and, accordingly, hate war. Either innately or socially given to "maternal thinking," women are viewed, explicitly or implicitly, as pacifists. At the dawn of civilization, women's values informed the gentle, noncompetitive Minoan society, which tragically succumbed to the aggressive assault of warrior bands whose values have dominated all subsequent human societies.[12] Women are less likely than men to engage in the violation of nature. Since the early glimmerings of industrialization in the sixteenth century, there has been a natural affinity between women and what we now call ecology. Men, not women, have mined (Mother) earth, have turned waterways from their natural courses, have raped the land.[13] Women, according to this view, identify primarily with other women, rather than with men. They have been less attuned than men to the modes of self-assertive individualism, in part because its privileges have been denied them. Women have been less likely than men to say or write "I" with conviction, much less with anger. Women shroud their judgments in "silences." In political action, women are more likely than men to defend the needs and claims of communities, including small children, and less likely to embark on personal or collective conquest.

Elizabeth Janeway has developed the more serious features of this line of thought into a systematic critique of power as it has been used and abused by the great political figures of the Western tradition, arguing that women have specialized in the "powers of the weak."[4] In sum, the attempts to identify a specific women's tradition have, by and large, resulted in the identification of women with the values of nurture, pacifism, collective life—the diametric opposites of what are taken to be the values of men, especially as encoded in the canon. Accordingly, many women—not, I think, including Janeway—are tempted to dismiss the plea that we reclaim that legacy with defiance: Since men have forged it, let them keep it if they choose. It has nothing to offer women. Or, in an alternate formulation, it has nothing to offer humanity, which it has brought to the brink of nuclear holocaust.

There is an irony in this view of women's collective identity and collective dissent from the reigning truths encoded in the canon. For the women who oppose the tradition are, in large measure, espousing the view of themselves that it propounds. Sophocles depicts Antigone as championing the principles of family religion—of clan and kin and their gods—against those of the state. And he carefully identifies the conflict of laws with a conflict between genders: If Antigone can thus "flout authority / Unpunished, I [Creon] am woman, she the man." And again: "No woman shall be master while I live."[5] In the event, Creon's victory—the victory of the male state as the preserve of order—proves Pyrrhic. Yet Sophocles casts the tale of Antigone's rebellion against that order as a tragedy because he finds legitimacy in both sets of claims. She lost because the claims she represented were archaic and impeded the progress of civilization. Creon lost because he could not find a place for them in the new order he was trying to build.

The sense that women and men represent distinct sets of values pervades the canon. Different authors represent women's values in different lights, some insisting that women primarily represent the disruptive force of sexuality, others insisting that they represent the claims of private relations and nurture. But whichever perspective authors adopt, they invariably insist that the work of civilization requires the suppression or at least the containment of women's values. Even Shakespeare, who portrays Portia as triumphant in the name of mercy in a situation in which the unmediated claims of justice would have required delivering up the pound of flesh, represents her triumph as anomalous. In the comedies in which he depicts a succession of vital, attractive heroines, he invariably restores order by having them accept marriage as the sign of their proper female identity.[16] In so doing, Shakespeare prefigures the central values of individualism, which granted women even less independence before returning them to their ordained domestic roles. Goethe, in the breathtakingly popular *Sorrows of Young Werther*, graphically represents Lotte's embodiment of domestic femininity by regularly associating her not merely with love in general but with the pouring of milk and the provision of nurture.[17]

Goethe, like many other late-eighteenth- and nineteenth-century writers, entertained a highly favorable view of women's innate values, which he saw as the necessary anchor for male individualism. Charles Dickens demonstrated that even the most disturbing sequence of events in the most disorderly world could be resolved by an appropriate marriage.[18] In his hands, women's domesticity emerged as the antidote to chaos and corruption, although the condition of its beneficent effects was its privacy. Women worked their magic in the home, soothing brows, loving men, nurturing children. Should they fail in that mission, should they attempt independent action even in the form of well-meaning charity, the order of the home— and with it the order of the world—would collapse.

Even social scientists, notably Auguste Comte, underscored the importance of women's special virtues to social and cultural order. In Comte's complex model of modern society, women did not figure as active participants in the basic public roles, yet a woman represented the ultimate goodness. Comte, like many of his contemporaries, was beginning to represent women's values as a residue. In a world governed by the "scientific" principles of sociology, religion, charity, and nurture had no place, so they were relegated to the margin where they could be celebrated—even worshiped, as Clothilde de Vaux was to be worshiped in his "Religion of Humanity"—but not allowed to intrude in the necessary business of running the world.[19]

Some of Dickens's and Comte's contemporaries were already worrying about the dangers of women's sexuality, worrying that women could not so easily be marginalized and contained. Many of their successors became increasingly preoccupied with the dangers that women represented. From Schopenhauer to Nietzsche ("go to women, but do not forget the whip") and beyond, a strong current of misogyny resurfaced amidst the dominant view of women as inherently passive, as willing accomplices in their own subordination. In *Civilization and Its Discontents*, Sigmund Freud, who forcefully insisted upon the natural differences between women and men, pointed out that the position civilization accorded to women made them its natural and inescapable enemies.[20]

Traces of the anxiety that informed these men's determination to keep women in their male-defined place can be found throughout the Western tradition, although they acquired special force with the consolidation of individualism. It has not been the canonical writers so much as their interpreters who have obscured the place of women in those writers' reflections on society and the polity. Even those conservatives who seek the pedigree of (male) individualism in Plato and Aristotle would acknowledge that gender plays a premier role in their different visions of the nature of the public good.[21] In one way or another, women or the representation of gender figured centrally in the thought of Machiavelli, Hobbes, Locke, and Hume, to name but a few.[22] Most of those who wrote of individualism for men, preeminently Jean-Jacques Rousseau, wrestled with the questions that trouble feminists today.[23] Contemporary feminists reject their answers but recognize that they sketched the contours of the problem. Even those who, like Karl Marx, did not especially concern himself with women, invite scrutiny for their silences.

Consider such familiar canonical texts as Thomas Hobbes's *Leviathan* and John Locke's *Second Treatise on Government.*[24] Both explicitly discuss the notion of sovereignty during the period of the English Revolution. Both deservedly rank as classics of political theory. On the simplest level, Hobbes can be taught as an apostle of authority, Locke as an apostle of reasonable freedom. Centuries of commentary have swathed the texts in conflicting readings, including conflicts about their authors' possible relations to specific political positions. Commentaries notwithstanding, Hobbes and Locke can be rendered compelling and even "relevant" to students. On the assumption that both accepted the essentials of what C. B. MacPherson has called "possessive individualism," both can be shown to have responded differently to its implications.[25] Taken together, they lay bare the essentials of the inescapable struggle between the claims of social order and the claims of individual right. On those grounds alone they deserve their honored place in a meaningful ("relevant") canon.

Hobbes and Locke saw the individual as prior to society but differed on the implications. For Hobbes, the growth of individualism required an increase in centralized authority. Individuals must sacrifice their sovereignty upon entering society in order to enjoy the benefits of peace. For Locke, who saw individualism as grounded in labor, including the congealed labor of absolute private property, sovereignty resided in the individual and his property, from which even the government derived its authority. These familiar outlines acquire new meaning when subjected to an analysis of gender. Both Hobbes and Locke assumed that the individual was male. Both also frankly discussed the relation of women to that individual and, perhaps more interesting, to individualism in general.

Repudiating the venerable notion that woman's inferiority to man derived from Eve's curse, both Hobbes and Locke used women's theoretical standing as individuals to invalidate the religious foundations for political sovereignty, as propounded by Sir Robert Filmer.[26] Both also rejected the related argument from patriarchy, namely that men were natural rulers because of their status as fathers. Hobbes pointed out, in accordance with his model of the state of nature as the "warre of all against all," that women, like weak men, could kill strong men through cunning. This fledgling argument for equality between the sexes in nature did not lead him to advocate their equality in political society, although he came close to advocating a kind of equality in submission to absolute authority. But, in addition to that submission, he suggested that women contractually subordinate themselves to men in the interests of protecting their children. Locke was less generous. Having also admitted an original equality of women with men, he rapidly passed to the assertion that since "law and the customs of the country" had, in practice, instituted women's political subordination to individual men, the matter could be left there.[27]

The extent to which these classic texts lend themselves to a serious discussion of the relations between women, gender, and political theory has gone largely unnoticed.[28] It is not necessary to stretch the intentions of the authors, since both Hobbes and Locke clearly identified the relations between men and women—and the role of gender relations in society—as a cornerstone of any polity. More important, in contributing to a revolutionary bourgeois political theory, both found it necessary to postulate the theoretical equality of women to men, however rapidly they brushed it aside. A reading of their texts in the light of that theoretical imperative compels one to ask innumerable questions about the relations between gender relations and political relations. In effect, Hobbes and Locke were precociously attacking the time-honored notions of female inferiority. They did not repudiate the political and social necessity for the subordination of women, but they justified it on new grounds and, in so doing, opened the way to subsequent notions of female individualism and equality.

Changing discourses created new opportunities for discussion. Hobbes and Locke, whatever their particular views on actual relations in the world, prefigured systematic critiques of deference, hierarchy, and the particularistic worldview. By attacking Filmer's arguments for divinely or humanly ordained structures of authority, they struck a decisive blow at patriarchy. To be sure, they dismissed the notion of women's equality with men in practice, but their having even briefly postulated that equality in theory exposed the inherent radicalism of their attack on the principles of hierarchy. Increasingly, their followers would argue that for a man to be a responsible citizen he must be morally and economically autonomous—must not depend upon the will of another man. Mary Wollstonecraft, possibly under the influence of Adam Smith, vigorously attacked the debilitating effects of fashion on women, since it reinforced their propensity to dependence. The critique of dependence would have a long career and culminate in the campaign for the abolition of slavery. Hobbes's and Locke's ideas of individualism lay at the core of that ideological current. If Hobbes and Locke cannot be taken directly to represent the thought of women, or of laboring men, they did both respond to the social and political changes of their era and formulate the ideological categories in the name of which successive struggles for fuller social and political participation would be waged.[29] Significantly, the early British feminist tradition of which Joan Kelly has written emerged out of the same cultural matrix.[30]

One after another of the writers and theorists who are now taken as canonical wove gender into their visions of society and the polity. Gertrude Himmelfarb, a leading defender of the great tradition, herself wrote an illuminating book that demonstrated the significance of Harriet Taylor Mill's ideas on women's equality for the development of John Stuart Mill's political thought.[31] Himmelfarb, in fact, deplores Harriet Taylor Mill's influence on her husband, which she credits with moving Mill from an admirable conservatism to a dangerous liberalism. Not everyone would agree with her assessment, but it should now be impossible to teach Mill without serious attention to the ways in which women's relation to individualism transformed his thought. And it should be impossible to teach Harriet Taylor Mill without serious attention to the ways in which she tried to claim individualism for women.

The preoccupation with gender that percolates through literature and even the most abstract texts in political theory testifies, however indirectly, to the ubiquitous presence of women in social and political life. The developments that have produced the feminist critique of the canon have also produced the new social history and the new historicism. And even if much of this work has been developed by men on the same male-centered principles that govern the canon, it has, in general, proved more hospitable to women than the "great men and great ideas" posture of the canon.

Take the case of the French Revolution, which can and has been taught with only passing reference, or none, to the women who played such an important role in its unfolding. For some the exclusion would be justified on the grounds that you cannot possibly attend to every small radical sect when your real mission is to provide a sense of the logic of events, of the outcome, of the abiding political and intellectual legacy. Those who are now remembered as the great leaders of the revolution did not make that mistake. They took anxious account of those radical sects and the disorderly women who plagued their political lives. To consider their decisions in splendid isolation is to denigrate their political genius by ignoring the stern challenges they confronted.

Women did decisively contribute to the origins, progress, and consequences of the French Revolution. Women organized the *salons* in which many of the liberal ideas of the day were developed and disseminated. Women participated in, and frequently launched, some of the most portentous popular uprisings. A woman, Charlotte Corday, assassinated the popular leader Marat. Mme. Roland prodded, poked, loved, and influenced the Girondists. Marie Antoinette embodied everything that people most opposed or defended. Olympe de Gouges drafted a statement on the rights of women that earned her the scaffold at the hands of the Montagnards during the Terror. Different revolutionary groups held very different positions on the "woman question," the disposition of which played an important role in the ultimate outcome of the revolution. Almost all of the principal revolutionary leaders, however violently they differed on other matters, agreed on the necessity of women's subservience to men, but they disagreed mightily on the nature of that subservience and on the identity of the men who were entitled to it.

To teach the French Revolution as an exclusively male story is not merely unfair to women, it is to distort the French Revolution itself, which touched all aspects of society and the polity, including gender relations. Contemporaries viewed particular women and womanhood in general as premier signs of the social and political transformation they were effecting or opposing. Marie Antoinette, long dismissed as little more than a curiosity of historical trivia, has recently been revealed as a central symbol in the revolutionary period. Radical male journalists, notably Le Père Duchesne, devoted considerable energy to exposing her as the wanton embodiment of destructive female independence: sexuality and self-indulgence run rampant. They argued that she had, by her want of domestic virtue, turned the king into a cuckold and thereby poisoned the fabric of national life. Initially calling for her forced domestication, they eventually insisted that only her death could purify the nation. And from the ashes of her defeat rose the figure of Marianne, the symbol of revolutionary virtue, and beyond her the ideal of bourgeois domesticity.[32]

In general, the new social history and the new historicism have tended to develop in conformity with feminist assumptions about women's distinct values, although recent work is revealing that many women did not fit the model at all. All that Queen Elizabeth I had in common with prevailing myths of womanhood was her mythical virginity. Catherine de Medici, Catherine the Great, Rosa Luxemburg, Dolores Ibarruri ("La Passionaria"), and Indira Gandhi were pacifists? They are only a few exemplars of a venerable tradition of battling women, including poor women who throughout history have rioted for bread and against taxes. More disturbing, although hardly surprising, other work, like Claudia Koonz's splendid study of Nazi women, is revealing that many women did not embrace the equality and identity of women across class and racial lines.[33] Social history abounds with women who did not view themselves as patient Griseldas and did not view all other women as sisters.

The emphasis on social history and the new historicism—the shift from text to context—enriches our understanding of the canon but cannot alone satisfy feminists' determination to recover women's voices and perspectives. Neither social history nor the new historicism intrinsically foregrounds women's experiences and values, although in sensitive hands they may. Neither social history nor the new historicism intrinsically captures women's subjective perspective or autobiographies. Both can, however, forcefully underscore the centrality of gender in the development and interpretation of history and culture.

As a mediator between men's and women's stories, gender constitutes a good deal more than the stalwarts of the tradition want to deal with and a good deal less than many feminists think is women's due. But gender does properly capture the ways in which the relations between women and men undergird any society, polity, or culture. Gender is an objective—social, cognitive, or epistemological—rather than a subjective category. And, as a language, it offers a social, economic, political, intellectual, and even psychological structure for personal experience. Gender thus organizes experience from the perspective first of society and second of the observer of society.

The introduction of gender as one of the essential ways of telling the story of the past need not distort the past. It need not substitute a problematic women's culture for what we have been taught to regard as high culture. And it cannot create more women generals, prime ministers, presidents, and popes than we know there to have been, although it may restore some queens to the serious attention they deserve and it will assuredly recuperate some women writers and intellectuals who never merited the oblivion into which they have fallen. Nor will it transform bellicose women "princes" or all aspiring women intellectuals into closet pacifists and maternal thinkers. It will not, in short, radically transform the past, but it will significantly revise our view of the past—what we accept as innate or natural, how we assess different groups' opportunities to display excellence. Above all, it will revise our view of the canon and of history as our common legacy, which in turn will shape our attitudes toward our own possibilities for creating a good society.

In the interests of creating a usable past for elite men, those who have dominated society and culture have defined the polity and the Republic of Letters, those monuments of the good society, as male and have tended to associate the forms of worship and organization that they were leaving behind—Antigone's clans and gods—with women. The canon, especially as constructed to validate the triumph of individualism, contains a good deal about the triumph of male "rationality" over female "disorder." Women can hardly be expected to accept the story from that perspective, however much, as a first step, we do need to know it. But we especially need to understand the ways in which it has decisively contributed to feminists' own interpretation of women's distinct stories. For if the canon has not normally represented women's self-assertion, and has even less frequently represented it approvingly (think of Lady Macbeth), feminist scholarship has not done much better. Most feminist scholars, in their determination to expose the canon's and our culture's androcentrism, have protested the ways in which they have denied women's political and cultural authority but have then turned around and constructed a feminist theory that disconcertingly represents women in the same terms that the canon represented them. And, however understandably, feminist scholars have risked distorting the complexity of women's own stories.

I now recognize that, as a child, I was guilty of a lamentable failure of imagination. I could not understand the fuss about adopted children's wanting to know who their real parents were. From my perspective, anyone who had parents, adopted or not, and a good home should be willing to accept things as they were. The existential and ontological questions "Who am I?" "Where do I come from?" moved me not at all. It was difficult enough to work with the world you had been given; why bother about the worlds "we know not of"? I also did not want to know that I could not realistically aspire to the roles, all male, with which I tended to identify. I have learned that I was wrong on both counts and that both kinds of being wrong are related, and are related to the future of any justification for teaching the great tradition.

The creators and exponents of the canon have presented it simultaneously as collective history and as autobiography. The political and social changes of the recent past have exposed its claims to be autobiography as outrageous and fraudulent. Erosion has reduced its claims to be collective history as fraudulent. Much of the revolt against the canon has been fueled by the refusal to accept someone else's autobiography as our own, and by the insistence that—whatever the world may say—our own autobiography matters. Both these responses command respect: the orphan—even the secure, adopted child—does need to know who he or she is. However painful the knowledge, orphans need to know—at least must try to know—of their natural parents and their own special legacy. Proverbially, orphans tend to have fantasies about extraordinarily important and powerful parents. The truth rarely confirms the fantasies, but one can only admire the courage that can face those anxieties squarely, especially when the coveted knowledge may demonstrate not that the real parents were dukes or counts but that they were unfortunates who had a drinking problem, or not enough money to get married, or worse.

Similarly, those who have been excluded by the canon need to know the cause. They need to know why their predecessors did not win, why they lacked the power or the resources to impose their views, why their own kind did not tell the story. Here, as with real-life orphans, we ought to be suspicious of romantic answers. Most women, for example, do not appear to have shared a distinctive culture or opposed the reigning values of their societies in a consistent and programmatic fashion. But the more important point lies elsewhere.

The recovery of women's past illuminates and transforms our reading of the canon. It does not substitute for it. No one's autobiography could substitute for collective history, nor could anyone hope to reconstruct a personal autobiography without such a history. We cannot reclaim the legacy of the canon unless we understand and revise the purposes for which it was constructed. It is neither innocent nor transcendent—above all, not graven in stone—but rather, as Rousseau said of constitutions, engraved in the hearts of citizens. Today, our republic has poor prospects for survival unless it recognizes women as well as men as citizens and educates them to identify with the polity, rather than to define themselves as its natural opponents.

The postmodernist assault on power in all forms has, in some circles, led to a newly ferocious attack on the canon as nothing more than another manifestation of colonization and imperialism. From the postmodernist perspective, the canon embodies not merely the gender hierarchy of men's domination of women and the class and racial hierarchies of elite men's domination of the rest, but the West's domination of the world. Attacking the suspect epistemological status of any official narrative of an infinitely complex past, postmodernists reject the canon's claims to be objective and, beyond them, its claims to embody universal values. Like all other stories that purport to be objective, the canon becomes just someone else's story—and a not very interesting one at that. Worse, it becomes a story by which imperialists justify their domination.

The postmodernist attack has broadened the feminist attack to include all of those whose experience and values the canon ignored or denied. To that extent, the attack is both broadening and narrowing its implicit definition of culture—broadening by vastly increasing the numbers of participants; narrowing by tending to reduce culture to unmediated personal narratives. And although it has much in common with the feminist attack, it has introduced significant new dimensions. For where feminism has tended to focus on woman's experience and values in general, postmodernism has strongly emphasized diversity. In so doing, postmodernists have taken a strong stand in favor of the personalist and liberationist tendencies that have

Claims of a Common Culture

figured in individualism from the start, thus stretching the metaphors of colonization and imperialism to cover power in all its forms.

Frantz Fanon, psychologist and theorist of revolution, invoked the toll of colonization and imperialism when he wrote movingly of the feelings of black children in Martinique who opened their textbooks to read: "Our ancestors the Gauls. . . ." The lords of empire appropriate the history and the culture of those they dominate and substitute the history and culture of the metropolis. To be worthy, to advance, is to think oneself white—and male—and to accept the identity of your conquerors. Fanon, who went on from his Martiniquais beginnings to a French medical education and immersion in existentialist philosophy, came to believe that colonized peoples must throw off European social, political, and, perhaps especially, cultural domination through a purging violence. To be "liberated" the human spirit must rid itself of the manacles of other peoples' traditions, histories, languages, and patterns of reasoning.[34]

As metaphors, colonization and imperialism nicely capture the way in which many feminists have viewed the canon and even the way in which many students view it today. This hostility helps to explain the conservatives' claims of a crisis in liberal education and the failure of many liberals, to say nothing of radicals, to understand the conservatives' gnashing of teeth and beating of breasts. For the liberal and radical left, liberal education is not in crisis, at least not in the kind of crisis the conservatives see: it is manifesting a healthy adaptation to changing times and constituencies. Those who cry crisis are derided as chained to outmoded and authoritarian notions of what a liberal education should be, to outmoded notions of a "traditional" canon. Thus those of the liberal and radical left deny that the canon, even if it could be identified, is worth saving.[35]

The left refuses to understand that to settle for education as personal autobiography or identity means tacitly to accept the worst forms of political domination. Fanon was criticizing the substitution of French history for Martiniquais history, the substitution of the history of the imperialist power for that of the colonized people. He was invoking the right of colonized children to their own collective history. Beyond that, he was pointing toward the experience of colonization as a framework for a broader collective history, that included "the wretched of the earth." He assuredly was not arguing for the collapse of collective identity into its constituent stories. To the contrary, he saw the struggle for a new definition of the collectivity as essential to the political purpose and will of colonized peoples.[36]

Claims of a Common Culture

As Fanon's own intellectual hegira demonstrates, it proved difficult entirely to shake the thralls of Western culture. Throughout his life, notwithstanding his increasingly radical posture, Fanon himself remained tied to the European intellectual traditions that permitted him to formulate his rage on behalf of his downtrodden brothers and sisters. The same currents of thought, notably existentialism, which in Paris and its satellites have led to deconstruction and beyond, shaped his characterization of oppression as, above all, psychological domination. For Fanon, colonization primarily concerned the spirit and the psyche, and he demanded a "liberation" from those "mind forg'd manacles." In the end, he came close to arguing that colonized people must, if necessary, destroy the elevators, the machines, and all of the products of Western technology. If, in the process, they sacrificed the economic progress that might ensure material advance, they would, at least, have freed their minds and thus prepared the way to the establishment of their own polities. But even at the extreme, he cherished the ideal of collective resistance and collective identity.

In our global society the challenge of the non-Western world remains morally and politically compelling. Among feminists, Gayatri Spivak has impressively argued those claims, insisting that we recognize and assume responsibility for the destructive effects that capitalism wreaks in the lives of women throughout the world.[37] Without pretending to summarize her complex reasoning, I should suggest that her work, like that of Fanon, underscores the importance of collective identity and its historical development. It is hard to read her as calling merely for the proliferation of personal voices, however much she enjoins us to attend to voices that differ from our own. She may profitably be evoked, then, as exposing the personalist attack on the canon within the United States as a luxury of a highly developed, materially wealthy nation. But it should not pass unnoticed that the attack on the canon also includes a denial of our privilege and the rejection of our responsibilities as colonizers. To deny our complicity with material power by reducing it to an artifact of language and dissolving it in a myriad of personal voices is to deny our collective responsibility to the world in which we live.

Those who are attacking the canon do not see it this way. For them, the proliferation of personal voices betokens attention to the claims of non-Western peoples. According to the implicit logic of their arguments, attention to the multiple stories of those whom our canon has excluded amounts to attention to the colonized in general. Has not, after all, our culture colonized women, African-Americans, and others in the same manner that Westerners have colonized the peoples of Africa, India, and South America? Their logic exposes the power and the inadequacy of metaphor. As a metaphor, colonization does capture aspects of the relations between the canon and its orphans. As a reality—with the partial exception of the special case of African-Americans—it does not.[38] To the extent that the opponents of the canon believe themselves to be operating out of a political morality, they are misguided. To the extent that they wish to reduce all politics to the politics of language, they are irresponsible.

Fanon's emphasis on the need for a purging violence derived at least in part from his understanding of the compelling hold of European ideas and institutions on the minds of the colonized. As a psychiatrist, he believed that an outpouring of anger would help to restore to the colonized possession of their own minds—would exorcise the demons of centuries of domination and dependency. Mao Tse-Tung acted on a similar insight when he encouraged the Chinese peasants to execute their former landlords. We might debate the value of such strategies for Third World revolutionaries, but our conclusions would not necessarily apply to the education we propose to offer to American students. In any event, developments around the world, most notably in China, clearly demonstrate that social revolutionaries and ex-colonial peoples above all need Western, that is capitalist, technology and science. Their challenge remains to appropriate those techniques and technical knowledge without becoming mired in the historically attendant social and cultural values, some of which have been repellent. However elusive the connections, Western society did engender the scientific and industrial revolutions, which did not originate by a kind of spontaneous combustion in different parts of the globe.

Very likely, many American students do feel colonized in relation to the elite Western culture that has constituted the backbone of our humanistic education. Women and minority students in particular are, as it were, being asked to look at someone else's picture and acknowledge it as their own mirror image. Toni Morrison marvelously captured the dilemma in her novel *The Bluest Eye*, which opens with the words of the ubiquitous primer: "There is the house. See the house. See Jane run."[39] Repeating the quote several times, she progressively runs it together until, in the last version, there are no spaces between words, no punctuation, and no capitalization. White culture thus becomes the seamless web that permeates the mind and shrouds the image of African-American children. Morrison's protagonist survives the onslaught to tell the story, but Pecola, victim of the material as well as the cultural expropriation of African-American people, goes mad in her quest for blue eyes. The problem, as Morrison delineates it, is to combine the heritage of African-American communities with enough of the dominant culture to emerge as a whole adult.

The war on the canon reflects the general crisis in our culture, specifically the crisis of individualism. An individualism designed for the benefit of the few, universalistic rhetoric notwithstanding, is having difficulty in accommodating the claims of the many. The war over the canon essentially consists in a war between those who would preserve the older model of individualism, which rested upon the exclusion of women, African-Americans, and other dispossessed people, and those who would extend the claims of individualism equally to all. The defenders of the canon bemoan the crisis in the interest of restoring lost forms of domination, in particular the public and private cultural domination of elite white men and their surrogates.

This nostalgia especially plagues conservative—and even some liberal male—academics who formed their own sense of self-respect from their identification with a particular canon. Some, in particular Allan Bloom, strive if anything to extend the hegemony of individualism throughout history even as they continue to restrict the numbers of those who legitimately speak in its name.[40] Thus Bloom, like many other conservatives, places great weight on classical culture, notably Plato and Aristotle, on the grounds that the classical world constituted the cradle of individualism. But his enthusiasm, appearances to the contrary notwithstanding, leads away from history, not toward it. For Bloom's determined quest for the classical embodiment of individualism tends to remove individualism from the realm of history in order to raise it to a fundamental value and measure of our humanity.

Certainly intelligent and well-educated conservatives know full well that non-Western cultures historically took a different road from that of Greece and Rome and that those cultures have come to embrace individualism—to the extent that they have embraced it—under the impact of the West's conquest of the world. They therefore attribute to the West a privileged world-historical role that it emphatically has had; and they attribute to the West a superiority that remains debatable. The politics and ideology that lie barely hidden beneath the surface of this strategy should be lost on no one, and blacks and other nonwhites have not been slow to charge imperialist apologetics. Among other niceties, the conservative argument implies, in a manner reminiscent of the linear theory of history advanced by dogmatic ("vulgar") Marxists, that the West has been civilizing the rest of the world by bringing it to a realization of its own humanity—humanity here equated with Western concepts of individualism. It is, moreover, worth noting that some feminists, who strongly oppose conservative politics and educational views in this country, implicitly follow the conservative commitment to the superiority of individualism by assuming that Western bourgeois feminism offers a superior model for women of the non-Western world.

This association of the canon with the essence of our humanity has generated a sharp reaction within elite academic circles. Those who explicitly reject the canon's anthropomorphic form especially oppose the assumptions of "bourgeois humanism" with its emphasis on the personal subject or author, or the "great leader." They offer instead society-as-text and text-as-society, and both as process or system. Attacking the concept of the independent self, or subject, they insist that the self should be understood as a "subject position," a shifting configuration within textuality or discourse. The self reduces to the articulation of specific social or textual possibilities. The words are there to be said; the subject (the one who says those particular words) just happens to be at that discursive place at that time. Although many exponents of these theories claim that "the deconstruction of identity is not the deconstruction of politics" but rather it "establishes as political the very terms through which identity is articulated," their views have contributed to the disillusionment with values that had been tailored to the measure of man.[41] And whatever their claims to speak in the name of the excluded and oppressed, they have done little or nothing to reestablish the accountability of the humanities to a society that can tolerate dissident voices.

From one perspective, these critics of the canon represent an attempt to shore up academic elitism by casting intellectual work in a highly specialized, abstract, and even arcane language. From another, they, if inadvertently, represent the cutting edge of a radical democratization that banishes the element of identification and turns the humanities into a depersonalized game that anyone with the proper analytic training can play. As for those who lack the special training and just like to read books, may God help them—democratically of course. When, in other words, the emphasis falls more on critical virtuosity than on the text itself, there is less need to understand the text in relation to the tradition as a whole—less need to have read a large number of texts.[42]

This democratization has more to do with the politics of the academy—

who has a chance to get a Ph.D., to teach, to receive tenure—than with the politics of the larger world. For, as Barbara Christian has argued, from the perspective of many of those previously excluded from identification with the canon, the death of the subject or the death of the author, however "democratic," seems somewhat premature, if, indeed, it does not look like the old elitist swindle in new democratic dress.[43] Surely it is no coincidence that significant elements of the Western white male elite proclaimed the death of the subject at precisely the moment at which it was being forced to share that status with women and with the peoples of other races and classes. And how wonderful that the announcement of the death of the author has come at precisely the moment at which the authorial claims of women and blacks have begun to gain recognition.

With the growing convergence between post-structuralism and postmodernism, those who are proclaiming the death of the subject seem increasingly to be joining forces with those who are proclaiming the proliferation of voices, although more out of cynicism and disillusionment than commitment. They thereby reinforce the position of those who oppose the canon out of commitment to the excluded voices and who, rather than abolishing the subject, would prefer to multiply it out of frankly political motives. Attacking the idea of the canon as the legitimate embodiment of our culture, they are attacking the residual notions of hierarchy that it embodied. In their view, the canon must be forcibly abolished, and in its place a thousand flowers must bloom, although they do have a disquieting tendency to dismiss voices of which they do not approve as "weeds." In this respect, they borrow from the militant psychology of liberation that Fanon and Mao were invoking.

Increasingly, the lines are being drawn between those who would retain the canon in its pristine purity and those who would demolish it. Both positions directly reflect important political tendencies within our society; both directly testify to the crisis of individualism; both irresponsibly bypass the main issue that confronts our culture, our education, and our conception of justice. If there is any good news to be drawn from the battle over the canon, it must be that culture and education matter, however poorly they are currently being served.

The canon we have inherited, whatever its contemporary limitations, has demonstrably articulated the values and the relations of power of Western civilization in general and our nation in particular. Today, under the impact of massive changes, its once-sturdy foundations are about as solid as quicksand. The conservative attempt to restore the canon by fiat is, as its detractors claim, a partisan political gambit with poor prospects. Nor is there any reason to believe that even if the restoration from above could be imposed it could successfully engage the imaginations of those we most need to draw into identification with our national purpose. More likely, a successful counterrevolution would result in ever widening alienation. In the present climate, it would be easy to abolish the canon, although in that summary abolition, we would be, first, denying our history, our links to our past, and, second, forsaking the ideal of a common culture. Unfortunately, these consequences themselves seem to enjoy widespread and ominous support on the left.

Unless we agree that there is a place for some canon in our culture and education, the demand to revise it to take account of gender, race, and class makes no sense. We would include or exclude references to these claims on a purely personal basis. Our decision would reflect whim, or perhaps character or politics, but little else. Paradoxically, those who reject the narrowness of the established canon but who remain committed to the validity of a canon—of some collection of texts that reflects a common culture—may well be the true custodians of liberal education and of the humanities. For those who insist on expanding the canon take seriously the political function of a humanistic education. They also doubtless believe that such an education must, in some measure, be accountable to the collectivity of its constituents—to a "national community," however internally variegated and periodically rent.

Contrary to the pretensions of romantics and cynics, myths serve poorly as foundations for identity, much less for political action. We who are teachers do our students no favor by pretending that the past consisted primarily of the popular cultures of laboring people or the personal writings of elite women. We do them no favor by ignoring kings and presidents and by pretending that our personal favorites rival Shakespeare as a poet or Plato as a philosopher.

To throw out the canon does not solve the problems of women and minority students any more than the expurgation of all traces of Western technology solves the problems of colonial peoples. Throwing out the received histories and culture only makes things worse. For, if you do not include a heavy dose of the history of elite white males, how do you explain why women and members of minorities are not running the world? Perhaps we could include white male history and culture as the story of the un-relieved imposition of force and violence, but, then, how do we explain thousands of years of submission by those we claim to honor and respect? One of the more difficult tasks that face those who have been excluded from the corridors of political and intellectual power is to accept the history of their oppression or exclusion and to transform it into a base for future action. In other words, the transformation of the canon in response to changing constituencies has less to do with rewriting the story than with reinterpreting it.

The appropriate place and function of the canon in our own culture and the attendant attempts to revise survey courses in the humanities present especially delicate problems. Motivation for revision stems in large part from the alienation of students from an elite culture that appears to have nothing to do with them. Recent experience suggests that we best succeed in engaging their imaginations by invoking their own experience—a step that is ordinarily essential to establish any student's relation to the humani-ties. But it is not enough. As a curriculum, the humanities must offer the student a perspective on personal experience; it must inspire pride from models the significance of which they can be taught to recognize. Today the canon no longer appears to offer that perspective or those models.

All the humanities focus on problems of values and human relations, problems of authority and freedom in society. The humanities as a canon, a body of principal texts, have taken shape in conjunction with the rising commitment to humanism as a form of individualism. The texts that have dominated the canon for at least the past century have privileged the ideals of responsible individualism, rationalism, and universalism. The emphasis on rationalism and universalism has proven decisive, for it has illuminated the extent to which the canon was developed as a weapon in the struggle against hierarchy, dependence, and particularism—the extent to which the canon we have inherited has been associated with the history of admirable modern Western notions of freedom, as well as with less admirable aspects of the ideology of individualism.

Blinded by their disputes over the appropriate texts to teach, both conser-vatives and liberals minimize the extent to which the idea of a liberal education, above all, has embodied the commitment to a common culture. And if our common culture, in contrast to specific texts, is the issue, then crisis there is, if only in the sense of fundamental change. Our culture as a whole suffers from a gap between words and things, between official discourses and the world. That gap has opened the space for the questions and proposed revisions of those who are challenging the status of the canon. The gap strengthens the case of those who view the canon as arbitrary, artificial, and politically biased. Perhaps more alarming, the gap strengthens the case of those who would abolish the idea of any canon at all.

The demand for relevance in education seems plausible. After all, the initial function of the canon was to provide selected individuals with a collective history, culture, and epistemology so that they could run the world effectively. The canon emerged as the privileged texts of what functioned as a collective autobiography and the foundation for identity. Individuals do require histories, cultures, and epistemologies to make informed choices and to act politically. But at some point the attack on the received canon shifted ground. Having initially been waged in the name of its orphans' right to know their own story, the war on the canon rapidly moved to the individual's right to education as a personal history, a parochial culture, and a private epistemology. Today, under the influence of postmodernism, that tendency is escalating into a full-scale repudiation of the possibility of distinguishing among the intrinsic merit of various texts. The combined impact of these radically personalist and historicist attacks has effectively sacrificed the ideal of collective identity that constituted the canon's most laudable feature.

Since in theory it should not be difficult for the canon to take account of the feminist challenge by introducing the essential woman as the counterpart of the essential man, it is difficult to understand the force of conservative opposition to such a move in simple class or racial terms. To the contrary, it should be easy to imagine a revitalized canon that celebrates women's admittedly belated progress toward individualism. And even if we accept the premise that by nature the essential woman differs from the essential man, as both the canon and feminist theory have been known to suggest, it should be possible to replace the unitary subject or (male) individual of the canon with a more complex vision that takes gender difference as central to both men's and women's identities. But today the attacks on the canon have moved well beyond such solutions.

The texts that constitute the canon owe their status to a process of selection. Although discriminations remain difficult, the criteria for selection seem to include some uneasy mixture of quality, theme, and representativeness.

Those who defend the inherited and unrevised canon would doubtless insist primarily on standards of quality: The selected texts, or at least the authors, enjoy their position as a result of the incontestable superiority of craft, reasoning, and execution. They are the best. Next, the defenders of the canon would insist that their preferred texts develop central themes in Western culture. Finally, they would offer the texts as representative of that culture.

Teaching the humanities in historical context offers the best—indispensable—way to introduce students to the tension between the tradition and the society that engendered it. Recent scholarly tendencies, not merely on the right, have frowned upon the reduction of texts to the putative influences that shaped them and have favored a return to something that resembles the New Criticism, which viewed texts as irreducible entities to be taken on their own terms. But there is a broad ground between the purist view of the text and the reduction of text to the life of its author. Texts can, legitimately, be taken as articulations of the societies that produced them. The strategy rests on the assumption that all authors are, in some sense, hostage to the society and culture in which they live. In this respect, authors work with the images and questions that lie to hand. Consequently, it becomes legitimate to probe a text for what it does not say as well as for what it does say. It also becomes legitimate to query the functions of the text in its broader context. Texts vary in their explicit indications of their contexts and silences. In instances in which the familiar texts present a seamless front, in which they fiercely resist their own deconstruction—and few successfully do so—other texts can be substituted.

The representativeness of canonical texts can be evaluated on various levels. The techniques of reader-response criticism permit attention to the relations between authors and those they thought they were addressing. An overwhelming proportion of our canonical texts have a polemical edge. Their authors are arguing in favor of one or another position. So what did authors argue for, whom did authors argue against, and who was likely to have composed their readership? The next step concerns the more general relation of authors' ideas to the ideas of their epoch. Here an admittedly less-than-precise analysis of correspondence could be helpful: specific formulations of ideas relate to other formulations of ideas. We cannot establish a causal relation between the two, but we can identify the correspondences and frequently even the likely paths of dissemination.

It may be misguided to insist upon too sharp a distinction between high and popular culture. The canonical texts of much of the Western tradition took shape against the backdrop of and in interaction with a predominantly oral popular culture. Indisputably, many intellectuals wrote only for other intellectuals, lay and clerical, but they did not write in isolation from the culture of the people among whom they lived. Above all, most, including clerics, did not write in isolation from the women of their own class.[44]

The possible correspondences between the texts of the canon and the broader culture at best suggest only that elite culture had something to do with the society from which it derived. Elite culture did not express the intentions, feelings, or perceptions of laboring people and rarely those of women, even elite women. Especially from the Renaissance on, elite culture tended to generalize from the experience of a very small group of men whom it identified with humanity, or "man." Yet that elite culture can be taught from the perspective of gender, class, and even race, if we are prepared to accept attention to issues of gender, class, and race as proxies for the subjective testimony of those excluded from the most exalted roles. For some, who would prefer to abolish the idea of elite culture entirely, that is a big "if."

Yet that elite culture functioned in relation to women, the lower classes, and some people of color analogously to the way in which imperialism functioned for colonized peoples. At worst, it denied the values and perceptions of all others and imposed itself as an absolute standard. It also exercised a powerful hegemony. Since those who developed it spoke in the name of power, progress, and, increasingly, rationalism, it commanded emulation or excited envy merely by virtue of that power. Even those who most intransigently opposed the individuals or classes for which the elite culture spoke frequently sought to claim its benefits for themselves. Significant numbers of intellectual women must surely have sought to "think like a man," for men had successfully identified themselves with the most sophisticated and compelling modes of thought. The successful identification is the point.

The canon, however we constitute it, can best be taught if recognized, at least in part, as a kind of political spoil. The canon, or the power to speak in the name of the collectivity, results from social and gender relations and struggles, not from nature. Those who fashioned our collective elite tradition were the victors of history. Their ability to write as authorities has derived from their social and political position, not so much as individuals but as members of a gender, a class, a race. Quality, in this perspective, was ascribed to those able to hone their voices and their crafts so that they emerged as the "best" among a previously restricted group. Their victory constituted an important feature of all our histories. If we remain bound to their accomplishment, they remain bound to our subordination. Hegel's discussion of lordship and bondage could serve us well here as the primary text.[45]

Any definition of the canon would include authors who produced texts that could appropriately be subjected to the analysis of gender, class, and race. Gender remains the easiest to decode, for gender constituted a primary category of social and cognitive organization for most peoples. Class and race pose greater but hardly insurmountable challenges. It is possible, with little difficulty, to select texts by standard canonical authors that discuss issues of gender, class, and race. It is possible, in the spirit of contemporary theory, to view teaching as an exercise in hermeneutics: we reread our texts from the perspective of contemporary concerns. And no—pace Mr. Bloom —such readings need not obliterate either the intrinsic quality of the texts or the specific concerns of their authors. After all, conservatives themselves engage in precisely such hermeneutical readings when they trace the lineage of individualism from Plato to our own time. Nor need we reject in toto the conservatives' argument that the truly great writers conveyed transcendent, timeless, and universal values. Even those who reject such absolutes ought to be able to recognize the world-historical power and continued relevance of the ideas of a Plato or Aristotle or Shakespeare. And what about the Bible, which, since the fall of Rome, has figured as the primary text for most Western women?

The entire focus of conventional courses can be changed by the themes we select. If one rejects all the pieties about the rise and triumph of the individual as the manifestation of progress and civilization, it should be possible, for example, to examine the tension between freedom and authority for society at large or to focus on the shift from particularism to individualism. Cynthia Jordan has recently demonstrated the rich possibilities of rereading familiar stories and including those of sisters as a counterpoint to those of brothers.[46] In short, it should be possible, without doing violence, to present the individual as the issue in the debate rather than as the predetermined result or teleological center.

In addition to reinterpretation or thematic reorganization, the canon must be expanded, although hardly by substituting popular ballads for Shakespeare, much less *Star Trek* for Faulkner. Because access to literacy has so frequently been limited by gender, class, and race, we do not have a large pool of women, working people, and people of color to draw upon, although the numbers expand considerably from the eighteenth century on. To the extent that women were long excluded from the organizations that engendered various professional discourses, especially philosophy, they were unlikely to have written much that could compete with the work of the outstanding men.[47] Or, to be blunt, women's opportunities more often than not led them to write in the margins of, when not in outright opposition to, the dominant culture. And when opportunity permitted them to write within it, they—Queen Elizabeth I, Mary Astell, and Louisa McCord— were likely to preach the necessity for women to subordinate themselves to their husbands.[48] Or perhaps, like Émilie du Châtelet, they might ignore women and gender entirely.[49] The exceptions to these general trends deserve a recognition that they too infrequently receive. Christine de Pizan, Mary Wollstonecraft, Harriet Taylor Mill, to name but a few of the most obvious, belong in the canon. After 1850, the choices become numerous. Virginia Woolf is a current favorite but can hardly stand for all the rest. What of Mme. de Staël, George Sand, Harriet Jacobs, George Eliot, Margaret Fuller, Anna J. Cooper, Charlotte Perkins Gilman, Simone de Beauvoir, Rosa Luxemburg, and Zora Neale Hurston? These are but a few random choices.

Marginalized and suppressed groups are, by definition, largely excluded from membership in the Republic of Letters. The excellence on which that Republic has prided itself remains embarrassingly bound by gender, race, and class. Its honorary members have usually been asked to leave their origins at the door. But it is in the nature of a vibrant culture to offer more than it intends. Modern criticism reminds us that even a "reactionary" text may raise contradictions that it imperfectly resolves, whereas even a "revolutionary" text may embody a deep commitment to the culture it is purportedly attacking.

The status of the canon has taken on unprecedented political significance. The canon has faltered, in large measure, as a consequence of the unprecedented expansion of higher education in our time. Those who are launching the attack on it claim to be speaking, as Robert Scholes has put it, in the name of the intrinsic interest of all forms of "human expressiveness."[50] Most of those who are defending it have been determined to reverse the expansion and to identify higher education, and our official culture, with a narrow elite. To defend the claims of personal experience in the face of that project is to fall victim to its most sinister implications and to dispossess the excluded as readily as the canon excluded the dispossessed. The challenge is not to condemn quality as anti-democratic—a miserable aim and a sure formula for well-deserved defeat—but to reclaim it for a reinvigorated national democracy. To reclaim the canon is to insist on the necessity for that common culture which defines us as the products of a common history and the members of a collectivity—the heirs of Western civilization.

Today, Western civilization has come under attack from within and without its confines. Its protracted monopoly of technology and attendant military might has permitted it to impose itself throughout the world. For the non-Western world, that imposition has consisted in conquest and colonization, a direct and indirect assault on the integrity and sovereignty of peoples and nations. Non-Western peoples have had enough, however much they sensibly acknowledge their dependence upon Western technology if only to improve the standard of living and self-defense of their people. Many Western peoples are also claiming to have had enough, without acknowledging that they have, however unequally, reaped substantial material benefits from Western dominance. Thus Western feminists who dismiss the canon as an exercise in colonization confuse the metaphor with the substance. Like it or not, in global perspective, we are the colonizers, not the colonized; the canon is the repository of the history of our people, not that of our conquerors. For better or worse, we are also, as recent events in Eastern Europe and China testify, the model for the aspirations of people around the world.

The moving finger, in this instance, having writ, will move on, independent of our piety or wit. No attack on the canon, nor even a successful repudiation of it, could change one iota of the distinct relations of domination and subordination among and within genders, classes, or races that have made us what we are. Nor could the expansion and reinterpretation of the canon change who and what we are, although they could help us to understand how we got to be the way we are and how we might do better. The unrevised canon, with all its faults, has represented a genuinely great civilization that has led the world in establishing the claims of individual rights while upholding the claims of social order. The challenge to the canon directly concerns the balance between individual right and social order and especially the interpretation of individualism. The defense of individual rights and the insistence that the state's claims against the individual be unambiguously justified are one thing. The celebration of the personalist and atomizing tendencies of the ideology of individualism are another. Under the guise of an effort to reclaim an American past rooted in the Western tradition, the struggle over the canon is emerging as a struggle for our present and future—for the contemporary interpretation of an individualism that has ruthlessly excluded countless numbers of our people, even as it offered them their highest aspirations. We are now playing for high stakes, which the contending parties are increasingly defining as common culture on the old terms or no common culture at all. Both are threatening our ability to take pride in our national culture and the larger tradition of which it is a part. Without that pride and the acknowledgment of the common culture on which it is based, we would lose the grounds for transforming it for our own times.

We can no longer restore the original version of the canon as everybody's autobiography. Nor, however great the temptations, can we afford to surrender to the anarchy of an infinite number of personal autobiographies. Our canon and the great tradition it embodies constitute the collective history without which none of our individual stories makes sense. We now face the challenge of rewriting it as a collective history that is not the monopoly of a single group, a single perspective. In our own time, as much if not more than ever, the relation between the individual and collective lives of peoples presents difficult problems of justice, morality, and politics. The task that confronts our canon's orphans is not to commit inadvertent suicide by destroying it but to reclaim it for themselves. For only they, and those who accept their just claims, can preserve the large part that remains indispensable and revitalize the whole for us all.

8

AMERICAN INDIVIDUALISM

BETWEEN COMMUNITY

AND FRAGMENTATION

Since the first half of the nineteenth century, if not earlier, the relation between American culture and the Western tradition has bedeviled American intellectuals. Most notably, Ralph Waldo Emerson tried to convince his fellow Americans that they could match Old World standards of cultural excellence while developing a distinct voice and perspective appropriate to their coming of age as a nation. Today, the concept of national culture seems, if anything, more elusive than ever, especially since the current attacks on the notion of a canon implicitly contest its validity. The emphasis on diversity of experience and multiplicity of voices suggests that to speak of a national culture is to privilege the experience of an elite at the expense of the many. This is nonsense. Americans, in all their diversity, have cherished a strong sense of national identity that, however fluid, has been firmly grounded in the Declaration of Independence, the American Revolution, and the ratification of the Constitution, grounded, that is, in the events that established the United States as something new under the sun—the first large democratic republic in history.

Through the years, this identity has expanded to encompass historically unprecedented waves of immigration and a material prosperity that have confirmed the image of the United States as the land of democracy and opportunity. National identity remains elusive, but, like love, if it remains impossible to define precisely, most people impart to it genuine meaning. For present purposes we may recognize that a commitment to freedom, democracy, and equality—however difficult to reconcile in theory and however much violated in practice—has placed a firm stamp on all our people, male and female, black, white, and "ethnic." That that political culture has its roots in the initial Anglo-Saxon and Celtic Protestant immigration to America changes nothing, although it speaks well for early Anglo-Saxon and Celtic Protestants.

Since World War II, American Studies has emerged as a distinct discipline that concerns the nature of our "Americanness" in all its varied manifestations, and that has, from the start, been tempted to see itself as the special custodian of our sense of ourselves as a people and a nation. (What does it mean to be an American?) Until recently, American Studies, like our culture at large, tended to answer that to be an American meant to be, or to aspire to become, white, Protestant, middle-class, male, and probably from the Northeast.[1] Longfellow, Whittier, and other representatives of the genteel tradition, and then Emerson, Hawthorne, Melville, and their successors, represented the presumed essence of American culture.

The last two decades have shattered those illusions and turned American Studies into a battleground, with the concept of American identity as the stakes. Today we recognize Americans as female as well as male, black as well as white, poor as well as affluent, Catholic or Jewish as well as Protestant, and of diverse national and ethnic backgrounds. On occasion, even southerners receive some attention, although white southerners rarely do, especially the more affluent. The last two decades have also witnessed a growing restiveness with the assumption that the culture of a privileged few could adequately represent the specific beliefs and practices of the many varieties of Americans.

Our new eclecticism has included considerable soul-searching about what we mean by culture, with a general tendency to move toward a broad definition that includes the sum of any people's activities, practices, and beliefs, and it has questioned the hierarchies that privilege some forms of cultural expression over others. The immediate casualty has been the willingness to accept the special place of "high" literary culture in our national self-representation.[2] The long-term casualty has been the possibility of acknowledging any American national culture at all.

The sharpness of the reaction against the equation of American culture with high literary culture testifies to the prior success in linking American culture with American identity even as it reflects the general mood that has led to the attacks on the canon of the Western tradition. Those who reject the literary canon as the primary embodiment of American identity reject it as "not my canon or that of my people." If that canon ignores or demeans African-American women, how can an African-American woman be expected to acknowledge it as the highest expression of her identity as an American? The notion of culture as a powerful articulation of identity has thus emerged from the debates essentially unscathed, even as the battle over whose identity continues to rage. Thus, the postmodernists stake their conception of a transformed culture on expanding the number of voices to which we attend in order to let groups that have been excluded speak directly of their own experience.[3]

That battle, which pits conservatives against liberals and is, as conservatives are wont to remind us, political to its core, is leading, directly or indirectly, to the replacement of a long-uncontested hegemony of white, male authors by a plurality of women, African-Americans, and members of various minority or marginalized groups. Increasingly, previously acknowledged canonical texts are, directly or indirectly, being replaced not merely by alternate texts such as domestic fiction and slave narratives but by films, television shows, folktales and songs, artifacts, quilts, even comic books. For if many conventional courses are persisting largely untransformed, they are losing their exclusive status and are being forced to compete with new courses devoted exclusively to new intellectual fashions. Increasingly, the conventional methods of history and literature are giving way to cultural anthropology, ethnography, oral history, the study of material culture, reader-response criticism, the sociology of literature. To its practitioners, the new American Studies embodies a welcome opening to pluralism; to its critics, it is little more than a modern Tower of Babel. The battle for American Studies thus intersects with and articulates the larger struggle that encompasses all of the humanities—our attitudes toward education, culture, texts, and criticism.[4]

Nationally, the struggle has attracted more attention than matters of cultural and educational policy normally warrant. From William Bennett's pronouncements on education to Allan Bloom's *The Closing of the American Mind* to the debate over the Stanford curriculum and beyond, tempers have flared over the purpose and content of teaching. Hence, the special case of American Studies has received careful scrutiny in the pages of *The Chronicle of Higher Education*.[5] Today the most pressing question appears to be whether any new synthesis is possible or even desirable. How, in other words, are we to weave the various cultures that we are learning to recognize and appreciate into a general view of American culture?

The possibility of synthesis remains confused by the perceptions of the participants in the debate, who frequently see it as a struggle among academic groups or generations as well as among ideas. Thus Joan Scott, in a forum at the American Historical Association, openly conflated the introduction of new perspectives with the accession of new people, and there is reason to believe that her position enjoys widespread support.[6] Today, both sides of the debate feel embattled: the "old guard" perceives a massive assault on its position and a disquieting triumph of new subjects and methods; the exponents of those new subjects and methods insist that they are defending a minority cause against entrenched powers. At a recent meeting of a national association, whose program reflected a substantial increase in sessions devoted to women, African-Americans, and popular culture and a concomitant decline in sessions devoted to high culture and formal politics, I had a long discussion with a young woman scholar who perceived the meeting as dominated by elderly, established, white men. She could not begin to understand that significant numbers of those whom she viewed as the custodians of orthodoxy were no longer even attending the association's meetings because they believed, with good reason, that the meetings had been captured by the newcomers.

Much of the recent work in American Studies has been framed by the larger battle and self-consciously intended as an assault on established academic power. In a necessary first step, this work has, above all, attempted to establish the cultural integrity of noncanonical culture. The determination to right perceived wrongs has frequently led to an identification with the excluded, but, ironically, that identification has obscured the extent to which the new perspectives have, in fact, triumphed. Today, those who claim to represent the claims of the "excluded" are riding high, while conservatives rank as the principal, embattled defenders of an unpopular position.

The new vision of American Studies rests on the assumption that the heretofore dominant tradition, which studiously ignored complex class, race, and gender relations, defended the prerogatives of a small elite to speak in the name of American society and culture as a whole. In so doing, it marginalized or silenced outright the voices of those who did not belong to the white, male elite. To rectify that neglect, scholars have succeeded in imaginatively reclaiming the voices, representations, productions, and values of the oppressed and excluded, and they have demonstrated the cultural strength and richness of those who have been ignored. Yet the conceptual implications of this work remain, on the whole, as fragmented as the individual studies on which they are based. As Linda Kerber insisted in her keynote address to the meeting of the American Studies Association in 1988, American Studies scholars have been "early to widen the definition of what constitutes a text," to understand the links among Emerson's essays, Harriet Wilson's *Our Nig*, and Campbell's soup cans but have, withal, "remained too much a part of the complacency and status quo we deplore."[7]

That next step must, in Kerber's sensible view, consist in understanding "difference as a series of relationships of power, involving domination and subordination," and must push us "to use our understanding of the power relations to reconceptualize both our interpretation and our teaching of American culture." But proponents of the new work have been slow to interest themselves in weaving their rich recoveries into a new view of American culture as a whole. Some promising exceptions notwithstanding, they have given rise neither to a new synthesis nor a clear theory.[8] Thus, for example, Werner Sollors's arresting study, *Beyond Ethnicity*, offers "consent" and "descent" as fruitful metaphors for understanding the relation of ethnic cultures to the dominant culture but says little about the specific writers and texts of the dominant culture or even about race and gender, much less class.[9] The challenge remains to understand the pattern of marginalized cultures in relation to each other as well as in relation to the canonical culture, and, especially, the relation between the canonical culture and the idea of a national culture.

The ideas of canonical and national have largely developed in tandem, although they have potentially different implications. The most recalcitrant defenders of canonical culture normally have in mind a Western tradition that begins with the Greeks, whereas the defenders of national culture have to wrestle with American culture's long-standing sense of itself as derivative, secondary, or "colonial" in relation to that tradition. The conservatives do not help much on this score, for they give scant attention to the new scholarship, except for occasional angry outbursts against its allegedly excessive claims and misreadings, and certainly do not propose a general theory or synthesis that would take account of its claims. The critics of the canon, for their part, normally conflate its specifics with its claim to represent all of American experience; accordingly, they dismiss the possibility of a core experience. The ghost of the canon lingers in their writing as an object of attack, but no successor has taken its place. Thus, the cultures of women, African-Americans, working people, and ethnic groups are normally considered for their specific dynamics and in relation to the canon or dominant groups that excluded, oppressed, or ignored them, but rarely in relation to other previously ignored groups. Identity in this perspective becomes primarily identity in relation to other members of the group, and community becomes primarily the community of the group itself. Emerson's goal of a national culture dissolves in the concern to appreciate the discrete (sub)cultures on their own terms. Emerson might wish to protest, but in truth he asked for it. His modern followers have merely carried out the logic of his romance with the individual.

In a sense, this attitude flows logically from many of the writings that are being rediscovered. Women, African-Americans, Jewish-Americans, and others who were seeking to capture their distinct experience normally focused on their relations as writers and as individuals with what they accepted as "American" culture—on their own experience of "twoness." Feminist and African-American literary studies have, perhaps, most directly and systematically explored the power of that sense of "twoness" among those whom they study.[10] They have especially attacked the assumption that the quintessential American self can be represented by the solitary white male individual and have focused on the distinct experience of those whose identities that representation denied.[11] In so doing, they have primarily sought to recreate the alternate senses of self and community of women and African-Americans and, in the process, to expand the conception of literary studies by deploying new methods and exploring a variety of new topics. They have especially questioned the assumption that texts may enjoy privileged status on the basis of their quality, as if they existed independent of society and history.

Frequently the new scholarship of race and gender, in insisting that the status of texts depends precisely upon society and history, appears to be questioning whether we can appropriately speak of a unified culture at all. In the event, much of the attack on the very idea of an American national culture has come from people on the left who have rushed to celebrate the national cultures of, say, China, Vietnam, Nicaragua, or Cuba, in full knowledge that those nations, which certainly do have admirable national cultures of their own, also display severe internal tensions of ethnicity, race, and gender. And who, even on the left, would deny that France or Germany have discernible, if not easily defined, national cultures? It seems that only in the United States is it "reactionary" or "elitist" or "chauvinistic" to take pride in one's national culture.

There is an exquisite irony in the way in which the argument has developed. Today, as perhaps never before in our history, our national identity is under assault. From persisting immigration to the power of multinational corporations, innumerable forces are eroding the concept of the nation as we have known it. Those from the left who criticize its cultural manifestations apparently have not fully noticed that the proliferation of Japanese automobile companies or of Japanese real estate purchases within the United States constitutes an integral aspect of what they celebrate as cultural pluralism. Those who have noticed might well argue that the nation must be recognized as the relic of an oppressive history the passing of which justifies no call for mourning. I remain unconvinced. The threatened decomposition of the Soviet Union and the Balkan States into their component warring nationalities offers scant promise of international stability, and the less immediately ominous, but nonetheless possible, decomposition of the United States offers no more. Today, as in the eighteenth century, the defense of our national identity carries portentous political implications.

Those who would bury the concept of a unified culture appear oblivious to, not to say contemptuous of, the deep and often appreciative consciousness of a dominant American culture that has been displayed by the finest women and African-American writers. Fully understanding that the idea of a prestigious, dominant culture was promoted by successive elites who had the political, social, and economic power to claim to speak in the name of American society as a whole, they nonetheless took its claims seriously and did not readily jettison its standards of excellence, even when they sought to influence them. For us similarly to recognize the hegemony of that culture is not to slight the claims of the innumerable discrete cultures, especially those of women and African-Americans; it is to recognize that the elite conception of American culture has been able to offer itself as the embodiment of our national aspirations as a people and as the standard against which all discrete cultures have had to define themselves, or at least as the standard that those who aspired to be taken seriously have had to match.

The dominant culture, in other words, challenged women and members of other excluded groups to frame their own experience at least in part according to its norms. For many, the response to that challenge required a form of bilingualism. Thus Henry Roth, in his brilliant novel, *Call It Sleep*, evoked a young Jewish boy's attempt to navigate between the language of his mother and the language of school.[12] His conundrum admitted no facile resolution. The voice of his mother was that of home, love, nurture, and the traditions of his forebears; the voice of school was that of the new country and his own advancement—the voice that would eventually permit him to recreate and master the specific conflicts and wonders of his childhood.

The general case of bilingualism carried special force and poignancy for women and for African-Americans. Between them, the specific feminist and African-American challenges to our inherited notion of a unified American culture largely define the main lines of the broader attacks on that culture. For if both contest the narrow elitism of the view of culture as a privileged, white male preserve, and if both insist upon the existence and integrity of alternate cultures, namely those of women and African-Americans, in the end they do so on somewhat different grounds. The feminist attack on established culture understandably emphasizes gender and sexuality, arguing that to understand culture from a male perspective ignores the experience and perceptions of half of humanity. The African-American attack, in contrast, emphasizes the importance of a minority people's distinct cultural legacy. The most extreme separatist claims notwithstanding, feminist scholarship does not necessarily challenge the predominance of white American Protestant culture; it challenges the ways in which individuals of different genders have experienced and elaborated that culture. African-American scholarship challenges precisely that predominance, although it does not often challenge the predominance of men over women. However different the perspectives and implications, the literary scholarship of race and gender each delineates an encompassing attack on a white, male canon that has denied the experience and identities of African-Americans and women.

The recent recuperation of the bilingualism of women and African-American writers has revealed rich and continuous strands in American culture that that culture itself had too long ignored. But this healthy enthusiasm for the previously ignored has tempted critics to treat newly recovered cultural currents as if they were wholly autonomous, whereas one of the great powers of the writers who are taken to represent discrete female or African-American cultures lies in the cultural tension that their works articulate. A close reading of any of their great "forgotten" texts reveals a sustained engagement with the dominant culture, including a determination to appropriate its most generous values and to challenge it to realize them for all.

Langston Hughes's "A Theme for English B" explores the complexities of that unequal bicultural or bilingual experience.[13] Hughes, representing himself as the only colored student in his class but as liking the same things as white students, wonders whether if being asked to write of himself within the context of white education does not amount to being asked to shape himself to fit the expectations of white America—to adopt white speech, a foreign tongue. How do you write your self in someone else's words? in another people's words? What can be the relation between the objective structure of our canon or tradition and the subjective experience of individuals? What can be the relation between the hallowed traditions of whites as a people and the experience of blacks as a people? "Being me, it will not be white. / But it will be / a part of you, instructor." The instructor is white, "yet a part of me, as I am a part of you. / That's American."[14]

Hughes thus raises, as a matter of personal experience and identity, the problem that Houston Baker has discussed in *Modernism and the Harlem Renaissance*.[15] How can a black student establish the links between his personal identity, what Baker calls "family history," and the language of his people's oppressors? Hughes, refusing to accept the racist implications of radical difference between the experience of his represented self and that of his white classmates, insists that he, too, likes bebop and Bach, that he is partially immersed in white culture as they are, in lesser degree, immersed in black. But writing the self presents a special challenge, for the codes of selfhood have been derived from white culture. The white modernism of Joyce and Eliot does not "sound" like the history of African-Americans. Baker's point is that the success of the Harlem Renaissance cannot fairly be measured by white, modernist criteria. Hughes's point is yet more complex and more fundamental. For Hughes, by writing his poem, does inscribe a representation of himself in the words of others and, in so doing, insists upon his independent right to claim their tradition as his own, even as he recognizes the ways in which it denies him.

Alice Walker develops similar themes in her story "A Sudden Trip Home in Spring," poignantly exploring the response of Sarah, a black student, to the white college that has no place for the writers who represent her tradition and experience.[16] Sarah's roommate has never heard of Richard Wright, nor of any black poets. For Sarah, Wright remains compelling especially because of his difficulty in dealing with his own father, whom in childhood he had seen, as children are wont to see fathers, as "Godlike," as "big, omnipotent, unpredictable and cruel," as "entirely in control of his universe," and whom in adulthood Wright had recognized as "just an old watery-eyed field hand." What, Sarah wondered with Wright, was "the duty of a son to a destroyed man?" Sarah herself could not draw pictures of black men, for she could not bear "to trace defeat onto blank pages." How could she now deal with the death of her own father, who, like Wright's, seemed to close the doors to the rooms of the mansion of this life and, by implication, the next?

Walker underscores Sarah's rootlessness and suspension between the Georgia of her people and the intellectual world of her own present and future. Where was Sarah's home? How could she claim as home a place in which she spent weeks trying "to sketch or paint a face that is unlike every other face around me?" Sarah's trip to Georgia for her father's funeral reminds her that among her people she is at home, even as it reminds her that college too has, in important ways, become her home.

So where was Sarah's home? What did she find in Georgia? And, having found it, why did she return to college? College, Walker suggests, had already given her something, if only the knowledge of Dylan Thomas that led her to wish a red coffin for her father, to wish him not to go "gentle into that good night." College, as her brother reminds her, is what her mother would have wanted for her, and her father too—the education she deserves. To spend weeks trying to draw one face is what education is about. Only when she has learned to draw that face—to represent the men of her people—will she be free to go where she chooses.

To rage, with Thomas, against the "dying of the light," Sarah had to learn to claim the history of black men, had to be able to see her grandfather in all his pride, simply as he was, *"his face turned proud and brownly against the light."* Having finally seen him that way, free from all the *"anonymous, meaningless people,"* she could paint him, or, better yet, plan to make him, as he himself suggested, up in stone. For his eyes spoke to her of yes as well as no, just as her brother's courage suddenly became her "door to all the rooms."

And, with the yes and no, Walker glancingly evokes another of Sarah's debts to her white education, for her insistence on seeing both yes and no in the eyes of the men of her people shows her having made the vision of Albert Camus her own, having recognized it as about her own life. From Camus, Sarah could borrow the fundamental insight of *The Rebel*: "What is a rebel? A man who says no. But if he refuses, he does not renounce: he is also a man who says yes, from his first movement."[17] Burying her father and planning to make her grandfather up in stone, Sarah had reclaimed the men of her own people and had thereby learned how to take from another people's education what she needed.

Langston Hughes and Alice Walker, exploring their own situations as writers between two cultures, followed in the tradition of their people.[18] For if, as Henry Louis Gates has argued in a bold theory of African-American literary criticism, African-American writers have largely learned to write by reading texts of the Western tradition, and have largely been trained "to think of the institution of literature essentially as a set of Western texts," they have also worked out of a black vernacular tradition that has provided them with central topoi and tropes and that they have shared with other African-American writers.[19] In *The Signifying Monkey*, Gates elaborates a theory for the systematic reading of the distinct African-American literary tradition and for understanding the relation between the African-American vernacular and literary traditions—primarily seeks ways to consider the African-American tradition on its own terms, to allow it to speak in its own voice.[20]

Gates, in other words, offers an elegant and challenging theory of African-American literature as poised and constantly mediating between a predominantly oral vernacular and a formal literary tradition. Although he avoids using "popular" as a category, he is clearly identifying its proper meaning as of the people, and thereby seeking to delineate the ties that bind a people's inherited sense of itself to its literary expression. In this respect, he is building upon W. E. B. Du Bois's notion of "twoness," but, in the end, Gates is more interested in recovering the distinct African roots of that twoness than in exploring African-Americans' engagement with elite American culture.

There can be no doubt, as the work of Toni Morrison demonstrates, that a distinct African-American oral tradition has persisted into our own time and informs the work and identities of innumerable African-American writers. But from the start, and especially since the mid-nineteenth century, African-American writers have also attended to the models of elite literate culture. The move from oral to written itself requires an act of translation and, as African-American writers effect it, they inescapably commit themselves to participating in some measure in a culture that is not of their own people's making. That act of translation further commits them, whatever their intentions, to viewing their people's community through the eyes of the observer. Like Zora Neale Hurston, who in *Jonah's Gourd Vine* carefully translates the more obscure words of dialect for her potential white readers, they must always think of how the vernacular should be spelled on the printed page.[21] Even if they remain direct participants in the oral culture of their youth, they necessarily do so in some measure as outsiders. The tragedy of twoness, which cannot be divorced from its potential richness, consists in that inevitable alienation.

The African-American literary tradition has developed through constant interaction with the dominant (white) culture, although the relations between African-American writers and that culture have changed in relation to changing historical conditions.[22] As Susan Willis has cogently argued, and as Toni Morrison's *Beloved* breathtakingly demonstrates, African-American women's fiction can only be understood as the product and (re)enactment of history, specifically of the South and "the essential characteristic of the system as a whole as it arose out of slavery."[23] The continuing engagement with slavery testifies to African-American women writers' continuing engagement with the central myth of modern American culture— the myth of individual freedom and equality.[24] From Harriet Jacobs to Frances Ellen Watkins Harper to Pauline Hopkins, and throughout the twentieth century, African-American women writers implicitly and explicitly have confronted the dominant white traditions—male and female— with their hypocrisy and bad faith.[25] But in doing so, they draw directly upon the proclaimed standards of the tradition itself—the Bible, fiction, and political theory.

Beginning with the poet Phillis Wheatley in the eighteenth century, they have also adopted the forms of that culture, adapting them to their own visions but also accepting most of their formal constraints and many of their cultural assumptions. These aspects of African-American women's writing have been slow to attract attention, most likely because the simple acknowledgment of their having been written required heroic efforts of demystification. Not surprisingly, most of the ground-breaking work has been devoted to the sustained project of recovery that established basic facts, notably that the first African-American novel, *Our Nig*, was written by a woman, and that the most highly crafted narrative by a slave woman, *Incidents in the Life of a Slave Girl*, was, as its title page proclaimed, "written by herself."[26] On these foundations scholars are now getting a clearer picture of the accomplishments of African-American women writers, as evidenced in the splendid Schomburg Library edition.[27]

For these women writers, alienation carried special and complex meanings. For if, as Hazel Carby has argued for Nella Larsen's *Quicksand*, alienation was experienced as a personal state of mind, it was never only that.[28] The alienation of African-American women writers inevitably has evoked the condition of their people and, especially, the implications of their own ties to them. Most, accordingly, intermingled sharp protests against degradation, exclusion, and oppression with direct testimony to their own ability to meet genteel social and literary standards. Harriet Wilson's *Our Nig*, which explodes with ill-contained anger, constitutes the principal exception to this tendency prior to the twentieth century, when first Zora Neale Hurston and then Toni Morrison and Alice Walker turned, albeit differently than Wilson, to the recovery of African-American folk culture.[29] But as Carby has also argued, to reduce the tradition of African-American women's writing exclusively to a romanticization of the rural folk is sorely to miss its point.[30]

In *Incidents*, Harriet Jacobs crafted a self-representation that she intended for the consumption of a white, northeastern, middle-class, female readership. Her text simultaneously cultivates and wars with the expectations of purity and gentility that she knew she had to meet in order to serve the cause of abolition and her own dignity. Jacobs took great pains to differentiate her protagonist, Linda Brent, from the ordinary women of the slave community, whose own admirable qualities she depicted. Depicting Brent as speaking in flawless English, Jacobs implicitly drew a sharp contrast between her and the other slave women on the plantation whom she depicted as speaking in dialect. And although less broadly educated than her northern free-black contemporary Charlotte Forten, like Forten, she evokes Anglo-American high culture as a means of locating her text within that general discourse and locating herself as author as a potential member of the Republic of Letters.

Jacobs could not suffer her readers to confuse Brent with the ordinary women of the slave community at least in part because of her determination to establish herself as author but also because of her determination to establish herself as a respectable woman. In *Incidents*, she makes much of the heavy cost of slavery for slave women whom it cast as mere objects. But she could not represent her protagonist—and implicitly herself—as an object. She could not, in other words, bear to represent the full subjective horror of a slave woman's experience as simply a sexual object. Accordingly, her story of Brent's relations with Dr. Flint abounds with implausibilities.[31] Jacobs's self-respect demanded that she represent herself as a woman with whom her northern readers could identify. Her rhetorical emphasis on her fall from "virtue" and her regrets constitute a deft and highly crafted self-representation. If she was intent upon painting slavery in its full horrors, she was also intent upon constructing a worthy and appealing representation of herself. A mere fall from virtue, under intolerable circumstances, pales in significance when compared with the admission that her condition rendered her nothing but a casual object of sexual desire. Her apparently confessional account of her lapse thus dissembles the infinitely more humiliating denial of her very human identity.[32]

Those who came after, including Frances Ellen Watkins Harper, Pauline Hopkins, Nella Larsen, and Jessie Fauset, more often than not similarly wrote in "standard" English for an educated middle-class audience. The consolidation of the African-American bourgeoisie influenced their concerns as well as their style, especially their determination to demonstrate their social and literary respectability. That concern with respectability did not undercut their concern for their people, nor did the larger society permit them to sever their identification with even the least polished members of that community, but they also refused to relinquish their own aspirations to respect and excellence as writers, as defined by the larger national and transatlantic culture. For these women, first slavery and then the plight of the African-American rural and urban working classes constituted an undeniable aspect of their own identity as African-Americans—a moral responsibility that they could never forsake—but never an alternative to elite culture.

Literate African-Americans have always engaged the dominant culture, although few have accepted its premises about themselves or countenanced its neglect of the vernaculars of their own kind. How could we expect them to have done otherwise? For the dominant culture advanced the prevailing standards of excellence and embodied the values of that Republic of Letters from which most writers have sought acceptance and respect. No less important, it enjoyed disproportionate control of the production and distribution of books.[33] Much of the tension and conflict that characterize powerful writing derives from the need to mediate between the writer's "mother" tongue and the language of formal culture. If written culture bears witness to the particular experience of the individual, it also aspires to that measure of universality or, yes, abstraction, that will make the individual's experience accessible to others.

The dominant culture has in truth exhibited an arrogant disdain for the contribution of women, African-Americans, and others to the unveiling of their particular cultures; worse, it has been blind and deaf to their explorations of the human condition. But if the particularity of such writers is scorned, how could their universality be recognized? The bigotry of the dominant culture has thus made a mockery of its greatest strength, namely its insistence that the representation of individual experience illuminate our understanding of what it means to be human.

More sharply than any other ethnic culture, the African-American tradition exposes the tensions that bind discrete American peoples to the dominant culture. For more than any other group, African-Americans have been individually and collectively stigmatized first by the experience of slavery and then by race.[34] Indeed, African-American women writers have consistently wrestled with both questions without ever feeling free to distance themselves as individuals or as members of the middle class from the condition of their people in general. In this respect, the power of the dominant culture to mask the reality and significance of class divisions, while simultaneously denying the legitimacy of black nationalism, has reinforced the notion of racial identity as the primary determinant of individual status. The recent literary studies of race have tended to follow that lead, albeit while reversing its values. Yet most African-American women writers have not seen their purpose as the celebration of oral culture, much less as the divorce of their own work from the dominant culture.

Feminist scholars, too, have castigated the dominant culture for its denial and silencing of women—for its pretensions that elite, white, male culture properly represents American identity. In Nina Baym's strong formulation, American critics have resolutely and purposefully misread our literary past in their determination, literally, to recreate it as a literature of beset manhood, or, as I should prefer to call it, of anxious male autobiography.[35] Following this lead, Jane Tompkins has demonstrated that Hawthorne's reputation derived in no small measure from the concerted efforts of his friends and relatives, from his position as a well-connected, white, northeastern male.[36] Tompkins juxtaposes the case of Hawthorne's fabricated reputation to that of Harriet Beecher Stowe, who, although she enjoyed remarkable popularity and even respect in her day, has been marginalized by literary posterity as one of those "scribbling women" whom Hawthorne jealously deplored.[37] Tompkins's point is well taken, but it does not follow that Hawthorne, by reasonable critical criteria, was not in fact a superior writer than those he deplored.

One feminist scholar after another has seconded Tompkins's views, insisting that the picture of a uniform American tradition or national destiny rests upon ideological choices, upon a willful simplification of complex realities and relations. They are, in effect, arguing that the principle of "to the victor belongs the spoils" has dominated culture and imagination as well as politics and economics. The prevailing view of literary merit primarily depends upon some people's vision of Americans as a people—upon some people's ability to impose their views on others.[38] American Studies based on the reading of Emerson, Hawthorne, Melville, Poe, and their successors amounts to little more than a usable past for a white, northeastern, male elite. In labeling this received notion of a usable past as a self-serving deception that has deprived most of us of our true culture, feminist critics are as one with African-American critics in contesting its claims to centrality.

In reaction to the excessive claims for the representativeness of the canon, feminist critics have sought to identify and explicate a distinct female literary tradition and its relation to women's distinct experience. In an impressively thoughtful and learned study, Mary Kelley adopted the rubric "literary domestics" to capture the spirit of women writers caught between their commitment to the privacy of women's nature and mission and their participation in the public world as successful writers. Annette Kolodny, also emphasizing women's domestic vision, has argued that women developed their own fantasies of the West, which differed significantly from those of men. Judith Fryer has traced the theme of women's perceptions of private and public—self and world—through Edith Wharton's and Willa Cather's "imaginative structures" and representations of space. And Cynthia Wolff has thoughtfully explored the ways in which Edith Wharton used writing—the mastery of words—to overcome her most deep-seated fears.[39] Although these scholars do not argue explicitly that women were negotiating between a vernacular and the literary culture in which they sought to inscribe themselves, they do draw heavily upon women's private, as well as published, writings to reconstruct the women's lives and values, which they view as radically different from those of men. Overwhelmingly, they emphasize what women shared as women as the mainspring of women's writing and imaginations.[40] They thus reinforce the tendency in feminist theory in general to see the pressing intellectual problem of our time as one of

recognizing and understanding difference and marginalization, as recuper-
ating the voices that our dominant culture has silenced.

Women, according to many of these critics, have developed a distinct
perspective on American society and, implicitly and explicitly, have held
dominant male values to account. Mindful of the stringent conditions that
have governed their possibilities for happiness and security, women have
normally refrained from open revolt against prevailing values but have
nonetheless found innumerable subtle ways of criticizing them. This view,
as some feminist critics are beginning to understand, risks submerging the
experience of different groups of women under a single, homogenizing
model.[41] In effect, the dominant tendency in literary studies of gender
inadvertently tends toward countering the dominant image of the elite,
white male self with a complementary image of an elite, white female self.
But this general model of the female self does not even account for the
experience and perceptions of elite, white southern women who, like their
men, normally opposed the very premises of white northeastern culture.[42]

Caroline Lee Hentz, a prolific and accomplished novelist, directly coun-
tered Harriet Beecher Stowe's influential *Uncle Tom's Cabin* with *The Planter's Northern Bride*. Feminist scholars have devoted considerable effort to
demonstrating the ways in which Harriet Beecher Stowe engaged the necessity of abolition from a distinct female perspective. Yet a comparison with
The Planter's Northern Bride clearly reveals that, however much Stowe spoke
in the female voice, she spoke in the female voice of her class, race, and
region. She never repudiated the values of the men of her community. For if
she chastised their mistakes and excesses, she nonetheless shared with them
an immersion in a specific form of white, Protestant, individualist culture.
Certainly Caroline Lee Hentz, a northeasterner by birth but a southerner by
choice and identification, purposefully echoed the elite, male culture of her
adopted region when she condemned the northern capitalist oppression of
labor and celebrated the superior qualities of the beneficent southern slaveholders.[43]

Throughout a career that extended from the 1850s until the early twentieth century, Augusta Jane Evans, even more dramatically than Hentz, engaged the high (male) culture of her day. In her first three novels, *Inez* (1855),
Beulah (1859), and *Macaria* (1864), she systematically and successively explored the problems of Catholicism, which she abhorred, of faith, which she
believed essential, and of the legitimacy of slavery and the southern cause in
the Civil War, which she unequivocally supported.[44] In each of these novels,

especially *Beulah*, she also explored the related problems of women's identity and independence.

Evans never questioned the importance of female strength, nor the importance, within acceptable bounds, of female initiative and self-accountability. But she sharply rejected the northeastern model of individualism and celebrated woman's acceptance of her proper role within marriage and, above all, her willing subordination to God, who guaranteed any worthy social order. Although *Beulah* includes some of the themes that were appearing in northeastern women's fiction, notably a critique of the prevailing obsession with fashionable values and hypocritical religious observance, in essential ways it departs radically from conventional domestic fiction. And although it seriously engages the implications of individualism for women, it endorses the distinctly southern values of hierarchy and particularism. Indeed, the novel can profitably be read as a gloss on early-nineteenth-century high culture, especially Coleridge and Carlyle, whom Evans deeply admired. Unabashedly learned, Evans used her fiction to explore the most serious intellectual and political issues of her day.

Hentz and Evans can no more be neatly fit into any general model of nineteenth-century womanhood than can Harriet Jacobs, however much they, like she, might occasionally borrow its forms for their own purposes. After the war, as before, southern white women, like African-American women, found themselves frequently at odds with the prevailing models of womanhood and might as easily turn for ideas and interchange to the writings of men as to those of other women. Women who took their own literary aspirations seriously especially turned to men, or possibly to Charlotte Brontë or George Eliot, for they sought recognition by a recognized literary elite. For them the canon that we are trying to dismantle enjoyed genuine literary and intellectual prestige. Their acceptance of its general merits did not, in their minds, include acceptance of all its specific attitudes, but they did see it as a legitimate representation of the pinnacle of national culture.

Women and African-Americans, including African-American women, have developed their own ways of criticizing the attitudes and institutions that have hedged them in. Confronted with rigidly class-, race-, and gender-specific models of acceptability, they have manipulated the language to speak in a double tongue, simultaneously associating themselves with and distancing themselves from the dominant models of respectability. Their continuous negotiation with the possibilities afforded by the culture has had nothing to do with a mindless acceptance of themselves as lesser. It has had everything to do with their determination to translate the traditions and values of their own communities into a language that would make them visible to others—and with their own determination to participate in national culture.

As conservatives insist, the central questions are political. In general, the new literary studies of race and gender have positioned themselves resolutely on the left end of the liberal spectrum, even as they have sharply distanced themselves from Marxism. Since Marxist thought had, until very recently, paid little attention to race, gender, and ethnicity per se, scholars who are primarily concerned with African-American, women's, and ethnic culture have some grounds for believing that Marxism does not directly or adequately engage the issues that most interest them.[45] But the real problem seems to lie with the general view of Marxism as at least as authoritarian as the earlier elitist consensus.[46] For, in general, the new literary studies in race and gender have focused on recovering personal experience rather than a systematic view of the central dynamics of American society and culture.[47] The haste to dismiss Marxism thus merges with a general disinclination to engage general theories of social and cultural relations and leaves many of the new studies hostage to the models that they are attacking.[48]

Rather than engaging the battle for American culture as a whole, many contemporary scholars have, if anything, enthusiastically embraced fragmentation, variously describing it as diversity or pluralism. They, accordingly, risk settling for a one-sided reading. At issue is neither the importance of recovering previously excluded voices nor the importance of demonstrating the integrity of African-American or women's cultures. African-American writers read and built upon other African-American writers just as women writers read and built upon other women writers. As Gates, himself building upon a tradition of African-American scholarship, has argued, African-American writers have retained strong ties to the vernacular cultures of their people. Similarly, women writers have retained close ties to the everyday lives of women. Neither African-Americans nor women unquestioningly accepted the negative views of themselves engendered by elite white men, even if those views occasionally caused some pain and anxiety. But these discrete cultures developed within a larger society and polity with which, in some measure, they identified. To sacrifice that context is to abandon the attempt to understand the ways in which African-Americans, women, and others related to each other and, especially, to those who wielded cultural as well as social and political power. It is, in effect, to lose the national dimension of the American of American Studies.

The cultures and communities that constitute America have notoriously permeable boundaries. If African-American and women writers have understood their identities to derive, in important ways, from the communities to which they have belonged, as writers they have not readily agreed that they should have access only to those communities to which others have assigned them. They have not accepted the view that they should be defined solely in terms of their race or gender. African-American writers have not read only other African-American writers; women writers did not read only other women writers. And if they have drawn upon their own experience to fashion narratives and visions, they have also sought to link that experience to the accepted central traditions of American—and beyond it Western—culture as a whole. The vast majority of African-American and women writers have not belonged to homogeneous communities. Literate African-Americans have never been able to avoid regular interaction with whites; literate women have never been able to avoid interaction with men. Whatever we may view as the boundaries of their immediate, affective communities, both African-Americans and women have lived in and belonged to more than one community—frequently to several interlocking social or cultural communities—all of which have been defined by their relation to each other and to the nation as a whole. Today, even those who most enthusiastically celebrate diversity implicitly confirm the persistence of this engagement in their commitment to a transformation of the academy in particular and our cultural life in general.

Werner Sollors's model of consent and descent engages the central issues but does not exhaust them, especially in the cases of race and gender, for which both consent and descent remained problematic. He has argued that we have overemphasized and actually misrepresented the significance of ethnicity in American culture, for ethnicity, far from being a distinct cultural identity based on community identification, has been the product of precisely that objectifying elite gaze which scholars of ethnic cultures have warred against. He can thus be read to suggest that mainstream American culture has created "ethnic" as a category for its own ends in order to explain American diversity to itself and perhaps even—Sollors does not put it this way—to ensure the marginalization or compartmentalization of subordinate cultural communities. If we push Sollors's insight to its logical conclusion, we should be forced to recognize that the very commitment of the new scholarship to acknowledging, naming, and appreciating ethnic—and I should add racial and gender—diversity risks confirming the exclusion of those groups from the cultural mainstream. The celebration of ethnicity amounts to a reinforcement of marginalization—a reinforcement of the idea that those who consent to join the dominant culture leave their culture of origin behind them.[49]

T. S. Eliot insisted that we cannot hope to understand culture if we thoughtlessly identify it with individual experience. He might have added that culture cannot be reduced to autobiography. Instead, he wisely insisted "that the culture of the individual is dependent upon the culture of a group or class, and that the culture of the group or class is dependent upon the culture of the whole society to which that group or class belongs. Therefore it is the culture of the society that is fundamental."[50] Culture must be understood as a manifestation of interlocking and hierarchically related communities. Relations of power color the ways in which we perceive ourselves in relation to others, ourselves in relation to the past, ourselves in relation to humanity. To put it differently, we know ourselves through the languages available to us, and the languages that we know influence what we perceive ourselves to be. Individual perception is not prior to or separate from collective identity. Individual perception is a function of collective identity.

Some scholars of the American literary tradition are beginning to explore its relation to prevailing social and economic relations, notably T. Michael Gilmore, Walter Benn Michaels, and others who share their perspective. Their work is revealing the ways in which American literature implicitly or explicitly has testified to the contradictions that undergird the celebration of the autonomous individual.[51] Sacvan Bercovitch has compellingly insisted on the relation between the American self and the history of American culture.[52] Bercovitch, together with Myra Jehlen and others, has also insisted that we even recognize the ideological dimension of the texts we most value.[53] Recently, Jeffrey Steele has offered a close investigation of the concept of the self in the American Renaissance.[54] For more than a decade, Carroll Smith-Rosenberg has been exploring the ways in which gender has structured American identity and social relations.[55] Amy Lang has charted the ways in which changing social and political preoccupations influenced the ways in which men (re)constructed Anne Hutchinson to embody their visions of gender and dissent.[56] And Gillian Brown has demonstrated that the language of domesticity in fact pervaded nineteenth-century American cultural consciousness, affecting even elite men's representation of their society.[57] Separately and together, these and similar undertakings, specific disagreements notwithstanding, point toward a new synthesis in literary studies.

The best of this scholarship is teaching us to recognize even the most revered texts as the products of society and—covertly, if not openly—as witnesses to its struggles. Thus, as David Reynolds has recently reminded us, even so-called canonical texts betray their deep engagement with the tensions of the world in which they were produced. Elements of popular culture, preoccupations with economic change, anxieties about social status and class position, all figure in texts that may not explicitly acknowledge either their debts or their anxieties.[58] Similarly, David Leverenz insists that the "vital relation between classic American writers and history" should be sought "in the broad pressures of class and gender ideologies." But even Leverenz takes pains to distance himself from the presumably old-fashioned view that the connection might also be sought in "the specific links between texts and political or cultural contexts"—as if ideologies could be separated from the political and cultural systems within which they develop and which they articulate.[59]

In general, even the most promising new scholarship has not fully answered the most pressing concerns voiced in the new literary studies of race and gender, particularly the determination to recover the subjective experience of those whom the dominant culture marginalized and silenced. It is as if they were moving from the preoccupation captured in William Andrews's title *To Tell a Free Story* to the preoccupation to "tell my own story," on the conviction that "free" embodies the values of the dominant society and thus distorts the individual's self-perception, or worse, on the conviction that "free" must mean personal autonomy and liberation. But to abandon "free" as the product of collective experience is to abandon the cultural, social, and political context that gives meaning to the individual story. It is to lose precisely what most concerned Langston Hughes and Alice Walker—the possibility of bridging "twoness."

Under the expanding influence of postmodernism and post-structuralism, the new literary studies of race and gender are increasingly extending the notion of text to cover all social relations. Adopting from literary criticism the theory that language is all of society or "reality" that we can hope to know, they are insisting that we attend to a plurality of voices on equal terms—that we introduce genuine "democracy" into our appreciation of diverse cultures.[60] This position embodies a commitment to the equal value of human beings in their particularity and diversity, but by rejecting the notion of a hierarchy of intrinsic worth, it also rejects the attempt to understand the structures of domination and subordination within which cultures are elaborated and articulated.[61] The new literary studies of race and gender are thus repudiating the dual focus of text and context that traditionally characterized American Studies. Leverenz's opposition of "ideologies" to "political and cultural contexts" is, therefore, sobering. For Leverenz admirably prides himself on writing "about something" in contrast to engaging in sterile exercises. He is not, disclaimers notwithstanding, repudiating context; he is renaming it under the pressure of postmodernist and poststructuralist currents.

Significantly, the most compelling results of the new literary studies of race and gender point back, albeit in new terms, toward the older paradigm of American Studies as some combination of history and literature. Yet too often they make the case for the value of the cultures of previously marginalized groups as if those cultures should be understood on their own terms, which, in part, is to say in isolation. Too often they appear to be seeking to replace the very idea of an American culture—and especially an American self—with a multiplicity of unrelated cultures and selves. Too often they assume that if it could be demonstrated that our dominant culture has resulted from the privilege and power of some, then that culture must be repudiated entirely. These conclusions do not follow from those premises.

The new literary studies of race and gender have, in general, insisted upon the claims of a myriad of subjective experiences and upon the cultural distinctiveness of marginalized or oppressed communities. Yet for all their insistence on community, they have not decisively challenged the commitment to individualism advanced by the dominant culture. In effect, they are proposing that we study new individuals, not that we study differently the ways in which individuals interact—their conflicts, but also their accommodations, and the ways in which the dominant discourses have obscured those interactions.

The most compelling lesson of this work should be the insistence that our inherited notion of American culture has arisen from historical struggles that have been won by some and lost by others, for such are the consequences of power.[62] Yet those who are attacking the canon have, in large measure, repudiated the very notion of power in favor of a radical democratization. If our dominant culture has indeed resulted from the silencing of those who lacked the power, prestige, or connections to ensure that their views would prevail, then it behooves us to understand the dominant culture as the product of conflict it has been. It also behooves us to understand that the very power which facilitated the dominant culture's triumph endowed it with an undeniable prestige in the eyes of those it excluded, and especially with the power to set the terms of any criticisms of it.

The American self of our tradition has been white and male, normally northeastern although occasionally western, normally elite although occasionally middle class or even poor but upwardly mobile. That self has functioned as a collective self-representation, even as it has functioned as the implicit autobiography of the men of the dominant class and race. Today we no longer accept it as an adequate self-representation. Those of us who are not members of a white, male, northeastern elite need to understand the conditions that have permitted it to prevail. To do so we must recognize that, in essential respects, it has in fact prevailed. The new literary studies of race and gender suggest that we should reexamine that national image from the perspective of those whose lives it did not reflect. Perhaps the most sobering lesson of such an examination will be the hegemony enjoyed by that image in which so many did not share. However sobering, that lesson could help to instruct us in the inescapable relations between culture and power and remind us that American identities, like American culture, have always been shaped by the conflicted relations of class as well as gender and race.

Race and gender should, in fact, enjoy privileged positions in our understanding of American culture, for they lie at the core of any sense of self. The incalculable advantage of the dominant culture has been its ability to deny their significance, to define the individual as not black and not female. Yet that very negative betrays the centrality of race and gender to any conception of the American self. American culture has developed as a celebration of freedom and individualism, as a repudiation of inequality. The measure of its success—its hegemony—can be seen in its ability to promote the ideal of American exceptionalism, to deny the existence of systematic or structural inequalities. Above all, its success has consisted in its ability to conflate the subjective notion of the self with the objective notion of national identity and thereby to exclude those who do not fit the subjective model from its objective corollary.

Understood as collective rather than strictly personal expression, our culture can permit different individuals to claim it as their own—not necessarily as an expression of their immediate personal experience but as an affirmation of their national identity. Our culture, like all cultures, has always been subject to change. To recognize its national and inherently political character is to understand that to be an American means something more than to belong to a specific group of Americans. To be an American is forthrightly to acknowledge a collective identity that simultaneously transcends and encompasses our disparate identities and communities. Unless we acknowledge our diversity, we allow the silences of the received tradition to become our own. Unless we sustain the ideal of a common culture, we reduce all culture to personal experience and sacrifice the very concept of being an American.

9

TOWARD A

FEMINIST CRITIQUE

OF INDIVIDUALISM

If, as Paul Ricoeur says, interpretation is "the intelligence of the double meaning," feminism promises to become interpretation par excellence.[1] For feminism has emerged from women's special experience of twoness—the painful living of "objecthood." Individualism, like the Western tradition from which it emerged and which enthusiasts celebrate as its supreme realization, has firmly cast women as other, even as it has afforded men models of subjecthood and authority that women have tried to adapt to their own ends. Yet women have always had to wrestle with the knowledge that individualism's prestigious models of authoritative subjectivity have refused female identification. Feminism, as an ideology, took shape in the context of the great bourgeois and democratic revolutionary tradition. It thus owes much to the male-formulated ideology of individualism, as it does to the special experiences of women who have been excluded from the benefits of individualism.

During the twentieth century, American women have steadily increased their independent participation in the labor force, society, and the polity. Increasingly cut loose from the "protection" of husbands, families, and communities, they are behaving more and more like "individuals." But their growing personal freedom and independence from male authority have not automatically resulted in the hoped-for full equality with men. "Difference" persists and colors every assessment of women's real needs and wishes. The tension between difference and equality, which has informed feminism from the start, has steadily escalated until it now dominates feminist theory and policy. As successive gains for women reveal the inadequacy of earlier optimistic assumptions, feminists are being forced ever more directly to confront the intractability of difference and the elusiveness of equality. In this process, the attention of feminists as well as their adversaries has tended to shift from specific policies and measures to the cardinal fact of difference itself.

The principal feminist responses have consisted in a celebration of difference and in a denial or repudiation of it. Feminist consciousness, confronting the massive legacy and present power of male culture, has tended either toward female separatism, with an emphasis on essentialism, or toward integration, with an emphasis on androgyny. Even those feminists who identify fully with neither tendency remain indebted to formulations that capture the intensities either of the angry rejections of male domination or the dreams of absolute equality. Feminist theory has built upon these tendencies and, in some hands, is now moving toward a postmodernist rejection of the very notion of difference as an unacceptable manifestation of power. Postmodernist feminism thus desperately drives the implications of female anger to their logical conclusion: the destruction of the entire house that man has built. Feminist theory, in attempting to wrest understanding from a difficult past, is increasingly asking how the staggering evidence of female exclusion from the dominant consciousness could be read to promise anything better. But before it entirely repudiates our collective past, it might also ask how women could afford to jettison all claims to the products and record of so many centuries of collective life.

Anger lies at the heart of the matter, for without anger there is no feminist consciousness at all. But the unloosing of anger continues to threaten many women, especially young women, who assume that to acknowledge anger is to be doomed to act it out and thereby jeopardize relations with boyfriends, husbands, lovers, and possibly fathers and mothers as well.[2] The refusal to acknowledge anger reinforces the message that "good girls" do not get raped because they do not invite it and thus reinforces the message that men's violence is, at bottom, a woman's problem. It is not: it is primarily a man's problem. Anger reflects the knowledge that a man who could rape one woman could rape any woman, that the provocation (and, like it or not, sometimes there is provocation) does not justify the act. That anger remains difficult, especially because it is so often accompanied by fear. Teachers are regularly and unjustifiably surprised by students, even sophisticated graduate students, who anxiously search the historical record for some evidence of sexual equality, some evidence of at least one society, at some place in some time, in which women genuinely functioned as men's equals. The students worry that if power and its attendant violence have always been monopolized by men, there may be grounds for believing that they always will be. How can women identify with a record of our collective life that is only a record of their collective suppression and frequent brutalization?

Sooner or later all feminists are compelled to face the inescapable, gut-wrenching angers that inform the aspirations of women, too long cast as impure, inferior, and inadequate and cast out from the sanctuaries of truth, law, knowledge, and the Word. This current in any feminism fuels female resentment of male prerogative and encourages women to accept one another's (and their own) pain. But when this anger crystallizes in separatist tendencies, it easily slips into indiscriminate attacks on "male knowledge" and "male values." It seeks beginnings in imagined pre-patriarchal utopias, histories in heresy, and futures in gynocentrism. It celebrates denial of the male text—and, hence, all male interpretation—as the essence of female consciousness. Frequently, it celebrates a metaphoric sisterhood, separate female communities, and a presumed autonomous female consciousness. Through love or through hate, it battles, to the edge of oblivion, with the dominant male culture. Its most important lessons are the hardest to bear: the full, self-conscious knowledge that we and our kind have been objects of men's scorn, fear, greed, lust, violence. To possess that knowledge is to be possessed by rage—and the impulse to violence that follows therefrom, for to possess that knowledge is to feel one's nonexistence.

Another feminist current, seeking to escape the anguish of anger, aspires to the "purer" spheres of androgyny: the true word knows neither male nor female, nor does the rational polity, the equitable task, or the order of the just. Carolyn Heilbrun's generous eye reveals androgyny in many of those great moments of literature in which the human spirit transcends the contingencies of the flesh, as in the transcendent act of creation itself. Indeed, any vigorous individualism carries androgynous overtones. It is a treat to see Heilbrun's fictional heroine, Kate Fansler, relish a martini rather than sipping a glass of white wine or a cup of herbal tea.[3] The individual, the citizen, and the artist all become, in part, abstractions from the immediacy of physical being. Their essential qualities never turn upon the sexual identity of their embodiments. If the citizen, from the time of Aristotle to the end of the nineteenth century, was male, there was nothing intrinsic to the concept of citizenship that dictated this sexual privilege. Even Machiavelli's condition that the citizen be able to bear arms in defense of the polity could have been met by women, had the community been willing to risk their reproductive abilities on the fields of battle.

The categories of individual, citizen, and artist refer to the self-conscious being, the political being, and the creative being in such a way that the attributive takes priority over the substantive—becomes the substantive. And once being is identified with its attribute and becomes in some sense categorical, being comes to be understood primarily as the unit of a system. Any variety of physical being (male, female, tall, short, black, white) may, theoretically speaking, occupy the category, for individuals become interchangeable. Or so traditional conservatives have always insisted in reproaching radical egalitarians. In this perspective, at the logical extreme, a woman may replace a man. Historically, women have found themselves overwhelmingly excluded from such systems, which have never provided logical reasons for the exclusion. The reasons have always been historical and contingent and thus often in violation of the principles of the systems themselves. Hence, feminism could simply urge the rightful and overdue inclusion of women in the preexisting androgynous slots so long monopolized by men.

I may here risk some violence to Heilbrun's conception of androgyny, and to Virginia Woolf's. But where they would claim that their vision of androgyny transcends the specificities of male being in the world and offers a model of human being that incorporates male and female elements, it still too closely resembles the model of the angels, or of rational politics, or of the occupational possibilities of multinational capitalism. It abstracts too much from the varieties of life in different human bodies, proposing homogenization of the ways of being—of male and female—rather than advocating free access to social and cultural categories for very different beings.

At its most compelling, the vision echoes the Christian conception of the soul, freed from the body, and promises a spiritual wholeness embraced by, but therefore dissolved in, eternity. There will be neither male nor female, black nor white, rich nor poor, weak nor strong. East and West, slave and free, alpha and omega, disappear. But shorn of the conviction of salvation and transcendence, the vision of androgyny collapses into the gray interchangeability of cogs in some machine. More concretely and ominously, elite women who can afford full-time, high-quality childcare can operate as the functional equivalents of men, leaving working-class women to shoulder the burdens of womanhood and consigning the poorest women to the androgynous misery of part-time (if any) labor and dependence upon crack. The principle of justice should not be made to hinge upon women's and men's identity of being.[4]

Feminism, in its many varieties, has derived from women's rejection of the poignant duality that rends the consciousness of female subjects, who live in a culture largely not of their own making. Like that tradition, it has given rise to contending views about the nature of and best means to attain social justice and recognition for women. In this respect, feminism has followed the path of individualism in viewing "man" and "woman" as absolutes, in building the ideal of the individual (or, in the case of woman, nonindividual) directly from biology. Man and woman, respectively, embody nature. Feminism's temptation to follow individualism in this abstraction flows naturally from individualism's commitment to reducing women to female sexuality and to justifying men's superiority as a consequence of male sexuality. This strategy is sometimes compelling in the measure that feminism engages our culture's dominant models of being as encoded in its most prestigious texts and traditions.

Unfortunately the strategy too frequently leads to the assumption that a single, "orthodox" feminism can embody the aspirations of all women and thus mocks the multiplicity of female experiences, the range of female consciousness, and the varying strategies for coping with what remains overwhelmingly a man's world. The attempt to define and impose a feminist orthodoxy implies a totalitarianism that negates the very point of the feminist revolt—that substitutes the experience of privileged individuals for the discrete claims of countless others.

Feminism does embody the claims of women on the basis of what they share as women—what we might view as the claims of the female individual. In this spirit, feminism is frequently viewed, in Mary Wollstonecraft's words, as the proclamation of the "rights of woman." But contemporary experience also reveals feminism to be something more and something less. The goal of "the rights of woman" has revealed itself as deceptive. Rights have not granted women equality with men, much less obliterated centuries of discrimination against women. Rights, above all, have not transformed men's—or women's—consciousness in the sense dreamed of by those who yearn for the "liberated woman" of radical utopian thought. The failure of the campaign for woman's rights to deliver "new worlds" has, in part, resulted from our inability to eradicate the fundamental sexual difference between women and men, whatever the scope of that difference may be. It has also resulted from the inherent limitations of individualism in ideology and in practice. Individualism, in jumping from personal identity to political right, has itself abstracted from difference of condition among men. Feminism can ill afford to accept that sleight of hand. To prevail, it will have to assimilate a recognition of difference among women to the core of its meaning and program.

Although feminist theory, in its multiple guises, has been attempting to wrestle with these complexities, it is only beginning to offer a sustained critique of that individualism from which it itself derives.[5] The postmodernist dismissal of individualist notions of difference, in one sense, comes closest, but its wholesale rejection of our history and traditions risks the substitution of dialectic for rhetoric and an attendant divorce from the most pressing problems of our time. Worse, notwithstanding its radical repudiation of previous traditions, it has failed to engage a systematic critique of individualism; to the contrary, it drives the logic of individualism to its utopian-liberationist conclusions.[6] A feminist critique of individualism must simultaneously engage the strengths and weaknesses of our tradition and help us to (re)engage the history of our people and culture on new terms. The point is not to deny women's suppression, much less their anger at it, but to suggest ways of focusing the knowledge and the anger so as to save us from the twin evils of complacent acceptance of things-as-they-are and an imaginative turning of our world into a mess of broken crockery.

Feminists have sought not merely the reappropriation of womanhood but the appropriation of purportedly neutral public and cultural space, the transformation of that space in conformity to the rights of women as much as to their visions and fantasies, and the translation of mystifying language into a common tongue. Contemporary feminism thus uneasily combines practical and theoretical goals. In addition to specific policies to improve the position of women, feminists seek new ways of understanding: an elucidation of male domination, a development of strategies for breaking out of the prison of otherness, and an appropriation of the dominant culture as a heritage for women as well as for men. By emphasizing the suppression of all women as women, feminists are attempting to understand the advantage and prerogative of some women by race, class, and nationality. The feminist project thus implies a (re)consideration of the relation between individual freedom and collective order—an understanding that would neither cloud oppression nor glorify victimization but that would permit the reappropriation of a difficult past in the interest of constructing an acceptable future.

Feminist knowledge of self as "one" and as "many" carries an edge that male individualism lacks. Feminist individualism arises from enslavement and comes weighted with its legacy of fear. To be sure, male as well as female experience of enslavement—of literal slavery, servitude, class exploitation, and simple denigration—has informed the origins and triumph of bourgeois individualism as well as its radical and social democratic offshoots. Mary Wollstonecraft borrowed the kernel of her discussion of fashion and its debilitating effect upon women from Adam Smith, who had waxed eloquent in his indictment of the self-abasing effects of fashion on men. The language of antislavery and of women's rights coalesced in the antebellum United States: the words of one cause served the intentions of the other. Men have their own experience of oppression and self-doubt, but, in their struggles to combat them, they have been able to draw legitimation from a dominant model of man as natural and divinely ordained lord of the universe. Successive male orderings of the public, political, and symbolic worlds have invariably come at the expense of women.

The otherness of women has provided an indispensable cement to the varieties of class formation and consolidation. In various guises, ruling-class hegemony has drawn an explicit and implicit binding force from the celebration of man, and hence from the negation of women. The wresting of consciousness, identification, and willed choice from a chaos of violence has always occurred in the name of an ideal man. Individualism strengthened that general historical rule by postulating man as an end in himself, as his own telos.

Feminist criticism gains force through its knowledge and appropriation of female subordination—the confinement of women within the male word—but only when it simultaneously insists on knowing the self in relation to others. Hegel, in his celebrated discussion of "lordship and bondage," preeminently insisted on the interrelation of opposing consciousness and thus offered a devastating critique of the myth of individualism, which he in other respects celebrated. "Self-consciousness has before it another self-consciousness; it has come outside itself. This has a double significance. First it has lost its own self, since it finds itself as an *other* being;

secondly, it has thereby sublated that other, for it does not regard the other as essentially real, but sees its own self in the other."[7]

But, if consciousness begins with the sublation of the other, with the sublation of the first double meaning, and becomes then a second double meaning, it must follow by sublating itself. For its certainty of self derives from the conquest and erasure of the other, which transforms the other into the self, which must, in turn, be sublated "for this other is itself." Hegel elaborated, "This sublation in a double sense of its otherness, in a double sense is at the same time a return in a double sense into its self." First, he argued, the self, "through sublation, gets back itself, because it becomes one with itself again through the cancelling of *its* otherness; but secondly, it likewise gives otherness back again to the other self-consciousness, for it was aware of being in the other, it cancels this its own being in the other and thus lets the other again go free."[8]

Metaphorically, Hegel's discussion of lordship and bondage offers an incomparable prism through which to read the encoding of female within male self-consciousness. Feminists can recognize fragments of themselves in the evocation of the fear of the bond servant. And they can plot a future in the recognition that labor anchors fear in such a way as to transform it into the foundations for an independent self, for, in Hegel's model, it is precisely through the labor that most appears to be coerced—to be dictated by an outside consciousness—that the laborer, the bond servant, becomes aware of having a consciousness that "exists in its own right and on its own account." Labor affords the bond servant the (re)discovery of herself by herself, of having and being a mind of her own. For Hegel, the radical fear of this condition cannot be separated from labor: "Without the discipline of service and obedience, fear remains formal and does not spread over the whole known reality of existence. Without the formative activity shaping the thing, fear remains inward and mute, and consciousness does not become objective for itself."[9]

As many feminists, most notably Simone de Beauvoir, have insisted, women exist as the other, the reflection for a dominant male consciousness.[10] This otherness, this self-alienation as subject, has cast women as potential experts in the double meaning, within which there is no resolution, only oblivion. The Hegelian model, itself both idealist and profoundly male-centered, postulates the ultimate reunion of the spirit with itself. A feminist version must aspire to the ultimate reunion of the spirit with a collectivity that embraces males and females.

Neither the tradition of the woman as representative of her class, family, or office, nor that of the woman extraordinaire—the overreacher of her sex—has proved adequate to the aspirations of modern feminists. Both traditions inform feminism, just as both temptations motivate individual feminists. But feminism has, above all, taken its stand upon the simultaneous recognition of women as women and the recognition of the rights of all female individuals. Neither the female delegate nor the female individual has successfully challenged the dominant social and political relations or the word. This failure results in part from the tenacity of male privilege and power to define opportunities for both men and women. But it also results in part from feminism's own difficulty in challenging the privilege and power at their root—in the fundamental principles of our society and culture. Feminism's reluctance to challenge individualism has left feminists torn between small patchwork gains on the margins of individualism and utopian negations of everything male. Yet it increasingly appears that to realize its own promise feminism must, in the spirit of "radical obedience," undertake that critique of individualism which men, of both the left and the right, seem to be avoiding.[11]

Women live routinely with having their own sexual identity called into question. Men's sexuality constitutes the weapon, the standard, and the goal of making history, whereas women's sexuality supposedly places them outside of history. Women thus know exclusion and inferiority as intrinsic properties of their being, as the necessary consequence of who they are. Men can interpret their own exclusion and inferiority as accidents or conspiracies of history, as a particular injustice, and as more than adequate grounds for social, political, and ideological revolution. For a woman, exclusion and inferiority are named as intrinsic to her being. The deepest anxieties for women, therefore, are grouped and externally defined as anxiety of being, of essence.

This pervasive female experience of being other carries the seed of a special redemption, for deep in female self-awareness lies the awareness of self as rooted in and inseparable from a collective—of, if you prefer, community—life that embraces both men and women. If one's sexuality alone provides justification for exclusion, if one's most basic features as a being in the world dictate one's inferiority, then, for all those who refuse the condemnation, the reappropriation of self can be reappropriation not just for the individual but for the community itself.

Many feminists indeed insist that women's experience carries the seeds of transformative notions and practices of justice, but they also overwhelmingly insist that transformation must come from the substitution of female for male standards. At the extreme, some even insist that the concept of justice is so heavily compromised by male abstraction as to require absolute repudiation. Such thinking resembles the arguments of postmodernist feminists who insist that the power of language to cast woman as the other requires the repudiation of all forms of binary thinking—all dualities, all conceptions of twoness—as the only way to circumvent the conundrum of equality and difference. Both arguments, however, share an abiding complicity with one especially objectionable aspect of individualism, notably its emphasis on personal, subjective experience. Within the individualist tradition, this radical personalism has coexisted with an abiding commitment to abstract uniform standards, preeminently the concept of justice, but also a variety of standards of quality and objectivity. It is easy to criticize the tensions and contradictions between those two tendencies in individualism, just as it is easy to criticize the bad faith that has confused abstract standards with the specific forms of male being. But, we do not solve the problem by the arbitrary abolition of one side of the tension, while we raise the other to an absolute law.

Justice as the articulation of personal experience does not provide an adequate substitute for justice as the articulation of abstract standards, even if we know that in practice the abstract standards have been heavily biased in favor of the personal experience of men. The concept of justice that male individualism has bequeathed us does not simply represent a crude disguise for men's self-interest and advantage. It also represents a serious attempt to move justice beyond the personal struggles of clans and the personal prerogatives of kings, to bring it out of the world of trials by fire and water, out of the world of feuds, and into a world in which it is at least possible to conceive of human rights.

There is no reason to assume that women's experience has been intrinsically superior to men's experience or that a concept of justice that derives solely from the experience of oppression would be preferable—or at least preferable enough—to one that derives solely from an experience of power. For men's experience of power has included much more than the oppression of others. Whatever crimes may be laid on the men who have led the human race in its struggle to build civilization, lead they did. It should be enough to note that any viable concept of justice we may devise would have to be built upon the collective historical experience to which both men and women are heir.

Some feminists have been tempted to assume that women, "naturally" more nurturing than men, can draw from their experience newly generous models of morality and justice. Truly, the danger in the individualist tradition has been the ease with which it has invited individuals to objectify everything that they perceive as other, to view other human beings as nothing more than obstacles in their path. Women, assigned the responsibility for children, have, it is said, a more immediate sense of the humanity of others, which they feel themselves bound to protect and nurture. This sense of compassion, and the attendant ability to identify with the unfortunate, constitutes the great gift of women's experience at its most generous. But we all know that it has not always been generous. To take an example not as trivial as it might seem to the uninitiated: those who have experienced dismissal by the junior high school girls' clique could hardly, with a straight face, claim generosity and nurture as a natural attribute of women. More grimly, could anyone who has ever seen a child who has been abused by her, or for that matter his, mother recommend oppression as the best preparation for generosity? As Thomas Wentworth Higginson, convinced abolitionist and leader of the first black Union regiment, wryly reflected: "If it be the normal tendency of bondage to produce saints like Uncle Tom, let us all offer ourselves at auction immediately."[12] No. Weakness, victimization, exclusion, and personalization hardly offer adequate models for collective justice.

Feminism can ill afford to repudiate women's past, but if it holds the historical context of that past to have been uniformly unjust, it cannot afford uncritically to glorify women's discrete part of it. Conversely, if there is much to admire in women's past, we cannot readily assume that the male-dominated historical context contributed nothing to it. If feminism indeed contains redemptive promise for our society and culture, it can only realize that promise by cultivating both a critical attitude toward the past and a commitment to our history—whatever its injustices—as the history of women as well as of men. The past (in the sense of tradition and authority) that women inherit consists overwhelmingly of male texts, scriptures, and institutions. To repudiate that past would impoverish, if not preclude, our understanding of the present and our possibilities for the future; conversely, to accept it uncritically by minimizing the pain of violence, rape, degradation, contempt, objectification, and humanity-defying idealization would be to betray ourselves.

Sherry Ortner, in a path-breaking article, "Is Female to Male as Nature Is to Culture?" suggested, in the tradition of Beauvoir, that men, subsuming women in nature, have built their culture in opposition to women, over women's bodies, and at the expense of women's minds.[13] In a complex process that has evolved in tandem with men's struggle to dominate nature, men have identified women with nature, projecting back and forth between their concepts of both. The myth denied female autonomy and rationality, just as it helped to bar women from the realm of politics, mind, and spirit that men were attempting to appropriate. More, it provided the cornerstone of their increasingly individualistic and instrumentalist attitude toward knowledge and truth. In denying women, men were denying the claims of a twoness that embodies the reality of the other—were using otherness to signify the negation of the other. They were thereby denying their own history. Hegel, after all, was not writing about women, nor even about slaves, but about the human condition.

Loath to recognize an equal but opposing female consciousness, the dominant male culture has generated a variety of images of women, all of which fall within the structural category of "not-man." Yet despite men's Herculean efforts at denial, the (negated) presence of woman pervades even the most outrageously male-centered texts. The construction of lordship has required not merely the bondage of women but the denial of alternate visions that might embody an opposing consciousness. Although lower-class men (peasants, slaves, serfs) did not participate in the unfolding lordship of the spirit, the hegemonic notion of "man" always held some promise for them. They were never represented as having an opposing consciousness, although they might occasionally be recognized as opposing specific distributions of power and wealth—as having some form of class consciousness. At their most dangerous, they might aspire to wrest the position of lordship from others, but they were not ordinarily assumed to embrace a radically different vision of consciousness.

Women, looking to the most prestigious texts of the Western tradition, confront misogyny, idealization, objectification, silence. The absence of female consciousness from that tradition challenges feminists to look beyond and through the texts, even as they claim the tradition as a collective legacy. The absence anchors one term of a double meaning. The silences, all the more difficult to restore because of the circuitous interpretation they call for, offer clues to the willed suppression of women. A hegemonic culture relies as much upon negation as upon positive affirmation for its binding force. The more negation can be inscribed in silence, the more binding it will be, for the explicit denigration of women constitutes an act of naming that permits differing views about the strength of the tie between name and thing, between sign and referent. Significantly Christine de Pizan's precocious defense of women's excellence was provoked by Jean de Meleun's *Roman de la Rose*—an explicit proclamation of misogyny. When women are explicitly denigrated, the naming of their aggression, sexuality, or deviance brings those aspects of their being into public discourse. Bourgeois individualism, in contrast to what preceded it, has represented women as "passionless," thus foreclosing any discussion—even negative—of female power.

Male unease with female power, or potential power, nonetheless laces even individualist discourses that represent women as nurturing and passive. An implicit evocation of female power refrains from naming female attributes that might not flatter male self-esteem, but it mobilizes male fear and anger in the service of binding a male audience to a positive assertion about womanhood. Thus the lithesome, virginal object of romantic adoration may figure not merely as a sign of inspiration but also as the (negated) sign of the repressed devouring mother—the castrating bitch. Restoring the negation is a first step, beyond which lies the task of restoring a female consciousness that is outside the polarity of "virgin" or "bitch"—a polarity constructed by a male consciousness fearful of women's independent consciousness.

Throughout the centuries, men have wrested their ideal of manhood from the turbulence of political, social, and sexual struggle and have ensconced it as the special sign of civilization and grace. And they have constructed a complementary myth of woman as the proper object of male subjectivity triumphant. Structurally bound, the two myths were intended to represent an idealized whole—mankind in his perfection. The preferred myth of woman emphasized the natural complicity of the weaker sex in its submission to the stronger: "Hee for God only, shee for God in him."[14] Submerged in the myth of woman, however, lies its negation, denied because of its implicit threat to the consciousness of man. Submerged in the myth of man lies the multiplicity of men and their unequal relations to the means of production, the modes of symbolization, the possibilities of power. Around the dominant myths percolate periodic denigrations of female evil and potential class and racial violence. But the dominant myth normally ascribes such dangers to innate female sinfulness, willfulness, and corruption, not to self-conscious and opposing female intentionality. Similarly, class opposition was customarily read in the spirit if not the precise formulation of Roland Mousnier's remarks on the causes of peasant rebellions: original sin and the inability of human beings to live according to the laws of God.[15]

Feminists must begin by decomposing the very myth of man, recognizing that to accept the unchanging polarity of woman and man is to succumb to the preferred structures of male domination. They must thus reclaim man for historical understanding as the only way to establish woman's historical presence. This reclamation points toward the recognition of gender relations as a fundamental aspect of societies, polities, and cultures. The emphasis on gender relations, building on but not accepting determination by the biological differences between the sexes, illuminates the interdependence of men and women in life and consciousness. It thus refuses the postmodernist dismissal of difference as an artifact of language and an abuse of power and insists that difference lies at the core of our humanity. By accepting difference, it insists that difference is historically as well as biologically grounded and interpreted—that the consequences of difference attributed by societies and polities are subject to constant reinterpretation.

The claim that difference does not naturally dictate specific relations of lordship and bondage leads directly to the recognition of the class and race relations with which gender relations interact and which they frequently reinforce. Recognition of social and political struggles enables us to understand some women's experience as pawns in the organized and purposeful struggles of men, and other women's experience as active participants in various relations of domination. It forces us to grapple with the domination that characterizes relations between mistress and servant, mistress and maid. For even as sex unites women, class and race divide them. Seeing men—outside the ideal "History of Man"—allows us to reappropriate our mothers' and grandmothers' lives in subordination as historical, not natural. The social and political dimension of male life reminds us that the oppression of women is no mere individual or psychological aberration but a social fact, a link in the shifting relations among humans. Above all, it reminds us that the cultural representations of sexuality and sexual identity are themselves abstractions from specific social and political relations.

Feminist Critique of Individualism

The path of feminist interpretation leads through the objectification of male culture to the recognition that the triumph of the Hegelian "spirit" resulted in the exploitation and the denial of female being. Feminist interpretation translates the language of the lord into the vision of the slave—man into woman, he into she. Logically, such translation constitutes no more than a reversal within prevailing structures. Women replace men, but lordship and bondage stand unshaken. In feminist terms, the translation may, in the manner of the reversals of the charivari, delight and purge, but it nonetheless deprives women of their history. And women's history, the lived experience of servitude, must be fought for, however painful its recollection. For without the knowledge of our own suppression, without the humiliation of our own exclusion, the dominant culture offers us nothing but the prefabricated structures and categories of male thought.

The question remains: What has the dominant tradition to offer beyond the history of our own suppression? On what terms can feminist interpretation appropriate a male culture? Women themselves have left disproportionately few cultural monuments, as they have left disproportionately few records of rule. Neither the pen nor the sword has been freely at their disposal. Tillie Olsen has written movingly of the silences in women's literary production: the silences imposed by the needs of others, the fulfillment of human responsibilities to children, the sick, the old; the silences imposed by the need to earn a living or to care for a house.[16]

The dominant culture that feminists confront was produced by men, not created by God or nature. To the extent that men have spoken for the collectivity, they have done so on the basis of their privileged access to the functions of literacy and rule, not on the basis of intrinsic sexual merit. Their social representations, their social and political institutions, replete with distortions, injustices, and self-adulations as they may be, nonetheless belong to our collective past. Depending upon the recognition of those stripped of their own voices and visions, the lords of creation have not existed independent of those they have suppressed. The servitude and labor, recovered as memory, permit the bond servant to appropriate the record of bondage and to transform it into a consciousness of strength. Women do need to reappropriate and relive the fears of our foremothers, which have frequently passed unrecorded and unacknowledged but which alone register the reality of their labors. In that remembrance, the objectification of male culture gives way to the subjective appropriation of the possibilities for women.

Feminism should, in this perspective, be seen as a strategy of interpretation—a translation, transformation, and appropriation of womanhood, understood as a social product—as the composite of women whose lives, while divided by class and race, are grounded in sexual similarity. Translating the denigration of mere womanhood, of the eternal female nature, into the proud vocabulary of shared pain, feminism insists upon pain and conflict as inherent rather than accidental to the human condition. This recognition permits the transformation of bondage into freedom, repudiating lordship as itself yet another form of bondage. Appropriating freedom in pain, not as a masochistic or ascetic distortion but as the foundation of social and political justice, feminism appropriates womanhood's history of bondage as the foundation of feminist consciousness.

Such interpretation formulates understanding by proposing a (re)reading of our tradition, of the texts, artifacts, and other visible remains of collective human life. Inevitably, there will be conflicting interpretations.[17] But, for those who take history seriously, the continuous reappropriation of the past remains a necessity. Feminists can draw strength from a recognition of the common tradition as in fact common—as the product of many labors and many subjectivities—but only on condition that we take the tradition seriously and struggle to appropriate it. We can ill afford to reject the tradition in toto, for, as with any great hegemonic tradition, it has irreversibly shaped the ways in which we think about ourselves and the people we have in fact become. By deconstructing the ideal of man, the individual, as the single subject—the hegemonic self-consciousness of the collective tradition—we are also deconstructing the ideal of woman that shapes our consciousness. Above all, we are groping toward an understanding of all individuals as hostage to the collectivities to which they belong and which alone give their identities meaning. We are thus challenging the residual narcissism that aspires to cast man's relation to his tradition as the reunion of the Spirit with the spirit of each individual interpretation. By understanding the tradition as a collective product, feminist interpretation challenges "male" interpretation—the relation of the lord, or ideal man, to his past. For the real message of lordship and bondage is that where one is lord, all are enslaved.

The individualism from which modern feminism was born has much to answer for but much in which to take pride. Individualism has decisively repudiated previous notions of hierarchy and particularism to declare the possibility of freedom for all. In so doing, it transformed slavery from one unfree condition among many into freedom's antithesis—thereby insisting that the subordination of one person to any other is morally and politically unacceptable. But the gradual extension of individualism and the gradual abolition of the remaining forms of social and political bondage have come trailing after two dangerous notions: that individual freedom could—indeed must—be absolute, and that social role and personal identity must be coterminous.

Following the principles of individualism, modern Western societies have determined that the persistence of slavery in any form violates the fundamental principle of a just society. But in grounding the justification in absolute individual right, they have unleashed the specter of a radical individualism that overrides the claims of society itself. To the extent that feminism, like antislavery, has espoused those individualistic principles, it has condemned itself to the dead ends toward which individualism is now plunging. Feminism, as the daughter of individualism, carries the potential of bringing individualism back to its social moorings by insisting that the rights of individuals derive from society rather than from their innate nature. Feminism, as the daughter of women's exclusion, understands that social opportunity must lie in access to the various roles that society offers. Above all, women, with the privileged knowledge of sexual asymmetry, which derives from their history of subordination, understand that justice must derive from a collectivity that grounds its deepest principles of individual right in the collectivity's commitment to honor and protected difference.

CONCLUSION

However much this book is intended as a feminist critique of individualism, it is bound to strike some—and perhaps many—as a critique of feminism. The risk is unavoidable. Feminism today has become so protean and wears so many faces that any notion of *a* feminist position has become utopian. Recognizing the danger that many other feminists, whose views differ from mine, may consider my criticisms disloyal, I can only hope that the scope of the movement permits the acceptance of divergent viewpoints as part of a continuing effort to make sense of what women need.

Today, the feminist critique of individualism is becoming ever more widespread. If my argument differs from those of others, it is primarily in my conviction that feminism, in all its guises, is itself the daughter of that (male) individualism which so many feminists are attacking. The attack on individualism has, in general, led to arguments that practices and values, from the organization of work to the law, should be refashioned and rethought to take account of women's distinct experience—perhaps even women's distinct nature. But our very conception of women's experience and nature has been filtered through the premises of individualism. For this reason, it seems to me that the metaphors of sisterhood and community that still enjoy much currency with many feminists should be recognized as, in some sense, hostage to the very institutions they are mobilized to oppose. Similarly, feminist politics have had difficulty in breaking with the legacy of individualism.

From my perspective, the central problem in the feminist critique of individualism lies in the difficulty of reimagining the collectivity—society as a whole—in such a way as to take account of women's legitimate needs. There can be no doubt that many, if not most, of our laws and institutions, including our vision of justice, have been constructed on the basis of men's experience. But it is a big step from an attack upon the biases inherent in those laws and institutions to a repudiation of the possibility of any "objective" standards. I am, accordingly, arguing that the dream of objectivity constitutes one of the great contributions of our civilization, however much it has been constructed by men for their own advantage.

This conviction that feminists have come perilously close to "throwing out the baby with the bath" also informs my discussion of the claims of a common culture. Feminism and postmodernism have both irrefutably demonstrated that, more often than not, the defense of a common culture has constituted the defense of the prerogatives and perspective of some over those of others. They have also taught us that culture is infinitely and richly diverse—that each of us has her or his own story. But to accept the overriding claims of those diverse stories is to accept a potentially dangerous and impoverishing fragmentation. It is also to risk the loss of our own history, which was, like it or not, fashioned in interaction with a dominant culture. In many academic circles, the Western tradition, not to mention the idea of an American national culture, enjoys scant popularity today. Yet neither feminism nor postmodernism are conceivable or comprehensible without them. To jettison them now means to forego the possibility of coming to terms with our history and perhaps the possibility of shaping our future as well.

American women are, as they always have been, members of American society and heirs to Western and American culture. The issue that confronts us is the terms of their membership in the present and future. That issue has led many feminists up against the dilemma posed by the juxtaposition of equality and difference. How can women, if they are different, ever hope to be equal? How can women, if they aspire to be equal, continue to insist that they are fundamentally different? In writing this book, I have become more convinced than I had previously been of the importance of difference. Even after discounting all of the ways in which our specific culture has constructed and represented difference, a biological difference remains. But the recognition of difference does not dictate the social consequences of difference. The consequences are a matter for the collective determination of society as a whole. We live in a world in which women must be able to support themselves and in which the survival of our species depends upon their bearing children. It is, accordingly, of the most pressing social concern that our laws and institutions permit them to do both.

In the end this book is not so much an argument for a chimerical equality, but for equity—and an argument that equity requires a broader and more generous social vision than individualism alone can provide. It is, in sum, an argument that the realization of equity for women requires a view of individual right as derivative from collective social life.

AFTERWORD

PERSONAL THOUGHTS

ON THE CONSEQUENCES

OF DIFFERENCE

Feminism today has everything to do with the education of our students and daughters—the subject with which I began this book—and with the education of ourselves. We must, as Carolyn Heilbrun has argued, "recognize what the past suggests: women are well beyond youth when they begin, often unconsciously, to create another story."[1] Too often, she suggests, young women live according to the familiar scripts that promise a happy ending in return for the acceptance of passivity and closure. Even those of us who are privileged (white, middle-class, securely employed) run the risk of "choosing to stay right where we are," listening to "our arteries hardening . . . seated comfortably in our tenured positions." So we stop, just when we should be ready "to make some use of our security, our seniority, to take risks, to make noise, to be courageous, to become unpopular."[2]

Today, in ways that would have pleased Christine de Pizan, women's stories are gaining an urgency and prestige that they have long been denied. For many, "feminism" constitutes the essence of those stories if only by underscoring the importance of women's distinct purposes and consciousness. But even today it is not possible to think seriously about women without also thinking seriously about men—and vice versa. For many, the very word "feminist" has an ominous ring, if only because so many still associate it with "bra-burners" and "lesbians" and, especially, with dissatisfaction and anger. For many, the very idea of being a feminist seems puzzling. What do we need it for? Or, as Sigmund Freud asked more than fifty years ago, with a note of despair, "What do women want?"

In truth, many women today want what many men want: to make a decent living, to have a rewarding personal life, and to get on in the world without rocking too many boats. And today at least those who are comfortably middle class have grown up in a world in which women have enjoyed many of the advantages that men enjoy. Today, women can plan to go to graduate school, law school, medical school, or business school without fearing that they will be denied admission simply because they are women. Today, women can get credit in their own names. Today, women can gain admission to almost any occupation—we may yet even see women priests in the Catholic church—and can call upon the government to assist them if they encounter at least flagrant discrimination. These possibilities would have seemed unattainable twenty years ago. But to take advantage of these possibilities, young women need what men have always had, namely, stories that help them to imagine specific ways of being a woman in the world—and the possibilities of laughter.

Looking back on the stories with which I was reared and recognizing the gap between them and the way in which my life has unfolded, I see that an education in feminism must include a measure of autobiography, if only to convince younger women that growing up as a woman, while it will never be easy, is possible.

As a little girl I had three main ambitions: to become the first woman president of the United States (and thereby prove that a woman could do anything that a man could do—probably better), to marry a black man (this, before the civil rights movement, was the best way I could think of to fight racial discrimination), and to have twenty-one children (and, of course, be a perfect mother to them all). In the event, I have done none of those things, but the ambitions remain instructive. They reveal how little I, like other children, understood about exactly what grown-ups do. And they reveal, even though I heard no talk of feminism at the time, how much I was concerned with what it meant to grow up to be a woman.

When I finally got to college, and might have been expected to have a better idea of what women do when they grow up, things were not much clearer. I still remember how anxiously my best friend and I scrutinized the women faculty members—since we were at a women's college, there were women faculty members—to find what today would be called role models. No luck. Our women professors were almost all single, and the few who were not had marriages that we could not make sense of—which was probably our problem not theirs. Our mothers were married but did not have careers. The choice was stark and distressing. When I got to graduate school, it looked even worse. There were no women professors, and I had almost no women classmates. To this day, I remember that one of my male classmates, now a well-known professor and a perfectly decent chap, asked me while we were standing in line to see one of our professors, "What is a nice girl like you doing in graduate school, taking a place that could go to a man with a wife and children to support?" In that climate women's history was unheard of, and women, with the exception of an occasional queen, were absent from the curriculum.

It was very confusing, and I had not the remotest conception of myself as a professional. What was I doing in graduate school? I was a good student—a role I had always known how to fill and in which I had always felt comfortable. But I was feeling increasingly less comfortable. What was I going to do when I grew up? Then, as always, the only answer seemed to be to get married and have children, to be the good wife and mother that I had been reared to be. Yet with each passing day I was inadvertently becoming more accomplished in and committed to my work, and thus, however unintentionally, I was limiting the number of men who might be interested in marrying me and perhaps limiting the time I would have to give to children. The language in which I thought about myself was radically opposed to what I was doing.

Predictably the consequences of this fundamental contradiction included a heavy dose of emotional and psychological tension. As it happened, I was extremely fortunate in meeting one of the increasingly small number of men who might be prepared to cope with an ambitious woman. For even if I did not know that I was ambitious, the men whom I dated assuredly did. So did my mother, who was visibly worried. During my weekly phone calls, she would regularly ask, "Are you having any fun?" To which I would respond, "Yes, I have just written a fascinating paper on the problem of taxation and royal power in medieval France," or on some equally scintillating topic. To which she would impatiently retort, "No, I mean are you having any *fun*?" What my mother, who loved me and who understood the harsh realities of the world much better than I, meant was, "Are you going out? Are you seeing anyone in particular?" My mother, best of intentions notwithstanding, thus reinforced my deep conviction that it would have to be marriage or career, and she reinforced my sense that marriage was the safer bet of the two.

In the mid-1960s, neither my mother nor I could predict the changes that were about to sweep over American society, although perhaps we should have suspected something. In fact, I met and married my husband before the feminist movement had attained much visibility or power. But even our wonderfully happy marriage did not solve the underlying problem. Not surprisingly, it took me a long time to get around to finishing my dissertation. The problem was not that I did not enjoy the work, but that, at some deep level, I did not want to finish. Finishing would once again confront me with the troubling question of what I was going to be when I grew up.

Along the way I devised an impressive array of feints and dodges. I took a job in publishing and another in the poverty program. I concentrated on being the model wife of a department chair—or "chairman," as he insisted on calling himself—entertaining frequently, cooking elaborately. I thought I might become a psychoanalyst, a plan that included the comforting necessity of starting my training all over again. Think of it, another ten years as a student! And withal, I went on reading history. At one point, I even drafted the manuscript for a short book. I did everything except finish my dissertation. The problem was not research or writing, both of which I enjoyed. The problem was finishing.

Eventually I did finish, primarily because of the steady, quiet encouragement of my husband, who understood what I wanted—or rather, what I could be—better than I. And, having finished, I got a job. There I was, willy-nilly, embarked on a professional career. But I still did not think of myself as a professional. Indeed, I still thought of myself as a girl, as anyone who probed beneath the surface would have discovered. Not that there was anything wrong with my thinking of myself as a girl, if by *girl* one means merely that I enjoyed being female in relation to males, that I liked clothes, that I had no objection to appearing feminine, that, to borrow Goldie Hawn's succinct formulation from "Private Benjamin," "I want[ed] to wear my sandals, I want[ed] to go out to lunch." The trouble with my thinking of myself as a girl lay in my reluctance to see myself either as an adult woman or as a serious professional capable of earning her own living and taking care of herself. It lay especially in my inability to understand that "woman" and "professional" were compatible.

I have risked this personal history because I believe that it reflects a widespread experience among those of my generation and that its consequences are with us still. Like the novelist Alix Kates Shulman, I belong to a generation of women for whom the main model of achievement was "prom queen" and who could not imagine what to do with themselves as "ex-prom queens," even if we never had a prayer of being prom queen in the first place. Women who have been reared to think of themselves primarily as girls normally cannot readily imagine their futures or what it might mean to grow up. Even women like those of the present generation who are being reared with the assumption that they will have careers and work for their livings, remain haunted by the experience of the women of my generation and the general assumptions of our culture.

The women's movement of the past two decades has made considerable progress in pulling down barriers to women's equal participation in society, but it has understandably tended to focus more on removing obstacles than on how we live with the changes. Feminists have often insisted that "the personal is political," by which they mean that personal relations must be understood as having political implications—for example, that marriage is not simply a personal matter, it is also a relation governed by law and subject to modification by political action. The personal as political also means that the inevitable conflicts between human beings must be understood in the context of a larger political pattern that advantages men over women. Thus, for example, rape should not be understood simply as the manifestation of a disturbed personality but, even more important, as the manifestation of structurally unequal relations between women and men.

This insight has permitted at least some women to recognize that their personal unhappiness has political or social roots and that the best way to ease it may not be to take another Valium. In fact, one of the early examples of the political dimension of personal experience was the recognition that doctors indeed prescribed Valium to much greater numbers of women than men, presumably on the assumption that men should be cured while women should be tranquilized. Over the years, we have accumulated numerous examples of the ways in which our society's inherited assumptions about men's and women's roles—and the greater importance ascribed to men's—have influenced everything from health care to medical research to the availability of credit to educational policy. We need not look for conspiracies in every corner to accept the evidence. It is overwhelming. Our society has been grounded in fundamental assumptions about the differences between women and men, and in enduring assumptions about the proper roles of women and men.

As a woman married to a Sicilian-American, I have no difficulty in recognizing the differences between women and men. My husband, even more than I, grew up in a world in which boys were boys and girls were girls and that was the end of that. In truth, I have always regarded his generous support for my own ambitions as a moving triumph of will over instinct—a triumph that did not come easily.

Early in our marriage we enjoyed playing gin rummy, and, as it happened, I frequently won. Now my husband enjoys winning as much as anyone I know. And one day, when I had not just won, but won big, he turned to me with a wicked gleam in his eye and said, "Yes, but you don't have a penis." We had a good laugh. Having been thoroughly trounced, albeit in a game, he took the high ground of anatomical difference. However much I won, I was still a girl. And we both enjoyed the joke immensely. But, as his case suggests, the real question is not whether there are differences. The question concerns the consequences of the differences. Are boys entitled to win just because they are boys? Should girls be reared, as they so frequently have been, to fear winning—and worse, to refrain from winning—out of respect for boys' superior anatomy?

Our culture has been grounded in the notion that the anatomical differences between women and men should have social consequences. That notion has not always resulted from mindless prejudice or sexism. For during much of our history, male strength and female reproductive capacity have been essential to the survival of society. Recent feminist scholars have taught us that previous scholars have frequently exaggerated the importance of male strength to society, that, for example, women gatherers rather than male hunters provided most of the food for the earliest human societies. But the basic point remains valid. In general, men's greater size and, especially, upper-body strength have fitted them better for certain kinds of heavy labor and armed combat and have certainly given them the advantage in direct physical competition with women. Louisa McCord captured the matter when, in a polemical attack on feminists who were claiming equality between women and men, she sardonically asked what could be the outcome of "pitting woman against man, in a direct state of antagonism, by throwing them into the arena together, stripped for the strife; by saying to the man, this woman is a man like yourself, your equal and similar, possessing all rights which you possess, and (of course . . .) possessing none others. In such a strife what becomes of corporeal weakness?" Louisa McCord did not doubt the outcome. Women would lose, and the world would become a "wrangling dog kennel."[3]

McCord was writing directly out of her experience in a southern slave society in which it was very difficult for women to step into male roles.

Women could not easily, for example, run plantations. They were simply never trained to assume such responsibilities, and in particular, in that rural slave society, the ability to exercise authority depended in important ways on the ability to impose one's will through physical combat if need be. Fully to exercise the authority of master depended upon the ability to whip your prime male field hand yourself. Most women, even if they had superb training in crop rotation and the vagaries of marketing cotton, could not. Most women, in a world in which physical violence was endemic, needed the protection of male strength. Under such conditions, the justification of men's prerogatives on the grounds of their superior strength made considerable sense.

Just as men's superior physical strength apparently justified male advantage, so did women's ability to bear children apparently justify the view that women's roles should primarily reflect their biological characteristics. Concerns about overpopulation understandably color the ways in which we think about reproduction today, although even we, apparently, should now be worrying about having an adequate supply of workers to support our elderly. In previous societies the concern for a viable rate of reproduction commanded primary attention. Since many children were stillborn or died in infancy, a woman had to go through many more pregnancies than she wanted just to make sure that enough children would survive beyond the age of five to replenish or even increase the next generation. For the same reasons, most societies preferred not to risk women's lives on the front line in warfare.

Men, from this perspective, are much more disposable than women: one man can impregnate any number of women. A woman normally can only bear one child at a time, and it takes her nine months to do so, not to mention the time she must devote to nursing. In many instances frequent childbearing tended to undermine women's health and strength. Finally, even women who chose to limit their fertility had access only to unreliable forms of contraception. As a result, many women in past societies spent a significant part of their adult years bearing and nursing children and, accordingly, needed—even if they often did not get—the special protection required by the vulnerability of pregnancy and nursing. Under these conditions, many women directed their energy and imagination to making the best of their "situation" by finding their sense of self-worth and self-respect in their roles as wives and mothers.

During the twentieth century the importance of the biological differences between men and women have lost most of their power to explain and justify the social, economic, and political differences between men and women. The modern technological and contraceptive revolutions have radically reduced the significance of biological difference for most aspects of life. Modern methods of contraception ensure that women no longer need bear more children than they choose, and most women in developed societies like our own choose to bear few. Modern technology ensures that there are very few occupations that women cannot perform as effectively as men. In what way, after all, is muscular strength a prerequisite for pushing the button that will unleash nuclear warfare? Or for flying a jet bomber? Women have proved fully capable of becoming astronauts. There is no biological reason that they should not serve at the highest levels of military command or business administration or political power.

Those who wish to argue from physiology to social role are rapidly being forced to argue that although men are indeed better suited than women to serve in the infantry or in heavy labor, they are hardly better suited to sit behind desks, making important decisions and earning mega-salaries. One of the most striking aspects of our society lies in the declining relevance of men's physical strength to the most important business of life, including the exercise of economic and political power. In an age addicted to weight lifting and bodybuilding, we are loath to talk very much about this simple fact. We might even fairly be charged with engaging in a vast cultural deception, but the facts are as inescapable as we seem to find them unsettling. Men do retain the advantage of physical strength over women, but the significance of the advantage has steadily decreased and is now questionable. Many men have found this change disturbing, especially since it has been accompanied by a significant increase in women's potential independence and economic power.

The women's movement and feminism have permitted us to displace the problem of the declining value of men's physical strength into a discussion of the differences between men and women. Typically, many people associate the pursuit of women's rights with the decline of femininity and the increase of female aggression. Women, it is said, no longer know how to be women, do not want doors or coats held for them, do not want to be women. Women who display a serious concern with their careers or, heaven forbid, seek advancement in them risk angry denunciations as "power bitches." The epithet suggests that when a woman pursues a goal with determination, she has automatically removed herself from the category of woman, has, in some way, masculinized herself. We—women as much as men—remain deeply uncomfortable with the idea that a woman might want to win, much less that she might want to beat a man. For when a man beats another man, the contest is accepted as one between individuals, whereas when a woman beats a man, the contest is seen as representative of the battle between the sexes. Even women, who in general have not been reared to understand the pleasures of winning, themselves remain anxious about the prospect—almost fearful that winning will indeed prove that they are not truly women.

It took me longer than I care to admit to understand that women were entitled to win and that winning could be as much fun for women as for men. And goodness knows I had an object lesson close to home. For years, the quality of my life depended upon the fate of the San Francisco Giants, who for the last two decades have proved on balance disappointing, notwithstanding the promise of Will Clark, Kevin Mitchell, and, if all goes well, Matt Williams. After all these years, I still have not been able to decide if the ignominy of marginally .500 ball is better or worse than the anxieties that attend their occasional, but ultimately unsuccessful, heroics. Years ago I learned that for a baseball fan the virtues of hard work, courage in the face of defeat, discrete displays of excellence—how, in short, you play the game—matter little, if at all. The point is to win. And if baseball infects fans with this passion, what must it do to the players?

Among its other virtues, which I think are legion, baseball embodies a dramatization of the beauty and daring of physical strength and skill. I do not say that it could never be a woman's game, especially since in 1989, for the first time, a woman made a competitive college baseball team. But like Louisa McCord, I remain doubtful that many women could ever successfully compete against men for spots in the starting lineup in the major leagues. I do, in other words, think that baseball will predominantly remain a man's game, not merely in the sense of men as players but also in the sense of a dramatization of an important aspect of male identity.

In baseball, male physical strength indisputably matters, as do physical and moral courage. Those who doubt the "moral courage" would do well to look into the astonishing career of the Giants' pitcher, Dave Dravecky, whose pitching arm had a cancer cut out of it but who, in defiance of every medical prognosis, returned to the major leagues eight months later. A devoutly religious Christian, his determination cost him a broken arm and a renewed threat of cancer that has forced his permanent retirement, but the outcome hardly diminishes the valor of his effort.

Roger Kahn, in his wonderful book *The Boys of Summer*, poignantly details the dimensions of and links between physical and moral courage and their significance for boys and men who are not themselves ball players. He skillfully interweaves a running account of his own fears, as a child, of the fastball his father threw at him with accounts of the players on the spectacular Dodger teams of the early 1950s. Suddenly the reader can see and feel what it took for Jackie Robinson, the first black player in the majors, to stand day after day at second base awaiting the raised cleats of the white players of the opposing team, awaiting the tear of cleats on his shins. Day after day, Jackie Robinson took his place at second base, and day after day he held his ground. When it was over, thanks to Jackie Robinson and Branch Rickey, baseball was integrated.

Women are unaccustomed to such tests of physical strength and endurance. Our models of courage are different, although no less important in their way. We need only think of the courage of a Rosa Parks, who quietly, simply refused to move from the seat on the bus that was reserved for white folks. Women, too, can appreciate baseball. Indeed I unhesitatingly count myself a fan. But watching baseball, we are not generally watching our own kind, not shaping our own identities. As fans, our enthusiasm, like that of men, is for a lived contest between spirit and flesh and for a competition women are unlikely to enter directly. Why should we recoil? Why should women not appreciate a specifically male version of the human condition? Why should we not recognize that, notwithstanding all the changes our world has undergone or may undergo, differences persist and can be enjoyed?

Professional sports rank among the few remaining arenas in modern life to which the biological differences between men and women are relevant. Sexual relations rank as another. By and large, the worlds of work and politics do not. Even women's primary responsibility for child rearing, which is currently receiving so much attention through discussions of the "mommy track," is more socially than biologically determined. And, although some studies suggest that boys outperform girls on some tests of mathematical ability, few are yet willing to credit biology with the difference. Even if biological difference could be established, it is hard to believe that it would be relevant below the level of genius. Thus although many of us, women as well as men, do not wish to see it that way, it remains true that the vast majority of our social roles result from social choices, not from the dictates of biology. This change in the relevance of men's physical strength, which has come upon us rapidly, causes unavoidable confusion, but we cannot afford to let our own confusion shape our future.

Afterword

Evidence abounds that men are finding these changes especially difficult to deal with. The growing attention to men's violence against women and children (rape, acquaintance rape, wife beating, child molestation, incest) directly testifies to our, and especially men's, discomfort with the dramatic changes in the relevance of male strength to social and political power. Some believe that these forms of violence are not actually increasing but are only being reported more frequently. We may doubt that an increase in reporting alone accounts for our sense of escalating violence, for there is good reason to believe that many men, frustrated by a world they have no hope of controlling in the wake of an erosion of their advantages and the social relevance of their physical superiority, are increasingly tempted to use that strength in the one situation in which it still clearly gives them an advantage—their personal relations with women. If I am correct in this suspicion, then we are looking at a tragedy of massive proportions.

I do not raise these questions in a spirit of condemnation. To the contrary, I believe that in general men face as many difficulties as women and are no better prepared to meet them. I also believe that women share the responsibility to rethink the relation between our biological characteristics and our social roles and responsibilities. Few men these days would want a wife who could not contribute to the family income and share the anxieties of having to do so. When my husband teasingly pretends to long for the days in which women kept to their proper places in the bedroom and kitchen, I solemnly remind him of my salary and contributions to the work we publish together. He sighs with feigned regret and grumbles that, forced to choose, he figures it is safer to put up with me.

He has lost a good deal in the way of service since the early days of our marriage. He is, in truth, more likely to do our everyday cooking than I, although on rare occasions I still prepare a fancy dinner. He has, I think, especially lost the right to be the one who is busier, who faces the greater demands from the outside world. Thank goodness he has not lost his sense of humor, although a few years ago, in making my own adjustments to new roles, I gave him a shock.

I am the proud mistress of a very large dog named Josef. As a puppy, Josef proved something of a handful. Big, bouncy, decidedly male, he had a strong will of his own. And I, having been raised to think like a girl, mistakenly thought that the appropriate way to deal with a young creature, a mere puppy, was to be gentle and speak softly—to nurture and cultivate this fledgling personality. I was wrong. As any dog-lover knows, the only way to train a dog is to establish yourself as master, which, in Josef's case, required a certain amount of brute force. I had to learn to raise my voice and to adopt a severe, commanding tone. I had to learn to pick him up by his jowls and deck him, flat on his back. At the worst, I had to learn to put on heavy leather gloves and to drag him out from under the table, where he was baring his forbidding teeth, in order to deck him again. Above all, I had to learn that I could never afford to lose a confrontation with him. In short, I had to win.

And as I went about these exercises in training, I would cheerfully say, "Who's boss, Josef?" My husband approved until one day I added, "Who's boss of all the bosses?" The specific formulation rather unsettled my husband, who was not used to thinking of our household from the perspective of me as boss. And I fear that my insistence that it was only a phrase to train the dog did not entirely put him at ease. My husband recovered his sense of humor. And I learned something I could never have imagined about the pleasures of winning without guilt. The lesson has stayed with me.

These fragments of autobiography carry no particular lesson, unless it be that much of our sense of the richness and joy of life comes from our appreciation of the differences between men and women, our appreciation of each other. But, to the best of my knowledge, that delightful difference between boys and girls—"you don't have a penis"—has few necessary consequences for political and economic roles in a world of adult women and men—a world that will never realize the dreams of radical egalitarianism but that can meet the tests of equity and justice.

The "other story" of my adult life is not, from one perspective, radically different from the story of my youth. From another perspective, it is another story entirely. For me, the space between the similarity and the difference is the space of necessary revision, of expanded questions, of new possibilities for those we are trying to educate. Feminism has helped to define that space for women—and for men—but has not alone caused it to open. Feminism can help us to rethink our history and to reimagine our politics, but it cannot alone do either. As a critique of the excesses of individualism, feminism potentially contributes to a new conception of community—of the relation between the freedom of individuals and the needs of society. The realization of that potential lies not in the repudiation of difference but in a new understanding of its equitable social consequences.

NOTES

INTRODUCTION

1. See, e.g., *Hypatia*; *Signs*; *Feminist Studies*; *Genders*; *Tulsa Studies in Women's Literature*; *Women and Politics*; *Journal of Women's History*. For an overview, see Minnich, O'Barr, and Rosenfeld, *Reconstructing the Academy*.

2. In fact, Black Studies paved the way, but the nationalist thrust of that movement has not prevailed and Black Studies programs have not been successful in mounting a comprehensive and theoretically coherent challenge.

3. Friedan, *Feminine Mystique*.

4. See, esp., Sandel, *Liberalism and the Limits of Justice*; MacIntyre, *After Virtue*; Wolgast, *Grammar of Justice*; Sandel, *Liberalism and Its Critics*.

5. The previous essays and articles are all listed in the bibliography.

CHAPTER 1

1. See essays in Jaggar and Bordo, *Gender/Body/Knowledge*, esp. Jaggar, "Love and Knowledge"; Tronto, "Women and Caring"; Arnault, "Radical Future of a Classic Moral Theory."

2. In so doing, they drew upon a long-standing female tradition. Sisterhood, as an everyday practice and as a metaphor, has existed since the beginnings of capitalist society, and before. But that ancient metaphor has acquired its specific meanings from specific social relations, and its meanings and implications continue to change as our society changes.

3. Eisler, *Chalice and the Blade*. But cf. Cynthia Fuchs Epstein, *Deceptive Distinctions*, pp. 185–86, who argues that, given the opportunity to wield political power, women have behaved very similarly to men.

4. Belenky, Clinchy, Goldberger, and Tarule, *Women's Ways of Knowing*; Gilligan, *In a Different Voice*; Kittay and Meyers, *Women and Moral Theory*. For a strong recent defense of emphasizing what women share across lines of class and race, see Bordo, "Feminism, Postmodernism, and Gender-Scepticism."

5. Gilligan, *In a Different Voice*; Kittay and Meyers, *Women and Moral Theory*; O'Brien, *Politics of Reproduction*. Elshtain, *Women and War*, also believes that women have developed an ethic of care. Both O'Brien and Elshtain, however, strenuously resist the pitfall of assuming that women are somehow "naturally" nice and gentle. See also Baier, "What Do Women Want in a Moral Theory?" These currents are especially strong in popular feminism; see Segal, *Is the Future Female?*, esp. pp. 1–37.

6. Fox-Genovese, *Within the Plantation Household*, pp. 290–333; Terborg-Penn, "Black Women in Resistance"; Bush, "'The Family Tree Is Not Cut.'"

7. Van Allen, "'Aba Riots' or Igbo 'Women's War'?," and "'Sitting on a Man.'"

8. See, e.g., Thomis and Grimmett, *Women in Protest*, and Hufton, "Women and the Family Economy." On the sexual division of labor and resistance in early modern society, see Natalie Zemon Davis, *Society and Culture*; Fox-Genovese, "Placing Women's History"; Fox-Genovese, "Gender, Class and Power"; Fox-Genovese, "Women and Work."

9. Rable, *Civil Wars*.

10. Kantorowicz, *The King's Two Bodies*; Aidoo, "Asante Queen Mothers." On the sexual division of labor in general, see Silverblatt's excellent discussion in *Moon, Sun, and Witches* and in her "Imperial Dilemmas." See also Segalen, *Mari et femme*.

11. Gutman, *Black Family*, uses the phrase to capture the enduring bonds of loyalty among black slaves whose family relations were too frequently sundered.

12. See, e.g., Yellin, *Women and Sisters*; Hewitt, "Feminist Friends"; Hersh, *Slavery of Sex*.

13. Morgan, *Sisterhood Is Powerful*. Cf. Heilbrun's discussion of women's conflicted feelings about power in *Writing a Woman's Life*, pp. 16–17.

14. See Shreve, *Women Together, Women Alone*, and Heilbrun, *Writing a Woman's Life*, pp. 44–46.

15. Ruth Schwartz Cowan, *More Work for Mother*; Strasser, *Never Done*.

16. Carolyn Heilbrun especially emphasizes the importance of anger in *Writing a Woman's Life*. Although her discussion is generally faithful to the experience of many women during the 1960s and early 1970s, it may not accurately capture the more complex attitudes of women of previous generations, many of whom may have taken more satisfaction in their lives than contemporary feminist critics allow. See also West, "Love, Rage, and Legal Theory," and Brownmiller, *Against Our Will*.

17. For a brilliant fictional representation of this collective middle-class female autobiography, see Shulman's *Memoirs* and her *Burning Questions*. For an overview of women's issues since World War II, see Harrison, *On Account of Sex*, and Echols, *Daring to Be Bad*. For essays that wonderfully capture the most generous spirit of the women's movement in the 1970s, see Stimpson, *Where the Meanings Are*.

18. See, e.g., Rich, "Compulsory Heterosexuality."

19. See, e.g., Chernin, *Obsession*, and *Hungry Self*.

20. Rich, *Of Woman Born*; Heilbrun, *Writing a Woman's Life*, p. 67.

21. Chodorow, *Reproduction of Mothering*; Dinnerstein, *Mermaid and the Minotaur*.

22. For a somewhat different reading of sisterhood as "political solidarity among women," see hooks, *Feminist Theory*, pp. 43–65.

23. For a fuller development of this argument, see chap. 5, below.

24. Hurston, *Dust Tracks*. For a parallel discussion of the birth of race as a concept, see Fields, "Slavery, Race, and Ideology."

25. Again, see chap. 5, below, for a development of the argument.

26. Kerber, "Separate Spheres." On the dangers of feminist views of women's powerlessness, see the insightful discussion of Jehlen, "Archimedes and the Paradox of Feminist Criticism," pp. 581–82.

27. On the general problem, see Spelman, *Inessential Woman*; Grimshaw, *Philosophy and Feminist Thinking*, pp. 75–100; Angela P. Harris, "Race and Essentialism";

Riley, *Am I That Name?* See also hooks, *Ain't I a Woman*; Angela Y. Davis, *Women, Race, and Class*; Joseph and Lewis, *Common Differences*; Bettina Aptheker, *Woman's Legacy*.

28. Felice N. Schwartz, "Management Women."

29. See, esp., Ehrenreich, *Hearts of Men*.

30. Fuchs, *Women's Quest for Economic Equality*. See also Robertson, "Strategies for Improving the Economic Situation of Women"; Lloyd and Niemi, *Economics of Sex Differentials*, pp. 240–311.

31. For a thoughtful discussion of nineteenth-century sisterhood, see Boydston, Kelley, and Margolis, *Limits of Sisterhood*.

32. Something analogous is happening in the African-American community. See William Julius Wilson, *Truly Disadvantaged*.

33. Leach, *True Love and Perfect Union*; Ginzberg, "'Joint Education of the Sexes.'" For a strong contemporary argument that emphasizes the ways in which women do adapt to public opportunities, see Cynthia Fuchs Epstein, *Deceptive Distinctions*.

34. For a recent, thoughtful discussion of the specific experience of working-class women, see Hochschild, *Second Shift*.

35. Flax, "Postmodernism and Gender Relations," and *Thinking Fragments*. Similarly, the "French feminists" are borrowing from a variety of French post-structuralist discourses, including Lacanian psychology. See, e.g., Moi, *Sexual/Textual Politics*; Moi, *French Feminist Thought*; Gallop, *Daughter's Seduction*; Gallop, "Heroic Images"; Gallop, *Reading Lacan*; Marks and de Courtivron, *New French Feminisms*.

36. Lerner, *Creation of Patriarchy*; Eisenstein, *Capitalist Patriarchy*; Folbre, "Logic of Patriarchal Capitalism"; Folbre, "Of Patriarchy Born"; Hartmann, "Capitalist Patriarchy." See also Fox-Genovese, "Socialist-Feminist American Women's History."

37. Segal, *Is the Future Female?*, p. 69.

38. Dinnerstein, *Mermaid and the Minotaur*; Chodorow, *Reproduction of Mothering*, and *Feminism and Psychoanalytic Theory*. See also Olivier, *Jocasta's Children*.

39. Rich, *Of Woman Born*; O'Brien, *Politics of Reproduction*; Ruddick, *Maternal Thinking*.

40. Elshtain, *Women and War*; Elshtain, "Feminist Discourse"; Elshtain, "Symmetry and Soporifics."

41. For the importance of parenting, see, e.g., Chodorow, *Reproduction of Mothering*. For the emphasis on difference, see, e.g., Gilligan, *In a Different Voice*; Eisler, *Chalice and the Blade*. For an especially sobering critique of androgyny, see Elshtain, "Against Androgyny."

42. For a forceful critique of assimilating the experience of all women to a middle-class norm, see Spelman, *Inessential Woman*. See also hooks, *Feminist Theory*.

43. See Fox-Genovese, "New Female Literary Culture." And, for especially interesting renditions of the common narrative, see Shulman's *Memoirs* and her *Burning Questions*.

44. Here, I am taking respectful exception to the views of my friend bell hooks. See, esp., her *Talking Back*. I do share her commitment to the importance of self-knowledge (autobiography) for individuals but doubt that it provides an adequate basis for a socially responsible feminist politics.

45. "Employers Are Looking Abroad"; Harrison and Bluestone, *The Great U-Turn*.

46. Rix, *American Woman*, includes a wide array of relevant statistics. See also Fuchs, *Women's Quest for Economic Equality*; Robertson, "Strategies for Improving the Economic Situation of Women."

47. Luker, *Abortion and the Politics of Motherhood*; Hewlett, *Lesser Life*.

48. Jameson, "Postmodernism, or the Cultural Legacy of Late Capitalism," and "Postmodernism and Consumer Society," tellingly suggests that postmodernism describes the conditions of our world.

49. See, e.g., West, "Jurisprudence and Gender"; "Authoritarian Impulse in Constitutional Law"; "Law, Rights, and Other Totemic Illusions." Robin West has emerged as one of the most original and forceful feminist legal theorists. For references to others, see chaps. 3 and 4, below. For West's critique of other tendencies in feminist jurisprudence, see her "Difference in Women's Hedonic Lives."

50. Segal, *Is the Future Female?*, p. 246.

CHAPTER 2

1. Klein, *Gender Politics*.

2. *Concise Oxford Dictionary*, p. 204.

3. Tönnies, *Community and Society*.

4. Tate, *Collected Essays*; Tate, *Essays of Four Decades*; Weaver, *Southern Tradition at Bay*; Bradford, *Remembering Who We Are*. The "conservatives" to whom I refer are the traditionalists, who in our country have been especially prominent in the South. Free-market liberals today call themselves conservatives, and the conservative political movement embraces many tendencies. With no pejorative intent, I exclude the free-market conservatives as irrelevant to the immediate problems, primarily because they have identified themselves as uncompromising defenders of individualism.

5. See, e.g., Marcuse, *One-Dimensional Man*, and MacIntyre's critique of his thought, *Herbert Marcuse*.

6. This tendency is particularly evident in discussions of slaves and working people. See, e.g., Blassingame, *Slave Community*; Gutman, *Black Family*; Thompson, *Making of the English Working Class*. Recall that Marx built his critique of the alienation inherent in the division of labor on the pioneering work of Adam Smith, whose own forebodings remain well worth reading. See Smith, *Wealth of Nations*, esp. pp. 14–15; and, for Marx's continuing dialogue with his predecessors in political economy, see *Theories of Surplus-Value*.

7. Marx, *Economic and Philosophic Manuscripts*; and, for a critique of this tendency, Fox-Genovese and Genovese, "Illusions of Liberation." Marx never repudiated his youthful utopianism, which reappeared in such later works as the *Critique of the Gotha Program*, but he did temper it considerably in the great works of his mature years. More important, the interpretation of history that emerges from *Capital*, *Theories of Surplus-Value*, and his historical essays bears little relation to his philosophical speculations, which, in effect, constitute a superimposition, not to say an

embarrassment. See, e.g., "Introduction to the New Edition," in Genovese, *In Red and Black*.

8. See, esp., Kerber, "Separate Spheres."

9. In recent years, many women's historians have been paying attention to the differences in women's experience by race and class. See, e.g., Stansell, *City of Women*; Barbara Leslie Epstein, *Politics of Domesticity*; Hewitt, "Beyond the Search for Sisterhood"; Janiewski, *Sisterhood Denied*; Fox-Genovese, *Within the Plantation Household*; and, for an overview of the developments, Fox-Genovese, "Socialist-Feminist American Women's History."

10. Jeffrey, *Frontier Women*, first developed this argument, which has been echoed in recent work.

11. Lebsock, *Free Women of Petersburg*.

12. Smith-Rosenberg, *Religion and the Rise of the American City*.

13. Yellin, *Women and Sisters*; Hersh, *Slavery of Sex*.

14. Fox-Genovese, *Within the Plantation Household*; Stansell, *City of Women*.

15. For an overview of white women's efforts, see Anne Firor Scott, *Southern Lady*.

16. Rouse, *Lugenia Burns Hope*, offers a much-needed biography of that important woman. See also Giddings, *When and Where I Enter*.

17. Clawson, "Nineteenth-Century Women's Auxiliaries," and *Constructing Brotherhood*, pp. 178–210.

18. For a recent discussion of the relation between social housekeeping and political feminism, see Cott, "What's in a Name?"

19. On the ways in which Americans have found "traditional liberalism" lacking "as a national public philosophy," see Rogers M. Smith, "'One United People.'" Sandel, *Liberalism and the Limits of Justice*, argues something similar, albeit in very different terms. See also MacIntyre, *After Virtue*.

20. The recent court decision, *Stanford* v. *Kentucky*, that permits teenagers to be sentenced to death for murder testifies to the same trend. See *Stanford* v. *Kentucky*; *Wilkins* v. *Missouri*. Much of the tremendous recent concern about the family implicitly derives from a recognition of the growing fragmentation and possibly contradictory interests of family members, but those who are concerned do not usually frame the discussion in terms of individualism. See, e.g., Okin, *Justice, Gender, and the Family*, which is primarily an attack on such conservatives as Sandel, Bloom, and MacIntyre. For a thoughtful attempt to reconsider the value and function of the family from the perspective of children, see Elshtain, "Political Theory Rediscovers the Family," and "'Thank Heaven for Little Girls.'"

21. Fleming, *Politics of Human Nature*. See also Sandel, *Liberalism and the Limits of Justice*; MacIntyre, *After Virtue*.

22. Friedman, "Women's Autobiographical Selves."

23. Gilligan, *In a Different Voice*, has most systematically developed this point of view, but it is an important current in much feminist thought. See, among many, Kittay and Meyers, *Women and Moral Theory*; Ruddick, "Maternal Thinking"; O'Brien, *Politics of Reproduction*; O'Brien, *Reproducing the World*; Flax, "Postmodernism and Gender Relations"; Belenky, Clinchy, Goldberger, and Tarule, *Women's Ways of Knowing*.

24. West, "Jurisprudence and Gender." See also Minnow, "1986 Supreme Court Term"; Okin, *Justice, Gender, and the Family*; Nedelsky, "Reconceiving Autonomy."

25. Nedelsky, "Reconceiving Autonomy," p. 7. For a similar view that defending women's interests might require a different conception of community, see Spaulding, "Anti-Pornography Law"; Rogers M. Smith, "'One United People.'" For the general critique of liberalism, see Sandel, *Liberalism and the Limits of Justice*; MacIntyre, *After Virtue*; Charles Taylor, *Philosophical Papers*, esp. chap. 7, "Atomism"; Sandel, *Liberalism and Its Critics*.

26. Sandel, *Liberalism and the Limits of Justice*, pp. 148–49. See also Rawls, "Justice as Fairness," and for the fullest picture of his views, *Theory of Justice*.

27. Jean Bethke Elshtain comes closest to this position, which she has been developing with considerable sophistication. Among her many publications, see, esp., "The Family Crisis" and "Symmetry and Soporifics."

28. See, esp., Weitzman, *Divorce Revolution*, and Hewlett, *Lesser Life*.

29. For a telling critique of essentialism, see Spelman, *Inessential Woman*. For an argument for greater attention to history in feminist theory, see Nicholson, *Gender and History*. For fuller developments of my own views, see Fox-Genovese, *Within the Plantation Household*; "Placing Women's History"; and "Culture and Consciousness."

30. Wollstonecraft, *Vindication of the Rights of Woman*.

31. See chap. 5, below, for a fuller discussion of particularism in women's experience and identities.

32. Van Allen, "'Aba Riots' or 'Igbo Women's War'?," and "'Sitting on a Man.'"

33. Hollander, *Seeing through Clothes*.

34. For the ways in which capitalism and imperialism undercut women's rights to collective resources and undermined their position relative to that of the men of their own communities, see, e.g., Boserup, *Woman's Role in Economic Development*. For the classic, if subsequently criticized, statement of the British case, see Clark, *Working Life of Women*; and for a sophisticated, recent view, see Boydston, "To Earn Her Daily Bread."

35. Baer, *Chains of Protection*.

36. In Blackstone's words, "By marriage, the husband and wife are one person in law: that is, the very being or legal existence of the woman is suspended during the marriage, or at least is incorporated and consolidated into that of the husband: under whose wing, protection, and *cover*, she performs every thing. . . . Upon this principle of an union of person in husband and wife, depend almost all the legal rights, duties, and disabilities, that either of them acquire by the marriage." See Blackstone, *Commentaries*, 1:430. See also Salmon, *Women and the Law of Property*.

37. For overviews, see Rhode, *Justice and Gender*, and Flexner, *Century of Struggle*. For the specific case of married women's property, see Basch, *In the Eyes of the Law*.

38. *California Federal Savings and Loan Association v. Guerra*.

39. See, e.g., Fox-Genovese, "Women and Agriculture during the Nineteenth Century."

40. Elshtain, "Family Crisis"; Martha May, "Historical Problem of the Family Wage."

41. Sandel, *Liberalism and the Limits of Justice*, p. 150.

42. On the boundaries that have, historically, protected communities, see Gerald E. Frug, "City as a Legal Concept." For a fuller discussion of particularism, see chap. 5, below.

43. Elshtain, *Public Man, Private Woman.*

44. In addition to *Public Man, Private Woman*, see her "Toward a Theory of the Family and Politics"; "Symmetry and Soporifics"; "'Thank Heaven for Little Girls.'"

45. Fleming, *Politics of Human Nature*, pp. 5, 1. For an elaboration of these remarks, see my "Ahistorical Admonitions," parts of which I have excerpted here. For a critique of conservative attacks on liberalism, see Gutmann, "Communitarian Critics of Liberalism."

46. Fleming, *Politics of Human Nature*, p. 6. Fleming's rejection of traditional doctrine is surprising from a southern conservative, and yet his specific doctrine does echo the thought of Albert T. Bledsoe, a prominent political theorist and theologian of the Old South.

47. See, esp., Eisler, *Chalice and the Blade.*

48. Fleming, *Politics of Human Nature*, p. 56.

49. Ibid., p. 155.

50. Ibid., p. 181.

51. Ibid., p. 198.

52. See chap. 3, below.

53. Jaggar, *Feminist Politics and Human Nature.* For a critique of socialist-feminism, see Segal, *Is the Future Female?*, pp. 38–69.

54. hooks, *Ain't I a Woman*; hooks, *Talking Back*; hooks, *Feminist Theory*; Spivak, *In Other Worlds.*

55. West, "Jurisprudence and Gender," pp. 13–14, 72.

56. Chodorow, *Reproduction of Mothering*, and *Feminism and Psychoanalytic Theory.* For a devastating critique of the functionalism of Chodorow's model, see Elshtain, "Symmetry and Soporifics," pp. 73–79. See also West, "Communities, Texts, and Law," which argues for the reformation of communities through "a greater attention to the narratives of those who have been excluded from legal discourse."

57. Okin, *Justice, Gender, and the Family*, pp. 170–71.

58. Nedelsky, "Reconceiving Autonomy," p. 36.

59. Smith-Rosenberg, "Female World of Love and Ritual."

60. For a general view of women's communities, see Bernard, *Female World.*

61. Rogers M. Smith, "'One United People.'"

CHAPTER 3

1. Cott, "What's in a Name?"

2. Cynthia Fuchs Epstein, *Deceptive Distinctions*, p. 240.

3. MacKinnon, *Toward a Feminist Theory of the State*, p. 249.

4. See chap. 3, above. Notwithstanding MacKinnon's sharply defined position, her work shares many assumptions with that of Gilligan, *In a Different Voice*; West, "Jurisprudence and Gender"; and others.

5. *Wimberly v. Labor and Industrial Relations Commission of Missouri.*

6. West, "Jurisprudence and Gender"; Littleton, "Equality and Feminist Legal Theory"; Littleton, "Restructuring Sexual Equality"; Nedelsky, "Reconceiving Autonomy." The perception that male experience pervades every aspect of our law has provoked a strong feminist current in legal education. See, e.g., Bender, "A Lawyer's Primer"; Erickson, "Sex Bias in Law School Courses"; Finley, "Break in the Silence"; Mary Jo Frug, "Re-Reading Contracts"; Coombs, "Crime in the Stacks." For a discussion of women's position in law schools, see Angel, "Women in Legal Education"; and for a general historical overview, Morello, *Invisible Bar.*

7. Sandel, *Liberalism and the Limits of Justice.* Nedelsky, "Reconceiving Autonomy," offers an important exception. MacKinnon, *Toward a Feminist Theory of the State,* points in the same direction, although she does not engage the issue directly.

8. On women's distinct worlds, see Smith-Rosenberg, "Female World of Love and Ritual." On the ties between women and men, see Rothman, *Hands and Hearts.*

9. Heated debates surround the meaning and intentions of Anglo-American political theory in the eighteenth century and beyond, but few have challenged—or even seriously discussed—the importance of the concept of the individual, although African-American and women's history have called attention to its limits. See Conkin, *Prophets of Prosperity*; Conkin, *Self-Evident Truths*, pp. 75–108; Kerber, *Women of the Republic*; Kettner, *Development of American Citizenship*; McDonald, *Novus Ordo Seclorum*; William B. Scott, *In Pursuit of Happiness.* For my own view of the relation between gender hierarchy and social role, see "For Feminist Interpretation."

10. For the classic discussion of the hostility to "factionalism," see Hofstadter, *Idea of a Party System.* For a more recent discussion, see Kohl, *Politics of Individualism.*

11. See Tocqueville, *Democracy in America,* and *Old Régime and the French Revolution.* Tocqueville's insights, which reflected his implicit comparison with the corporatist and hierarchical social structure of pre-Revolutionary France, have cast a long shadow over subsequent scholarship.

12. Lousse, *Société d'Ancien Régime.*

13. Some American historians have tried to emphasize the corporatist features and values of early American experience, albeit frequently without using the word. See Bailyn, *New England Merchants*; Henretta, "Families and Farms"; Waters, "Traditional World." Horwitz, *Transformation of American Law,* explicitly addresses the move from corporatist to individualist principles in law; Tushnet, *American Law of Slavery,* addresses the distinct character and influence of slavery on southern law.

14. Fitzhugh, *Sociology for the South.* See also Genovese, *World the Slaveholders Made*; Genovese and Fox-Genovese, "Slavery, Economic Development, and the Law"; Genovese and Fox-Genovese, "Religious Ideals"; Fox-Genovese and Genovese, "Divine Sanction of Social Order." Henry Hughes envisioned a modern corporatism, which he called "warranteeism," that, in some respects, foreshadowed fascism. See Hughes, *Treatise on Sociology,* and *Selected Writings.*

15. See Tönnies, *Community and Society,* and chap. 2, above.

16. Basch, *In the Eyes of the Law.*

17. See Pole, *Pursuit of Equality.*

18. Fee, "Science and the Woman Problem"; John David Smith, *Old Creed for the New South.*

19. Frug, "City as a Legal Concept."

20. Fields, "Ideology and Race," and "Slavery, Race, and Ideology."

21. Fields, "Slavery, Race, and Ideology."

22. In the Old South, the churches forcefully opposed "scientific" racism on the same basis that they supported slavery—the Bible. Thus although most believed African people to be especially suited to enslavement, they did not accept the doctrine of the diversity of the races that was being propounded by Josiah Nott and others, and many did believe that, were black Africans not available, some whites would have to be enslaved.

23. The key development was the decision of the Ford Company in 1905 to pay a select group of male workers enough to support their families without financial contributions from their wives. See Martha May, "Historical Problem of the Family Wage."

24. Ralph E. Smith, *Subtle Revolution*; Oppenheimer, *Female Labor Force*; Smuts, *Women and Work in America*; Wandersee, *Women's Work and Family Values*; and, for an overview, Kessler-Harris, *Out To Work*. Both world wars, especially World War II, created a heightened demand for female labor that evaporated with their end, but even these special situations did not dramatically affect the secular tendency. War or no war, women have participated in the labor force in increasing numbers. On the contemporary situation, see Fuchs, *Women's Quest for Economic Equality*.

25. Rix, *American Woman*, p. 127. The specific figure is 53.4 percent.

26. Ibid., p. 137.

27. Formal barriers to middle-class women's participation in the public sphere began to fall during this period, notably in education and the professions. See, e.g., Cott, *Grounding of Modern Feminism*, and Rosenberg, *Beyond Separate Spheres*. On developments following World War II, see Harrison, *On Account of Sex*, and Klein, *Gender Politics*. But on the persisting resistance, see Mansbridge, *Why We Lost the ERA*, and on the conflicts between women's goals and liberalism, see Rogers M. Smith, " 'One United People.' "

28. Woolf, *A Room of One's Own*, pp. 33–34, 88–89.

29. See, e.g., Radford, "Sex Stereotyping."

30. MacKinnon, *Toward a Feminist Theory of the State*, p. 248.

31. See Friedan, *It Changed My Life*, p. 318; Ehrenreich, *Hearts of Men*; Weitzman, *Divorce Revolution*. Historians have frequently assumed that women required the same access to divorce as men in order to achieve independence as individuals. See Basch, *In the Eyes of the Law*; Censer, " 'Smiling through Her Tears.' " But they have less commonly discussed the protection that marriage afforded women. Marriage normally becomes an issue when women perceive, or are taken to perceive, it as a constraint. For a sensitive discussion of the view of women who still take marriage as their primary source of social identity and role, see Luker, *Abortion and the Politics of Motherhood*. See also Hewlett, *Lesser Life*; Sidel, *Women and Children Last*.

32. Foremost among these disabilities ranked married women's inability, at common law, to hold property in their own names or to control their own wages. See Kanowitz, *Women and the Law*. But cf. Beard, *Women as Force in History*, p. 137, who argued that common law did not weigh heavily on married women, who could always resort to courts of equity for marriage settlements. Recent scholarship has

sharply attacked Beard's position. See, esp., Salmon, *Women and the Law of Property*. For the related problem of protective legislation for women, see Baer, *Chains of Protection*.

33. For early examples of church intervention in family relations, see McCurry, "In Defense of Their World"; Kasserman, *Fall River Outrage*. For the emergence of specialized, secular intervention in family affairs in the twentieth century, see Gordon, *Heroes of Their Own Lives*; Odem, "Delinquent Daughters."

34. Women have always figured among the fiercest critics of the women's movement. In the middle of the nineteenth century, the staunchly proslavery southerner Louisa McCord published fierce polemics against those she dismissed as "bloomerites." See, e.g., McCord, "Enfranchisement of Women," and Fox-Genovese, *Within the Plantation Household*. On the late-nineteenth-century opposition to woman suffrage, see Camhi, "Women against Women." For our own time, see Didion, *White Album*, p. 109; Schlafly, *Power of the Christian Woman*, p. 17; Felsenthal, *Sweetheart of the Silent Majority*.

35. Traditional, especially southern, conservatives and members of the working class frequently respond in this fashion. See note 13, above; Fleming, *Politics of Human Nature*; and Luker, *Abortion and the Politics of Motherhood*, pp. 110–18, on the structural change brought about by women in the work force.

36. The various class action suits that have accompanied individual grievance suits surely rest upon collective principles. See, e.g., *Equal Employment Opportunity Commission* v. *Sears, Roebuck & Co.*, p. 1264. See Joan Wallach Scott, *Gender and the Politics of History*, pp. 167–77; Wiener, "Sears Case," p. 161; Rosenberg, "Exchange," p. 394.

37. Affirmative action is not a monolith, but a complex series of disparate programs. See Rhode, *Justice and Gender*, p. 184. Some forms of affirmative action have been implemented under court order; some under Executive Order No. 11,246; some under national, state, and local government mandates; and some under private, voluntary programs.

38. See, e.g., Walzer, *Spheres of Justice*, and Fox-Genovese, "Some Are More Equal than Others."

39. The figures for the various professions regularly appear in surveys of academic employment and newspaper articles. See, e.g., Carter and Carter, "Women's Recent Progress"; Cynthia Fuchs Epstein, *Women in Law*, p. 53; Menkel-Meadow, "Women in Law?"; Cynthia Fuchs Epstein, "Epstein Responds"; Knowles, "Legal Status of Women in Alabama"; Knowles, "Legal Status of Women in Alabama, II."

40. See Rogan, *Mixed Company*; Goodman, "Women, War, and Equality," pp. 243, 249; Yoder and Adams, "Women Entering Nontraditional Roles," p. 260.

41. *Regents of the University of California* v. *Bakke*; *Grove City College* v. *Bell*; Civil Rights Restoration Act of 1987; 20 U.S.C. §§ 1681–86 (1982). One commentator, foreshadowing the *Grove City* decision, argued that Title IX did not cover employment and should not be extended from the specific program to the institution receiving federal funds as a whole. See also Crow, "Title IX," pp. 1099, 1131; Daly, "Some Runs, Some Hits, Some Errors"; Carter and Carter, "Women's Recent Progress."

42. Selig, "Affirmative Action in Employment"; Herman Schwartz, "1986 and 1987 Affirmative Action Cases"; Rutherglen and Ortiz, "Affirmative Action."

43. *Johnson v. Transportation Agency, Santa Clara County, California.*

44. Radford, "Sex-Stereotyping"; *Craft* v. *Metromedia, Inc.*; *Hishon* v. *King and Spaulding*; and *Price Waterhouse* v. *Hopkins, reversing and remanding.*

45. 42 U.S.C. §§ 2000e–2000e-17 (1982); 29 U.S.C. § 206(d) (1982). On comparable worth, see Livernash, *Comparable Worth*; Feldberg, "Comparable Worth," p. 311; chap. 2, above.

46. Milkman, "Women's History and the Sears Case"; Joan Wallach Scott, *Gender and the Politics of History*, pp. 167–77; Haskell and Levinson, "Academic Freedom and Expert Witnessing"; Kessler-Harris, "*Academic Freedom and Expert Witnessing*"; Haskell and Levinson, "On Academic Freedom and Hypothetical Pools."

47. Walzer, *Spheres of Justice*; Justice Antonin Scalia's dissenting opinion in *Johnson* v. *Transportation Agency, Santa Clara County, California*. See also "The Week," p. 12.

48. Ronald Dworkin, "DeFunis v. Sweatt," p. 82.

49. See, e.g., Goldman, "Affirmative Action," p. 209, who argues that affirmative action seeks to redress past wrongs to groups by providing equal or preferential opportunity to individuals.

50. The argument for collective or group distinctiveness has not yet surfaced as an important tendency in the theoretical legal literature among those who favor affirmative action for blacks and women, although issues such as maternity leave are forcing renewed attention to it. For thoughtful discussions of many of the questions that concern me, see Spaulding, "Anti-Pornography Law," and West, "Jurisprudence and Gender." Law, "Rethinking Sex and the Constitution," defends some notion of group distinctiveness for affirmative action, although with respect to pornography and abortion, she takes high individualist ground. Separatist feminists have based their claims for collective identity on the common abuse that women have suffered from the "patriarchal" beliefs and practices of American society but have failed to link their cause to a systematic critique of individualism. In the Sears case, Rosalind Rosenberg based her testimony against the EEOC and for Sears on the grounds that women, as a group, have different employment preferences—specifically that they would turn down potentially lucrative jobs in commission sales—from men, as a result of cultural attitudes, socialization, and conflicting priorities, including family responsibilities. Perhaps the most thoughtful, if not the most analytically rigorous, general argument has been advanced by Elizabeth Janeway, *Powers of the Weak*, who looks to the "weak" to provide new attitudes and forms of organization to address social problems and the abuse of power.

51. Black nationalists, drawing upon a wide variety of theories, have been able to demonstrate a strong tradition of national identity within the black experience, even though their position has not intrinsically challenged the broad individualist principles of American society. See, e.g., Vincent Harding, *There Is a River*; Stuckey, *Slave Culture*.

52. Kessler-Harris, "Just Price," p. 237. Reaffirming her conviction that "social and cultural differences between women and men surely exist," she nonetheless concluded that "their abstract expression is less instructive than clear-eyed analysis in

historical context." Nor, she added, should this analysis "be allowed to obscure differences among women and the historically specific ways in which they manifest themselves and serve as sources of tension and change" (p. 247).

53. Milkman, "Women's History and the Sears Case," pp. 394–95.

54. Joan Wallach Scott, "Deconstructing Equality-Versus-Difference," p. 43.

55. Ibid., p. 46.

56. Wolgast, *Grammar of Justice*; Sandel, *Liberalism and the Limits of Justice*. MacIntyre, *After Virtue*, also offers a comprehensive critique, albeit from a particular perspective.

57. Minnow, "1986 Supreme Court Term," esp. pp. 12–13, 71–72. See also Eisenstein, *Female Body*, p. 54.

58. See chap. 7, below, for a development of this tendency in the debates over the canon.

59. Kennedy, "Racial Critiques," pp. 1816–18.

60. Scanlan, "Illusions of Job Segregation." On reverse discrimination, see Tur, "Justifications of Reverse Discrimination"; Wolgast, "Is Reverse Discrimination Fair?"; Teichman, "Reverse Discrimination"; Tur, "Concluding Remarks."

61. See, e.g., Martha Minnow's discussion of *Johnson v. Transportation Agency, Santa Clara County, California* in Minnow, "1986 Supreme Court Term," p. 91.

62. Wolgast, *Grammar of Justice*, p. 41.

63. Sandel, *Liberalism and the Limits of Justice*, p. 147.

64. See Rix, *American Woman*, pp. 348, 393. In 1986, the median income of year-round, full-time women workers was just under $17,000, that of their male counterparts was almost $26,000 (p. 348). See also Fuchs, *Women's Quest for Economic Equality*.

65. Aldrich and Buchele, *Economics of Comparable Worth*, p. xx. Kirp, Yudof, and Franks, *Gender Justice*, read the evidence more positively than most, claiming that "personal characteristics such as training, experience, and family-induced limitations explain most of the disparity [in the wage gap between women and men], even without taking an individual's occupation into account" (p. 172).

66. The "caused by discrimination" is the heart of the matter, for comparable worth does not address disparities that are not caused by discrimination. Comparable worth requires that discrimination exist, be proved, and be rectified by the courts or by legislation. Economic studies from various perspectives suggest that discrimination does play a role in the disparity in male and female wages, but even sympathetic economists cannot agree on how large a role.

67. See chap. 2, above.

68. At the time that the Equal Pay Act of 1963 was being debated, the issue of comparable worth emerged and was rejected. Title VII of the Civil Rights Act was more ambiguous. In *County of Washington, Oregon v. Gunther* (1981), Justice Brenner for the court affirmed that the female prison guards' claims "of discriminatory undercompensation are not barred" by Title VII merely because they "do not perform work equal to that of male guards." Thus, although the court did not resolve the specific dispute, it did leave open the possibility for suits on the grounds of comparable worth. It also left the basis for such suits very ambiguous.

69. Evans and Nelson, *Wage Justice*, esp. pp. 39, 173. "By August 1987 20 states and 166 localities (outside of Minnesota) had implemented comparable worth and 26 additional states were in the earliest stages of action" (p. 173). The two key court cases were *County of Washington, Oregon* v. *Gunther* and *AFSCME* v. *Washington*.

70. Scanlan, "Illusions of Job Segregation."

71. Evans and Nelson, *Wage Justice*, p. 172.

72. Kirp, Yudof, and Franks, *Gender Justice*, p. 166.

73. For a discussion of productivity as a matter of pressing concern, see the series of articles by Ferleger and Mandle: "Addressing the Productivity Problem," "Confronting the Productivity Crisis," "Democracy and Productivity," and "Savings Shortfall."

74. This fundamental problem in any labor theory of value emerged at the dawn of bourgeois political economy. See Adam Smith, *Wealth of Nations*.

75. My friend and colleague Eleanor Main developed this distinction at a session on comparable worth in which we both participated at the conference Women and the Constitution in Atlanta, February 1988.

76. See Mill, *Utilitarianism*; Himmelfarb, *On Liberty and Liberalism*, p. 205; Mill, "Subjection of Women," pp. 123, 125. See also Bentham, *Introduction*, and Rawls, *Theory of Justice*.

77. Even many "socialist-feminists" remain wedded to the illusion of individual autonomy for women. See, e.g., Eisenstein, *Radical Future of Liberal Feminism*, pp. 237–38. For a pessimistic assessment of women's real gains, see Hall, *Classroom Climate*, and Sandler, *Campus Climate Revisited*.

78. Wolgast, *Equality and the Rights of Women*, pp. 42–44, 103, 108. But cf. McMillan, *Women, Reason, and Nature*, pp. ix, 35, 38–39, who suggests that the thrust of the feminist argument rests on the belief that there are no important differences between the sexes. Law, "Rethinking Sex and the Constitution," pp. 1007–13, argues that the constitutional equality doctrine must distinguish between laws drawing explicit sex-based lines and laws governing real biological differences.

79. The fundamental argument derives from John Locke, especially his "Second Treatise on Government." See also Dumont, *From Mandeville to Marx*; Fox-Genovese and Genovese, *Fruits of Merchant Capital*, pp. 272–98; Macpherson, *Political Theory of Possessive Individualism*; Renner, *Institutions of Private Law*, pp. 90–93; chap. 5, below.

80. Ginsburg, *Contested Lives*, p. 216. *Roe* v. *Wade*, which granted women a limited right to the choice to have an abortion, failed to take a stand on many of the most divisive issues. See, on the issues it bypassed, Ricks, "New French Abortion Pill."

81. *Webster* v. *Reproductive Health Services*. For a general review of reproductive legislation, see Cohen and Taub, *Reproductive Laws*. The broader appeal of choice as a matter of individual right apparently accounts for Douglas Wilder's election as the first black governor of Virginia.

82. Cf. MacKinnon, *Toward a Feminist Theory of the State*, pp. 184–94, who argues that since sexual relations are inherently unequal and determined by men, there can be no sexual freedom for women and that, in effect, the woman's right to an abortion does not liberate women's sexuality, it liberates men's aggression.

83. Luker, *Abortion and the Politics of Motherhood*.

84. Ginsburg, *Contested Lives*, p. 216.

85. For significant exceptions, see Petchesky, *Abortion and Woman's Choice*, and Glendon, *Abortion and Divorce*. For a review of the legal issues, see Milbauer, *Law Giveth*.

86. Petchesky, in her important book *Abortion and Woman's Choice*, esp. pp. 1–18, also questions the appropriateness of individual right as a defense of a woman's right to abortion. See also Gordon, *Woman's Body, Woman's Right*.

87. Nedelsky, "Reconceiving Autonomy."

88. Ruddick, "Maternal Thinking."

89. Ibid., p. 342. The state of Connecticut has recently written a woman's right to an abortion into law, limiting that right only by the "viability" of the fetus and thus implicitly offering a definition of life.

90. Gilligan, *In a Different Voice*.

91. On the right to abortion as a matter of individual (religious) conscience, see Beverly Wildung Harrison, *Our Right to Choose*.

92. William Julius Wilson, *Truly Disadvantaged*.

CHAPTER 4

1. Wolfe, "Dirt and Democracy," p. 27.

2. Griffin, *Pornography and Silence*.

3. For a thought-provoking discussion of the distinction between pornography as a psychological and a sociological phenomenon, see Randall, *Freedom and Taboo*, and for its Sadeian aspects, see Angela Carter, *Sadeian Woman*.

4. Hawkins and Zimring, *Pornography in a Free Society*, pp. 30–73; U.S. Department of Justice, *Final Report*, p. 1353. The most commonly used figures suggest that the annual revenues from pornography amount to seven or eight billion dollars.

5. Hawkins and Zimring, *Pornography in a Free Society*, p. 72.

6. For a sampling of feminist views on pornography, see Gubar and Hoff, *For Adult Users Only*; Eisenstein, *Female Body*; Smart, *Feminism and the Power of the Law*, esp. pp. 114–37; Kappeler, *Pornography of Representation*; Carter, *Sadeian Woman*; Burstyn, *Women against Censorship*; Griffin, *Pornography and Silence*; Andrea Dworkin, *Pornography*; MacKinnon, *Feminism Unmodified*; Diamond, "Pornography and Repression."

7. *Jacobellis v. Ohio*, (Stewart, J., concurring), cited by MacKinnon, *Toward a Feminist Theory of the State*, p. 197.

8. Donnerstein, Linz, and Penrod, *Question of Pornography*, p. 3.

9. MacKinnon, *Toward a Feminist Theory of the State*, p. 194.

10. MacKinnon, *Feminism Unmodified*, p. 146.

11. Randall, *Freedom and Taboo*, p. 4.

12. For a full discussion of the positions and the issues at stake, see Copp and Wendell, *Pornography and Censorship*, esp. Garry, "Pornography and Respect for Women," Berger, "Pornography, Sex, and Censorship," Feinberg, "Pornography and the Criminal Law," and Scanlon, "Freedom of Expression." On the relation between

regulation and attitudes, see Pritchard, "Beyond the Meese Commission Report."

13. On public opinion, see Burton, "Public Opinion and Pornography Policy."

14. In full recognition of the terminological problems, I am using "radical" feminists narrowly here—to refer to those, notably Andrea Dworkin and Catharine MacKinnon, who emphasize sexual oppression and exploitation as the most important and intractable forms of social hierarchy. See, e.g., Dworkin, *Pornography*, and MacKinnon, *Toward a Feminist Theory of the State*. For the conservative view, see, e.g., U.S. Department of Justice, *Final Report*. See also West, "Feminist-Conservative Anti-Pornography Alliance."

15. And let it be noted that, in the past, the socialist left generally agreed, in accordance with its own principles of social order, however much it now seems to espouse the radical individualism it originally arose to combat and, in fact, long militantly did combat.

16. The clearest exposition of these views can be found in MacKinnon, *Toward a Feminist Theory of the State*. For a general evaluation of feminist critiques of pornography, see Eckersley, "Whither the Feminist Campaign?"

17. See, e.g., Wendell, "Pornography and Freedom of Expression"; Feinberg, "Pornography and the Criminal Law"; Dunlap, "Sexual Speech and the State"; Sunstein, "Pornography and the First Amendment"; and, for a general discussion of the issues, Soble, *Pornography*.

18. See, e.g., Fleming, *Politics of Human Nature*, and MacKinnon, *Toward a Feminist Theory of the State*, p. 193.

19. Montesquieu, *Spirit of the Laws*. See also Kra, "Montesquieu and Women."

20. The phrase, originally coined by Robin Morgan, has gained wide currency. See Morgan, *Going Too Far*, p. 169. See also Lederer, *Take Back the Night*.

21. MacKinnon is less than clear on this matter. I am very grateful to Sharon McCoy for pointing the inconsistency out to me.

22. MacKinnon, "Complicity," pp. 89–93.

23. MacKinnon, *Toward a Feminist Theory of the State*, p. 197.

24. Griffin, *Pornography and Silence*, pp. 201–2.

25. The formulation is that of Wolfe, "Dirt and Democracy," p. 28; but see Andrea Dworkin, *Pornography*, for confirmation that he does not exaggerate, and Dworkin, *Letters from a War Zone*, pp. 197–322, e.g., p. 308: "The war is men against women, the country is the United States."

26. MacKinnon, *Toward a Feminist Theory of the State*, p. 197.

27. Duggan, Hunter, and Vance, "False Promises," p. 134; Eisenstein, *Female Body*, p. 170.

28. For a full discussion, see Downs, *New Politics of Pornography*; for a brief discussion of the Indianapolis ordinance and the issue of pornography as an infringement of women's civil rights, see Rhode, *Justice and Gender*, pp. 268–70. For a sympathetic view of the attempt and the judgment that it failed "because we have been unwilling to decide that the equality of women (or other groups) is a sufficiently strong interest to justify the abridgement of individual speech rights," see Spaulding, "Anti-Pornography Law."

29. *American Booksellers Association* v. *Hudnut*. See also Downs, *New Politics of*

Pornography, for a general discussion, and Seator, "Judicial Indifference."

30. See the essays in Burstyn, *Women against Censorship*. See also Rhode, *Justice and Gender*, pp. 269–70.

31. See, for an instructive example, the furor provoked by Gore's book, *Raising PG Kids in an X-Rated Society*.

32. Donnerstein, Linz, and Penrod, *Question of Pornography*, p. 144, conclude that research to date has not produced enough evidence to prove that exposure to nonviolent pornography increases men's aggression against women, and that the data on the effects of exposure to violent pornography are inadequate to conclude anything, although they do believe there are grounds for assuming that it causes an increase in men's aggressive feelings toward women. Since most of the research has been conducted in laboratories, we are permitted some skepticism about its precise relation to what goes on in the world. For the view that there might be some correlation between the circulation of sex magazines and rape, see Baron and Straus, *Four Theories of Rape*, pp. 95–124. See also Einsiedel, "Social Science and Public Policy."

33. See, e.g., U.S. Department of Justice, *Final Report*.

34. Protective labor legislation may have been implemented, with the support of many women, to spare women from the most physically debilitating forms of labor, but it also excluded them from many of the best-paying jobs and, consequently, actually raised barriers against their economic equality with men. The heated debates about maternity leave, and even the "mommy track," are once again raising the issue. Felice N. Schwartz, "Management Women"; Rogers M. Smith, "'One United People.'"

35. *Miller* v. *California*.

36. Wolfe, "Dirt and Democracy," p. 28.

37. Feinberg, "Pornography and the Criminal Law."

38. Wolgast, *Grammar of Justice*, p. 112.

39. On problems of zoning, see Christiansen, "Zoning and the First Amendment."

40. The key case in this matter is *City of Renton* v. *Playtime Theaters, Inc.* See also "Content Analysis Distinction" and Christiansen, "Zoning and the First Amendment."

41. See Wasserstrom, "Racism, Sexism, and Preferential Treatment," p. 48, who argues that rights are "distinctive moral 'commodities,'" and Hart, "Are There Any Natural Rights?," p. 19, who argues that rights "are typically conceived of as *possessed* or *owned by* or *belonging to* individuals." For a telling critique of this position, see Wolgast, *Grammar of Justice*, pp. 28–49, esp. pp. 29–30. And for a discussion of the relation between individualistic conceptions of right and the thought of the Enlightenment, see MacIntyre, *After Virtue*, pp. 68–70.

42. Elshtain, "Victim Syndrome." According to her evidence, if not her rhetoric, societies with low levels of pornography are more likely to be socialist than bourgeois, and it is entirely possible that in the modern world the institutions that are inculcating habits of restraint and decency are not preeminently those of the bourgeois family. See also Elshtain, "New Porn Wars," and her contribution to Lapham, "Place of Pornography."

43. Ehrenreich, *Hearts of Men*.

44. Eisler, *Chalice and the Blade*.

45. See, e.g., Chodorow, *Reproduction of Mothering*; Chodorow, *Feminism and Psychoanalytic Theory*; Dinnerstein, *Mermaid and the Minotaur*; Olivier, *Jocasta's Children*.

46. Fleming, *Politics of Human Nature*; Elshtain, *Public Man, Private Woman*; Elshtain, *Women and War*.

47. The early influential formulation was that of Ortner, "Is Female to Male as Nature Is to Culture?," but the debate pervades feminist scholarship.

48. For interesting feminist attempts to come to terms with evolution and sociobiology, see Hrdy, *Woman That Never Evolved*, and Nancy Makepeace Tanner, *On Becoming Human*.

49. But see Elshtain, *Women and War*, pp. 163–93.

50. See, e.g., O'Brien, *Politics of Reproduction*.

51. See, for a view similar to my own, West, "Pornography as a Legal Text."

52. Tribe, *Constitutional Choices*.

53. Berns, "Pornography vs. Democracy."

54. On the possibilities within our law, see Robel, "Pornography and Existing Law."

55. For an excellent discussion of the problem of children's rights, see Wolgast's discussion of "wrong rights" in *Grammar of Justice*, pp. 28–49. The Supreme Court has recently held that it is a crime to own pornographic pictures of children, thus moving in the direction of regulating even the private possession of specific pornographic commodities in the interests of protecting children from exploitation. See Greenhouse, "Justices, 6 to 3."

56. *Stanford* v. *Kentucky*; *Wilkins* v. *Missouri*.

57. See Sandel, *Liberalism and the Limits of Justice*; MacIntyre, *After Virtue*.

58. Kappeler, *Pornography of Representation*, p. 219. See also West, "Jurisprudence and Gender"; Nedelsky, "Reconceiving Autonomy"; Littleton, "Restructuring Sexual Equality"; Wolgast, *Grammar of Justice*; and, most militantly, MacKinnon, *Toward a Feminist Theory of the State*.

59. Kappeler, *Pornography of Representation*, p. 219.

CHAPTER 5

1. George Eliot, *Middlemarch*, "Prelude."

2. Ibid.

3. Heilbrun, *Writing a Woman's Life*; Fox-Genovese, "New Female Literary Culture."

4. George, *One Woman's "Situation."*

5. Natalie Zemon Davis, "Ghosts, Kin, and Progeny"; DuPont de Nemours, *Autobiography*.

6. Ulrich, *Good Wives*.

7. Estates, unlike classes, were legally defined social groups, similar to although

never as rigid as castes. See, e.g., Dumont, *Homo Hierarchicus*, and *From Mandeville to Marx*. See also Duby, *Société aux XIème et XIIème siècles*.

8. The word *individualism*, it should be noted, was not used until the 1820s in France and was not invoked in relation to the United States until Tocqueville's *Democracy in America* in the 1840s.

9. For an excellent discussion of particularist and universalist ideologies and institutions in women's experience, see Natalie Zemon Davis, *Society and Culture*, esp. pp. 65–95.

10. Baier, "What Do Women Want in a Moral Theory?"; West, "Jurisprudence and Gender"; Nedelsky, "Reconceiving Autonomy."

11. Gilligan, *In a Different Voice*.

12. Homans, *Bearing the Word*.

13. Rubin, "Traffic in Women"; Rosaldo, "Use and Abuse of Anthropology." In recent years, this position has gained wide currency among feminist scholars. For insightful discussions, see Newton and Rosenfelt, *Feminist Criticism and Social Change*, esp. Barrett, "Ideology and the Cultural Production of Gender," pp. 65–86; Kauffman, *Gender and Theory*. For a critique, see Bordo, "Feminism, Postmodernism, and Gender-Scepticism."

14. Fox-Genovese, *Within the Plantation Household*, and "My Statue, My Self."

15. The Reformation did engender a variety of radical politics, including a serious peasant revolt in Germany, but Luther himself repudiated that revolt and did his best to convince the German princes that Protestantism did not challenge the traditional foundations of their political power. Ozment, *Age of Reform*. For the implications of Calvinism for women, see Douglass, *Women, Freedom, and Calvin*, and Potter, "Gender Equality and Gender Hierarchy."

16. Many feminists have sharply criticized the mentality of science, notably its tendency to transform nature into an object of exploitation, and have associated it with male in contradistinction to female modes of thought. The most subtle discussion of these issues can be found in Sandra Harding, *Science Question in Feminism*. See also Keller, *Reflections on Gender and Science*, and Schiebinger, *The Mind Has No Sex?*

17. The classic, and widely criticized, formulation is that of Weber, *Protestant Ethic*.

18. Pocock, *Machiavellian Moment*; Macpherson, *Political Theory of Possessive Individualism*.

19. Ozment, *When Fathers Ruled*.

20. For one of the most powerful, see West, "Jurisprudence and Gender."

21. Those who did favor the rights of women included Olympe de Gouges and the Marquis de Condorcet. See, among many, Landes, *Women and the Public Sphere*.

22. Fox-Genovese, "Property and Patriarchy."

23. Cott, "Passionlessness."

24. Salvaggio, *Enlightened Absence*, p. 5.

25. Badinter, *Émilie, Émilie*, and *Unopposite Sex*; Fox-Genovese and Genovese, *Fruits of Merchant Capital*, chap. 11, "The Ideological Bases of the Domestic Economy: The Representation of Women and the Family in the Age of Expansion," pp. 299–336; Kerber, "Separate Spheres"; Irene Q. Brown, "Domesticity, Feminism,

and Friendship"; Lindemann, "Love for Hire"; Lindemann, "Maternal Politics." See also Kristeva, "Stabat Mater."

26. Polanyi, *Great Transformation*.

27. Staves, "British Seduced Maidens"; Miller, *Heroine's Text*; Castle, *Clarissa's Cyphers*; Tony Tanner, "Julie and 'La maison paternelle'"; Wexler, "'Made for Man's Delight.'"

28. A compelling source for these views can be found in novels. For women novelists' support of responsible motherhood and domesticity, see, among many, Edgeworth, *Belinda*, and Charlotte Smith, *Emmeline*. For a male novelist's critique of aristocratic women's license, see Laclos, *Liaisons dangereuses*.

29. Kerber, *Women of the Republic*.

30. For general discussions, see Poovey, *Proper Lady and the Woman Writer*, and Newton, *Women, Power, and Subversion*. For specific novels, see Austen, *Persuasion*; Charlotte Smith, *Emmeline*; Edgeworth, *Belinda*.

31. Macaulay, *Letters on Education*; Sophia, a Person of Quality, *Woman Not Inferior to Man*.

32. Beauvoir, *Second Sex*.

33. Shanley, "'One Must Ride Behind'"; Shanley, *Feminism, Marriage, and the Law*; Basch, *In the Eyes of the Law*.

34. Fleming, *Politics of Human Nature*; MacIntyre, *After Virtue*; Sandel, *Liberalism and the Limits of Justice*.

35. Belsey, "Constructing the Subject," p. 50.

36. On previous British feminists, see Moira Ferguson, *First Feminists*.

37. Kelly, "Early Feminist Theory."

38. De Pizan, *Book of the City of Ladies*.

39. Perry, *Celebrated Mary Astell*; Astell, *Some Reflections upon Marriage*.

40. Kelly, "Did Women Have a Renaissance?" For new readings of gender in the Renaissance, see Margaret W. Ferguson, Introduction to *Rewriting the Renaissance*, pp. xv–xxxi; and Rigolot, "Gender or Sex Difference," pp. 287–98.

41. See, e.g., Wemple's excellent study, *Women in Frankish Society*.

42. E.g., Solomon, *In the Company of Educated Women*; Spencer, "Women and Education"; Karant-Nunn, "Continuity and Change"; Linda L. Clark, "Socialization of Girls"; Offen, "Second Sex and the Baccalauréat."

43. See Perry, *Celebrated Mary Astell*; Ezell, *Patriarch's Wife*; and, for France, Sonnet, *L'Éducation des filles*.

44. King and Rabil, *Her Immaculate Hand*; Warnicke, *Women of the English Renaissance*; Margaret W. Ferguson, Introduction to *Rewriting the Renaissance*, pp. xv–xxxi; Rigolot, "Gender Sex Difference," pp. 287–98; Travitsky, *Paradise of Women*; Suzanne W. Hull, *Chaste, Silent, and Obedient*; Hilda L. Smith, *Reason's Disciples*.

45. See Atkinson, *Mystic and Pilgrim*. On the general problem of women's self-representations, see Sidonie Smith, *Poetics of Women's Autobiography*.

46. Shepherd, *Amazons and Warrior Women*; Dugaw, *Warrior Women and Popular Balladry*.

47. Ezell, *Patriarch's Wife*.

48. Warner, *Joan of Arc*.

49. Larner, *Enemies of God*; Wiltenberg, "Disorderly Women and Female Power."

50. Pitkin, *Fortune Is a Woman*; Saxonhouse, *Women in the History of Political Thought*.

51. Herrin, "Women and the Faith in Icons," demonstrates that women especially defended icon worship because it could be carried on at home. See also her *Formation of Christendom*, pp. 307–11.

52. Some women, e.g., established a special relation to the dominant tradition that excluded them without directly challenging it by "mothering" men's minds. Perry and Brownley, *Mothering the Mind*.

53. Schibanoff, "Comment on Kelly's 'Early Feminist Theory,'" p. 324.

54. Heilbrun, *Writing a Woman's Life*.

55. Mellor, *Romanticism and Feminism*; Goldberg, *Sex and Enlightenment*; Fox-Genovese and Genovese, *Fruits of Merchant Capital*, chap. 11, "The Ideological Bases of the Domestic Economy: The Representation of Women and the Family in the Age of Expansion," pp. 299–336; Schiebinger, "Skeletons in the Closet." See also the fine articles by Lindemann, "Love for Hire," and "Maternal Politics." On England, see Caroline Davidson, *A Woman's Work Is Never Done*; Irene Q. Brown, "Domesticity, Feminism, and Friendship"; Mendelson, "Stuart Women's Diaries and Occasional Memoirs"; Crawford, "Women's Published Writings, 1600–1700"; George, *Women in the First Capitalist Society*.

56. Rogers, *Feminism in Eighteenth-Century England*; Poovey, *Proper Lady and the Woman Writer*; Newton, *Women, Power, and Subversion*; Armstrong, "Rise of Feminine Authority in the Novel"; Miller, "Emphasis Added"; Stewart, "Novelists and Their Fictions."

57. Armstrong, *Desire and Domestic Fiction*. See also Douglas, *Feminization of American Culture*.

58. Hilda Smith, writing about seventeenth-century intellectual and literary women, especially deplores the sentimentalization of women's writings in the eighteenth century. See Smith, *Reason's Disciples*. For one example of the essentialist current, see Bonnie G. Smith, "Contribution of Women to Modern Historiography." For a discussion of the pitfalls of essentialism, see Spelman, "Woman as Body," and, esp., *Inessential Woman*.

59. See Offen, "Depopulation, Nationalism, and Feminism," and Sherman, *Women as Interpreters of the Visual Arts*.

60. For a comparative account, see Rendall, *Origins of Modern Feminism*. See also Barbara Taylor, *Eve and the New Jerusalem*; Moses, "Saint-Simonian Men/Saint-Simonian Women"; Moses, *French Feminism*; Zucker, "German Women and the Revolution of 1848."

61. Ross and Rapp, "Sex and Society"; Arnstein, *Protestant versus Catholic in Mid-Victorian England*; Sayers, *Biological Politics*. First-person accounts for working women remain sparse, but see Michel, *Red Virgin*, and Cullwick, *Diaries*.

62. Koonz, *Mothers in the Fatherland*; Bock, "Racism and Sexism in Nazi Germany"; Bridenthal, Grossmann, and Kaplan, *When Biology Became Destiny*.

63. For a revealing example of this indebtedness, as well as a preliminary attempt to wrestle with it, see Jardine, *Gynesis*.

CHAPTER 6

1. Du Bois, *Souls of Black Folk*, p. 1.

2. Ibid., p. 3.

3. For the similarities, see Stimpson, *Where the Meanings Are*, pp. 11–37.

4. Kelly, "Doubled Vision of Feminist Theory."

5. David Brion Davis, *Problem of Slavery in Western Culture*.

6. The debates about the representations of women and the opportunities afforded women within Western Christianity remain complex. See, e.g., Ruether, *Religion and Sexism*; Warner, *Alone of All Her Sex*; Tavard, *Woman in Christian Tradition*; Atkinson, Buchanan, and Miles, *Immaculate and Powerful*; Bynum, *Jesus as Mother*; Natalie Zemon Davis, *Society and Culture*, pp. 65–95; Fox-Genovese, "Culture and Consciousness."

7. See, e.g., West, "Jurisprudence and Gender"; Nedelsky, "Reconceiving Autonomy." See also Wolgast, *Grammar of Justice*; Sandel, *Liberalism and the Limits of Justice*; MacIntyre, *After Virtue*.

8. Heilbrun, *Writing a Woman's Life*; Miller, *Subject to Change*, pp. 47–64.

9. Miller, *Subject to Change*, p. 55.

10. For critiques of the limitations of the model of separate spheres, see Hewitt, "Beyond the Search for Sisterhood," and Fox-Genovese, "Socialist-Feminist American Women's History." For a preliminary attempt to introduce women's history into Western civilization, see Fox-Genovese and Stuard, *Restoring Women to History*.

11. For a trenchant critique of nonfeminist history of women, see Stuard, "The Annales School and Feminist History." For review articles, see Joan Wallach Scott, "Women in History"; Hufton, "Women in History"; Fox-Genovese, "Culture and Consciousness."

12. Resurgence, because women's history has a much longer tradition than is commonly recognized. See Bonnie G. Smith, "Contribution of Women to Modern Historiography." For a critique of social history, see Fox-Genovese and Genovese, *Fruits of Merchant Capital*, pp. 179–212.

13. Fox-Genovese, "Culture and Consciousness"; Veeser, *New Historicism*.

14. On the Sears case, in which the EEOC brought suit against Sears Roebuck for its failure to promote sufficient numbers of women to commission sales, see, among many, Haskell and Levinson, "Academic Freedom and Expert Witnessing"; Kessler-Harris, "*Academic Freedom and Expert Witnessing*"; Haskell and Levinson, "On Academic Freedom and Hypothetical Pools"; Milkman, "Women's History and the Sears Case." On the impact of post-structuralism and postmodernism, see Palmer, *Descent into Discourse*; Joan Wallach Scott, "Deconstructing Equality-Versus-Difference"; Stansell, "Response to Joan Scott"; Koonz, "Post Scripts"; Jehlen, "Patrolling the Borders"; Hartsock, "Foucault on Power."

15. Lerner, *Creation of Patriarchy*; Joan Wallach Scott, *Gender and the Politics of History*.

16. Hartmann, "Capitalist Patriarchy"; Hartmann, "Unhappy Marriage of Marxism and Feminism"; Folbre, "Logic of Patriarchal Capitalism." See also Mann, "Slavery, Sharecropping, and Sexual Inequality," who is developing a view of many patriarchies.

17. Lerner, *Creation of Patriarchy*, p. 239.

18. Ibid., p. 229.

19. See Maclean, *Renaissance Notion of Woman*. Cf. Guinsburg, "Counterthrust to Sixteenth-Century Misogyny," and the subtle analysis of Crawford, "Attitudes to Menstruation."

20. Rowbotham, "Trouble with 'Patriarchy'"; Okin, "Patriarchy and Married Women's Property."

21. Spender, *Women of Ideas*, p. 5.

22. Rosaldo, "Use and Abuse of Anthropology," esp. p. 394, argues that male dominance characterizes so much of known human social organization as to function as a general rule—for which, as with all rules, there may be an occasional exception, but no systematic disproof.

23. Jaggar, *Feminist Politics and Human Nature*; Tong, *Feminist Thought*; Young, "Socialist Feminism and the Limits of Dual Systems Theory."

24. Stansell, *City of Women*; Boydston, "To Earn Her Daily Bread"; Gordon, *Heroes of Their Own Lives*; Milkman, *Gender at Work*. See also Boydston, Kelley, and Margolis, *Limits of Sisterhood*, and Fox-Genovese, "Socialist-Feminist American Women's History."

25. For forceful critiques of essentialism, see Spelman, *Inessential Woman*; Grimshaw, *Philosophy and Feminist Thinking*; Riley, *Am I That Name?*; Angela P. Harris, "Race and Essentialism." For a view similar to my own on the limitations of patriarchy, see Cocks, *Oppositional Imagination*.

26. Thus Mary Poovey, in *Uneven Developments*, p. 23, apparently feels obliged to defend herself against political complacency by arguing that her use of gender "is not a function of the absolute and ahistorical importance of gender."

27. Joan Wallach Scott, *Gender and the Politics of History*, p. 41.

28. See, e.g., Toril Moi's discussion of Hélène Cixous. Moi, *Sexual/Textual Politics*, esp. pp. 104–7.

29. See, e.g., Schor, *Breaking the Chain*, pp. 1–28.

30. See Jardine, *Gynesis*; Salvaggio, *Enlightened Absence*, esp. pp. 128–32.

31. Joan Wallach Scott, *Gender and the Politics of History*, pp. 5, 2.

32. Flax, "Postmodernism and Gender Relations," p. 633. For a fuller development, see also her *Thinking Fragments*. See also Eisenstein and Jardine, *Future of Difference*.

33. Flax, "Postmodernism and Gender Relations," p. 643.

34. Joan Wallach Scott, *Gender and the Politics of History*, p. 26.

35. See the interchange between the two: Himmelfarb, "Some Reflections on the New History," and Joan Wallach Scott "History in Crisis?" See also Joan Wallach Scott, Review of *New History and the Old*, by Himmelfarb.

36. The single most influential figure in cultural studies has probably been Michel Foucault, whose extensive publications include *The Order of Things*, *Discipline and Punish*, and *History of Sexuality*. The key figure in post-structuralist literary criticism is Jacques Derrida. See, among many, his *Of Grammatology*. For feminist skepticism about Foucault, see Hartsock, "Foucault on Power"; Fox-Genovese, "Gender, Class, and Power."

37. Palmer, *Descent into Discourse*.

38. Dalton, "Where We Stand," p. 11.

39. For a general history and analysis, see Moi, *Sexual/Textual Politics*. For skeptical views of the uses of post-structuralism for feminist critics, see Showalter, "Feminist Criticism in the Wilderness"; Christian, "Race for Theory"; Bordo, "Feminism, Postmodernism, and Gender-Scepticism."

40. See, among many, Cixous, "Laugh of the Medusa"; Irigaray, *Speculum de l'autre femme*; Irigaray, *Ce sexe qui n'en est pas un*.

41. On postmodernism in general, see, among many, Jameson, "Postmodernism and Consumer Society"; Arac, *Postmodernism and Politics*; Hassan, *Dismemberment of Orpheus*; Andrew Ross, *Universal Abandon?*; Margolis, "Postscript on Modernism and Postmodernism, Both"; Hutcheon, *Poetics of Postmodernism*; Hutcheon, "Postmodern Problematizing of History." For recent arguments in favor of the intimate relation between feminism and postmodernism, see Waugh, *Feminine Fictions*; Owens, "The Discourse of Others"; and Dalton, "Where We Stand," p. 7, who unequivocally states, "Feminism is, I believe, at its most powerful and best as a postmodern project." For a variety of views on the relation between feminism and postmodernism, see Nicholson, *Feminism/Postmodernism*.

42. Christian, "Race for Theory," pp. 67, 71.

43. See, esp., Spivak, *In Other Worlds*. See also Marks and de Courtivron, *New French Feminisms*, and Jardine, *Gynesis*.

44. Joan Wallach Scott, "History in Crisis?," p. 691.

45. Ibid., p. 682.

46. Ibid., p. 691.

47. Himmelfarb, "Some Reflections on the New History," p. 669.

48. Ibid.

49. Significantly, an enthusiastic and self-congratulatory account of this process can be found in the official journal of the Organization of American Historians (Wiener, "Radical Historians"). See also Novick, *That Noble Dream*.

50. Himmelfarb, *New History and the Old*, pp. 21, 18.

51. Joan Wallach Scott, Review of *New History and the Old*, by Himmelfarb, p. 699.

52. Collins, "Social Construction of Black Feminist Thought," p. 770.

53. Ibid., p. 772.

54. Ibid., p. 773.

55. Bloom, *Closing of the American Mind*, p. 30.

56. Poovey, "Feminism and Deconstruction," p. 63.

57. On the pitfalls of essentialism, see Spelman, *Inessential Woman*, and Riley, *Am I That Name?* I have elsewhere argued against the essentialist reading of women's historical and contemporary experience. See, e.g., *Within the Plantation Household*, and "Culture and Consciousness."

58. Poovey, *Uneven Developments*, offers a fine discussion of aspects of this process and of its general consequences.

59. The classic formulation is that of Rubin, "Traffic in Women."

60. Fox-Genovese, *Within the Plantation Household*.

61. The phrase comes from Lampedusa's novel, *The Leopard*.

62. Joan Wallach Scott, "Deconstructing Equality-Versus-Difference," pp. 33–34.

63. Ibid., p. 43.

64. Ibid., p. 46.

65. Jehlen, "Patrolling the Borders," p. 32–33. See also her fine article "Archimedes and the Paradox of Feminist Criticism."

66. Jehlen, "Patrolling the Borders," p. 36.

67. Heilbrun, *Toward a Recognition of Androgyny*; most recently, Cynthia Fuchs Epstein, *Deceptive Distinctions*; Okin, *Justice, Gender, and the Family*; and for a combination of androgyny and postmodernism, Joan Wallach Scott, *Gender and the Politics of History*.

68. Littleton, "Equality and Feminist Legal Theory," pp. 1052, 1057.

69. Weaver, *Language Is Sermonic*, p. 182.

70. Ibid., p. 161.

71. Ibid., p. 181.

72. Homans, *Bearing the Word*, p. 4.

73. Ibid., p. 13.

74. Fields, "Ideology and Race."

75. There are those who have tried to make the case, although their numbers seem to be decreasing even among lesbian feminists. For the utopian dimension of female separatism, see Gilman, *Herland*.

76. Miller, *Subject to Change*, pp. 47–64.

77. Armstrong, *Desire and Domestic Fiction*; Douglas, *Feminization of American Culture*.

78. Tilly, "Paths of Proletarianization," pp. 400–417.

79. Tilly, "People's History," pp. 471–72.

CHAPTER 7

1. The terms *canon* and *great tradition* both invite confusion. Canon is increasingly being used as shorthand for an ill-defined group of "great" texts with which all students should be familiar. For some, the term means little more than the history of Western civilization. For others it means the history of great ideas or great books. For most it probably means some combination of political and intellectual history—great men and great books. The lists of works worth including vary considerably. Both Columbia University and the University of Chicago have well-known core curricula based on their ideas of the high points of Western civilization. Recently Stanford University has, with considerable publicity, revised its course in Western Civilization. For a range of recent positions on the place of the canon in education, see "Canon Busting and Cultural Literacy," and, esp., Bennett, "Why Western Civilization?"

2. Fox-Genovese, "Feminist Challenge to the Canon." See also my "Great Tradition and Its Orphans" and "Claims of a Common Culture," from which this chapter is, in part, drawn.

3. Salinger, *Catcher in the Rye*.

4. Harriet A. Jacobs, *Incidents in the Life of a Slave Girl*. For a thorough discussion of Jacobs's references to the dominant (white) culture, see McCaskill, "To Rise above

Race." Antebellum southern men who went to college appear to have received a version of the history of Western civilization—notably as formulated by Thomas Roderick Dew, president of William and Mary—that did not differ radically from what my generation was taught in the late 1950s and early 1960s and certainly differed little at all from what was taught at Harvard or the University of Wisconsin or the University of Virginia, or for that matter, Smith or Vassar or Tuskegee in the 1890s or the 1930s. See, e.g., Dew, *Digest of the Laws*.

5. Fuller, *Letters of Margaret Fuller*; Haight, *George Eliot*; Redinger, *George Eliot*; Hemenway, *Zora Neale Hurston*. Eliot translated Feuerbach and Strauss; Fuller's letters abound with references to the elite culture of her day, which she frequently links to her deep admiration for Shakespeare.

6. Gita May, *Madame Roland*, discusses how, as a girl, Madame Roland read Plutarch's *Lives* and, later, Jean-Jacques Rousseau's *Confessions*, imaginatively transforming their message to fit her own aspirations.

7. For one fine discussion of the ways in which liberal values were self-consciously forged in combat with the legacy of feudalism, see Houghton, *Victorian Frame of Mind*.

8. In this respect, the impetus informing feminist scholarship very much resembles that informing African-American and other forms of ethnic studies, and indeed the social history of the common people. For a similar argument, see Stimpson, *Where the Meanings Are*, pp. 11–37.

9. See mentions in chap. 5, above. For a review of recent work, see Fox-Genovese, "Culture and Consciousness." For substantive discussions, see, among many, King and Rabil, *Her Immaculate Hand*, and Gibson, "Educating for Silence."

10. See, e.g., Tompkins, *Sensational Designs*.

11. See, esp., Spender, *Women of Ideas*.

12. Eisler, *Chalice and the Blade*. For a fuller development of my critique, see also Fox-Genovese, Review of *Chalice and the Blade*.

13. Merchant, *Death of Nature*. The most balanced discussion of these issues can be found in Sandra Harding, *Science Question in Feminism*. See also Keller, *Reflections on Gender and Science*. For a nuanced discussion that nonetheless emphasizes the opposition between science and "femininity," see Schiebinger, *Mind Has No Sex?*; for an investigation of the ways in which science and medicine treated gender, see Jordanova, *Sexual Visions*; and for the experience of women in science, see Rossiter, *Women Scientists in America*.

14. Janeway, *Powers of the Weak*. See also Fox-Genovese, "Power and Authority."

15. Sophocles, *Antigone*, ll. 483–84, 525.

16. Shakespeare's views had much in common with the "popular" culture of his day, which frequently depicted temporary reversals in male and female roles as a means of confirming their conventional order. On reversals, see Natalie Zemon Davis, *Society and Culture*, pp. 124–51. On the interaction of "high" and "popular" culture, see Bakhtin, *Rabelais and His World*.

17. Goethe, *Sorrows of Young Werther*.

18. The tendency to credit a happy domestic ending with the power to restore order is evident throughout Dickens's fiction, as indeed throughout Victorian fiction

in general. See, among many, Dickens, *Our Mutual Friend*, and *Bleak House*. For the social context of the domestic ending, see Gallagher, *Industrial Reformation*; for twentieth-century women writers' attempts to break through the domestic ending, see DuPlessis, *Writing Beyond the Ending*. See also Armstrong, *Desire and Domestic Fiction*.

19. Comte, *Auguste Comte and Positivism*; Kofman, *Abérrations*.

20. Freud, *Civilization and Its Discontents*.

21. For some examples of work on women in classical philosophy, see Okin, *Women in Western Political Thought*; Spelman, "Woman as Body"; Spelman, *Inessential Woman*; Saxonhouse, *Women in the History of Political Thought*.

22. On Machiavelli's concern with gender, see Pitkin, *Fortune Is a Woman*.

23. Joel Schwartz, *Sexual Politics of Jean-Jacques Rousseau*.

24. Hobbes, *Leviathan*; Locke, "Second Treatise."

25. Macpherson, *Political Theory of Possessive Individualism*.

26. Filmer, *Patriarcha*.

27. I developed a fuller version of this argument in Fox-Genovese, "Property and Patriarchy." Since that time, a number of feminist scholars have also explored the role of gender in classical political theory and have arrived at similar judgments. See, e.g., Eisenstein, *Radical Future of Liberal Feminism*; Nicholson, *Gender and History*. Of special interest, and from a somewhat different perspective than my own, is Elshtain, *Public Man, Private Woman*.

28. In addition to Elshtain, *Public Man, Private Woman*, see Schochet, *Patriarchalism*.

29. Wollstonecraft, *Thoughts on the Education of Daughters*.

30. Kelly, "Early Feminist Theory." See also Moira Ferguson, *First Feminists*; Hilda L. Smith, *Reason's Disciples*; Frankel, "Damaris Cudworth Masham."

31. Himmelfarb, *On Liberty and Liberalism*.

32. Colwill, "Just Another *Citoyenne*?" See also Landes, *Women and the Public Sphere*; Fox-Genovese and Genovese, *Fruits of Merchant Capital*, chap. 11, "The Ideological Bases of the Domestic Economy: The Representation of Women and the Family in the Age of Expansion," pp. 299–336; Applewhite and Levy, "Women, Democracy, and Revolution."

33. Koonz, *Mothers in the Fatherland*. See also Janiewski, *Sisterhood Denied*, and Fox-Genovese, *Within the Plantation Household*.

34. Fanon, *Studies in a Dying Colonialism*. On Fanon, see Gendzier, *Frantz Fanon*. On the liberationist implications of his thought, see Fox-Genovese and Genovese, "Illusions of Liberation."

35. See, e.g., Scholes, "Aiming a Canon at the Curriculum." For various points of view, see also "Canon Busting and Cultural Literacy."

36. Fanon, *Wretched of the Earth*.

37. Spivak, *In Other Worlds*.

38. See, e.g., Genovese, *In Red and Black*, and Harding, *There Is a River*.

39. Morrison, *Bluest Eye*, pp. 7–8.

40. Bloom, *Closing of the American Mind*.

41. Butler, *Gender Trouble*, p. 148.

42. This tendency may partially help to explain how academic virtuosity can coex-

ist with a general failure of "cultural literacy." See E. D. Hirsch, Jr., *Cultural Literacy*. See also the thoughtful discussion of these problems in Cain, *Crisis in Criticism*.

43. Christian, "Race for Theory." See also Hartsock, "Foucault on Power."

44. Zedler, "The Three Princesses."

45. Hegel, *Phenomenology of Mind*. See also chap. 9, below.

46. Jordan, *Second Stories*.

47. On women philosophers, see McAlister, "History of Women in Philosophy" (special issue of *Hypatia*).

48. On Queen Elizabeth, see Haigh, *Elizabeth I*, pp. 8–11, 21–25; on Astell, see Perry, *Celebrated Mary Astell*; on McCord, see Fox-Genovese, *Within the Plantation Household*.

49. Gardiner, "Women in Science."

50. Scholes, "Aiming a Canon at the Curriculum."

CHAPTER 8

1. The similarity of the response never meant that American identity as embodied in American culture was not subject to contest, but that even as the favored authors shifted from those of the genteel tradition to those of Matthiessen's *American Renaissance*, the chosen continued to belong to the northeastern, WASP tradition. See, e.g., Cheyfitz, "Matthiessen's *American Renaissance*."

2. Wise, "'Paradigm Dramas.'"

3. See, among many, Collins, "Social Construction of Black Feminist Thought," esp. p. 770: "Living life as an African-American woman is a necessary prerequisite for producing Black feminist thought because within Black women's communities thought is validated and produced with reference to a particular set of historical, material, and epistemological conditions." See also Joan Wallach Scott, *Gender and the Politics of History*, and Flax, "Postmodernism and Gender Relations."

4. For a thoughtful assessment of the general problem, see, esp., Cain, *Crisis in Criticism*, and, for the sharpest formulation of the conservative position, Bloom, *Closing of the American Mind*. For overviews of the status and mission of American Studies, see, e.g., Berkhofer, "New Context"; Wise, "'Paradigm Dramas'"; Michael Cowan, "Boundary as Center"; Lenz, "American Studies and the Radical Tradition"; Mussell, "Social Construction of Reality."

5. Bennett, *Our Children and Our Country*; Bennett, *To Reclaim a Legacy*; Bloom, *Closing of the American Mind*. For a discussion in the press over Stanford University's struggle over the curriculum, see "Bennett Says Stanford Was Intimidated." For a discussion of the state of American Studies, see "Bennett Calls Stanford's Curriculum Revision 'Capitulation' to Pressure."

6. Joan Wallach Scott, "History in Crisis?" Discussions of this confusion between points of view and the professional promotion of those who advance them are proliferating. Unfortunately, they themselves usually reflect the confusion. See, e.g., Wiener, "Radical Historians," and Novick, *That Noble Dream*. See also D'Emilio, "Not a Simple Matter."

7. Kerber, "Diversity and the Transformation of American Studies."

8. Many of the most promising exceptions to the tendency are strongly rooted in history, notably Stansell, *City of Women*; Leverenz, *Manhood and the American Renaissance*; Smith-Rosenberg, *Disorderly Conduct*; Lang, *Prophetic Woman*; Bercovitch, *Puritan Origins of the American Self*; Bercovitch, *American Jeremiad*.

9. Sollors, *Beyond Ethnicity*. I do not wish to slight the significance of Sollors's general argument but am struck by how little attention he gives to Hawthorne, Emerson, Poe, Melville, Whitman, and company. For random examples, Theodore Dreiser, Edith Wharton, Harriet Jacobs, Pauline Hopkins, Susan Warner, Fanny Fern (Ruth Hall), Augusta Evans Wilson, and William Gilmore Simms do not appear in his index. Nor do gender or women.

10. Du Bois, *Souls of Black Folk*, p. 11.

11. Fiedler, *Love and Death*, and *Return of the Vanishing American*.

12. Roth, *Call It Sleep*.

13. Langston Hughes, "Theme for English B." As Stephen J. Whitfield has reminded me, there is a problem in using "bilingualism" to describe women's relation to the dominant culture. I trust that it is clear that I do not, in fact, believe that women speak a different language from the men of their community. Feminist scholarship has, however, insisted that in important ways women write out of a different cultural experience than men and even confront a language that frequently denies their subjectivity and authority. I am, accordingly, using bilingualism in a metaphoric rather than a literal sense in an attempt to capture the ways in which at least some women experience and appropriate a common language differently than men.

14. Ibid., p. 109.

15. Baker, *Modernism and the Harlem Renaissance*.

16. The story is included in Walker, *You Can't Keep a Good Woman Down*, pp. 124–37.

17. Camus, *L'Homme révolté*, p. 25. The translation is my own.

18. Harriet A. Jacobs, *Incidents in the Life of a Slave Girl*; Fox-Genovese, *Within the Plantation Household*, epilogue. And many of Jacobs's black, female successors did the same.

19. Gates, *Signifying Monkey*, p. xxii.

20. Ibid.

21. Hurston, *Jonah's Gourd Vine*.

22. Among the works in history and culture, see, esp., Genovese, *Roll, Jordan, Roll*; Levine, *Black Culture and Black Consciousness*; Raboteau, *Slave Religion*; White, *Ar'n't I a Woman?*; Fox-Genovese, *Within the Plantation Household*. On slave narratives and African-American autobiographies, see, esp., Andrews, *To Tell a Free Story*; Cain, "Forms of Self-Representation," pp. 201–22; Davis and Gates, *Slave's Narrative*; Fox-Genovese, "My Statue, My Self"; Martin, *Mind of Frederick Douglass*; Sekora and Turner, *Art of the Slave Narrative*; Stepto, *From Behind the Veil*. For recent work in African-American literary criticism, see, esp., Gates, *Figures in Black*; Gates, *Signifying Monkey*; Baker, *Journey Back*; Baker, *Modernism and the Harlem Renaissance*; Carby, *Reconstructing Womanhood*; Christian, *Black Feminist Criticism*; McCaskill, "To Rise above Race"; Pryse and Spillers, *Conjuring*; Wade-Gayles, *No Crystal Stair*.

23. Willis, *Specifying*, p. 10.

24. From the Revolution on, individual freedom and equality began to emerge as the dominant myth of American culture, but it long coexisted with older visions of the primacy of community and, especially, with the southern defense of hierarchy and particularism.

25. For the relevant texts, see the wonderful Schomburg Library of Nineteenth-Century Black Women Writers. In some ways the most challenging and disturbing text of all is Harriet Wilson's *Our Nig*.

26. Harriet E. Wilson, *Our Nig*; Harriet A. Jacobs, *Incidents in the Life of a Slave Girl*. See also Yellin, "Texts and Contexts," and *"Written by Herself."*

27. Schomburg Library of Nineteenth-Century Black Women Writers. Each of the thirty volumes contains an introduction to the specific work by a scholar in the field.

28. Carby, *Reconstructing Womanhood*, esp. pp. 169–73.

29. On the difficulties of *Our Nig* in particular and the tradition of nineteenth-century African-American women's writing in general, see McCaskill, "To Rise above Race."

30. Carby, *Reconstructing Womanhood*, pp. 174–75.

31. The idea that he did not have his way with her sexually, if indeed he wanted her, is highly improbable; the idea that he wrote her letters and generally attempted to court her—to win her consent—is yet more improbable. See the fuller discussion in Fox-Genovese, *Within the Plantation Household*, pp. 372–96.

32. Hine, "Rape and the Inner Lives of Black Women."

33. Saxton, "Problems of Class and Race"; Zboray, "Transportation Revolution"; Zboray, "Antebellum Reading."

34. Reasons of space preclude my doing full—or indeed any—justice to the work on specific ethnic groups, although the work on Hispanic-Americans and Native Americans in particular justifies serious treatment.

35. Baym, "Melodramas of Beset Manhood." For the strength of that male tradition, see Townsend, "Francis Parkman."

36. Tompkins, *Sensational Designs*. That Hawthorne's reputation was largely fabricated does not mean, at least in my judgment, that his work was not as good as advertised. That is another question. It is also, in large measure, another question that Hawthorne's work was ideologically charged. For a discussion of his hostile treatment of Margaret Fuller, see Chevigny, "To the Edges of Ideology." For an insightful discussion of the reception of Stowe's *Uncle Tom's Cabin* in time and place, see Baym, *Novels, Readers, and Reviewers*; and, for new readings of the novel, see Sundquist, *New Essays on "Uncle Tom's Cabin."*

37. On the scribbling women, see Douglas, *Feminization of American Culture*. Most feminist critics have been more sympathetic to antebellum women writers than Douglas. See, e.g., Tompkins, *Sensational Designs*; Baym, *Woman's Fiction*; Kelley, *Private Woman, Public Stage*.

38. Kolodny, "Integrity of Memory"; Kolodny, *Land Before Her*; Cathy N. Davidson, *Revolution and the Word*; Cathy N. Davidson, "Introduction." See also references to Tompkins and Baym in note 37, above.

39. Kelley, *Private Woman, Public Stage*; Kolodny, *Land Before Her*; Fryer, *Felicitous Space*; Wolff, *Feast of Words*.

40. For other examples of this position, see Fetterley, Introduction to *Provisions*,

pp. 1–40; Meese, *Crossing the Double-Cross*; Pollak, *Dickinson*; Radway, *Reading the Romance*; Dobson, "Hidden Hand"; Samuels, "Family, the State, and the Novel." On the general tendency in feminist theory, see, e.g., Homans, *Bearing the Word*, pp. 4–13.

41. For a thoughtful discussion of the limits of the Northeastern model of woman's sphere, see Boydston, Kelley, and Margolis, *Limits of Sisterhood*.

42. See, e.g., Fox-Genovese, *Within the Plantation Household*.

43. Stowe, *Uncle Tom's Cabin*; Hentz, *Planter's Northern Bride*. See also Douglas, *Feminization of American Culture*; Gillian Brown, "Getting in the Kitchen With Dinah"; Sundquist, *New Essays on "Uncle Tom's Cabin."*

44. On Wilson, see Fidler, *Augusta Evans Wilson*; Jones, *Tomorrow Is Another Day*; Kelley, *Private Woman, Public Stage*.

45. Obviously, Marxists have paid considerable attention to the political rights of blacks and women, but they have normally attempted, without much success, to incorporate them within their established theoretical framework. But for path-breaking work, see Herbert Aptheker, *American Negro Slave Revolts*, and "Resistance and Afro-American History."

46. Denning, "'Special American Condition.'" The distancing has been of a very special kind, for, as Denning argues, much of the most innovative recent work in American Studies is heavily indebted to Marxist thought, even when it offers itself as a substitute for Marxism. In general, even those scholars who are working with Marxist concepts have refrained either from calling themselves Marxists or from accepting an integrated Marxist theory.

47. See, esp., David Brion Davis, *Problem of Slavery in the Age of Revolution*. In general, although references to "hegemony" have become fairly common, and although references to the consciousness of working people abound, they are not normally linked, as Davis links them, to economics and politics.

48. As an amusing sidelight, the more shrill conservatives are denouncing these radical individualists as "Marxists," which does not contribute to a serious discussion of the issues. For if Marxists of various stripes and conservatives of various stripes share anything at all—and they share much more than most care to admit—it is a commitment to an integrated social and cultural vision.

49. Sollors, *Beyond Ethnicity*. See also his "Region, Ethnic Group, and American Writers" and "Theory of American Ethnicity," esp. the discussion of ethnicity and class on pp. 263–66. Here, Gates's observations on the relations of African-American writers to the Western and vernacular traditions respectively (in *Signifying Monkey*) require development. For a thoughtful treatment of a specific instance in the relations between white and black culture, see Mahar, "Black English in Early Blackface Minstrelsy."

50. T. S. Eliot, *Christianity and Culture*.

51. Gilmore, *American Romanticism and the Marketplace*; Michaels, *Gold Standard and the Logic of Naturalism*.

52. Bercovitch, *Puritan Origins of the American Self*.

53. Bercovitch and Jehlen, *Ideology and Classic American Literature*.

54. Steele, *Representation of the Self*. See also Gillian Brown, *Domestic Individualism*.

55. Smith-Rosenberg, *Disorderly Conduct*.

56. Lang, *Prophetic Woman*.

57. Gillian Brown, *Domestic Individualism*.

58. Reynolds, *Beneath the American Renaissance*. See also, e.g., Jordan, *Second Stories*; Michaels, *Gold Standard and the Logic of Naturalism*; Michaels and Pease, *American Renaissance Reconsidered*.

59. Leverenz, *Manhood and the American Renaissance*, p. 3.

60. Joan Wallach Scott, "History in Crisis?"

61. For a sharp critique of the growing hold of postmodernism, see Palmer, *Descent into Discourse*.

62. It should be noted that what applies to blacks and women also applies to southern culture, which has been shamefully neglected.

CHAPTER 9

1. Ricoeur, *De L'Interprétation*, p. 18.

2. For a related discussion of women's anger, see Heilbrun, *Writing a Woman's Life*.

3. Kate Fansher is the heroine of the mystery novels that Heilbrun has written under the name of Amanda Cross. See also Heilbrun's discussion of creating her heroine in *Writing a Woman's Life*.

4. Heilbrun, *Toward a Recognition of Androgyny*. See also Cynthia Fuchs Epstein, *Deceptive Distinctions*, and Okin, *Justice, Gender, and the Family*.

5. In this regard, feminist jurisprudence and some feminist political theory is leading the way. See, e.g., Wolgast, *Grammar of Justice*; West, "Jurisprudence and Gender"; Nedelsky, "Reconceiving Autonomy"; Littleton, "Equality and Feminist Legal Theory." The widespread critique of normative "male" morality might be read to point in this direction but does not, as a rule, fundamentally question individualist premises. Rather, it seems to be developing a theory of female individualism. See, e.g., Gilligan, *In a Different Voice*; Kittay and Meyers, *Women and Moral Theory*.

6. See, e.g., Flax, *Thinking Fragments*; Joan Wallach Scott, *Gender and the Politics of History*; Dalton, "Where We Stand." For criticisms of the implications of postmodernism for feminism, see, e.g., Hartsock, "Foucault on Power," and Di Stefano, "Dilemmas of Difference." And, for an introduction to the debates, see Nicholson, *Feminism/Postmodernism*.

7. Hegel, *Phenomenology of Mind*, p. 229.

8. Ibid., pp. 229–30.

9. Ibid., p. 239.

10. Beauvoir, *Second Sex*.

11. The phrase is that of Rosemary Ruether and Eleanor McLaughlin in the introduction to their *Women of Spirit*, p. 19. See also MacIntyre, *After Virtue*, and Sandel, *Liberalism and the Limits of Justice*.

12. Higginson, *Black Rebellion*, cited in James McPherson's introduction, p. vii.

13. Ortner, "Is Female to Male as Nature Is to Culture?," pp. 67–88.

14. Milton, *Paradise Lost*, bk. 4, l. 299.

15. Mousnier, *Peasant Uprisings*, p. 306: "The underlying cause of seditions, and of

what gives rise to them, is original sin and man's refusal to obey the commandments of God."

16. Olsen, *Silences*.

17. Ricoeur, *De L'Interprétation*, pp. 29–44.

AFTERWORD

1. Heilbrun, *Writing a Woman's Life*, p. 109.

2. Ibid., p. 131.

3. McCord, "Woman and Her Needs," p. 275.

BIBLIOGRAPHY

FEDERAL STATUTES

Civil Rights Restoration Act of 1987, Pub. L. No. 100-259, 102 Stat. 28 (1988).
20 U.S.C. §§ 1681–86 (1982).
29 U.S.C. § 206(d) (1982).
42 U.S.C. §§ 2000e–2000e-17 (1982).

EXECUTIVE ORDER

Executive Order No. 11,246, 3 C.F.R. 339 (1964–65), *reprinted in* 42 U.S.C. § 2000e note at 28–31 (1982).

COURT CASES

AFSCME v. *Washington*, 770 F.2d 1401 (9th Cir. 1985).
American Booksellers Association v. *Hudnut*, 771 F.2d 323 (7th Cir. 1985).
California Federal Savings and Loan Association v. *Guerra*, 479 U.S. 272 (1987).
City of Renton v. *Playtime Theatres, Inc.*, 475 U.S. 41 (1986).
County of Washington, Oregon v. *Gunther*, 452 U.S. 161 (1981).
Craft v. *Metromedia, Inc.*, 766 F.2d 1205 (8th Cir. 1985).
Equal Employment Opportunity Commission v. *Sears, Roebuck & Co.*, 628 F. Supp. 1264 (N.D. Ill. 1986).
Fort Wayne Books, Inc. v. *Indiana*, 109 S.Ct. 916 (1989).
FW/PBS v. *City of Dallas* 110 S.Ct. 596 (1990).
Grove City College v. *Bell*, 465 U.S. 555 (1984).
Hishon v. *King and Spaulding*, 467 S.Ct. 69 (1984).
Jacobellis v. *Ohio*, 378 U.S. 184 (1964).
Johnson v. *Transportation Agency, Santa Clara County, California*, 480 S.Ct. 166 (1987).
Miller v. *California*, 413 U.S. 15 (1973).
Mississippi University for Women v. *Hogan*, 458 U.S. 718 (1982).
North Haven Board of Education v. *Bell*, 456 U.S. 512 (1982).
Paris Adult Theater I v. *Slaton*, 413 U.S. 49 (1973).
Price Waterhouse v. *Hopkins*, 109 S.Ct. 1775 (1989).
Regents of the University of California v. *Bakke*, 438 S.Ct. 265 (1978).
Roe v. *Wade*, 410 U.S. 113 (1973).
Stanford v. *Kentucky*, 109 S.Ct. 2969 (1989).

Stanley v. *Georgia*, 394 U.S. 557 (1969).
Webster v. *Reproductive Health Services*, 109 S.Ct. 3040 (1989).
Wilkins v. *Missouri*, 109 S.Ct. 2969 (1989).
Wimberly v. *Labor and Industrial Relations Commission of Missouri*, 479 U.S. 511 (1987).

BOOKS AND ARTICLES

Aidoo, Agnes Akosua. "Asante Queen Mothers in Government and Politics in the Nineteenth Century." In *The Black Woman Cross-Culturally*, edited by Filomina Chioma Steady, pp. 65–77. Cambridge, Mass.: Schenkman, 1981.

Aldrich, Mark, and Robert Buchele. *The Economics of Comparable Worth*. Cambridge, Mass.: Ballinger, 1986.

Ames, Kenneth L. "American Decorative Arts/Household Furnishings." *American Quarterly* 35, no. 3 (bibliography 1983): 280–303.

Andrews, William L. *To Tell a Free Story: The First Century of Afro-American Autobiography, 1760–1865*. Urbana: University of Illinois Press, 1986.

Angel, Mariana. "Women in Legal Education: What It's Like to Be Part of a Perpetual First Wave or the Case of the Disappearing Women." *Temple Law Quarterly* 61, no. 3 (Fall 1988): 799–846.

Angelou, Maya. *I Know Why the Caged Bird Sings*. New York: Random House, 1969.

Applewhite, Harriet B., and Darline Gay Levy. "Women, Democracy, and Revolution in Paris, 1789–1794." In *French Women and the Age of Enlightenment*, edited by Samia I. Spencer, pp. 64–79. Bloomington: Indiana University Press, 1984.

Aptheker, Bettina. *Woman's Legacy: Essays on Race, Sex, and Class in American History*. Amherst: University of Massachusetts Press, 1982.

Aptheker, Herbert. *American Negro Slave Revolts*. 5th ed. New York: International Publishers, 1987.

———. "American Negro Slave Revolts: Fifty Years Gone." *Science and Society* 51, no. 1 (Spring 1987): 68–72.

———. "Resistance and Afro-American History: Some Notes on Contemporary Historiography and Suggestions for Further Research." In *In Resistance: Studies in African, Caribbean, and Afro-American History*, edited by Gary Y. Okihiro, pp. 10–20. Amherst: University of Massachusetts Press, 1986.

Arac, Jonathan, ed. *Postmodernism and Politics*. Minneapolis: University of Minnesota Press, 1986.

Armstrong, Nancy. *Desire and Domestic Fiction: A Political History of the Novel*. New York: Oxford University Press, 1987.

———. "The Rise of Feminine Authority in the Novel." *Novel* 15, no. 2 (Winter 1982): 127–45.

Arnault, Lynne S. "The Radical Future of a Classic Moral Theory." In *Gender/Body/Knowledge: Feminist Reconstructions of Being and Knowing*, edited by Alison M. Jaggar and Susan R. Bordo, pp. 188–206. New Brunswick, N.J.: Rutgers University Press, 1989.

Arnstein, Walter L. *Protestant versus Catholic in Mid-Victorian England: Mr. Newdegate and the Nuns*. Columbia: University of Missouri Press, 1982.

Astell, Mary. *Some Reflections upon Marriage*. 1730. Reprint. New York: Source Books Press, 1970.

Atkinson, Clarissa W. *Mystic and Pilgrim: The Book and the World of Margery Kempe*. Ithaca, N.Y.: Cornell University Press, 1983.

Atkinson, Clarissa W., Constance H. Buchanan, and Margaret R. Miles, eds. *Immaculate and Powerful: The Female in Sacred Image and Social Reality*. Boston: Beacon Press, 1985.

Austen, Jane. *Persuasion*. 1818. Reprint. Boston: Little, Brown, 1903.

Badinter, Elisabeth. *Émilie, Émilie: L'Ambition féminine au XVIIIème siècle*. Paris: Flammarion, 1983.

———. *The Unopposite Sex: The End of the Gender Battle*. Translated by Barbara Wright. New York: Harper and Row, 1989.

Baer, Judith A. *Chains of Protection: The Judicial Response to Women's Labor Legislation*. Westport, Conn.: Greenwood Press, 1978.

Baier, Annette C. "What Do Women Want in a Moral Theory?" *Noûs* 9, no. 1 (March 1985): 53–63.

Bailyn, Bernard. *The New England Merchants in the Seventeenth Century*. Cambridge, Mass.: Harvard University Press, 1955.

Baker, Houston A., Jr. *The Journey Back: Issues in Black Literature and Criticism*. Chicago: University of Chicago Press, 1980.

———. *Modernism and the Harlem Renaissance*. Chicago: University of Chicago Press, 1987.

Bakhtin, Mikhail. *Rabelais and His World*. Translated by Helene Iswolsky. Cambridge, Mass.: MIT Press, 1968.

Baron, Larry, and Murray A. Straus. *Four Theories of Rape in American Society: A State-Level Analysis*. New Haven, Conn.: Yale University Press, 1989.

Barrett, Michèle. "Ideology and the Cultural Production of Gender." In *Feminist Criticism and Social Change: Sex, Class, and Race in Literature and Culture*, edited by Judith Newton and Deborah Rosenfelt, pp. 65–85. New York: Methuen, 1985.

Basch, Norma. *In the Eyes of the Law: Women, Marriage, and Property in Nineteenth-Century New York*. Ithaca, N.Y.: Cornell University Press, 1982.

Baym, Nina. "Melodramas of Beset Manhood: How Theories of American Fiction Exclude Women Authors." *American Quarterly* 33, no. 2 (Summer 1981): 123–39.

———. *Novels, Readers, and Reviewers: Responses to Fiction in Antebellum America*. Ithaca, N.Y.: Cornell University Press, 1984.

———. *Woman's Fiction: A Guide to Novels by and about Women in America, 1820–1870*. Ithaca, N.Y.: Cornell University Press, 1978.

Beard, Mary R. *Women as Force in History: A Study in Traditions and Realities*. New York: Macmillan, 1947.

Beauvoir, Simone de. *The Second Sex*. Translated by H. M. Parshley. New York: Knopf, 1953.

Belenky, Mary Field, Blythe McVicker Clinchy, Nancy Rule Goldberger, and Jill Mattuck Tarule. *Women's Ways of Knowing: The Development of Self, Voice, and Mind*. New York: Basic Books, 1986.

Belsey, Catherine. "Constructing the Subject: Deconstructing the Text." In *Feminist Criticism and Social Change: Sex, Class, and Race in Literature and Culture*, edited by Judith Newton and Deborah Rosenfelt, pp. 45–64. New York: Methuen, 1985.

Bender, Leslie. "A Lawyer's Primer on Feminist Theory and Tort." *Journal of Legal Education* 38, nos. 1 and 2 (March/June 1988): 3–37.

Bennett, William J. *Our Children and Our Country: Improving America's Schools and Affirming Our Common Culture.* New York: Simon and Schuster, 1988.

———. *To Reclaim a Legacy: A Report on the Humanities in Higher Education.* Washington, D.C.: National Endowment for the Humanities, 1984.

———. "Why the West?" *National Review*, 27 May 1988, pp. 37–39.

———. "Why Western Civilization?" *National Forum* 69, no. 3 (Summer 1989): 3–6.

"Bennett Calls Stanford's Curriculum Revision 'Capitulation' to Pressure." *Chronicle of Higher Education*, 27 April 1988, p. A2.

"Bennett Says Stanford Was Intimidated into Changing Courses." *New York Times*, 19 April 1988, p. A18.

Bentham, Jeremy. *An Introduction to the Principles of Morals and Legislation.* Edited by J. H. Burns and H. L. A. Hart. New York: Oxford University Press, 1970.

Bercovitch, Sacvan. *The American Jeremiad.* Madison: University of Wisconsin Press, 1978.

———. *The Puritan Origins of the American Self.* New Haven, Conn.: Yale University Press, 1975.

Bercovitch, Sacvan, and Myra Jehlen, eds. *Ideology and Classic American Literature.* Cambridge: Cambridge University Press, 1986.

Berger, Fred R. "Pornography, Sex, and Censorship." In *Pornography and Censorship*, edited by David Copp and Susan Wendell, pp. 83–104. Buffalo, N.Y.: Prometheus Books, 1983.

Berger, Raoul. *Government by Judiciary: The Transformation of the Fourteenth Amendment.* Cambridge, Mass.: Harvard University Press, 1977.

Berkhofer, Robert F., Jr. "A New Context for a New American Studies?" *American Quarterly* 41, no. 4 (December 1989): 588–613.

Bernard, Jesse. *The Female World.* New York: Free Press, 1981.

Berns, Walter. "Pornography vs. Democracy: The Case for Censorship." *Public Interest*, no. 22 (Winter 1971): 3–24.

Blackstone, William. *Commentaries on the Laws of England.* 4 vols. 1765–69. Reprint. Chicago: University of Chicago Press, 1979.

Blassingame, John W. *The Slave Community: Plantation Life in the Antebellum South.* Rev. and enl. ed. New York: Oxford University Press, 1979.

Bloom, Allan. *The Closing of the American Mind: How Higher Education Has Failed Democracy and Impoverished the Souls of Today's Students.* New York: Simon and Schuster, 1987.

Bock, Gisela. "Racism and Sexism in Nazi Germany: Motherhood, Compulsory Sterilization, and the State." *Signs* 8, no. 3 (Spring 1983): 400–421.

Bordo, Susan. "Feminism, Postmodernism, and Gender-Scepticism." In *Feminism/Postmodernism*, edited by Linda J. Nicholson, pp. 133–56. New York: Routledge, 1990.

Bibliography

Boserup, Ester. *Woman's Role in Economic Development*. New York: St. Martin's Press, 1970.

Boydston, Jeanne. "To Earn Her Daily Bread: Housework and Antebellum Working-Class Subsistence." *Radical History Review*, no. 35 (April 1986): 7–25.

Boydston, Jeanne, Mary Kelley, and Anne Margolis. *The Limits of Sisterhood: The Beecher Sisters on Women's Rights and Woman's Sphere*. Chapel Hill: University of North Carolina Press, 1988.

Bradford, M. E. *Remembering Who We Are: Observations of a Southern Conservative*. Athens: University of Georgia Press, 1985.

Bridenthal, Renate, Atina Grossmann, and Marion Kaplan, eds. *When Biology Became Destiny: Women in Weimar and Nazi Germany*. New York: Monthly Review Press, 1984.

Brown, Gillian. *Domestic Individualism: Nineteenth-Century American Politics of Self*. Berkeley and Los Angeles: University of California Press, 1990.

———. "Getting in the Kitchen with Dinah: Domestic Politics in *Uncle Tom's Cabin*." *American Quarterly* 36, no. 4 (Fall 1984): 503–23.

Brown, Irene Q. "Domesticity, Feminism, and Friendship: Female Aristocratic Culture and Marriage in England, 1660–1760." *Journal of Family History* 7, no. 4 (Winter 1982): 406–24.

Brownmiller, Susan. *Against Our Will: Men, Women and Rape*. New York: Simon and Schuster, 1975.

Burstyn, Varda, ed. *Women against Censorship*. Vancouver: Douglas and McIntyre, 1985.

Burton, Doris-Jean. "Public Opinion and Pornography Policy." In *For Adult Users Only: The Dilemma of Violent Pornography*, edited by Susan Gubar and Joan Hoff, pp. 133–46. Bloomington: Indiana University Press, 1989.

Bush, Barbara. "'The Family Tree Is Not Cut': Women and Cultural Resistance in Slave Family Life in the British Caribbean." In *In Resistance: Studies in African, Caribbean, and Afro-American History*, edited by Gary Y. Okihiro, pp. 117–32. Amherst: University of Massachusetts Press, 1986.

Butler, Judith. *Gender Trouble: Feminism and the Subversion of Identity*. New York: Routledge, 1990.

Bynum, Caroline Walker. *Jesus as Mother: Studies in the Spirituality of the High Middle Ages*. Berkeley and Los Angeles: University of California Press, 1982.

Cain, William E. *The Crisis in Criticism: Theory, Literature, and Reform in English Studies*. Baltimore, Md.: Johns Hopkins University Press, 1984.

———. "Forms of Self-Representation in Booker T. Washington's *Up from Slavery*." *Prospects* 12 (1987): 201–22.

Camhi, Jane Jerome. "Women against Women: American Antisuffragism, 1880–1920." Ph.D. dissertation, Tufts University, 1973.

Camus, Albert. *L'homme révolté*. Paris: Gallimard, 1951.

"Canon Busting and Cultural Literacy." *National Forum* 69, no. 3 (Summer 1989): 2–38.

Capper, Charles. "Margaret Fuller as Cultural Reformer: The Conversations in Boston." *American Quarterly* 39, no. 4 (Winter 1987): 509–28.

Carby, Hazel V. *Reconstructing Womanhood: The Emergence of the Afro-American*

Woman Novelist. New York: Oxford University Press, 1987.

Carter, Angela. *The Sadeian Woman and the Ideology of Pornography.* New York: Pantheon Books, 1978.

Carter, Michael J., and Susan Boslego Carter. "Women's Recent Progress in the Professions or, Women Get a Ticket to Ride after the Gravy Train Has Left the Station." *Feminist Studies* 7, no. 3 (Fall 1981): 477–504.

Castle, Terry. *Clarissa's Ciphers: Meaning and Disruption in Richardson's "Clarissa."* Ithaca, N.Y.: Cornell University Press, 1982.

Censer, Jane Turner. "'Smiling through Her Tears': Ante-Bellum Southern Women and Divorce." *American Journal of Legal History* 25, no. 1 (January 1981): 24–47.

Chernin, Kim. *The Hungry Self: Women, Eating, and Identity.* New York: Times Books, 1985.

———. *The Obsession: Reflections on the Tyranny of Slenderness.* New York: Harper and Row, 1981.

Chevigny, Bell Gale. "To the Edges of Ideology: Margaret Fuller's Centrifugal Evolution." *American Quarterly* 38, no. 2 (Summer 1986): 173–201.

Cheyfitz, Eric. "Matthiessen's *American Renaissance*: Circumscribing the Revolution." *American Quarterly* 41, no. 2 (June 1989): 341–61.

Chodorow, Nancy J. *Feminism and Psychoanalytic Theory.* New Haven, Conn.: Yale University Press, 1989.

———. *The Reproduction of Mothering: Psychoanalysis and the Sociology of Gender.* Berkeley and Los Angeles: University of California Press, 1978.

Christian, Barbara. *Black Feminist Criticism: Perspectives on Black Women Writers.* New York: Pergamon Press, 1985.

———. "The Race for Theory." *Feminist Studies* 14, no. 1 (Spring 1988): 67–79.

Christiansen, David J. "Zoning and the First Amendment Rights of Adult Entertainment." *Valparaiso University Law Review* 22, no. 3 (Spring 1988): 695–724.

Cixous, Hélène. "Laugh of the Medusa." *Signs* 1, no. 4 (Summer 1976): 875–93.

Clark, Alice. *Working Life of Women in the Seventeenth Century.* 1919. Reprint. London: Cass, 1968.

Clark, Linda L. "The Socialization of Girls in the Primary Schools of the Third Republic." *Journal of Social History* 15, no. 4 (Summer 1982): 685–97.

Clawson, Mary Ann. *Constructing Brotherhood: Class, Gender, and Fraternalism.* Princeton, N.J.: Princeton University Press, 1989.

———. "Nineteenth-Century Women's Auxiliaries and Fraternal Orders." *Signs* 12, no. 1 (Autumn 1986): 40–61.

Cocks, Joan. *The Oppositional Imagination: Feminism, Critique, and Political Theory.* New York: Routledge, 1989.

Cohen, Lester H. "Mercy Otis Warren: The Politics of Language and the Aesthetics of Self." *American Quarterly* 35, no. 5 (Winter 1983): 481–98.

Cohen, Sherrill, and Nadine Taub, eds. *Reproductive Laws for the 1990s.* Clifton, N.J.: Humana Press, 1989.

Collins, Patricia Hill. "The Social Construction of Black Feminist Thought." *Signs* 14, no. 4 (Summer 1989): 745–73.

Colwill, Elizabeth. "Just Another *Citoyenne*?: Marie-Antoinette on Trial, 1790–

1793." *History Workshop*, no. 28 (Autumn 1989): 63–87.

Comte, Auguste. *Auguste Comte and Positivism: The Essential Writings*. Edited by Gertrude Lenzer. New York: Harper and Row, 1975.

Concise Oxford Dictionary of Current English. 7th ed. Edited by J. B. Sykes. New York: Oxford University Press, 1982.

Conkin, Paul K. *Prophets of Prosperity: America's First Political Economists*. Bloomington: Indiana University Press, 1980.

———. *Self-Evident Truths: Being a Discourse on the Origins and Development of the First Principles of American Government—Popular Sovereignty, Natural Rights, and Balance and Separation of Powers*. Bloomington: Indiana University Press, 1974.

"The Content Analysis Distinction in Free Speech Analysis after *Renton*." *Harvard Law Review* 102, no. 8 (June 1989): 1904–24.

Coombs, Mary Irene. "Crime in the Stacks: A Feminist Response to a Criminal Law Textbook." *Journal of Legal Education* 38, nos. 1 and 2 (March/June 1988): 117–35.

Copp, David, and Susan Wendell, eds. *Pornography and Censorship*. Buffalo, N.Y.: Prometheus Books, 1983.

Cott, Nancy F. *The Grounding of Modern Feminism*. New Haven, Conn.: Yale University Press, 1987.

———. "Passionlessness: An Interpretation of Victorian Sexual Ideology, 1790–1850." *Signs* 4, no. 2 (Winter 1978): 219–36.

———. "What's in a Name?: The Limits of 'Social Feminism,' or, Expanding the Vocabulary of Women's History." *Journal of American History* 76, no. 3 (December 1989): 809–29.

Cowan, Michael. "Boundary as Center: Inventing an American Studies Culture." *Prospects* 12 (1987): 1–20.

Cowan, Ruth Schwartz. *More Work for Mother: The Ironies of Household Technology from the Open Hearth to the Microwave*. New York: Basic Books, 1983.

Crawford, Patricia. "Attitudes to Menstruation in Seventeenth-Century England." *Past and Present*, no. 91 (May 1981): 47–73.

———. "Women's Published Writings, 1600–1700." In *Women in English Society, 1500–1800*, edited by Mary Prior, pp. 211–82. New York: Methuen, 1985.

Crow, Cheri L. "Does Title IX of the Education Amendments of 1972 Prohibit Employment Discrimination—An Analysis." *Boston College Law Review* 22, no. 5 (July 1981): 1099–1132.

Cullwick, Hannah. *The Diaries of Hannah Cullwick, Victorian Maidservant*. Edited by Liz Stanley. New Brunswick, N.J.: Rutgers University Press, 1984.

Dalton, Clare. "Where We Stand: Observations on the Situation of Feminist Legal Thought." *Berkeley Women's Law Journal* 3 (1987–88): 1–13.

Daly, Mary C. "Some Runs, Some Hits, Some Errors—Keeping Score in the Affirmative Action Ballpark from *Weber* to *Johnson*." *Boston College Law Review* 30, no. 1 (December 1988): 1–97.

Davidson, Caroline. *A Woman's Work Is Never Done: A History of Housework in the British Isles 1650–1950*. London: Chatto and Windus, 1982.

Davidson, Cathy N. "Introduction: Towards a History of Books and Readers."

American Quarterly 40, no. 1 (March 1988): 7–17.

———. *Revolution and the Word: The Rise of the Novel in America.* New York: Oxford University Press, 1986.

Davis, Angela Y. *Women, Race, and Class.* New York: Random House, 1981.

Davis, Charles T., and Henry Louis Gates, Jr., eds. *The Slave's Narrative.* New York: Oxford University Press, 1985.

Davis, David Brion. *The Problem of Slavery in the Age of Revolution, 1770–1823.* Ithaca, N.Y.: Cornell University Press, 1975.

———. *The Problem of Slavery in Western Culture.* Ithaca, N.Y.: Cornell University Press, 1966.

Davis, Natalie Zemon. "Ghosts, Kin, and Progeny: Some Features of Family Life in Early Modern France." *Daedalus* 106, no. 2 (Spring 1977): 87–114.

———. *Society and Culture in Early Modern France.* Stanford, Calif.: Stanford University Press, 1975.

D'Emilio, John. "Not a Simple Matter: Gay History and Gay Historians." *Journal of American History* 76, no. 2 (September 1989): 435–42.

D'Emilio, John, and Estelle B. Freedman. *Intimate Matters: A History of Sexuality in America.* New York: Harper and Row, 1988.

Denning, Michael. "'The Special American Condition': Marxism and American Studies." *American Quarterly* 38, no. 3 (bibliography 1986): 356–80.

De Pizan, Christine. *The Book of the City of Ladies.* Translated by Earl Jeffrey Richards. New York: Persea Books, 1982.

Derrida, Jacques. *Of Grammatology.* Translated by Gayatri Chakravorty Spivak. Baltimore, Md.: Johns Hopkins University Press, 1976.

Dew, Thomas. *A Digest of the Laws, Customs, Manners, and Institutions of the Ancient and Modern Nations.* 1852. Reprint. New York: D. Appleton, 1884.

Diamond, Irene. "Pornography and Repression: A Reconsideration." *Signs* 5, no. 4 (Summer 1980): 686–701.

Dickens, Charles. *Bleak House.* 1853. Reprint. New York: Oxford University Press, 1948.

———. *Our Mutual Friend.* 1865. Reprint. New York: Oxford University Press, 1952.

Didion, Joan. *The White Album.* New York: Simon and Schuster, 1979.

Dinnerstein, Dorothy. *The Mermaid and the Minotaur: Sexual Arrangements and Human Malaise.* New York: Harper and Row, 1976.

Di Stefano, Christine. "Dilemmas of Difference: Feminism, Modernity, and Postmodernism." In *Feminism/Postmodernism,* edited by Linda J. Nicholson, pp. 63–82. New York: Routledge, 1990.

Dobson, Joanne. "The Hidden Hand: Subversion of Cultural Ideology in Three Mid-Nineteenth-Century American Women's Novels." *American Quarterly* 38, no. 2 (Summer 1986): 223–42.

Donnerstein, Edward, Daniel Linz, and Steven Penrod. *The Question of Pornography: Research Findings and Policy Implications.* New York: Free Press, 1987.

Douglas, Ann. *The Feminization of American Culture.* New York: Knopf, 1977.

Douglass, Jane Dempsey. *Women, Freedom, and Calvin.* Philadelphia: Westminster Press, 1985.

Downs, Donald Alexander. *The New Politics of Pornography*. Chicago: University of Chicago Press, 1989.

Du Bois, W. E. B. *The Souls of Black Folk*. 1953. Reprint. Millwood, N.Y.: Kraus-Thompson Organization, 1973.

Duby, Georges. *La société aux XIème et XIIème siècles dans la Région Mâconnaise*. Paris: Librairie Armand Colin, 1953.

Dugaw, Dianne. *Warrior Women and Popular Balladry, 1650–1850*. Cambridge: Cambridge University Press, 1989.

Duggan, Lisa, Nan Hunter, and Carole S. Vance. "False Promises: Feminist Anti-pornography Legislation in the U.S." In *Women against Censorship*, edited by Varda Burstyn, pp. 130–51. Vancouver: Douglas and McIntyre, 1985.

Dumont, Louis. *From Mandeville to Marx: The Genesis and Triumph of Economic Ideology*. Chicago: University of Chicago Press, 1977.

———. *Homo Hierarchicus: The Caste System and Its Implications*. Rev. ed. Translated by Mark Sainsbury, Louis Dumont, and Basia Galati. Chicago: University of Chicago Press, 1980.

Dunlap, Mary C. "Sexual Speech and the State: Putting Pornography in Its Place." *Golden Gate University Law Review* 17, no. 3 (Fall 1987): 359–78.

DuPlessis, Rachel Blau. *Writing Beyond the Ending: Narrative Strategies of Twentieth-Century Women Writers*. Bloomington: Indiana University Press, 1985.

Du Pont de Nemours, Pierre Samuel. *The Autobiography of Du Pont de Nemours*. Translated by Elizabeth Fox-Genovese. Wilmington, Del.: Scholarly Resources, 1984.

Dworkin, Andrea. *Intercourse*. New York: Free Press, 1987.

———. *Letters from a War Zone: Writings, 1976–1989*. New York: Dutton, 1989.

———. *Pornography: Men Possessing Women*. New York: Perigree Books, 1981.

———. *Woman Hating*. New York: E. P. Dutton, 1974.

Dworkin, Ronald. "DeFunis v. Sweatt." In *Equality and Preferential Treatment*, edited by Marshall Cohen, Thomas Nagel, and Thomas Scanlon, pp. 63–83. Princeton, N.J.: Princeton University Press, 1977.

Echols, Alice. *Daring to Be Bad: Radical Feminism in America, 1967–1975*. Minneapolis: University of Minnesota Press, 1989.

Eckersley, Robyn. "Whither the Feminist Campaign?: An Evaluation of Feminist Critiques of Pornography." *International Journal of the Sociology of the Law* 15, no. 2 (May 1987): 149–78.

Edgeworth, Maria. *Belinda*. 1801. Reprint. New York: Pandora Press, 1986.

Ehrenreich, Barbara. *The Hearts of Men: American Dreams and the Flight from Commitment*. Garden City, N.Y.: Anchor Press/Doubleday, 1983.

Einsiedel, Edna F. "Social Science and Public Policy: Looking at the 1986 Commission on Pornography." In *For Adult Users Only: The Dilemma of Violent Pornography*, edited by Susan Gubar and Joan Hoff, pp. 87–107. Bloomington: Indiana University Press, 1989.

Eisenstein, Hester, and Alice Jardine, eds. *The Future of Difference*. Boston: G. K. Hall, 1980.

Eisenstein, Zillah R. *The Female Body and the Law*. Berkeley and Los Angeles: University of California Press, 1988.

_____. *Feminism and Sexual Equality: Crisis in Liberal America*. New York: Monthly Review Press, 1984.

_____. *The Radical Future of Liberal Feminism*. New York: Longman, 1981.

_____, ed. *Capitalist Patriarchy and the Case for Socialist Feminism*. New York: Monthly Review Press, 1979.

Eisler, Riane. *The Chalice and the Blade: Our History, Our Future*. San Francisco: Harper and Row, 1987.

Eliot, George. *Middlemarch*. Edited by David Carroll. New York: Oxford University Press, 1986.

Eliot, T. S. *Christianity and Culture: The Idea of a Christian Society and Notes towards the Definition of Culture*. New York: Harcourt Brace Jovanovich, 1960.

Ellis, Kate, Beth Jaker, Nan D. Hunter, Barbara O'Dair, and Abby Tallmer, eds. *Caught Looking: Feminism, Pornography and Censorship*. 2d ed. Seattle, Wash.: Real Comet Press, 1988.

Elshtain, Jean Bethke. "Acid Stomachs and Breines' Bromides." *Telos*, no. 47 (Spring 1981): 211–14.

_____. "Against Androgyny." *Telos*, no. 47 (Spring 1981): 5–21.

_____. "The Family Crisis, the Family Wage, and Feminism: Historical and Theoretical Considerations." In *The Family Wage: Work, Gender, and Children in the Modern Economy*, edited by Bryce J. Christensen, pp. 59–77. Rockford, Ill.: Rockford Institute, 1988.

_____. "Feminist Discourse and Its Discontents: Language, Power, and Meaning." *Signs* 7, no. 3 (Spring 1982): 603–21.

_____. "The New Porn Wars." *New Republic*, 25 June 1984, pp. 15–20.

_____. "Political Theory Rediscovers the Family." Preface to *The Family in Political Thought*, edited by Jean Bethke Elshtain, pp. 1–6. Amherst: University of Massachusetts Press, 1982.

_____. *Public Man, Private Woman: Women in Social and Political Thought*. Princeton, N.J.: Princeton University Press, 1981.

_____. "Reflections on Abortion, Values, and the Family." In *Abortion: Understanding Differences*, edited by Sidney Callahan and Daniel Callahan, pp. 47–72. New York: Plenum Press, 1984.

_____. "Reflections on War and Political Discourse: Realism, Just War, and Feminism in a Nuclear Age." *Political Theory* 13, no. 1 (February 1985): 39–57.

_____. "Symmetry and Soporifics: A Critique of Feminist Accounts of Gender Development." In *Capitalism and Infancy: Essays on Psychoanalysis and Politics*, edited by Barry Richards, pp. 55–91. Atlantic Highlands, N.J.: Humanities Press, 1984.

_____. "'Thank Heaven for Little Girls': The Dialectics of Development." In *The Family in Political Thought*, edited by Jean Bethke Elshtain, pp. 288–302. Amherst: University of Massachusetts Press, 1982.

_____. "Toward a Theory of the Family and Politics." Introduction to *The Family in Political Thought*, edited by Jean Bethke Elshtain, pp. 7–30. Amherst: University of Massachusetts Press, 1982.

_____. "The Victim Syndrome: A Troubling Turn in Feminism." *Progressive* 46, no. 6 (June 1982): 42–47.

_____. *Women and War*. New York: Basic Books, 1987.

"Employers Are Looking Abroad for the Skilled and the Energetic." *New York Times*, 15 July 1989, p. E4.

Epstein, Barbara Leslie. *The Politics of Domesticity: Women, Evangelism, and Temperance in Nineteenth-Century America*. Middletown, Conn.: Wesleyan University Press, 1981.

Epstein, Cynthia Fuchs. *Deceptive Distinctions: Sex, Gender, and the Social Order*. New Haven, Conn: Yale University Press, 1988.

_____. "Epstein Responds to Menkel-Meadow's Review Essay on *Women in Law*." *American Bar Foundation Research Journal* 1983, no. 4 (Fall): 1006–8.

_____. *Women in Law*. New York: Basic Books, 1981.

Erickson, Nancy S. "Sex Bias in Law School Courses: Some Common Issues." *Journal of Legal Education* 38, nos. 1 and 2 (March/June 1988): 101–16.

Evans, Augusta J. *Beulah*. 1859. Reprint. New York: Dillingham, 1887.

_____. *Inez: A Tale of the Alamo*. 1855. Reprint. New York: Dillingham, 1897.

_____. *Macaria*. 1864. Reprint. New York: G. W. Dillingham, 1888.

Evans, Sara M., and Barbara J. Nelson. *Wage Justice: Comparable Worth and the Paradox of Technocratic Reform*. Chicago: University of Chicago Press, 1989.

Ezell, Margaret J. M. *The Patriarch's Wife: Literary Evidence and the History of the Family*. Chapel Hill: University of North Carolina Press, 1987.

Fanon, Frantz. *Studies in a Dying Colonialism*. Translated by Haakon Chevalier. New York: Monthly Review Press, 1965.

_____. *The Wretched of the Earth*. Preface by Jean-Paul Sartre. Translated by Constance Farrington. New York: Grove Press, 1965.

Fee, Elizabeth. "Science and the Woman Problem: Historical Perspectives." In *Sex Differences: Social and Biological Perspectives*, edited by Michael S. Teitelbaum, pp. 175–223. Garden City, N.Y.: Anchor Books/Doubleday, 1976.

Feinberg, Joel. "Pornography and the Criminal Law." In *Pornography and Censorship*, edited by David Copp and Susan Wendell, pp. 105–37. Buffalo, N.Y.: Prometheus Books, 1983.

Feldberg, Roslyn L. "Comparable Worth: Toward Theory and Practice in the United States." *Signs* 10, no. 2 (Winter 1984): 311–28.

Felsenthal, Carol. *The Sweetheart of the Silent Majority: The Biography of Phyllis Schlafly*. Garden City, N.Y.: Doubleday, 1981.

Felski, Rita. "Feminist Theory and Social Change." *Theory Culture and Society* 6 (May 1989): 219–40.

Ferguson, Margaret W., with Maureen Quilligan and Nancy J. Vickers. Introduction to *Rewriting the Renaissance: The Discourses of Sexual Difference in Early Modern Europe*, edited by Margaret W. Ferguson, Maureen Quilligan, and Nancy J. Vickers, pp. xv–xxxi. Chicago: University of Chicago Press, 1986.

Ferguson, Moira, ed. *First Feminists: British Women Writers, 1578–1799*. Bloomington: Indiana University Press, 1985.

Ferleger, Lou, and Jay R. Mandle. "Addressing the Productivity Problem in the 1990s." *Challenge* 33, no. 4 (July/August 1990): 17–21.

_____. "Confronting the Productivity Crisis." *Socialist Review*, no. 95 (September/October 1987): 122–27.

————. "Democracy and Productivity in the Future American Economy." *Review of Radical Political Economics* 19, no. 4 (Winter 1987): 1–15.

————. "The Savings Shortfall." *Challenge* 32, no. 2 (March/April 1989): 57–59.

Fetterley, Judith. Introduction to *Provisions: A Reader from 19th-Century American Women*, edited by Judith Fetterley, pp. 1–40. Bloomington: Indiana University Press, 1985.

Fidler, William Perry. *Augusta Evans Wilson, 1835–1909*. University: University of Alabama Press, 1951.

Fiedler, Leslie A. *Love and Death in the American Novel*. Rev. ed. New York: Stein and Day, 1966.

————. *The Return of the Vanishing American*. New York: Stein and Day, 1968.

Fields, Barbara Jeanne. "Ideology and Race in American History." In *Region, Race, and Reconstruction: Essays in Honor of C. Vann Woodward*, edited by J. Morgan Kousser and James M. McPherson, pp. 143–77. New York: Oxford University Press, 1982.

————. "Slavery, Race, and Ideology." *New Left Review*, no. 181 (1990): 95–118.

Filmer, Robert. *Patriarcha and Other Political Works*. Edited by Peter Laslett. Oxford: Basil Blackwell, 1949.

Findlay, Len. "Otherwise Engaged: Postmodernism and the Resistance to History." *English Studies in Canada* 14, no. 4 (December 1988): 383–99.

Finley, Lucinda. "A Break in the Silence: Including Women's Issues in a Torts Course." *Yale Journal of Law and Feminism* 1, no. 1 (Spring 1989): 41–74.

Fitzhugh, George. *Sociology for the South, Or the Failure of Free Society*. 1854. Reprint. New York: Burt Franklin, 1967.

Flax, Jane. "Postmodernism and Gender Relations in Feminist Theory." *Signs* 12, no. 4 (Summer 1987): 621–43.

————. *Thinking Fragments: Psychoanalysis, Feminism, and Postmodernism in the Contemporary West*. Berkeley and Los Angeles: University of California Press, 1990.

Fleming, Thomas. *The Politics of Human Nature*. New Brunswick, N.J.: Transaction Books, 1988.

Flexner, Eleanor. *Century of Struggle: The Woman's Rights Movement in the United States*. Rev. ed. Cambridge, Mass.: Harvard University Press, 1975.

Folbre, Nancy. "The Logic of Patriarchal Capitalism." Paper presented at the conference, Rural Women in the Transition to Capitalism, Northern Illinois University, De Kalb, Ill., 31 March–2 April 1989.

————. "Of Patriarchy Born: The Political Economy of Fertility Decisions." *Feminist Studies* 9, no. 2 (Summer 1983): 261–84.

Foster, Frances Smith. *Witnessing Slavery: The Development of Ante-Bellum Slave Narratives*. Westport, Conn.: Greenwood Press, 1979.

Foucault, Michel. *Discipline and Punish: The Birth of the Prison*. Translated by Alan Sheridan. New York: Pantheon Books, 1977.

————. *The History of Sexuality*. 3 vols. Translated by Robert Hurley. New York: Pantheon Books, 1978–86.

————. *The Order of Things: An Archaeology of the Human Sciences*. New York: Pantheon Books, 1970.

Fox-Genovese, Elizabeth. "Ahistorical Admonitions." Review of *The Politics of Human Nature*, by Thomas Fleming. *Chronicles: A Magazine of American Culture* 13, no. 1 (January 1989): 34–37.

————. "The Claims of a Common Culture: Gender, Race, Class and the Canon." *Salmagundi*, no. 72 (Fall 1986): 31–43.

————. "Culture and Consciousness in the Intellectual History of European Women." *Signs* 12, no. 3 (Spring 1987): 529–47.

————. "The Feminist Challenge to the Canon." *National Forum* 69, no. 3 (Summer 1989): 32–34.

————. "For Feminist Interpretation." *Union Seminary Quarterly Review* 35, nos. 1 and 2 (Fall/Winter 1979–80): 5–14.

————. "Gender, Class and Power: Some Theoretical Considerations." *History Teacher* 15, no. 2 (February 1982): 255–76.

————. "The Great Tradition and Its Orphans, Or Why the Defense of the Traditional Curriculum Requires the Restoration of Those It Excluded." In *The Rights of Memory: Essays on History, Science, and American Culture*, edited by Taylor Littleton, pp. 185–213. University: Alabama University Press, 1986.

————. "My Statue, My Self: Autobiographical Writings of Afro-American Women." In *The Private Self: Theory and Practice of Women's Autobiographical Writings*, edited by Shari Benstock, pp. 63–89. Chapel Hill: University of North Carolina Press, 1988.

————. "The New Female Literary Culture." *Antioch Review* 38, no. 2 (Spring 1980): 193–217.

————. "Placing Women's History in History." *New Left Review*, no. 133 (May/June 1982): 5–29.

————. "Power and Authority." *Nation*, 22 November 1980, pp. 549–52.

————. "Property and Patriarchy in Early Bourgeois Political Culture." *Radical History Review* 4, nos. 2 and 3 (Spring/Summer 1977): 36–59.

————. Review of *The Chalice and the Blade*, by Riane Eisler. *New York Times Book Review*, 4 October 1987, p. 32.

————. Review of *The Creation of Patriarchy*, by Gerda Lerner. *Journal of the American Academy of Religion* 55, no. 3 (Fall 1987): 608–12.

————. "Socialist-Feminist American Women's History: A Review Essay." *Journal of Women's History* 1, no. 3 (Winter 1990): 181–210.

————. "Some Are More Equal Than Others." *Village Voice Literary Supplement* 28, no. 17 (May 1983): 8.

————. *Within the Plantation Household: Black and White Women of the Old South*. Chapel Hill: University of North Carolina Press, 1988.

————. "Women and Agriculture in the Nineteenth Century." In *Agriculture and National Development: Views on the Nineteenth Century*, edited by Louis Ferleger. Ames: Iowa State University Press, 1990.

————. "Women and Work." In *French Women and the Age of Enlightenment*, edited by Samia I. Spencer, pp. 111–27. Bloomington: Indiana University Press, 1984.

Fox-Genovese, Elizabeth, and Eugene D. Genovese. "The Divine Sanction of Social Order: Religious Foundations of the Southern Slaveholders' World View." *Journal of the American Academy of Religion* 55, no. 2 (Summer 1987): 211–33.

————. *Fruits of Merchant Capital: Slavery and Bourgeois Property in the Rise and Expansion of Capitalism*. New York: Oxford University Press, 1983.

————. "Illusions of Liberation: The Psychology of Colonialism and Revolution in the Work of Octave Mannoni and Frantz Fanon." In *Rethinking Marxism: Struggles in Marxist Theory: Essays for Harry Magdoff and Paul Sweezy*, edited by Stephen Resnick and Richard Wolff, pp. 127–50. New York: Autonomedia, 1985.

Fox-Genovese, Elizabeth, and Susan Mosher Stuard with Rufus Fears and Marc Mayer. *Restoring Women to History*. Vol. 1, *Western Civilization I*. Bloomington, Ind.: Organization of American Historians, 1982.

Freud, Sigmund. "Civilization and Its Discontents." In *The Standard Edition of the Complete Psychological Works of Sigmund Freud*, edited by James Strachey, 21:64–145. 24 vols. London: Hogarth Press, 1966–74.

Friedan, Betty. *The Feminine Mystique*. Twentieth anniversary ed. New York: Norton, 1983.

————. *It Changed My Life: Writings on the Women's Movement*. New York: Random House, 1976.

Friedman, Susan Stanford. "Women's Autobiographical Selves: Theory and Practice." In *The Private Self: Theory and Practice of Women's Autobiographical Writings*, edited by Shari Benstock, pp. 34–62. Chapel Hill: University of North Carolina Press, 1988.

Frug, Gerald E. "The City as a Legal Concept." *Harvard Law Review* 93, no. 6 (April 1980): 1059–1154.

Frug, Mary Jo. "Re-Reading Contracts: A Feminist Analysis of a Contracts Casebook." *American University Law Review* 34, no. 4 (Summer 1985): 1065–1140.

Fryer, Judith. *Felicitous Space: The Imaginative Structures of Edith Wharton and Willa Cather*. Chapel Hill: University of North Carolina Press, 1986.

Fuchs, Victor R. *Women's Quest for Economic Equality*. Cambridge, Mass.: Harvard University Press, 1988.

Fuller, Margaret. *The Letters of Margaret Fuller*. Edited by Robert N. Hudspeth. 5 vols. Ithaca, N.Y.: Cornell University Press, 1983–88.

Gallagher, Catherine. *The Industrial Reformation of English Fiction: Social Discourse and Narrative Form 1832–1867*. Chicago: University of Chicago Press, 1985.

Gallop, Jane. *The Daughter's Seduction: Feminism and Psychoanalysis*. Ithaca, N.Y.: Cornell University Press, 1982.

————. "Heroic Images: Feminist Criticism, 1972." *American Literary History* 1, no. 3 (Fall 1989): 612–36.

————. *Reading Lacan*. Ithaca, N.Y.: Cornell University Press, 1985.

Gardiner, Linda. "Women in Science." In *French Women and the Age of Enlightenment*, edited by Samia I. Spencer, pp. 181–93. Bloomington: Indiana University Press, 1984.

Garry, Ann. "Pornography and Respect for Women." In *Pornography and Censorship*, edited by David Copp and Susan Wendell, pp. 61–81. Buffalo, N.Y.: Prometheus Books, 1983.

Gates, Henry Louis, Jr. *Figures in Black: Words, Signs, and the "Racial" Self*. New York: Oxford University Press, 1987.

Bibliography

_____. *The Signifying Monkey: A Theory of Afro-American Literary Criticism*. New York: Oxford University Press, 1988.

Geertz, Clifford. *The Interpretation of Cultures: Selected Essays*. New York: Basic Books, 1973.

Gendzier, Irene L. *Frantz Fanon: A Critical Study*. New York: Pantheon Books, 1973.

Genovese, Eugene D. *In Red and Black: Marxian Explorations in Southern and Afro-American History*. 2d ed. Knoxville: University of Tennessee Press, 1984.

_____. *Roll, Jordan, Roll: The World the Slaves Made*. New York: Pantheon Books, 1974.

_____. *The World the Slaveholders Made: Two Essays in Interpretation*. 2d ed. Middletown, Conn.: Wesleyan University Press, 1988.

Genovese, Eugene D., and Elizabeth Fox-Genovese. "The Religious Ideals of Southern Slave Society." *Georgia Historical Quarterly* 70, no. 1 (Spring 1986): 1–16.

_____. "Slavery, Economic Development, and the Law: The Dilemma of the Southern Political Economists, 1800–1860." *Washington and Lee Law Review* 41, no. 1 (Winter 1984): 1–29.

George, Margaret. *One Woman's "Situation": A Study of Mary Wollstonecraft*. Urbana: University of Illinois Press, 1970.

_____. *Women in the First Capitalist Society: Experiences in Seventeenth-Century England*. Urbana: University of Illinois Press, 1988.

Gibson, Joan. "Educating for Silence: Renaissance Women and the Language Arts." *Hypatia* 4, no. 1 (Spring 1989): 9–27.

Giddings, Paula. *When and Where I Enter: The Impact of Black Women on Race and Sex in America*. New York: William Morrow, 1984.

Gilligan, Carol. *In a Different Voice: Psychological Theory and Women's Development*. Cambridge, Mass.: Harvard University Press, 1982.

Gilman, Charlotte Perkins. *Herland*. 1915. Reprint. New York: Pantheon Books, 1979.

Gilmore, Michael T. *American Romanticism and the Marketplace*. Chicago: University of Chicago Press, 1985.

Ginsburg, Faye D. *Contested Lives: The Abortion Debate in an American Community*. Berkeley and Los Angeles: University of California Press, 1989.

Ginzberg, Lori D. "The 'Joint Education of the Sexes': Oberlin's Original Vision." In *Educating Men and Women Together: Coeducation in a Changing World*, edited by Carol Lasser, pp. 67–80. Urbana: University of Illinois Press, 1987.

Glendon, Mary Ann. *Abortion and Divorce in Western Law*. Cambridge, Mass.: Harvard University Press, 1987.

Goethe, Johann Wolfgang von. *The Sorrows of Young Werther*. Translated by Michael Hulse. New York: Penguin, 1989.

Goldberg, Rita. *Sex and Enlightenment: Women in Richardson and Diderot*. Cambridge: Cambridge University Press, 1984.

Goldman, Alan H. "Affirmative Action." In *Equality and Preferential Treatment*, edited by Marshall Cohen, Thomas Nagel, and Thomas Scanlon, pp. 192–209. Princeton, N.J.: Princeton University Press, 1977.

Goodman, Jill Laurie. "Women, War, and Equality: An Examination of Sex Discrimination in the Military." *Women's Rights Law Reporter* 5, no. 4 (Summer 1979): 243–69.

Gordon, Linda. *Heroes of Their Own Lives: The Politics and History of Family Violence, Boston, 1880–1960*. New York: Viking Books, 1988.

————. *Woman's Body, Woman's Right: A Social History of Birth Control in America*. New York: Grossman, 1976.

Gore, Tipper. *Raising PG Kids in an X-Rated Society*. Nashville, Tenn.: Abingdon Press, 1987.

Greenhouse, Linda. "Justices, 6 to 3, Restrict Rights to Pornography." *New York Times*, 19 April 1990, pp. A1, A12.

Griffin, Susan. *Pornography and Silence: Culture's Revenge against Nature*. New York: Harper and Row, 1981.

Grimshaw, Jean. *Philosophy and Feminist Thinking*. Minneapolis: University of Minnesota Press, 1986.

Groneman, Carol, and Mary Beth Norton, eds. *"To Toil the Livelong Day": American Women at Work, 1780–1980*. Ithaca, N.Y.: Cornell University Press, 1987.

Gubar, Susan, and Joan Hoff, eds. *For Adult Users Only: The Dilemma of Violent Pornography*. Bloomington: Indiana University Press, 1989.

Guinsburg, Arlene Miller. "The Counterthrust to Sixteenth-Century Misogyny: The Work of Agrippa and Paracelsus." *Historical Reflections/Réflexions Historiques* 8, no. 1 (Spring 1981): 3–28.

Gutman, Herbert G. *The Black Family in Slavery and Freedom, 1750–1925*. New York: Pantheon Books, 1976.

————. *Work, Culture, and Society in Industrializing America: Essays in American Working-Class and Social History*. New York: Knopf, 1976.

Gutmann, Amy. "Communitarian Critics of Liberalism." *Philosophy and Public Affairs* 14, no. 3 (Summer 1985): 308–22.

Haigh, Christopher. *Elizabeth I*. New York: Longman, 1988.

Haight, Gordon S. *George Eliot, a Biography*. New York: Oxford University Press, 1968.

Hall, Roberta M., with Bernice R. Sandler. *The Classroom Climate: A Chilly One for Women?* Washington, D.C.: Project on the Status and Education of Women, Association of American Colleges, 1982.

Hanen, Marsha, and Kai Nielsen, eds. *Science, Morality, and Feminist Theory*. Calgary: University of Calgary Press, 1987.

Harding, Sandra. *The Science Question in Feminism*. Ithaca, N.Y.: Cornell University Press, 1986.

Harding, Vincent. *There Is a River: The Black Struggle for Freedom in America*. New York: Harcourt Brace Jovanovich, 1981.

Harris, Angela P. "Race and Essentialism in Feminist Legal Theory." *Stanford Law Review* 42, no. 3 (February 1990): 581–616.

Harris, Trudier. *Exorcising Blackness: Historical and Literary Lynching and Burning Rituals*. Bloomington: Indiana University Press, 1984.

Harrison, Bennett, and Barry Bluestone. *The Great U-Turn: Corporate Restructuring and the Polarizing of America*. New York: Basic Books, 1988.

Bibliography

Harrison, Beverly Wildung. *Our Right to Choose: Toward a New Ethic of Abortion*. Boston: Beacon Press, 1983.

Harrison, Cynthia. *On Account of Sex: The Politics of Women's Issues, 1945–1968*. Berkeley and Los Angeles: University of California Press, 1988.

Hart, H. L. A. "Are There Any Natural Rights?" *Philosophical Review* 64, no. 2 (April 1955): 175–91.

Hartmann, Heidi. "Capitalist Patriarchy and Job Segregation by Sex." In *Women and the Workplace: The Implications of Occupational Segregation*, edited by Martha Blaxall and Barbara Reagan, pp. 137–69. Chicago: University of Chicago Press, 1976.

_____. "The Unhappy Marriage of Marxism and Feminism: Towards a More Progressive Union." *Capital and Class* 8 (Summer 1979): 1–22.

Hartsock, Nancy. "Foucault on Power: A Theory for Women?" In *Feminism/Postmodernism*, edited by Linda J. Nicholson, pp. 157–75. New York: Routledge, 1990.

Haskell, Thomas, and Sanford Levinson. "Academic Freedom and Expert Witnessing: Historians and the Sears Case." *Texas Law Review* 66, no. 7 (June 1988): 1629–59.

_____. "On Academic Freedom and Hypothetical Pools: A Reply to Alice Kessler-Harris." *Texas Law Review* 67, no. 7 (June 1989): 1591–1604.

Hassan, Ihab. *The Dismemberment of Orpheus: Toward a Postmodern Literature*. 2d ed. Madison: University of Wisconsin Press, 1982.

Hawkins, Gordon, and Franklin E. Zimring. *Pornography in a Free Society*. Cambridge: Cambridge University Press, 1988.

Hegel, G. W. F. *The Phenomenology of Mind*. Translated by J. B. Baillie. 2d ed., rev. New York: Humanities Press, 1931.

Heilbrun, Carolyn G. *Toward a Recognition of Androgyny*. New York: Knopf, 1973.

_____. *Writing a Woman's Life*. New York: Norton, 1988.

Hemenway, Robert E. *Zora Neale Hurston: A Literary Biography*. Urbana: University of Illinois Press, 1977.

Henretta, James A. "Families and Farms: *Mentalité* in Pre-Industrial America." *William and Mary Quarterly*, 3d ser. 35, no. 1 (January 1978): 3–32.

Hentz, Caroline Lee. *The Planter's Northern Bride*. 1854. Reprint. Chapel Hill: University of North Carolina Press, 1970.

Herlihy, David, and Christiane Klapische-Zuber. *Tuscans and Their Families: A Study of the Florentine Castato of 1427*. New Haven, Conn.: Yale University Press, 1985.

Herrin, Judith. *The Formation of Christendom*. Princeton, N.J.: Princeton University Press, 1987.

_____. "Women and the Faith in Icons in Early Christianity." In *Culture, Ideology, and Politics: Essays for Eric Hobsbawm*, edited by Raphael Samuel and Gareth Stedman-Jones, pp. 56–83. Boston: Routledge and Kegan Paul, 1982.

Hersh, Blanche Glassman. *The Slavery of Sex: Feminist-Abolitionists in America*. Urbana: University of Illinois Press, 1978.

Hewitt, Nancy A. "Beyond the Search for Sisterhood: American Women's History in the 1980s." *Social History* 10, no. 3 (October 1985): 299–321.

_____. "Feminist Friends: Agrarian Quakers and the Emergence of Woman's

Rights in America." *Feminist Studies* 12, no. 1 (Spring 1986): 27–49.

Hewlett, Sylvia Ann. *A Lesser Life: The Myth of Women's Liberation in America*. New York: William Morrow, 1986.

Higginson, Thomas Wentworth. *Black Rebellion*. Edited by James M. McPherson. New York: Arno Press, 1969.

Himmelfarb, Gertrude. *The New History and the Old*. Cambridge, Mass.: Harvard University Press, 1987.

――――. *On Liberty and Liberalism: The Case of John Stuart Mill*. New York: Knopf, 1974.

――――. "Some Reflections on the New History." *American Historical Review* 94, no. 3 (June 1989): 661–70.

Hine, Darlene Clark. "Rape and the Inner Lives of Black Women in the Middle West: Preliminary Thoughts on the Culture of Dissemblance." *Signs* 14, no. 4 (Summer 1989): 912–20.

Hirsch, E. D., Jr. *Cultural Literacy: What Every American Needs to Know*. Boston: Houghton Mifflin, 1987.

Hirsch, Marianne. *The Mother/Daughter Plot: Narrative, Psychoanalysis, Feminism*. Bloomington: Indiana University Press, 1989.

Hobbes, Thomas. *Leviathan*. Edited by C. B. Macpherson. Baltimore, Md.: Penguin Books, 1968.

Hochschild, Arlie, with Anne Machung. *The Second Shift: Working Parents and the Revolution at Home*. New York: Viking Press, 1989.

Hoffman, Eric. "Feminism, Pornography, and Law." *University of Pennsylvania Law Review* 133, no. 2 (January 1985): 497–534.

Hofstadter, Richard. *The Idea of a Party System: The Rise of Legitimate Opposition in the United States, 1780–1840*. Berkeley and Los Angeles: University of California Press, 1969.

Hollander, Anne. *Seeing through Clothes*. New York: Viking Press, 1978.

Homans, Margaret. *Bearing the Word: Language and Female Experience in Nineteenth-Century Women's Writing*. Chicago: University of Chicago Press, 1986.

hooks, bell. *Ain't I a Woman: Black Women and Feminism*. Boston: South End Press, 1981.

――――. *Feminist Theory from Margin to Center*. Boston: South End Press, 1984.

――――. *Talking Back: Thinking Feminist, Thinking Black*. Boston: South End Press, 1989.

Horwitz, Morton J. *The Transformation of American Law, 1780–1860*. Cambridge, Mass.: Harvard University Press, 1977.

Houghton, Walter E. *The Victorian Frame of Mind, 1830–1870*. New Haven, Conn.: Yale University Press, 1957.

Howell, Martha C. *Women, Production, and Patriarchy in Late Medieval Cities*. Chicago: University of Chicago Press, 1986.

Hrdy, Sarah Blaffer. *The Woman That Never Evolved*. Cambridge, Mass.: Harvard University Press, 1981.

Hufton, Olwen. "Women and the Family Economy in Eighteenth-Century France." *French Historical Studies* 9, no. 1 (Spring 1975): 1–22.

_____. "Women in History: Early Modern Europe." *Past and Present*, no. 101 (November 1983): 125–41.

Hughes, Henry. *Selected Writings of Henry Hughes: Antebellum Southerner, Slavocrat, Sociologist.* Edited by Sanford M. Lyman. Jackson: University Press of Mississippi, 1985.

_____. *Treatise on Sociology: Theoretical and Practical.* 1854. Reprint. New York: Negro Universities Press, 1968.

Hughes, Langston. "Theme for English B." In *The Langston Hughes Reader*, pp. 108–9. New York: Braziller, 1958.

Hull, Gloria T. *Color, Sex, and Poetry: Three Women Writers of the Harlem Renaissance.* Bloomington: Indiana University Press, 1987.

Hull, Suzanne W. *Chaste, Silent, and Obedient: English Books for Women, 1475–1640.* San Marino, Calif.: Huntington Library, 1982.

Hurston, Zora Neale. *Dust Tracks on a Road: An Autobiography.* Edited by Robert Hemenway. 2d ed. Urbana: University of Illinois Press, 1984.

_____. *Jonah's Gourd Vine.* 1934. Reprint. Philadelphia: Lippincott, 1971.

_____. *Their Eyes Were Watching God.* Urbana: University of Illinois Press, 1978.

Hutcheon, Linda. *A Poetics of Postmodernism: History, Theory, Fiction.* New York: Routledge, 1988.

_____. "The Postmodern Problematizing of History." *English Studies in Canada* 14, no. 4 (December 1988): 365–82.

Huyssen, Andreas. *After the Great Divide: Modernism, Mass Culture, Postmodernism.* Bloomington: Indiana University Press, 1986.

Irigaray, Luce. *Ce sexe qui n'en est pas un.* Paris: Éditions de Minuit, 1977.

_____. *Speculum de l'autre femme.* Paris: Éditions de Minuit, 1974.

Jacobs, Caryn. "Patterns of Violence: A Feminist Perspective on the Regulation of Pornography." *Harvard Women's Law Journal* 7, no. 1 (Spring 1984): 5–55.

Jacobs, Harriet A. *Incidents in the Life of a Slave Girl, Written by Herself.* Edited by Jean Fagan Yellin. Cambridge, Mass.: Harvard University Press, 1987.

Jaggar, Alison M. *Feminist Politics and Human Nature.* Totowa, N.J.: Rowman and Allanheld, 1983.

_____. "Love and Knowledge: Emotion in Feminist Epistemology." In *Gender/Body/Knowledge: Feminist Reconstructions of Being and Knowing*, edited by Alison M. Jaggar and Susan R. Bordo, pp. 145–71. New Brunswick, N.J.: Rutgers University Press, 1989.

Jaggar, Alison M., and Susan R. Bordo, eds. *Gender/Body/Knowledge: Feminist Reconstructions of Being and Knowing.* New Brunswick, N.J.: Rutgers University Press, 1989.

Jameson, Fredric. "Postmodernism and Consumer Society." *Amerikastudien/American Studies* 29, no. 1 (1984): 55–73.

_____. "Postmodernism, or the Cultural Legacy of Late Capitalism." *New Left Review*, no. 146 (July/August 1984): 53–92.

Janeway, Elizabeth. *Powers of the Weak.* New York: Knopf, 1980.

Janiewski, Dolores E. *Sisterhood Denied: Race, Gender, and Class in a New South Community.* Philadelphia: Temple University Press, 1985.

Jardine, Alice A. *Gynesis: Configurations of Woman and Modernity*. Ithaca, N.Y.: Cornell University Press, 1985.

Jeffrey, Julie Roy. *Frontier Women: The Trans-Mississippi West, 1840–1880*. New York: Hill and Wang, 1979.

Jehlen, Myra. "Archimedes and the Paradox of Feminist Criticism." *Signs* 6, no. 4 (Summer 1981): 575–601.

———. "Patrolling the Borders: Feminist Historiography and the New Historicism." *Radical History Review*, no. 43 (Winter 1989): 31–37.

Johnson, Barbara. *A World of Difference*. Baltimore, Md.: Johns Hopkins University Press, 1987.

Jones, Anne Goodwyn. *Tomorrow Is Another Day: The Woman Writer in the South, 1859–1936*. Baton Rouge: Louisiana State University Press, 1981.

Jordan, Cynthia S. *Second Stories: The Politics of Language, Form, and Gender in Early American Fictions*. Chapel Hill: University of North Carolina Press, 1989.

Jordanova, Ludmilla. *Sexual Visions: Images of Gender in Science and Medicine between the Eighteenth and Twentieth Centuries*. Madison: University of Wisconsin Press, 1989.

Joseph, Gloria I., and Jill Lewis. *Common Differences: Conflicts in Black and White Feminist Perspectives*. Garden City, N.Y.: Anchor Books/Doubleday, 1981.

Kanowitz, Leo. *Women and the Law: The Unfinished Revolution*. Albuquerque: University of New Mexico Press, 1969.

Kanter, Rosabeth Moss. *Men and Women of the Corporation*. New York: Basic Books, 1977.

Kantorowicz, Ernst H. *The King's Two Bodies: A Study in Mediaeval Political Theology*. Princeton, N.J.: Princeton University Press, 1957.

Kappeler, Susanne. *The Pornography of Representation*. Minneapolis: University of Minnesota Press, 1986.

Karant-Nunn, Susan C. "Continuity and Change: Some Effects of the Reformation on the Women of Zwickau." *Sixteenth Century Journal* 13, no. 2 (Summer 1982): 17–42.

Kasserman, David Richard. *Fall River Outrage: Life, Murder, and Justice in Early Industrial New England*. Philadelphia: University of Pennsylvania Press, 1986.

Kauffman, Linda, ed. *Gender and Theory: Dialogues on Feminist Criticism*. Oxford: Basil Blackwell, 1989.

Keller, Evelyn Fox. *Reflections on Gender and Science*. New Haven, Conn.: Yale University Press, 1985.

Kelley, Mary. *Private Woman, Public Stage: Literary Domesticity in Nineteenth-Century America*. New York: Oxford University Press, 1984.

Kelly, Joan. "Did Women Have a Renaissance?" In *Becoming Visible: Women in European History*, edited by Renate Bridenthal and Claudia Koonz, pp. 137–64. Boston: Houghton Mifflin, 1977.

———. "The Doubled Vision of Feminist Theory: A Postscript to the 'Women and Power' Conference." *Feminist Studies* 5, no. 1 (Spring 1979): 216–27.

———. "Early Feminist Theory and the *Querelle des Femmes*, 1400–1789." In *Women, History, and Theory: The Essays of Joan Kelly*, pp. 65–109. Chicago: University of Chicago Press, 1984.

———. *Women, History and Theory: The Essays of Joan Kelly*. Chicago: University of Chicago Press, 1984.

Kennedy, Randall L. "Racial Critiques of Legal Academia." *Harvard Law Review* 102, no. 8 (June 1989): 1745–1819.

Kerber, Linda K. "Diversity and the Transformation of American Studies." *American Quarterly* 41, no. 3 (September 1989): 415–31.

———. "Separate Spheres, Female Worlds, Woman's Place: The Rhetoric of Women's History." *Journal of American History* 75, no. 1 (June 1988): 9–39.

———. *Women of the Republic: Intellect and Ideology in Revolutionary America*. Chapel Hill: University of North Carolina Press, 1980.

Kessler-Harris, Alice. "*Academic Freedom and Expert Witnessing*: A Response to Haskell and Levinson." *Texas Law Review* 67, no. 2 (December 1988): 429–40.

———. "The Just Price, the Free Market, and the Value of Women." *Feminist Studies* 14, no. 2 (Summer 1988): 235–50.

———. *Out to Work: A History of Wage-Earning Women in the United States*. New York: Oxford University Press, 1982.

Kettner, James H. *The Development of American Citizenship, 1608–1870*. Chapel Hill: University of North Carolina Press, 1978.

King, Margaret L., and Albert Rabil, Jr., eds. *Her Immaculate Hand: Selected Works by and about the Women Humanists of Quattrocento Italy*. Binghamton, N.Y.: Center for Medieval and Early Renaissance Studies, State University of New York, 1983.

Kirp, David L., Mark G. Yudof, and Marlene Strong Franks. *Gender Justice*. Chicago: University of Chicago Press, 1986.

Kittay, Eve Felder, and Diana T. Meyers, eds. *Women and Moral Theory*. Totowa, N.J.: Rowman and Littlefield, 1987.

Klein, Ethel. *Gender Politics: From Consciousness to Mass Politics*. Cambridge, Mass.: Harvard University Press, 1984.

Knowles, Marjorie Fine. "The Legal Status of Women in Alabama: A Crazy Quilt." *Alabama Law Review* 29, no. 2 (Winter 1978): 427–515.

———. "The Legal Status of Women in Alabama, II: A Crazy Quilt Restitched." *Alabama Law Review* 33, no. 2 (Winter 1982): 375–406.

Kofman, Sarah. *Aberrations: Le devenir-femme d'Auguste Comte*. Paris: Flammarion, 1978.

Kohl, Lawrence Frederick. *The Politics of Individualism: Parties and the American Character in the Jacksonian Era*. New York: Oxford University Press, 1989.

Kolodny, Annette. "The Integrity of Memory: Creating a New Literary History of the United States." *American Literature* 57, no. 2 (May 1985): 291–307.

———. *The Land Before Her: Fantasy and Experience of the American Frontiers, 1630–1860*. Chapel Hill: University of North Carolina Press, 1984.

Koonz, Claudia. *Mothers in the Fatherland: Women, the Family, and Nazi Politics*. New York: St. Martin's Press, 1987.

———. "Postscripts." *Women's Review of Books* 6 (January 1989): 19–20.

Kra, Pauline. "Montesquieu and Women." In *French Women and the Age of Enlightenment*, edited by Samia I. Spencer, pp. 272–84. Bloomington: Indiana University Press, 1984.

Kristeva, Julia. "Stabat Mater." In *The Female Body in Western Culture: Contempo-rary Perspectives*, edited by Susan Rubin Suleiman, pp. 99–118. Cambridge, Mass.: Harvard University Press, 1985.

Laclos, Choderlos de. "Les liaisons dangereuses." In *Oeuvres complètes*, edited by Maurice Allem, pp. 29–423. 1782. Reprint. Paris: Bibliothèque de la Pléiade, 1951.

Lampedusa, Giuseppe di. *The Leopard*. Translated by Archibald Colquhoun. New York: Pantheon Books, 1960.

Landes, Joan B. *Women and the Public Sphere in the Age of the French Revolution*. Ithaca, N.Y.: Cornell University Press, 1988.

Lang, Amy Schrager. *Prophetic Woman: Anne Hutchinson and the Problem of Dissent in the Literature of New England*. Berkeley and Los Angeles: University of Cali-fornia Press, 1987.

Lapham, Lewis H., Al Goldstein, Midge Decter, Erica Jong, Susan Brownmiller, Jean Bethke Elshtain, and Aryeh Neier. "The Place of Pornography." *Harper's Magazine* 269 (November 1984): 31–45.

Larner, Christina. *Enemies of God: The Witch-hunt in Scotland*. Baltimore, Md.: Johns Hopkins University Press, 1981.

Law, Sylvia A. "Rethinking Sex and the Constitution." *University of Pennsylvania Law Review* 132, no. 5 (June 1984): 955–1040.

Leach, William. *True Love and Perfect Union: The Feminist Reform of Sex and Society*. New York: Basic Books, 1980.

Lebsock, Suzanne. *The Free Women of Petersburg: Status and Culture in a Southern Town, 1784–1860*. New York: Norton, 1984.

Lederer, Laura, ed. *Take Back the Night: Women on Pornography*. New York: William Morrow, 1980.

Leland, Dorothy. "Lacanian Psychoanalysis and French Feminism: Toward an Ade-quate Political Psychology." *Hypatia* 3 (Winter 1989): 81–103.

Lenz, Guenter H. "American Studies and the Radical Tradition: From the 1930s to the 1960s." *Prospects* 12 (1987): 20–58.

Lerner, Gerda. *The Creation of Patriarchy*. New York: Oxford University Press, 1986.

Leverenz, David. *Manhood and the American Renaissance*. Ithaca, N.Y.: Cornell University Press, 1989.

Levine, Lawrence W. *Black Culture and Black Consciousness: Afro-American Folk Thought from Slavery to Freedom*. New York: Oxford University Press, 1977.

Lindemann, Mary. "Love for Hire: The Regulation of the Wet-Nursing Business in Eighteenth-Century Hamburg." *Journal of Family History* 6, no. 4 (Winter 1981): 379–95.

———. "Maternal Politics: The Principles and Practice of Maternity Care in Eigh-teenth-Century Hamburg." *Journal of Family History* 9, no. 1 (Spring 1984): 44–63.

Littleton, Christine A. "Equality and Feminist Legal Theory." *University of Pitts-burgh Law Review* 48, no. 4 (Spring 1987): 1043–59.

———. "Restructuring Sexual Equality." *California Law Review* 75, no. 4 (July 1987): 1279–1337.

Livernash, E. Robert, ed. *Comparable Worth: Issues and Alternatives.* 2d ed. Washington, D.C.: Equal Employment Advisory Council, 1984.

Lloyd, Cynthia B., and Beth T. Niemi. *The Economics of Sex Differentials.* New York: Columbia University Press, 1979.

Locke, John. "Second Treatise of Government." In *Two Treatises of Government*, edited by Peter Laslett, pp. 285–446. 2d ed. Cambridge: Cambridge University Press, 1967.

Long, Elizabeth. "Women, Reading, and Cultural Authority: Some Implications of Audience Perspective on Cultural Studies." *American Quarterly* 38, no. 4 (Fall 1986): 591–612.

Lousse, Émile. *La société d'Ancien Régime: Organisation et représentation corporatives.* Louvain: Éditions Universitas, 1943.

Luker, Kristin. *Abortion and the Politics of Motherhood.* Berkeley and Los Angeles: University of California Press, 1984.

McAlister, Linda Lopez, ed. "Some Remarks on Exploring the History of Women in Philosophy." Introduction to the special issue of *Hypatia*, "The History of Women in Philosophy" 4, no. 1 (Spring 1989): 1–5.

Macaulay, Catharine. *Letters on Education, with Observations on Religious and Metaphysical Subjects.* 1790. Reprint. New York: Garland Publishing, 1974.

McCaskill, Barbara Ann. "To Rise above Race: Black Women Writers and Their Readers, 1850–1939." Ph.D. dissertation, Emory University, 1988.

McCord, Louisa S. [L. S. M.]. "Enfranchisement of Woman." *Southern Quarterly Review* 21 (April 1852): 322–41.

_____. "Woman and Her Needs." *De Bow's Review* 13, no. 1 (September 1852): 267–91.

McCurry, Stephanie. "In Defense of Their World: Gender, Class, and the Yeomanry of the South Carolina Low Country, 1820–1860." Ph.D. dissertation, State University of New York at Binghamton, 1988.

McDonald, Forrest. *Novus Ordo Seclorum: The Intellectual Origins of the Constitution.* Lawrence: University Press of Kansas, 1985.

MacIntyre, Alasdair. *After Virtue: A Study in Moral Theory.* 2d ed. Notre Dame, Ind.: University of Notre Dame Press, 1984.

_____. *Herbert Marcuse: An Exposition and a Polemic.* New York: Viking Press, 1970.

MacKinnon, Catharine A. "Complicity: An Introduction to Andrea Dworkin, 'Abortion,' Chapter 3, Right-Wing Women." *Law and Inequality* 1, no. 1 (June 1983): 89–93.

_____. *Feminism Unmodified: Discourses on Life and Law.* Cambridge, Mass.: Harvard University Press, 1987.

_____. *Toward a Feminist Theory of the State.* Cambridge, Mass.: Harvard University Press, 1989.

Maclean, Ian. *The Renaissance Notion of Woman: A Study in the Fortunes of Scholasticism and Medical Science in European Intellectual Life.* Cambridge: Cambridge University Press, 1980.

McMillan, Carol. *Women, Reason, and Nature: Some Philosophical Problems with*

Feminism. Princeton, N.J.: Princeton University Press, 1982.

Macpherson, C. B. *The Political Theory of Possessive Individualism: Hobbes to Locke.* New York: Oxford University Press, 1962.

Mahar, William J. "Black English in Early Blackface Minstrelsy: A New Interpretation of the Sources of Minstrel Show Dialect." *American Quarterly* 37, no. 2 (Summer 1985): 260–85.

Main, Eleanor. "Conceptions of Justice and Comparable Worth." Paper presented at the Women and the Constitution conference, Atlanta, Ga., February 1988.

Mann, Susan A. "Slavery, Sharecropping, and Sexual Inequality." *Signs* 14, no. 4 (Summer 1989): 774–98.

Mansbridge, Jane J. *Why We Lost the ERA*. Chicago: University of Chicago Press, 1986.

Marcuse, Herbert. *One-Dimensional Man: Studies in the Ideology of Advanced Industrial Society*. Boston: Beacon Press, 1964.

Margolis, Joseph. "Postscript on Modernism and Postmodernism, Both." *Theory Culture and Society* 6, no. 1 (February 1989): 5–30.

Marks, Elaine, and Isabelle de Courtivron, eds. *New French Feminisms: An Anthology*. Amherst: University of Massachusetts Press, 1980.

Martin, Waldo E., Jr. *The Mind of Frederick Douglass*. Chapel Hill: University of North Carolina Press, 1984.

Marx, Karl. *Capital: A Critique of Political Economy*. Translated by Samuel Moore and Edward Aveling. 3 vols. Moscow: Foreign Languages Publishing House, 1961–72.

————. *Critique of the Gotha Program*. In *Collected Works*, by Karl Marx and Frederick Engels. Vol. 24, *Marx and Engels: 1874–83*, pp. 77–99. Translated by Peter and Betty Ross. New York: International Publishers, 1989.

————. *Economic and Philosophic Manuscripts of 1844*. In *Collected Works*, by Karl Marx and Frederick Engels. Vol. 3, *Marx and Engels: 1843–44*, pp. 231–346. Translated by Martin Milligan and Dirk J. Struik. New York: International Publishers, 1975.

————. *Theories of Surplus-Value*. Translated by Emile Burns, Jack Cohen, and S. W. Ryazanskaya. Edited by S. W. Ryazanskaya and Richard Dixon. 3 vols. Moscow: Progress Publishers, 1963–71.

Maschke, Karen J. *Litigation, Courts, and Women Workers*. New York: Praeger, 1989.

Mascia-Lees, Frances E., Patricia Sharpe, and Colleen Ballerino Cohen. "The Postmodern Turn in Anthropology: Cautions from a Feminist Perspective." *Signs* 15, no. 1 (Autumn 1989): 7–33.

May, Gita. *Madame Roland and the Age of Revolution*. New York: Columbia University Press, 1970.

May, Martha. "The Historical Problem of the Family Wage: The Ford Motor Company and the Five Dollar Day." *Feminist Studies* 8, no. 2 (Summer 1982): 399–424.

Meese, Elizabeth A. *Crossing the Double-Cross: The Practice of Feminist Criticism*. Chapel Hill: University of North Carolina Press, 1986.

Mellor, Anne K., ed. *Romanticism and Feminism*. Bloomington: Indiana University Press, 1988.

Bibliography

Mendelson, Sara Heller. "Stuart Women's Diaries and Occasional Memoirs." In *Women in English Society 1500–1800*, edited by Mary Prior, pp. 181–210. New York: Methuen, 1985.

Menkel-Meadow, Carrie. "Women in Law? A Review of Cynthia Fuchs Epstein's *Women in Law.*" *American Bar Foundation Research Journal* 1982, no. 1 (Winter):189.

Merchant, Carolyn. *The Death of Nature: Women, Ecology, and the Scientific Revolution.* San Francisco: Harper and Row, 1980.

Michaels, Walter Benn. *The Gold Standard and the Logic of Naturalism: American Literature at the Turn of the Century.* Berkeley and Los Angeles: University of California Press, 1987.

Michaels, Walter Benn, and Donald E. Pease, eds. *The American Renaissance Reconsidered.* Baltimore, Md.: Johns Hopkins University Press, 1985

Michel, Louise. *The Red Virgin: Memoirs of Louise Michel.* Translated and edited by Bullitt Lowry and Elizabeth Ellington Gunter. University: University of Alabama Press, 1981.

Milbauer, Barbara, with Bert N. Obrentz. *The Law Giveth: Legal Aspects of the Abortion Controversy.* New York: McGraw-Hill, 1983.

Milkman, Ruth. *Gender at Work: The Dynamics of Job Segregation by Sex during World War II.* Urbana: University of Illinois Press, 1987.

———. "Women's History and the Sears Case." *Feminist Studies* 12, no. 2 (Summer 1986): 375–400.

Mill, John Stuart. "The Subjection of Women." In *Essays on Sex Equality*, edited by Alice S. Rossi, pp. 123–242. Chicago: University of Chicago Press, 1970.

———. "Utilitarianism." In *Collected Works of John Stuart Mill.* Vol. 10, *Essays on Ethics, Religion and Society*, edited by J. M. Robson, pp. 205–59. Toronto: University of Toronto Press, 1969.

Miller, Nancy K. "Emphasis Added: Plots and Plausibilities in Women's Fiction." *PMLA* 96, no. 1 (January 1981): 36–48.

———. *The Heroine's Text: Readings in the French and English Novel, 1722–1782.* New York: Columbia University Press, 1980.

———. *Subject to Change: Reading Feminist Writing.* New York: Columbia University Press, 1988.

Milton, John. *Paradise Lost.* In *Complete Poems and Major Prose*, edited by Merrit Y. Hughes. New York: Odyssey Press, 1957.

Minnich, Elizabeth, Jean O'Barr, and Rachel Rosenfeld, eds. *Reconstructing the Academy: Women's Education and Women's Studies.* Chicago: University of Chicago Press, 1988.

Minnow, Martha. "The 1986 Supreme Court Term—Foreward: Justice Engendered." *Harvard Law Review* 101, no. 1 (November 1987): 10–95.

Moi, Toril. *Sexual/Textual Politics: Feminist Literary Theory.* New York: Methuen, 1985.

———, ed. *French Feminist Thought: A Reader.* New York: Basil Blackwell, 1987.

Montesquieu, Charles Louis de Secondat de. *The Spirit of the Laws.* Translated and edited by Anne M. Cohler, Basia Carolyn Miller, and Harold Samuel Stone.

Cambridge: Cambridge University Press, 1989.

Morello, Karen Berger. *The Invisible Bar: The Woman Lawyer in America, 1638 to the Present.* New York: Random House, 1986.

Morgan, Robin. *Going Too Far: The Personal Chronicle of a Feminist.* New York: Random House, 1977.

————, ed. *Sisterhood Is Powerful: An Anthology of Writings from the Women's Liberation Movement.* New York: Random House, 1970.

Morrison, Toni. *Beloved.* New York: Random House, 1990.

————. *The Bluest Eye.* New York: Holt, Rinehart and Winston, 1970.

Moses, Claire Goldberg. *French Feminism in the Nineteenth Century.* Albany: State University of New York Press, 1984.

————. "Saint-Simonian Men/Saint-Simonian Women: The Transformation of Feminist Thought in 1830s' France." *Journal of Modern History* 54, no. 2 (June 1982): 240–67.

Mousnier, Roland. *Peasant Uprisings in Seventeenth-Century France, Russia, and China.* Translated by Brian Pearce. New York: Harper and Row, 1970.

Mussell, Kay. "The Social Construction of Reality and American Studies: Notes toward Consensus." *Prospects* 9 (1984): 1–16.

Nedelsky, Jennifer. "Reconceiving Autonomy: Sources, Thoughts and Possibilities." *Yale Journal of Law and Feminism* 1, no. 1 (Spring 1989): 7–36.

Newton, Judith, and Deborah Rosenfelt, eds. *Feminist Criticism and Social Change: Sex, Class, and Race in Literature and Culture.* New York: Methuen, 1985.

Newton, Judith Lowder. *Women, Power, and Subversion: Social Strategies in British Fiction, 1778–1860.* Athens: University of Georgia Press, 1981.

Nicholson, Linda J. *Gender and History: The Limits of Social Theory in the Age of the Family.* New York: Columbia University Press, 1986.

————, ed. *Feminism/Postmodernism.* New York: Routledge, 1990.

Novick, Peter. *That Noble Dream: The "Objectivity Question" and the American Historical Profession.* Cambridge: Cambridge University Press, 1988.

O'Brien, Mary. *The Politics of Reproduction.* Boston: Routledge and Kegan Paul, 1981.

————. *Reproducing the World: Essays in Feminist Theory.* Boulder, Colo.: Westview Press, 1989.

Odem, Mary Ellen. "Delinquent Daughters: Sexual Regulation of Female Minors, 1880–1930." Ph.D. dissertation, University of California at Berkeley, 1989.

Offen, Karen. "Depopulation, Nationalism, and Feminism in Fin-de-Siècle France." *American Historical Review* 89, no. 3 (June 1984): 648–76.

————. "The Second Sex and the Baccalauréat in Republican France, 1800–1924." *French Historical Studies* 13, no. 2 (Fall 1983): 252–86.

Okin, Susan Moller. *Justice, Gender, and the Family.* New York: Basic Books, 1989.

————. "Patriarchy and Married Women's Property in England: Questions on Some Current Views." *Eighteenth-Century Studies* 17, no. 2 (Winter 1983/84): 121–38.

————. *Women in Western Political Thought.* Princeton, N.J.: Princeton University Press, 1979.

Olivier, Christiane. *Jocasta's Children: The Imprint of the Mother.* Translated by

George Craig. New York: Routledge, 1989.

Olsen, Tillie. *Silences*. New York: Delacorte Press, 1978.

Oppenheimer, Valerie Kincade. *The Female Labor Force in the United States: Demographic and Economic Factors Governing Its Growth and Changing Composition*. Berkeley: Institute of International Studies, University of California, 1970.

Ortner, Sherry B. "Is Female to Male as Nature Is to Culture?" In *Woman, Culture, and Society*, edited by Michelle Zimbalist Rosaldo and Louise Lamphere, pp. 67–87. Stanford, Calif.: Stanford University Press, 1974.

Owens, Craig. "The Discourse of Others: Feminists and Postmodernism." In *The Anti-Aesthetic: Essays on Postmodern Culture*, edited by Hal Foster, pp. 57–82. Port Townsend, Wash.: Bay Press, 1983.

Ozment, Steven. *The Age of Reform, 1250–1550: An Intellectual and Religious History of Late Medieval and Reformation Europe*. New Haven, Conn.: Yale University Press, 1980.

———. *When Fathers Ruled: Family Life in Reformation Europe*. Cambridge, Mass.: Harvard University Press, 1983.

Palmer, Bryan D. *Descent into Discourse: The Reification of Language and the Writing of Social History*. Philadelphia: Temple University Press, 1990.

Perry, Ruth. *The Celebrated Mary Astell: An Early English Feminist*. Chicago: University of Chicago Press, 1986.

Perry, Ruth, and Martine Watson Brownley, eds. *Mothering the Mind: Twelve Studies of Writers and Their Silent Partners*. New York: Holmes and Meier, 1984.

Petchesky, Rosalind Pollack. *Abortion and Woman's Choice: The State, Sexuality, and Reproductive Freedom*. New York: Longman, 1984.

Pitkin, Hanna Fenichel. *Fortune Is a Woman: Gender and Politics in the Thought of Niccolò Machiavelli*. Berkeley and Los Angeles: University of California Press, 1984.

Pocock, J. G. A. *The Machiavellian Moment: Florentine Political Thought and the Atlantic Republican Tradition*. Princeton, N.J.: Princeton University Press, 1975.

Polanyi, Karl. *The Great Transformation*. New York: Farrar and Rinehart, 1944.

Pole, J. R. *The Pursuit of Equality in American History*. Berkeley and Los Angeles: University of California Press, 1978.

Pollak, Vivian R. *Dickinson: The Anxiety of Gender*. Ithaca, N.Y.: Cornell University Press, 1984.

Poovey, Mary. "Feminism and Deconstruction." *Feminist Studies* 14, no. 1 (Spring 1988): 51–65.

———. *The Proper Lady and the Woman Writer: Ideology as Style in the Works of Mary Wollstonecraft, Mary Shelley, and Jane Austen*. Chicago: University of Chicago Press, 1984.

———. *Uneven Developments: The Ideological Work of Gender in Mid-Victorian England*. Chicago: University of Chicago Press, 1988.

Posner, Richard A. "The Ethical Significance of Free Choice: A Reply to Professor West." *Harvard Law Review* 99, no. 7 (May 1986): 1431–48.

Potter, Mary. "Gender Equality and Gender Hierarchy in Calvin's Theology." *Signs* 11, no. 4 (Summer 1986): 725–39.

Pritchard, David. "Beyond the Meese Commission Report: Understanding the

Variable Nature of Pornography Regulation." In *For Adult Users Only: The Dilemma of Violent Pornography*, edited by Susan Gubar and Joan Hoff, pp. 163–77. Bloomington: Indiana University Press, 1989.

Pryse, Marjorie, and Hortense J. Spillers, eds. *Conjuring: Black Women, Fiction, and Literary Tradition*. Bloomington: Indiana University Press, 1985.

Rabkin, Peggy A. *Fathers to Daughters: The Legal Foundations of Female Emancipation*. Westport, Conn.: Greenwood Press, 1978.

Rable, George C. *Civil Wars: Women and the Crisis of Southern Nationalism*. Urbana: University of Illinois Press, 1989.

Raboteau, Albert J. *Slave Religion: The "Invisible Institution" in the Antebellum South*. New York: Oxford University Press, 1978.

Radford, Mary F. "Sex Stereotyping and the Promotion of Women to Positions of Power." *The Hastings Law Journal* 4 (March 1990): 471–535.

Radway, Janice A. *Reading the Romance: Women, Patriarchy, and Popular Literature*. Chapel Hill: University of North Carolina Press, 1984.

Randall, Richard S. *Freedom and Taboo: Pornography and the Politics of a Self Divided*. Berkeley and Los Angeles: University of California Press, 1989.

Rawls, John. "Justice as Fairness." *Philosophical Review* 67, no. 2 (April 1958): 167–94.

———. *A Theory of Justice*. Cambridge, Mass.: Harvard University Press, 1971.

Redinger, Ruby V. *George Eliot: The Emergent Self*. New York: Knopf, 1975.

Rendall, Jane. *The Origins of Modern Feminism: Women in Britain, France and the United States, 1780–1860*. New York: Schocken Books, 1984.

Renner, Karl. *The Institutions of Private Law and Their Social Functions*. Translated by Agnes Schwarzschild. Boston: Routledge and Kegan Paul, 1949.

Reynolds, David S. *Beneath the American Renaissance: The Subversive Imagination in the Age of Emerson and Melville*. New York: Knopf, 1988.

Rhode, Deborah L. *Justice and Gender: Sex Discrimination and the Law*. Cambridge, Mass.: Harvard University Press, 1989.

Rich, Adrienne. "Compulsory Heterosexuality and Lesbian Existence." *Signs* 5, no. 4 (Summer 1980): 631–60.

———. *Of Woman Born: Motherhood as Experience and Institution*. Tenth anniversary ed. New York: Norton, 1986.

Ricks, Sarah. "The New French Abortion Pill: The Moral Property of Women." *Yale Journal of Law and Feminism* 1, no. 1 (Spring 1989): 75–99.

Ricoeur, Paul. *De L'Interprétation: Essai sur Freud*. Paris: Éditions du Seuil, 1965.

Rigolot, François. "Gender Sex Difference in Louise Labé's Grammar of Love." In *Rewriting the Renaissance: The Discourse of Sexual Difference in Early Modern Europe*, edited by Margaret W. Ferguson, Maureen Quilligan, and Nancy J. Vickers, pp. 287–98. Chicago: University of Chicago Press, 1986.

Riley, Denise. *Am I That Name?: Feminism and the Category of "Women" in History*. London: Macmillan, 1988.

Rix, Sara E., ed. *The American Woman, 1988–89: A Status Report*. New York: Norton, 1988.

Robel, Lauren. "Pornography and Existing Law: What the Law Can Do." In *For*

Bibliography

Adult Users Only: The Dilemma of Violent Pornography, edited by Susan Gubar and Joan Hoff, pp. 178–97. Bloomington: Indiana University Press, 1989.

Robertson, Peter C. "Strategies for Improving the Economic Situation of Women: Systemic Thinking, Systemic Discrimination, and Systemic Enforcement." In *Equal Employment Policy for Women: Strategies for Implementation in the United States, Canada, and Western Europe*, edited by Ronnie Steinberg Ratner, pp. 128–42. Philadelphia: Temple University Press, 1980.

Rogan, Helen. *Mixed Company: Women in the Modern Army*. New York: Putnam's, 1981.

Rogers, Katherine M. *Feminism in Eighteenth-Century England*. Urbana: University of Illinois Press, 1982.

Rosaldo, Michelle Zimbalist. "The Use and Abuse of Anthropology: Reflections on Feminism and Cross-cultural Understanding." *Signs* 5, no. 3 (Spring 1980): 389–417.

Rosenberg, Rosalind. *Beyond Separate Spheres: Intellectual Roots of Modern Feminism*. New Haven, Conn.: Yale University Press, 1982.

———. "Exchange: A Feminist for Sears." *Nation*, 26 October 1985, p. 394.

Ross, Andrew, ed. *Universal Abandon?: The Politics of Postmodernism*. Minneapolis: University of Minnesota Press, 1988.

Ross, Ellen, and Rayna Rapp. "Sex and Society: A Research Note from Social History and Anthropology." In *Powers of Desire: The Politics of Sexuality*, edited by Ann Snitow, Christine Stansell, and Sharon Thompson, pp. 51–73. New York: Monthly Review Press, 1983.

Rossiter, Margaret W. *Women Scientists in America: Struggles and Strategies to 1940*. Baltimore, Md.: Johns Hopkins University Press, 1982.

Roth, Henry. *Call It Sleep*. 1934. Reprint. New York: Avon Books, 1964.

Rothman, Ellen K. *Hands and Hearts: A History of Courtship in America*. New York: Basic Books, 1984.

Rouse, Jacqueline Anne. *Lugenia Burns Hope: Black Southern Reformer*. Athens: University of Georgia Press, 1989.

Rowbotham, Sheila. "The Trouble with 'Patriarchy.'" In *People's History and Socialist Theory*, edited by Raphael Samuel, pp. 364–69. Boston: Routledge and Kegan Paul, 1981.

Rubin, Gayle. "The Traffic in Women: Notes on the 'Political Economy' of Sex." In *Toward an Anthropology of Women*, edited by Rayna R. Reiter, pp. 157–210. New York: Monthly Review Press, 1975.

Ruddick, Sara. "Maternal Thinking." *Feminist Studies* 6, no. 2 (Summer 1980): 342–67.

———. *Maternal Thinking: Toward a Politics of Peace*. Boston: Beacon Press, 1989.

Ruether, Rosemary Radford, ed. *Religion and Sexism: Images of Woman in the Jewish and Christian Traditions*. New York: Simon and Schuster, 1974.

Ruether, Rosemary Radford, and Eleanor McLaughlin, eds. *Women of Spirit: Female Leadership in the Jewish and Christian Traditions*. New York: Simon and Schuster, 1979.

Rutherglen, George, and Daniel R. Ortiz. "Affirmative Action under the Constitution and Title VII: From Confusion to Convergence." *UCLA Law Review* 35, no. 3 (February 1988): 467–518.

Salinger, J. D. *The Catcher in the Rye.* Boston: Little, Brown, 1951.

Salmon, Marylynn. *Women and the Law of Property in Early America.* Chapel Hill: University of North Carolina Press, 1986.

Salvaggio, Ruth. *Enlightened Absence: Neoclassical Configurations of the Feminine.* Urbana: University of Illinois Press, 1988.

Samuels, Shirley. "The Family, the State, and the Novel in the Early Republic." *American Quarterly* 38, no. 3 (bibliography 1986): 381–95.

Sandel, Michael J., ed. *Liberalism and Its Critics.* New York: New York University Press, 1984.

———. *Liberalism and the Limits of Justice.* Cambridge: Cambridge University Press, 1982.

Sandler, Bernice R., with Roberta M. Hall. *The Campus Climate Revisited: Chilly for Women Faculty, Administrators, and Graduate Students.* Washington, D.C.: Project on the Status and Education of Women, Association of American Colleges, 1986.

Saxonhouse, Arlene W. *Women in the History of Political Thought: Ancient Greece to Machiavelli.* New York: Praeger, 1985.

Saxton, Alexander. "Problems of Class and Race in the Origins of the Mass Circulation Press." *American Quarterly* 36, no. 2 (Summer 1984): 211–34.

Sayers, Janet. *Biological Politics: Feminist and Anti-Feminist Perspectives.* New York: Tavistock, 1982.

Scanlan, James P. "Illusions of Job Segregation." *Public Interest,* no. 93 (Fall 1988): 54–69.

Scanlon, T. M., Jr. "Freedom of Expression and Categories of Expression." In *Pornography and Censorship,* edited by David Copp and Susan Wendell, pp. 139–65. Buffalo, N.Y.: Prometheus Books, 1983.

Schibanoff, Susan. "Comment on Kelly's 'Early Feminist Theory and the *Querelle des Femmes,* 1400–1789.'" *Signs* 9, no. 2 (Winter 1983): 320–26.

Schiebinger, Londa. *The Mind Has No Sex?: Women in the Origins of Modern Science.* Cambridge, Mass.: Harvard University Press, 1989.

———. "Skeletons in the Closet: The First Illustrations of the Female Skeleton in Eighteenth-Century Anatomy." *Representations,* no. 14 (Spring 1986): 42–82.

Schlafly, Phyllis. *The Power of the Christian Woman.* Cincinnati, Ohio: Standard Publishing, 1981.

Schlereth, Thomas J. "American Studies and Students of American Things." *American Quarterly* 35, no. 3 (bibliography 1983): 236–41.

Schochet, Gordon J. *Patriarchalism in Political Thought: The Authoritarian Family and Political Speculation and Attitudes Especially in Seventeenth-Century England.* New York: Basic Books, 1975.

Scholes, Robert. "Aiming a Canon at the Curriculum." *Salmagundi,* no. 72 (Fall 1986): 101–17.

Schomburg Library of Nineteenth-Century Black Women Writers. Edited by Henry Louis Gates, Jr. 30 vols. New York: Oxford University Press, 1988.

Schor, Naomi. *Breaking the Chain: Women, Theory, and French Realist Fiction*. New York: Columbia University Press, 1985.

Schwartz, Felice N. "Management Women and the New Facts of Life." *Harvard Business Review* 67, no. 1 (January/February 1989): 65–76.

Schwartz, Herman. "The 1986 and 1987 Affirmative Action Cases: It's All Over but the Shouting." *Michigan Law Review* 86, no. 3 (December 1987): 524–76.

Schwartz, Joel. *The Sexual Politics of Jean-Jacques Rousseau*. Chicago: University Of Chicago Press, 1984.

Scott, Anne Firor. *The Southern Lady: From Pedestal to Politics 1830–1930*. Chicago: University of Chicago Press, 1970.

Scott, Joan Wallach. "Deconstructing Equality-Versus-Difference: Or, the Uses of Poststructuralist Theory for Feminism." *Feminist Studies* 14, no. 1 (1988): 33–50.

———. *Gender and the Politics of History*. New York: Columbia University Press, 1988.

———. "History in Crisis?: The Others' Side of the Story." *American Historical Review* 94, no. 3 (June 1989): 680–92.

———. Review of *The New History and the Old*, by Gertrude Himmelfarb. *American Historical Review* 94, no. 3 (June 1989): 699–700.

———. "Women in History: The Modern Period." *Past and Present*, no. 101 (November 1983): 141–57.

Scott, William B. *In Pursuit of Happiness: American Conceptions of Property from the Seventeenth Century to the Twentieth Century*. Bloomington: Indiana University Press, 1977.

Seator, Penelope. "Judicial Indifference to Pornography's Harm: *American Booksellers v. Hudnut*." *Golden Gate University Law Review* 17, no. 3 (Fall 1987): 297–358.

Segal, Lynne. *Is the Future Female?: Troubled Thoughts on Contemporary Feminism*. New York: Peter Bedrick Books, 1987.

Segalen, Martine. *Mari et femme dans la société paysanne*. Paris: Flammarion, 1980.

Sekora, John, and Darwin T. Turner, eds. *The Art of the Slave Narrative: Original Essays in Criticism and Theory*. N.p.: Western Illinois University Press, 1982.

Selig, Joel. L. "Affirmative Action in Employment: The Legacy of a Supreme Court Majority." *Indiana Law Journal* 63, no. 2 (Spring 1988): 301–68.

Shanley, Mary Lyndon. *Feminism, Marriage, and the Law in Victorian England, 1850–1895*. Princeton, N.J.: Princeton University Press, 1989.

———. "'One Must Ride Behind': Married Women's Rights and the Divorce Act of 1857." *Victorian Studies* 25, no. 3 (Spring 1982): 355–76.

Shepherd, Simon. *Amazons and Warrior Women: Varieties of Feminism in Seventeenth-Century Drama*. New York: St. Martin's Press, 1981.

Sherman, Claire Richter, with Adele M. Holcomb, eds. *Women as Interpreters of the Visual Arts, 1820–1979*. Westport, Conn.: Greenwood Press, 1981.

Showalter, Elaine. "Feminist Criticism in the Wilderness." *Critical Inquiry* 8, no. 2 (Winter 1981): 179–205.

Shreve, Anita. *Women Together, Women Alone: The Legacy of the Consciousness-Raising Movement*. New York: Viking Press, 1989.

Shulman, Alix Kates. *Burning Questions*. New York: Knopf, 1978.

————. *Memoirs of an Ex-Prom Queen*. New York: Knopf, 1977.

Sidel, Ruth. *Women and Children Last: The Plight of Poor Women in Affluent America*. New York: Viking Press, 1986.

Silverblatt, Irene. "Imperial Dilemmas, the Politics of Kinship, and Inca Reconstructions of History." *Comparative Studies in Society and History* 30, no. 1 (January 1988): 83–102.

————. *Moon, Sun, and Witches: Gender Ideologies and Class in Inca and Colonial Peru*. Princeton, N.J.: Princeton University Press, 1987.

Smart, Carol. *Feminism and the Power of the Law*. New York: Routledge, 1989.

Smith, Adam. *An Inquiry into the Nature and Causes of the Wealth of Nations*. Edited by R. H. Campbell, A. S. Skinner, and W. B. Todd. 2 vols. New York: Oxford University Press, 1976.

Smith, Bonnie G. "The Contribution of Women to Modern Historiography in Great Britain, France, and the United States, 1750–1940." *American Historical Review* 89, no. 3 (June 1984): 709–32.

Smith, Charlotte. *Emmeline, the Orphan of the Castle*. Edited by Anne Henry Ehrenpreis. New York: Oxford University Press, 1971.

Smith, Hilda L. *Reason's Disciples: Seventeenth-Century English Feminists*. Urbana: University of Illinois Press, 1982.

Smith, John David. *An Old Creed for the New South: Proslavery Ideology and Historiography, 1865–1918*. Westport, Conn.: Greenwood Press, 1985.

Smith, Ralph E., ed. *The Subtle Revolution: Women at Work*. Washington, D.C.: Urban Institute, 1979.

Smith, Rogers M. "'One United People': Second-Class Female Citizenship and the American Quest for Community." *Yale Journal of Law and the Humanities* 1, no. 2 (May 1989): 229–93.

Smith, Sidonie. *A Poetics of Women's Autobiography: Marginality and the Fictions of Self-Representation*. Bloomington: Indiana University Press, 1987.

————. *Where I'm Bound: Patterns of Slavery and Freedom in Black American Autobiography*. Westport, Conn.: Greenwood Press, 1974.

Smith, Valerie. *Self-Discovery and Authority in Afro-American Narrative*. Cambridge, Mass.: Harvard University Press, 1987.

Smith-Rosenberg, Carroll. *Disorderly Conduct: Visions of Gender in Victorian America*. New York: Knopf, 1985.

————. "The Female World of Love and Ritual: Relations between Women in Nineteenth-Century America." *Signs* 1, no. 1 (Autumn 1975): 1–29.

————. *Religion and the Rise of the American City: The New York City Mission Movement, 1812–1870*. Ithaca, N.Y.: Cornell University Press, 1971.

Smuts, Robert W. *Women and Work in America*. New York: Columbia University Press, 1959.

Soble, Alan. *Pornography: Marxism, Feminism, and the Future of Sexuality*. New Haven, Conn.: Yale University Press, 1986.

Sollors, Werner. *Beyond Ethnicity: Consent and Descent in American Culture*. New York: Oxford University Press, 1986.

————. "Region, Ethnic Group, and American Writers: From 'Non-Southern' and

'Non-Ethnic' to Ludwig Lewisohn; or the Ethics of Wholesome Provincialism." *Prospects* 9 (1984): 441–62.

———. "Theory of American Ethnicity, Or: '? S Ethnic?/Ti and American /Ti, De or United (W) States S Sı and Theor?'" *American Quarterly* 33, no. 3 (bibliography 1981): 257–83.

Solomon, Barbara Miller. *In the Company of Educated Women: A History of Women and Higher Education in America.* New Haven, Conn.: Yale University Press, 1985.

Sonnet, Martine. *L'Éducation des filles au temps des lumières.* Paris: Les Éditions du Cerf, 1987.

Sophia, a Person of Quality. *Woman Not Inferior to Man.* 1739. Reprint. London: Brentham Press, 1975.

Sophocles. *Antigone.* Loeb Classical Library. 1912.

Spaulding, Christina. "Anti-Pornography Law as a Claim for Equal Respect: Feminism, Liberalism and Community." *Berkeley Women's Law Journal* 4 (1988–89): 128–65.

Spelman, Elizabeth V. *Inessential Woman: Problems of Exclusion in Feminist Thought.* Boston: Beacon Press, 1988.

———. "Woman as Body: Ancient and Contemporary Views." *Feminist Studies* 8 (Spring 1982): 109–31.

Spencer, Samia I. "Women and Education." In *French Women and the Age of Enlightenment,* edited by Samia I. Spencer, pp. 83–96. Bloomington: Indiana University Press, 1984.

Spender, Dale. *Women of Ideas and What Men Have Done to Them: From Aphra Behn to Adrienne Rich.* Boston: Routledge and Kegan Paul, 1982.

Spivak, Gayatri Chakravorty. *In Other Worlds: Essays in Cultural Politics.* New York: Methuen, 1987.

Stansell, Christine. *City of Women: Sex and Class in New York, 1789–1860.* New York: Knopf, 1986.

———. "A Response to Joan Scott." *International Labor and Working-Class History,* no. 31 (Spring 1987): 24–29.

Staves, Susan. "British Seduced Maidens." *Eighteenth-Century Studies* 14, no. 2 (Winter 1980/81): 109–34.

Steele, Jeffrey. *The Representation of the Self in the American Renaissance.* Chapel Hill: University of North Carolina Press, 1987.

Stepto, Robert B. *From Behind the Veil: A Study of Afro-American Narrative.* Urbana: University of Illinois Press, 1979.

Stewart, Judith Hinde. "The Novelists and Their Fictions." In *French Women and the Age of Enlightenment,* edited by Samia I. Spencer, pp. 197–211. Bloomington: Indiana University Press, 1984.

Stimpson, Catharine R. *Where the Meanings Are: Feminism and Cultural Spaces.* New York: Methuen, 1988.

Stowe, Harriet Beecher. *Uncle Tom's Cabin Or, Life among the Lowly.* Edited by Ann Douglas. New York: Penguin Books, 1981.

Strasser, Susan. *Never Done: A History of American Housework.* New York: Pantheon Books, 1982.

Stuard, Susan Mosher. "The Annales School and Feminist History: Opening Dialogue with the American Stepchild." *Signs* 7, no. 1 (Autumn 1981): 135–43.

Stuckey, Sterling. *Slave Culture: Nationalist Theory and the Foundations of Black America*. New York: Oxford University Press, 1987.

Sundquist, Eric J., ed. *New Essays on "Uncle Tom's Cabin."* Cambridge: Cambridge University Press, 1986.

Sunstein, Cass R. "Pornography and the First Amendment." *Duke Law Journal* 1986, no. 4 (September): 589–627.

Tanner, Nancy Makepeace. *On Becoming Human: A Model of the Transition from Ape to Human and the Reconstruction of Early Human Social Life*. Cambridge: Cambridge University Press, 1981.

Tanner, Tony. "Julie and 'La maison paternelle': Another Look at Rousseau's 'La nouvelle Héloïse.'" *Daedalus* 105, no. 1 (Winter 1976): 23–45.

Tate, Allen. *Collected Essays*. Denver: Alan Swallow, 1959.

———. *Essays of Four Decades*. Chicago: Swallow Press, 1968.

Tavard, George H. *Woman in Christian Tradition*. Notre Dame, Ind.: University of Notre Dame Press, 1973.

Taylor, Barbara. *Eve and the New Jerusalem: Socialism and Feminism in the Nineteenth Century*. New York: Pantheon Books, 1983.

Taylor, Charles. *Philosophical Papers*. Vol. 2, *Philosophy and the Human Sciences*. Cambridge: Cambridge University Press, 1985.

Teichman, Jenny. "Reverse Discrimination." In *Law, Morality, and Rights*, edited by M. A. Stewart, pp. 315–22. Boston: D. Reidel, 1983.

Terborg-Penn, Rosalyn. "Black Women in Resistance: A Cross-Cultural Perspective." In *In Resistance: Studies in African, Caribbean, and Afro-American History*, edited by Gary Y. Okihiro, pp. 188–209. Amherst: University of Massachusetts Press, 1986.

Thomis, Malcolm I., and Jennifer Grimmett. *Women in Protest, 1800–1850*. New York: St. Martin's Press, 1982.

Thompson, E. P. *The Making of the English Working Class*. London: Victor Gollancz, 1980.

Tilly, Louise A. "Paths of Proletarianization: Organization of Production, Sexual Division of Labor, and Women's Collective Action." *Signs* 7, no. 2 (Winter 1981): 400–417.

———. "People's History and Social Science History." *Social Science History* 7, no. 4 (Fall 1983): 457–74.

Tocqueville, Alexis de. *Democracy in America*. Translated by George Lawrence. Edited by J. P. Mayer and Max Lerner. New York: Harper and Row, 1966.

———. *The Old Régime and the French Revolution*. Translated by Stuart Gilbert. Garden City, N.Y.: Anchor Books/Doubleday, 1955.

Tompkins, Jane. *Sensational Designs: The Cultural Work of American Fiction, 1790–1860*. New York: Oxford University Press, 1985.

Tong, Rosemarie. *Feminist Thought: A Comprehensive Introduction*. Boulder, Colo.: Westview Press, 1989.

Tönnies, Ferdinand. *Community and Society (Gemeinschaft und Gesellschaft)*. Translated and edited by Charles P. Loomis. East Lansing: Michigan State University Press, 1957.

Townsend, Kim. "Francis Parkman and the Male Tradition." *American Quarterly* 38, no. 1 (Spring 1986): 97–113.

Trachtenberg, Alan. *The Incorporation of America: Culture and Society in the Gilded Age*. New York: Hill and Wang, 1982.

Travitsky, Betty, ed. and comp. *The Paradise of Women: Writings by Englishwomen of the Renaissance*. Westport, Conn.: Greenwood Press, 1981.

Tribe, Laurence H. *Constitutional Choices*. Cambridge, Mass.: Harvard University Press, 1985.

Tronto, Joan C. "Women and Caring: What Can Feminists Learn about Morality from Caring?" In *Gender/Body/Knowledge: Feminist Reconstructions of Being and Knowing*, edited by Alison M. Jaggar and Susan R. Bordo, pp. 172–87. New Brunswick, N.J.: Rutgers University Press, 1989.

Tur, Richard H. S. "Concluding Remarks." In *Law, Morality, and Rights*, edited by M. A. Stewart, pp. 323–30. Boston: D. Reidel, 1983.

———. "Justifications of Reverse Discrimination." In *Law, Morality, and Rights*, edited by M. A. Stewart, pp. 259–94. Boston: D. Reidel, 1983.

Tushnet, Mark V. *The American Law of Slavery, 1810–1860: Considerations of Humanity and Interest*. Princeton, N.J.: Princeton University Press, 1981.

Ulrich, Laurel Thatcher. *Good Wives: Image and Reality in the Lives of Women in Northern New England, 1650–1750*. New York: Knopf, 1982.

U.S. Department of Justice. Attorney General's Commission on Pornography. *Final Report*. 2 vols. Washington, D.C.: Government Printing Office, 1986.

Upton, Dell. "The Power of Things: Recent Studies in American Vernacular Architecture." *American Quarterly* 35, no. 3 (bibliography 1983): 262–79.

Van Allen, Judith. "'Aba Riots' or Igbo 'Women's War'?: Ideology, Stratification, and the Invisibility of Women." In *Women in Africa: Studies in Social and Economic Change*, edited by Nancy J. Hafkin and Edna G. Bay, pp. 59–85. Stanford, Calif.: Stanford University Press, 1976.

———. "'Sitting on a Man': Colonialism and the Lost Political Institutions of Igbo Women." *Canadian Journal of African Studies* 6, no. 2 (1972): 165–81.

Veeser, H. Aram, ed. *The New Historicism*. New York: Routledge, 1989.

Wade-Gayles, Gloria. *No Crystal Stair: Visions of Race and Sex in Black Women's Fiction*. New York: Pilgrim Press, 1984.

Walker, Alice. *You Can't Keep a Good Woman Down*. New York: Harcourt Brace Jovanovich, 1981.

Walzer, Michael. *Spheres of Justice: A Defense of Pluralism and Equality*. New York: Basic Books, 1983.

Wandersee, Winifred D. *Women's Work and Family Values, 1920–1940*. Cambridge, Mass.: Harvard University Press, 1981.

Warner, Marina. *Alone of All Her Sex: The Myth and the Cult of the Virgin Mary*. New York: Knopf, 1976.

———. *Joan of Arc: The Image of Female Heroism*. New York: Knopf, 1981.

Warnicke, Retha M. *Women of the English Renaissance and Reformation*. Westport,

Conn.: Greenwood Press, 1983.

Wasserstrom, Richard A. "Racism, Sexism, and Preferential Treatment: An Approach to the Topics." *UCLA Law Review* 24, nos. 5 and 6 (June/August 1977): 581–622.

Waters, John J. "The Traditional World of the New England Peasants: A View from Seventeenth-Century Barnstable." *New England Historical and Genealogical Register* 130, no. 1 (January 1976): 3–21.

Waugh, Patricia. *Feminine Fictions: Revisiting the Postmodern.* New York: Routledge, 1989.

Weaver, Richard M. *Language Is Sermonic: Richard M. Weaver on the Nature of Rhetoric.* Edited by Richard L. Johannesen, Rennard Strickland, and Ralph T. Eubanks. Baton Rouge: Louisiana State University Press, 1970.

———. *The Southern Tradition at Bay: A History of Postbellum Thought.* Edited by George Core and M. E. Bradford. New Rochelle, N.Y.: Arlington House, 1968.

Weber, Max. *The Protestant Ethic and the Spirit of Capitalism.* Translated by Talcott Parsons. New York: Scribner's, 1930.

"The Week." *National Review,* 9 August 1985, pp. 12–16.

Weitzman, Lenore J. *The Divorce Revolution: The Unexpected Social and Economic Consequences for Women and Children in America.* New York: Free Press, 1985.

Wemple, Suzanne Fonay. *Women in Frankish Society: Marriage and the Cloister, 500 to 900.* Philadelphia: University of Pennsylvania Press, 1981.

Wendell, Susan. "Pornography and Freedom of Expression." In *Pornography and Censorship,* edited by David Copp and Susan Wendell, pp. 167–83. Buffalo, N.Y.: Prometheus Books, 1983.

West, Robin L. "The Authoritarian Impulse in Constitutional Law." *University of Miami Law Review* 42, no. 3 (January 1988): 531–52.

———. "Authority, Autonomy, and Choice: The Role of Consent in the Moral and Political Visions of Franz Kafka and Richard Posner." *Harvard Law Review* 99, no. 2 (December 1985): 384–428.

———. "Communities, Texts, and Law: Reflections on the Law and Literature Movement." *Yale Journal of Law and the Humanities* 1, no. 1 (December 1988): 129–56.

———. "The Difference in Women's Hedonic Lives: A Phenomenological Critique of Feminist Legal Theory." *Wisconsin Women's Law Journal* 3 (1987): 81–145.

———. "Economic Man and Literary Woman: One Contrast." *Mercer Law Review* 39, no. 3 (Spring 1988): 867–78.

———. "The Feminist-Conservative Anti-Pornography Alliance and the 1986 Attorney General's Commission on Pornography Report." *American Bar Foundation Research Journal,* no. 4 (Fall 1987): 681–711.

———. "Jurisprudence and Gender." *University of Chicago Law Review* 55, no. 1 (Winter 1988): 1–72.

———. "Law, Rights, and Other Totemic Illusions: Legal Liberalism and Freud's Theory of the Rule of Law." *University of Pennsylvania Law Review* 134, no. 4 (April 1986): 817–82.

———. "Liberalism Rediscovered: A Pragmatic Definition of the Liberal Vision." *University of Pittsburgh Law Review* 46, no. 3 (Spring 1985): 673–738.

———. "Love, Rage, and Legal Theory." *Yale Journal of Law and Feminism* 1, no. 1 (Spring 1989): 101–10.

———. "Pornography as a Legal Text: Comments from a Legal Perspective." In *For Adult Users Only: The Dilemma of Violent Pornography*, edited by Susan Gubar and Joan Hoff, pp. 108–30. Bloomington: Indiana University Press, 1989.

———. "Submission, Choice, and Ethics: A Rejoinder to Judge Posner." *Harvard Law Review* 99, no. 7 (May 1986): 1449–56.

Wexler, Victor G. "'Made for Man's Delight': Rousseau as Antifeminist." *American Historical Review* 81, no. 2 (April 1976): 266–91.

White, Deborah Gray. *Ar'n't I a Woman?: Female Slaves in the Plantation South.* New York: Norton, 1985.

Wiener, Jonathan M. "Radical Historians and the Crisis in American History, 1959–1980." *Journal of American History* 76, no. 2 (September 1989): 399–434.

———. "The Sears Case: Women's History on Trial." *Nation*, 7 September 1985, p. 161.

Willis, Susan. *Specifying: Black Women Writing the American Experience.* Madison: University of Wisconsin Press, 1987.

Wilson, Harriet E. *Our Nig: or, Sketches from the Life of a Free Black.* Edited by Henry Louis Gates, Jr. New York: Random House, 1983.

Wilson, William Julius. *The Truly Disadvantaged: The Inner City, the Underclass, and Public Policy.* Chicago: University of Chicago Press, 1987.

Wiltenberg, Joy Deborah. "Disorderly Women and Female Power in the Popular Literature of Early Modern England and Germany." Ph.D. dissertation, University of Virginia, 1984.

Wise, Gene. "'Paradigm Dramas' in American Studies: A Cultural and Institutional History of the Movement." *American Quarterly* 23, no. 3 (bibliography 1979): 293–337.

Wolfe, Alan. "Dirt and Democracy." *New Republic*, 19 February 1990, pp. 27–31.

Wolff, Cynthia Griffin. *A Feast of Words: The Triumph of Edith Wharton.* New York: Oxford University Press, 1977.

Wolgast, Elizabeth H. *Equality and the Rights of Women.* Ithaca, N.Y.: Cornell University Press, 1980.

———. *The Grammar of Justice.* Ithaca, N.Y.: Cornell University Press, 1987.

———. "Is Reverse Discrimination Fair?" In *Law, Morality, and Rights*, edited by M. A. Stewart, pp. 295–313. Boston: D. Reidel, 1983.

Wollstonecraft, Mary. *Thoughts on the Education of Daughters.* 1787. Reprint. Clifton, N.J.: Augustus M. Kelley, 1972.

———. *A Vindication of the Rights of Woman.* Edited by Carol H. Poston. 2d ed. New York: Norton, 1988.

Woolf, Virginia. *A Room of One's Own.* 1929. Reprint. New York: Harcourt Brace, Harbinger Books, n.d.

Yellin, Jean Fagan. "Texts and Contexts of Harriet Jacobs' *Incidents in the Life of a Slave Girl: Written by Herself.*" In *The Slave's Narrative*, edited by Charles T. Davis and Henry Louis Gates, Jr., pp. 262–82. New York: Oxford University Press, 1985.

———. *Women and Sisters: The Antislavery Feminists in American Culture.* New Haven, Conn.: Yale University Press, 1989.

————. *"Written by Herself:* Harriet Jacobs' Slave Narrative." *American Literature* 53, no. 3 (November 1981): 479–86.

Yetman, Norman R. "Ex-Slave Interviews and the Historiography of Slavery." *American Quarterly* 36, no. 2 (Summer 1984): 181–210.

Yoder, Janice D., and Jerome Adams. "Women Entering Nontraditional Roles: When Work Demands and Sex-Roles Conflict: The Case of West Point." *International Journal of Women's Studies* 7, no. 3 (May/June 1984): 260–72.

Young, Iris. "Socialist Feminism and the Limits of Dual Systems Theory." *Socialist Review*, nos. 2 and 3 (March–June 1980).

Zboray, Ronald J. "Antebellum Reading and the Ironies of Technological Innovation." *American Quarterly* 40, no. 1 (March 1988): 65–82.

————. "The Transportation Revolution and Antebellum Book Distribution Reconsidered." *American Quarterly* 38, no. 1 (Spring 1986): 53–71.

Zedler, Beatrice H. "The Three Princesses." *Hypatia* 4, no. 1 (Spring 1989): 28–63.

Zillmann, Dolf, and Jennings Bryant, eds. *Pornography: Research Advances and Policy Considerations*. Hillside, N.J.: Erlbaum, 1989.

Zucker, Stanley. "German Women and the Revolution of 1848: Kathinka Zitz-Halein and the Humania Association." *Central European History* 13, no. 3 (September 1980): 237–54.

INDEX

Abelard, Peter, 170

Abolitionism: and individual right, 8, 38, 62, 128, 178, 190, 241; and sisterhood, 13; and women, 13, 36; and *Incidents in the Life of a Slave Girl*, 211; and *Uncle Tom's Cabin*, 215, 234; language of, 231

Abortion, 2, 10, 97, 100, 110; and *Webster* decision, 7; and pro-choice, 22, 84; and minors, 38, 81; and individual right, 57, 81–85; and pro-life, 81; opponents of, 81, 82; and right to life, 83; and *Roe* v. *Wade*, 269 (n. 80)

Abstract: standards, 12, 31, 234; gender category, 18, 39, 41, 116, 119, 162, 267 (n. 52); justice, 33, 57, 85, 234; community, 54; rights, 55, 122; individual as, 77, 118, 122, 138, 159; life in the, 84; language, 188. *See also* Community; Individual; Justice; Language; Man; Rights; Woman

Abuse, 19, 24, 83, 100, 104, 267 (n. 50); of children, 1, 47, 66, 67, 99; sexual, 1, 63, 66, 92

Academia, 4, 149, 150. *See also* Colleges

Academic: standards, 1; canon, 9; feminism, 31, 70; freedom, 60; disciplines, 145; discourse, 152; elitism, 188; power, 202

Accountability, 6, 127, 129, 188, 216

Acquaintance rape, 22, 99, 255

Addams, Jane, 37

Affirmative action, 56, 57, 66–76, 78, 80, 110, 266 (n. 37), 267 (n. 50)

Africa, 13, 186

African-Americans, 37, 61, 62, 68, 69, 73, 74, 86, 139, 161, 186, 187, 202, 204–7, 209, 212, 213, 216–18, 267 (n. 50), 286 (n. 45); women, 17–19, 35, 36, 62, 148, 152, 201, 210, 211, 213, 216; men, 18, 58, 208; history, 139, 160, 207, 208, 264 (n. 9); experience, 139, 161, 267 (n. 51); scholarship, 170, 209, 281 (n. 8); children, 186; communities, 187; culture, 204–7, 209, 210–13, 214, 216–18, 286 (n. 49)

Africans, 148, 265 (n. 22)

Aggression, 14, 21, 49, 237, 252

Alcohol, 27; and pregnancy, 82

Alcoholism: and feminism, 1

Alienation, 35, 118, 135, 190, 191, 210, 211, 232, 260 (n. 6)

Alimony, 2, 80

Althusius, 49

American Historical Association, 149, 202

American Renaissance, 219

American Revolution, 7, 58, 62, 81, 171, 199, 285 (n. 24)

Americans, 19, 27, 29, 36, 38, 57, 59, 61, 62, 66, 68, 69, 73, 74, 79, 83, 86, 105, 110, 111, 121, 139, 148, 161, 169, 186, 187, 199–202, 204–7, 209, 212–14, 216–18, 223; society, 2, 29, 30, 33, 37, 38, 56, 62, 66, 68, 87, 139, 202, 205, 215, 217, 248, 267 (nn. 50, 51); women, 2, 3, 53, 62, 81, 135, 152, 201, 210, 211, 213, 216, 225; tradition, 9, 25, 122; history, 9, 54, 58, 139, 198, 219, 230; feminism, 17, 148, 167; laws, 18; flag, 110; colonies, 116, 120; culture, 123–24, 199–206, 244, 283 (n. 1), 285 (n. 24); national identity, 139, 199–201, 207, 267 (n. 51), 283 (n. 1); education, 167, 186. *See also* African-Americans; Italian-Americans; Jewish-Americans

American Studies, 200–203, 214, 218, 221, 286 (n. 46)

Index

Index